A HISTORY OF THA

This lively, accessible book is the first new history of Thailand in English for two decades. Drawing on new Thai-language research, it ranges widely over political, economic, social, and cultural themes.

Chris Baker and Pasuk Phongpaichit reveal how a world of mandarin nobles and unfree labour evolved into a rural society of smallholder peasants and an urban society populated mainly by migrants from southern China. They trace how a Buddhist cosmography adapted to new ideas of time and space, and a traditional polity was transformed into a new nation-state under a strengthened monarchy.

The authors cover the contests between urban nationalists, ambitious generals, communist rebels, business politicians, and social movements to control the nation-state and redefine its purpose. They describe the dramatic changes wrought by a booming economy, globalization, and the evolution of mass society. Finally, they show how Thailand's path is still being contested by those who believe in change from above and those who fight for democracy and liberal values.

Chris Baker taught Asian history at Cambridge University, and has lived in Thailand for over twenty years. He is now an independent writer, researcher, and translator. **Pasuk Phongpaichit** is Professor of Economics at Chulalongkorn University, Bangkok. She has written widely in Thai and English on the Thai economy, sex industry, corruption, illegal economy, and social movements. Together, they have co-authored *Thailand: Economics and Politics*, *Thailand's Boom and Bust*, *Thailand's Crisis*, and *Thaksin: The Business of Politics in Thailand*.

A HISTORY OF THAILAND

CHRIS BAKER
PASUK PHONGPAICHIT

CAMBRIDGE
UNIVERSITY PRESS

CAMBRIDGE UNIVERSITY PRESS
The Edinburgh Building, Cambridge CB2 2RU, UK
40 West 20th Street, New York, NY 10011–4211, USA
477 Williamstown Road, Port Melbourne, VIC 3207, Australia
Ruiz de Alarcón 13, 28014 Madrid, Spain
Dock House, The Waterfront, Cape Town 8001, South Africa

http://www.cambridge.org

First published by Cambridge University Press 2005
Reprinted 2005 (twice), 2006, 2007, 2008

Printed in China through Everbest

A catalogue record for this book is available from the British Library

National Library of Australia Cataloguing in Publication data
    Baker, Christopher John, 1948-.
    A history of Thailand.
    Includes Index.
    ISBN-13 978-0-521-81615-1 hardback
    ISBN-10 0-521-81615-7 hardback
    ISBN-13 978-0-521-01647-6 paperback
    ISBN-10 0-521-01647-9 paperback
    1. Thailand - History. I. Pasuk Phongpaichit. II. Title.
959.3

ISBN-13 978-0-521-81615-1 hardback
ISBN-10 0-521-81615-7 hardback

ISBN-13 978-0-521-01647-6 paperback
ISBN-10 0-521-01647-9 paperback

Contents

Illustrations

FIGURES

MAPS

CHARTS

Preface

History was invented for the nation-state. It has a tendency to imagine 'the false unity of a self-same, national subject evolving through time' (Prasenjit Duara). All too easily, the nation becomes something natural which always existed but was only properly realized in the nation-state. In reaction against this tendency, historians today prefer to write about people, things, ideas, localities, regions, or the globe – anything but the nation. Or else they write reflective histories about the interplay between the nation and the production of its own history.

The approach adopted here is to make the career of the nation-state the explicit focus of the story. One of the themes of this book is about how the idea of the nation and the machinery of the nation-state were established in Thailand, and then how different social forces tried to make use of it – by reinterpreting what the nation meant, and by seeking to control or influence the use of state power. The second major theme is about the evolution of the social forces involved. After the introductory chapter, the chapters alternate between these two themes, though the division is rough not rigid.

The publishers want the books in this series to be accessible to a wide readership, not too long and not overloaded with academic referencing. Our policy has been to limit footnoting to the sources for direct quotations. The appendix of 'Readings' cites major published works in English, but rather little has been published in English on modern Thailand over the past generation. In Thai there has been a huge amount, and even more exists in unpublished theses in both Thai and English. Our dependence on these works should be easily recognizable by their authors and other experts. Some of the most important are: Srisak Vallibhotama, Geoff Wade, Phiset Jiajanphong, Sratsawadi Ongsakun on early history; Nidhi Eoseewong, Saichon Sattayanurak on early Bangkok society; Davisakdi Puaksom, Attachak Sattayanurak, Rujaya Abhakorn on the Chulalongkorn reform era; Phimpraphai Phisanbut, Chamnongsri Rutnin, Panni Bualek on city society; Chatthip Nartsupha, David Johnston,

Atsushi Kitahara on rural society; Nakharin Mektrairat, Eiji Murashima, Thamrongsak Petchloetanan, Chanida Phromphayak Puaksom, Saichon Sattayanurak, Chaloemkiat Phianuan, Morakot Jewachinda, Vichitvong na Pombejra, Phenphisut Inthraphirom, Matt Copeland on nationalisms; Chalong Soontravanich, Somsak Jeamteerasakul, Suthachai Yimprasoet, Charnvit Kasetsiri on the American era; Praphat Pintobtaeng, Thirayuth Boonmi, Anek Laothamatas, Ubonrat Siriyuvasak, James Ockey, Kasian Tejapira, Thongchai Winichakul on Thailand since 1975. We would like to record our appreciation and thanks, along with apologies for any short-comings in our use of these works.

The book was written in Thailand but with indispensable help from forays to libraries and research centres. We are especially grateful to the Center of Southeast Asian Studies at Kyoto University, Nordic Institute of Asian Studies in Copenhagen, Johns Hopkins SAIS in Washington, and the libraries of the Australian National University and Cambridge University.

We would like to thank Kevin Hewison, Craig Reynolds, Malcom Falkus, Grant Evans, Andrew Brown, and John Funston who commented on earlier drafts of the manuscript.

For help in finding the illustrations, thanks to the Thailand National Archives, Thammasat University Archives, *Bangkok Post*, *The Nation*, Siam Society, Anake Nawikamune, Charnvit Kasetsiri, Chatchawan Chatsuthichai, Daoruang Naewthong, Ekkarin Latthasaksiri, Kane Sarika, Kovit Sanandaeng, Krairoek Nana, Nantiya Tangwisutijit, Pana Janviroj, Piriya Krairiksh, Sa-ard Angkunwat, Sakdina Chatrakul na Ayudhya, Sanga Luchapatthanakon, Sharon O'Toole, Somsuda Leyavanija, Steve Van Beek, Subhatra Bhumiprabhas, Thamrongsak Petchloetanan, and Warunee Osatharam.

NOTE ON TRANSLITERATION AND NAMES

Official spellings are used for kings and places, and conventional forms for some well-known names. Otherwise, Thai is translated using the Royal Institute system, with the exception of using 'j' for *jo jan*.

Abbreviations

BAAC	Bank for Agriculture and Agricultural Cooperatives
CDA	Constitution Drafting Assembly
CEO	chief executive officer
CIA	Central Intelligence Agency
CP	Charoen Pokphand group of companies
CPD	Campaign for Popular Democracy
CPT	Communist Party of Thailand
GDP	gross domestic product
IMF	International Monetary Fund
ISOC	Internal Security Operations Command
ITV	Independent Television
JPPCC	Joint Private Public Consultative Committee
KMT	Kuomintang
MP	member of parliament
NESDB	National Economic and Social Development Board, the planning agency
NGO	non-governmental organization
NIO	National Identity Office
NPKC	National Peacekeeping Council
PFT	Peasants Federation of Thailand
PPB	Privy Purse Bureau
SEATO	Southeast Asia Treaty Organization
TRT	Thai Rak Thai Party (Thai love Thai)
UN	United Nations
USAID	US Agency for International Development

Glossary

angyi	Chinese secret society
baht	unit of currency
barami	charisma, innate authority
Bodhisatta	a future Buddha
cakkavatin	the universal emperor in Buddhist cosmology
chaiyaphum	'victorious emplacement'; the science of siting a city
Chakri	the name of the Bangkok dynasty; adapted from King Rama I's former title as a minister of the military
chaophraya	one of the highest non-royal titles in traditional ranking system
chat	birth, race, nation
chatprathet	nation-state
chedi	stupa, reliquary temple
choduek	traditional title for head of the Chinese community
compradore	agent of colonial firm, liaising with local partners or customers
corvée	labour exacted by a feudal lord
ekkarat	a unified and independent kingdom
farang	westerner, European, foreigner
Isan	the northeast region
itthiphon	influence
jao	lord, ruler; member of the royal family/clan
jao pho	godfather, mafia
jao sua	merchant prince, especially Chinese (Thai adaptation of a Chinese phrase)
jap jong	process of staking a claim to unused land

jataka	collection of tales of the former lives of the Buddha; often used for preaching, or as the subjects of temple murals
jek	pejorative term for Chinese in Thailand
kamnan	the head of a group of villages
kanmueang ning	quiet or calm politics
kathin	ceremony of presenting new robes to Buddhist monks
kha ratchakan	bureaucrat; originally, the servant of the king
khon samai mai	modern people
khun nang	nobility; collective term for the old service bureaucracy
khwaen	a confederation of *mueang*
lak ratchakan	the principle of service to the king
lak wicha	the principle of law and rationality
luk thung	'child of the field', a music style
lukjin	'child of China', term for Thai-born descendants of a Chinese immigrant
mahanakhon	'great cities'
mankhong	security
manutsayatham	humanitarianism, or a belief in people
muang fai	weir-and-channel irrigation system
mueang	a political unit, originally a city-state, but applicable to countries
munnai	overseer
naga	mythological serpent
nai	boss, overseer
nakleng	tough guy
nibbana	nirvana, release from worldly existence in Buddhist teaching
nirat	a poetic form combining travel, remembrance of loved one(s), and observation of nature
phatthana	development
phleng phua chiwit	songs for life
pho khun	a paternal ruler in the legendary mode of the Sukhothai kings
pho liang	patron
pho yu pho kin	'enough to live and eat', sufficiency
phrai	in the traditional order, a freeman commoner bound to corvée

phrai mangmi	rich commoners
phrakhlang	the royal treasury (and its minister) in traditional government
phramahakasat	great king
phu di	'good people'; the aristocracy
phu noi	little (ordinary) people
phu yai	big (powerful) people
phumibun	'man of merit', person of special or supernatural power, sometimes leader of millenarian revolt
phung ton eng	self-reliance
prachakhom	people's assemblies
prathet	country
prathetchat	nation-state
protégé	someone under the protection of a colonial power (Britain, France) under the extraterritorial provisions of colonial treaties
rachasap	'royal language'; a specialized vocabulary for addressing kings
rai	unit of area, = 0.16 hectare
ratchathani	abode of kings; the inner, core kingdom
ratthaniyom	cultural mandate; state edict
sae	Chinese clan name
sakdina	'power over fields'; traditional system of numerical ranks; sometimes used as referent for Thai equivalent of feudalism
samakkhi(tham)	unity
samakhom lap	secret society
sanchat thai	of Thai nationality
sawatdi	greeting
Seri Thai	Free Thai, resistance movement against the Japanese during Second World War
siwilai	Thai adaptation of the word 'civilized', encapsulating aspirations for 'progress'
sukhaphiban	sanitary districts
tambon	administrative unit consisting of a group of villages
thamma	dharma, the teachings of the Buddha; righteous conduct
thammaracha	dharmaraja, a ruler adhering to Buddhist morality
thammathut	ambassadors of *thamma*

that	slave
thesaphiban	'control over territory'
thotsaphit ratchatham	the ten laws of royal conduct
thudong	pilgrimage
Traiphum	'Three Worlds'; an early Buddhist cosmology, perhaps written in the fourteenth century
wat	Buddhist temple, monastery
wiang	fortified settlement
wihan	assembly hall in a Buddhist temple
winaya	the code of discipline for Buddhist monks

Chronology

1351   Legendary foundation of Ayutthaya
1569   First fall of Ayutthaya to the Burmese
1767   Second fall of Ayutthaya
1782   New capital established at Bangkok; accession of King Yotfa, Rama I
1822   First trade treaty with Britain, negotiated by John Crawfurd
1851   Accession of King Mongkut, Rama IV
1855   Bowring treaty
1863   French protectorate of Cambodia
1868   Accession of King Chulalongkorn, Rama V
1872   Chulalongkorn's visit to India
1874   Front Palace Incident; Anglo-Siam Treaty over Chiang Mai; edict abolishing slavery
1885   Prince Prisdang's memorial on a constitution
1890   Establishment of Privy Purse Bureau
1892   Formation of ministerial council
1893   French gunboats threaten Bangkok (Paknam Incident); foundation of Ministry of Interior
1897   Chulalongkorn's first visit to Europe
1901   Ubon *phumibun* revolt
1902   Phrae revolt; southern states revolt; Sangha Act
1905   Conscription edict
1908   Sun Yat Sen visit to Bangkok
1909   Anglo-Siamese Treaty finalizes Siam's boundaries
1910   Accession of King Vajiravudh, Rama VI; Chinese strike in Bangkok
1912   Plot uncovered in military
1913   Nationality Act; Surname Act; Vajiravudh's *The Jews of the East*
1916   Foundation of Chulalongkorn University

1917   Siamese contingent to fight on Allied side in Europe; first
        'political newspaper' published
1920   First publication of Prince Damrong's *Our Wars with the Burmese*
1923   Press Act; W. C. Dodd's *The Tai Race* published
1925   Accession of King Prajadhipok, Rama VII
1927   People's Party founded in Paris
1928   Kulap Saipradit's *Luk phu chai* (A real man); Khun
        Wichitmatra's *Lak thai* (Origins of the Thai); Wichit
        Wathakan's *Mahaburut* (Great men); boycott of Japanese goods
1930   Ho Chi Minh (intermittently in Siam since 1928 organizing
        Vietnamese émigrés) forms Communist Party of Siam
1932   Revolution converts absolute to constitutional monarchy
        (24 June)
1933   Boworadet Revolt
1934   Foundation of Thammasat University; Phibun becomes
        minister of defence and army chief
1935   Abdication of King Prajadhipok
1936   Wichit Wathakan's play *Luat suphan* (Blood of Suphanburi)
1937   Second boycott of Japanese imports
1938   Phibun becomes prime minister; Thai Rice Company formed
1939   Siam renamed as Thailand; series of state edicts starts;
        Constitution Monument completed
1941   Japanese army enters Thailand; Thailand declares war on Allies;
        battle with French
1942   Phibun's Sangha Act; Communist Party of Thailand refounded
1944   Seri Thai network established; Phibun ousted as prime minister;
        foundation of Bangkok Bank
1945   Seni Pramoj recalled from US to front peace negotiations
1946   Pridi's constitution; death of King Ananda Mahidol, Rama VIII;
        accession of King Bhumibol Adulyadej, Rama IX
1946   First May Day rally
1947   First national labour federation; coup returns Phibun to power
1948   Troubles in Muslim south after Haji Sulong's arrest; CPT adopts
        Maoist strategy
1949   Palace Rebellion, Pridi flees
1950   Phibun's sweep against Peace Movement
1951   King Rama IX returns to Thailand; Silent or Radio Coup; first
        US military aid
1954   SEATO formed
1955   Phibun's democracy interlude

1957   Sarit Thanarat takes power by coup; completion of Mitraphap highway

1958   Sarit's second coup and repression

1960   Thai troops fight in Laos

1961   Khrong Chandawong executed; CPT forms first rural base in Phuphan

1962   Sarit's Sangha Act; Rusk-Khoman agreement confirms US security alliance

1963   Death of Sarit, succeeded by Thanom Kittikhachon; *Social Science Review* founded

1964   First air strike on Vietnam flown from Thailand

1965   'First shot' of communist insurgency

1966   Jit Phumisak shot dead in Phuphan

1967   Thai troops fight in South Vietnam; Hmong rebellion in northern hills

1968   Restoration of constitution

1971   Thanom coup against own government and abrogation of constitution; Village Scouts formed

1972   Student protest against Japanese goods, and for restoration of constitution

1973   Student uprising fells Thanom (14 October)

1974   Peasants Federation of Thailand formed; Dusit Thani strike

1975   Elected governments headed by Kukrit and Seni Pramoj; *Nawaphon* and Red Gaurs formed; US troops start to depart

1976   Massacre at Thammasat University and military coup (6 October)

1979   Restoration of elections and parliament

1980   Prem Tinsulanond as prime minister; political policy to end insurgency

1981   Failed April Fool's Day Coup

1984   Devaluation of baht

1985   Failed coup; Chamlong Srimuang elected mayor of Bangkok

1986   Nidhi Eoseewong's study of King Taksin published

1987   Remnants of CPT arrested; Sujit Wongthet's *Jek pon lao* published

1988   Chatichai Choonhavan becomes first elected prime minister since 1976; Nam Choan dam project cancelled

1991   Military coup by NPKC; Anand Panyarachun as prime minister

1992   NPKC prime minister Suchinda Kraprayun forced out by street demonstrations of 'Black May'; *Kho Jo Ko* protest against forest resettlement; death of Phumpuang Duangjan; Chuan Leekpai as prime minister

1994   Thai Culture Promotion Year; King Bhumibol's sufficiency farming scheme; Pak Mun dam completed

1995   Establishment of Constitution Drafting Assembly; Assembly of the Poor founded

1996   Banharn Silpa-archa ousted after no-confidence debate

1997   Assembly of the Poor 99-day protest; passage of 'People's Constitution'; onset of economic crisis

1998   Foundation of Thai Rak Thai Party by Thaksin Shinawatra

2001   Thaksin Shinawatra becomes prime minister

I

Before Bangkok

The name Thailand was invented in 1939. The country it described, formerly called Siam, had been defined by borders drawn in the 1890s and 1900s. Its capital, Bangkok, had been founded in 1782 in succession to an older city, Ayutthaya, destroyed fifteen years earlier. Ayutthaya had been one of the great port cities of Asia, with trading links stretching from Persia to China, and a political and economic hinterland focused on the basin of the Chaophraya river system.

The society of this hinterland had evolved over prior centuries in a pattern which was similar throughout Southeast Asia. The landscape was dominated by tropical and subtropical forest. People clustered in city-states. Society was organized around personal ties of service and protection. An era of warfare from the thirteenth to sixteenth centuries saw the emergence of a powerful militaristic kingship buttressed by Brahmanical ritual, trading profits, and systems for marshalling forced labour. But since the seventeenth century, this social and political order had begun to shift with the expansion of a commercial economy, a loosening of labour ties, the emergence of an aristocracy, and the new vitality of Theravada Buddhism.

PEOPLING THE CHAOPHRAYA BASIN

Mainland Southeast Asia is one of the most fertile and biodiverse areas of the planet. To the north, hill ranges divide the region from China, and splay southwards, subdividing the region like the fingers of a hand (Map 1). The plains between these ranges are heated to tropical and subtropical temperatures, while five great rivers carry snowmelt from the high mountains of inner Asia, and monsoons sweep the region with four to six months of heavy rainfall a year. High temperatures and plentiful moisture create a spectacularly abundant environment. The natural vegetation is thick forest – deciduous in the north, merging into tropical rainforest further south,

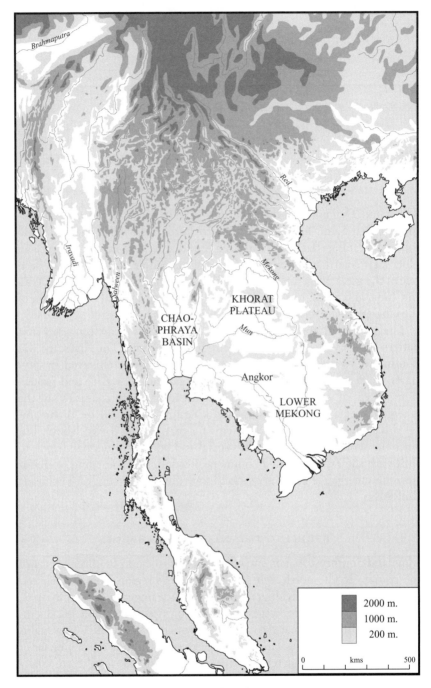

Brahmaputra

Red

Irawadi

Salween

Mekong

KHORAT
PLATEAU

CHAO-
PHRAYA
BASIN

Mun

Angkor

LOWER
MEKONG

2000 m.
1000 m.
200 m.

0   kms   500

Map 1: Mainland Southeast Asia

and dense mangrove along the coast. In the past, many species found this a much better habitat than man, including elephants, wild cattle, deer, monkeys, tigers, snakes, crocodiles, and a vast range of parasitical insects and micro-organisms.

The human population remained sparse until late in the region's history. There are traces of hunter-gatherers sojourning in mountain caves up to 180,000 years ago, but the traces are few and faint. Settlements increased with the coming of rice agriculture and bronze from around 2500 BC, and even more with the arrival of iron around 500 BC.

These metal age settlements were sited on a raised mound and surrounded by a moat, perhaps for defence, perhaps for water storage. The people grew rice, kept cattle and dogs, continued to hunt and gather in the forests, and traded valuable goods such as beads and ceremonial drums over long distances. Archaeologists suspect that new people may have spread through the region in this era, bringing rice agriculture, metalworking, domestic animals, and the languages we now call the Mon-Khmer group. They probably spread along the coasts, but also forged inland along the rivers to the upland plains which were easier to clear and healthier to settle.

From around the last century BC, these people had trade contacts with India which eventually brought ideas and technologies from a region where urban centres had already developed. Larger settlements began to appear, especially in the lower Mekong basin, and to the west in an area stretching from the lower Chaophraya basin across the hills on the neck of the peninsula to its western coast. In the sixth century AD, by adapting scripts borrowed from southern India, these two areas began to write the languages of Khmer and Mon, respectively. In the Khmer country, the farmers became expert at trapping and storing water from rainfall, lakes, and rivers to support a dense population. Rulers marshalled this manpower, along with Indian ideas about urban living, construction, religion, and statecraft to create new urban centres, state systems, and monarchies. The magnificent capital at Angkor became a model which was honoured and mimicked by smaller centres scattered westwards across the Khorat Plateau and the Chaophraya river system.

This early Mon-Khmer tradition was anchored on the coast and spread inland. A second inflow of people and culture came from the north through the hills.

The group of languages now known as Tai probably originated among peoples who lived south of the Yangzi River before the Han Chinese spread from the north into the area from the sixth century BC. As the Han armies came to control China's southern coastline in the first few centuries AD, some of these peoples retreated into the high valleys in the hills behind the coast. Then, over many centuries, some moved westwards, spreading Tai language dialects along a 1000-kilometre arc from the Guangxi interior to the Brahmaputra valley. They probably took with them some expertise in growing rice using the water flow from mountain streams. Certainly they chose to settle in the mountain basins where this technique could be put to good use. Their communities became identified with rice growing. They may also have acquired some martial skills from their encounters with the Chinese because other peoples saw them as fierce warriors. Some of the earlier, mainly Mon-Khmer inhabitants retreated upwards into the hills. Others coexisted with this farmer-warrior elite, often adopting a Tai language and gradually losing their own separate identity.

The Tai groups generally settled in the broad river basins in the hills. Only around the Mekong River did they move south – along the river itself, but also over low watersheds into the foothills around the upper tributaries of the Chaophraya river system. Possibly they were pushed southwards by Mongol raids in the late twelfth century. Possibly they were pulled by trade, or just drifted into a relatively empty area. They paused initially along the line where the hills fall into the plain. Here they could still site their settlements at the foot of a sacred hill, and use the waters flowing down for cultivation. Eventually, however, they spread further into the lowland plain.

Probably they coexisted with earlier inhabitants because their different techniques of rice growing dictated a preference for different types of land. The Mon-Khmer trapped rainfall in ponds. The Tai adapted their skill with water flows to using the rivers. Eventually the Tai language now known as 'Thai' became dominant in the Chaophraya basin. Yet the language itself suggests that various groups blended into this area's society. Thai has absorbed so many basic words, grammatical rules, and syntactical principles from Khmer (and possibly from Mon too) that it is sharply different from any other language in the Tai family (one linguist dubbed it Khmero-Tai). Early European visitors thought many of the people were Mon. Chinese settlers were present by the thirteenth century. The timings of these people movements and language shifts are unknown. The first known written use of Thai dates from the thirteenth century in the southern fringe of the hills. Further south on the plain, all records are in Khmer or Indian languages until the fifteenth century, suggesting these languages still commanded prestige. By the early sixteenth century, the Portuguese were told the lower Chaophraya basin was known as *mueang thai*, the Thai country.

Even after these inflows, the population of the Chaophraya basin was still very sparse. When the forest was cleared, these tracts were very fertile. But in their natural state they teemed with predators, including the germs of malaria and other jungle fevers. The long hot season made survival difficult anywhere distant from a permanent water source. Settlements were strung sparsely along the rivers and around the coasts. Most of the region remained as untouched forest until the last century.

This sparseness meant there was always space for newcomers who continually added to the social complexity over following centuries. The Karen came to occupy the hills marking the western boundary of the Chaophraya basin, though when they came and where from has been forgotten. Groups of Mon regularly moved eastwards across the same hills in refuge from political troubles. Malay seafarers from the archipelago beached on the coasts of the peninsula and settled. Chinese traders merged into the societies of the ports all around the gulf and down the peninsula. The Khorat Plateau began to be populated in the eighteenth century by Lao and Kui people moving westwards across the Mekong River. Hill dwellers filtered into the highlands, nudged by the southward expansion of the Chinese.

The sparseness also underlay slavery, slave raiding, and war. Settlements needed a certain scale to keep the forest and the predators at bay. Leaders needed people as warriors, farmers, artisans, builders, and servants. In early maritime trade, slaves were imported from China and from the Malay archipelago. Wars were often launched to seize people. Victorious armies returned home with piles of loot and strings of prisoners. Artisans were especially prized. Ordinary war prisoners were used as personal retainers, or settled in pioneer colonies to raise food production and increase the numbers available for recruitment. Down to the nineteenth century, some communities specialized as slave raiders, grabbing people from hill communities or neighbouring states and selling them in the lowland capitals.

MUEANG

Areas of settlement were separated from one another by stretches of mountain, forest, or sea. The basic political unit of the region became the city-state, known in Thai as *mueang*. The model evolved in the mountain basins, where the original *mueang* was often a fortified town, the home of the ruler or *jao*. Rather than spreading across the landscape, villages stayed clustered around the *mueang* centres for defence against enemies, animals, and diseases.

Some have argued that the sparse population meant land was a freely abundant good and had no value. Not at all. Land of good fertility and good location was highly prized. In the early stages of a *mueang*, the *jao* acted just like a landlord, managing the land and directing cultivation. As the settlement became larger and more complex, the *jao* became more of a ruler. Villages managed the land, holding it communally and redistributing it to match the labour supply and food needs of families. Villagers cooperated, often over a wide area, to build weir-and-channel systems (*mueang fai*) which supplied irrigation for rice growing. Hierarchy developed. The original settlers often became an elite which had privileged rights in land in return for the obligation to carry arms when required. Later settlers might have access to land only as dependants of this elite. War captives or purchased slaves might have no access at all. People were obliged to render dues to the *jao*, mostly in kind, and also labour services for such tasks as building and repairing the palace. Kin of the *jao* or other established families who helped to administer the *mueang* were allotted the dues and labour services of particular villages.

The settlements which appeared along the rivers in the lowlands and around the coasts differed only in detail. The favoured site was on a river meander, with a canal cut to complete a moat. Compared with the hill *mueang*, more of the population depended on trade rather than agriculture. Rulers might be selected for their wealth and trading skill more than for their lineage or martial quality.

Few places developed into larger cities over time, probably because sizeable settlements became vulnerable to epidemic disease or looting raids. In the legendary early history of Sukhothai, the whole population migrates to the Mon country after an epidemic. In that of Hariphunchai (Lamphun), the whole population is carried away by a victorious army. The Mun river valley in the northeast had several hundred settlements before the thirteenth century, but seems to have been virtually depopulated for the following 400 years. The ports along the coastline were always vulnerable to attack by enemies or pirates. In the early part of Nakhon Si Thammarat's chronicle, the city is repeatedly founded, deserted, and refounded. Songkhla was 'destroyed' twice in the seventeenth century alone. Changes in the landscape could also be disruptive. Satingpra, one of the biggest prehistoric settlements on the peninsula, was abandoned, probably when the coastline shifted. Many town sites in the Chaophraya basin were abandoned or moved when rivers changed course as the delta developed.

A few places defied this tendency for the population to slip and slide across the landscape. Partly this was due to the quality of their location. The idea of *chaiyaphum*, literally 'victorious emplacement', was a specific branch of local science. A site's *chaiyaphum* included defensive features (ease of moating), sacred features (hills, river junctions), water and food supplies, and local climate. Rulers could add to these natural attractions. In Sukhothai's famous (and controversial) Inscription One the ruler advertises his city to prospective settlers by describing his contributions to its *chaiyaphum*: he boasts of his own martial qualities as a protector; guarantees the food supplies ('there are fish in the water and rice in the fields'); promises fair justice, low taxes, and freedom to trade; lists the entertainments and festivals ('whoever wants to make merry, does so; whoever wants to laugh, does so'); and finally catalogues the religious places, emphasizing their number, splendour, and variety.[1]

RULERS AND STATES

Between the thirteenth and fifteenth centuries, there was a revolution in warfare which enabled ambitious rulers to expand their dominions. Part of this revolution was the arrival of firearms – first, cannon from China and Arabia, and later muskets and better cannon from the Portuguese. But the revolution also came from greater use of elephants for transport, better recruitment techniques, and perhaps simply more people available for recruitment as a result of a benign phase of climate.

Ambitious rulers first brought groups of adjacent *mueang* together in confederations. In the hills, these *khwaen* were formed by linking together the *mueang* in successive basins along one river. The ruler often sent his sons or other relatives to rule over the defeated *mueang*. He captured or attracted artisans with the skills to make his own *mueang* more splendid and famous than the others. He often patronized Buddhism, which enjoyed a surge of urban popularity in this era. Buddhism had originally come to the Chaophraya basin by the fifth century, but in a package of Indic gods which was probably not clearly defined into separate sects and traditions. In the thirteenth century, monks again brought the Theravada Buddhist tradition from Sri Lanka and, according to the religious chronicles, it spread like wildfire on a wave of popular enthusiasm. Rulers patronized the construction of splendid temples, venerated monks with a reputation for learning, and collected relics and images of the Buddha which were seen as concentrations of spiritual power.

These emerging capitals gradually became centres of loosely defined but distinct political zones. On the upper reaches of the Chaophraya system, the dominant place was Chiang Mai. It was founded officially in 1296, at a site with excellent *chaiyaphum*, by Mangrai, probably a Tai prince with some Mon-Khmer blood, who consolidated a *khwaen* along the Ping River, and began to subordinate chiefs along other rivers to the east. At death, Mangrai metamorphosed into the founder-ancestor spirit of this enlarged *khwaen*, and future rulers were chosen from his sacred lineage for almost the next two centuries. Chiang Mai only truly became the dominant place under his successors, who embellished the city with splendid *wat*, and built a network of marriage alliances with chiefs stretching east to the Nan River, and north across the Mekong River. The region became known as Lanna, a million ricefields. Further east, the lineage of Fa Ngum at Luang Prabang developed the state of Lanchang stretching along the Mekong and its tributaries.

To the south, the Tai states along the lower fringe of the hills developed another confederation. At first the dominant place was Sukhothai, where the lineage of the legendary founder-ancestor Phra Ruang built a resplendent religious capital. Later the focus and the lineage shifted to Phitsanulok, probably because strategy became a more important element in *chaiyaphum* than sacredness in this warlike era. This area acquired no distinctive name, but was dubbed *mueang nua* or the 'northern cities' by its neighbours to the south.

Another federation formed among port towns on the lower reaches of the rivers in the Chaophraya basin, and around the upper coasts of the gulf, especially four places which had been founded or refounded under Khmer influence around the eleventh century: Phetchaburi, Suphanburi, Lopburi, and Ayutthaya. After a struggle between the ruling families of these places, Ayutthaya emerged as the dominant centre in the late fourteenth century. The Chinese called this region Xian, which the Portuguese converted into Siam.

Each of these centres expanded its influence over neighbouring *mueang*, but in a particular form. The subordinate ruler was usually left in place. He might have to send a daughter or sister to become his overlord's wife, and perhaps a son to serve in his overlord's retinue; these charges served as hostages for the subordinate's continued loyalty. In privileged cases, the overlord might bestow on the subordinate a royal or noble wife who could also serve as an informant. The subordinate would deliver an annual tribute, usually some exotic or rare item. Later this payment was often standardized into ornamental trees made of silver and gold, a Malay practice. In reciprocation, the overlord would give insignia and ritual items which added to the subordinate ruler's status, and perhaps also useful items such as weapons and administrative systems. The overlord would guarantee to defend the subordinate *mueang* and its ruler from outside threats, and the subordinate in return would undertake to supply troops whenever the overlord needed to mobilize an army. But, in practice, the fulfilment of these agreements was never certain.

The overriding principle of these political alliances was that the subordinate ruler was not crushed out of existence, but strengthened so he could become a more stable and useful dependant. The subordinate *mueang* was not destroyed, but contained within a larger unit, and thus added to that larger unit's power and splendour. Rulers boasted not of the extent of their territory, but the number of their dependent rulers. Georges Condominas called this 'emboxment'. By this principle, the village is contained within a *mueang*, and the *mueang* within the influence of a superior *mueang*, possibly up through several levels. The terms 'mandala', 'segmentary state', and 'galactic polity' have been used for this political form, but emboxment describes the underlying mechanism.

This system probably evolved within the world of the Tai hill states, but it was embellished by features borrowed from the Chinese tributary system in which the coastal states of the region had been involved since the third century AD. The Chinese emperor demanded that 'barbarian states' deliver tribute, request confirmation of a new ruler's succession, and receive instruction about the superiority of Chinese civilization. In return, the emperor conferred regalia and undertook to defend the tributary. In practice, the emperor almost never sent troops to discipline a refractory tributary or defend a beleaguered one. But 'barbarian' states complied because tributary status gave them access to the Chinese market, by far the biggest source of demand for trade goods. On this pattern, some port *mueang* developed tributary relations with emerging centres of power in order to gain access to their growing markets. The rulers of these power centres listed such tributaries in their inscriptions and chronicles to vaunt their far-flung influence.

These webs of military and commercial relations were flexible and fluid. Centres rose and fell. At the margins, *mueang* developed parallel relations with two or more centres of power, and the relative importance of these various ties fluctuated over time.

From the late fourteenth century, the four emerging confederations in and around the Chaophraya basin (Lanna, Lanchang, Mueang Nua, Siam) began to contest against one another, beginning an era of intermittent warfare. Over the next century, people were submitted to systems of mass conscription, the size of armies escalated, societies became more militarized, and a warrior ethic prevailed. Great armies traversed the landscape, destroying cities, forcibly moving people, devastating crops, and provoking epidemics. Ultimately, these wars were inconclusive. The Ayutthaya forces finally conquered Chiang Mai in the late fifteenth century but to no avail. These centres could destroy one another and cart away people, famous Buddha images, and wealth, but over these distances they could not 'embox' one another permanently. In the late fifteenth century, these wars petered out.

ASCENDANCY OF THE COAST

Wealth generated by trade had a more lasting impact on the geopolitics. With improved shipbuilding, maritime trade increased. From the thirteenth century, Ayutthaya raided down the peninsula and northwards into the interior to command supplies of the exotic produce of tropical forests in great demand in China – aromatic woods, ivory, rhino horn, brilliant bird feathers. By playing the Chinese tribute system well, Ayutthaya became China's favoured trading partner. Then, in the later fifteenth century, Ayutthaya took control of a portage route across the neck of the peninsula, creating a new trade connection between east and west, avoiding the longer and pirate-infested route through the Melaka Straits. Ayutthaya prospered as an entrepot where goods were exchanged between the east (China), west (India and Arabia), and south (Malay archipelago). The Portuguese, who arrived in the early sixteenth century, marked Ayutthaya as one of the three great powers of Asia, along with China and the Indian empire of Vijayanagar.

Over the fifteenth and sixteenth centuries, Ayutthaya extended its power over the northern cities. Yet this was not a simple conquest and incorporation, but a more subtle merging of traditions. Wealth and trade links gave Ayutthaya the military advantage of access to supplies of Portuguese guns and mercenaries. But the northern cities probably had larger manpower reserves for recruitment, and tougher martial traditions. Some northerners were forcibly swept south to the rising port capital, but others probably moved of their own accord to share in the city's prosperity. The ruling families of the northern cities became entwined in marriage links with the

Ayutthayan dynasty. Northern warriors served as Ayutthaya's troop commanders. Northern nobles settled in the port capital, and blended into the official elite. Ayutthaya gradually absorbed administrative systems, architectural tastes, religious practices, and probably also the everyday language from its northern neighbours. Because of its prime location for trade, Ayutthaya was the capital of this enlarged federation. But the northern city of Phitsanulok operated as a second capital (the Portuguese sometimes described them as twin states) because of its strategic location for the wars against Lanna. Eventually northern nobles became the king-makers in Ayutthaya. In 1559 they finally dislodged the old dynasty and took control.

Over the same era, trade provoked east–west rivalries. The southward drift of people and power in the Chaophraya basin was matched on either side. To the west in the Irawadi basin, Pegu became dominant over the old Burman centre of Ava. To the east, the Khmer capital of Angkor was abandoned in favour of Lawaek-Udong in the Mekong delta. The three port capitals of Pegu, Ayutthaya, and Lawaek-Udong competed to control the interior sources for exotic forest goods demanded in the China trade.

Their rulers also competed for sheer precedence. With treasuries stocked from trade profits, armies swollen with recruits from the hinterland, personal guards manned by foreign mercenaries, temples embellished with images and gold looted from their conquered neighbours, the rulers of these places imagined themselves as *cakkavatin*, the unique world-conquering emperor described in Buddhist texts like the *Traiphum* (Three worlds). In this east–west competition, west had the advantage, probably because that direction was the source of the Portuguese mercenaries and cannon. Siam sent armies which battered the Khmer capital and placed submissive princes on the Khmer throne. Pegu demanded Siam accept similar tributary status, then allied with the northern nobles to besiege and take Ayutthaya in 1559. Pegu hauled away people, artisans, Buddha images, and loot; seized valuable elephants as symbolic tribute; and took members of the Ayutthayan ruling family as wives and hostages.

But over these distances, and across greater barriers of cultural difference, emboxment was even more difficult to sustain. Siam's domination of Cambodia declined once Vietnam became a countervailing power on the Khmers' other flank. Similarly, Naresuan, the Siamese prince taken away as hostage to Pegu, escaped, abrogated the tributary relationship with Pegu, and spent most of his fifteen-year reign (1590–1605) on campaign, resisting further Burmese inroads, and re-establishing Ayutthaya's dominance in the lower Chaophraya basin.

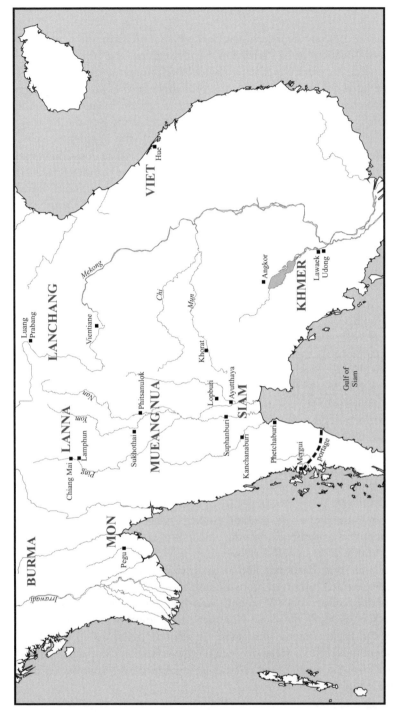

Map 2: Early political geography

By the start of the seventeenth century, this era of warfare had reached a stalemate. Most of the ruling centres across mainland Southeast Asia had been sacked one or more times over the preceding century. People began more effectively to resist being slaughtered for the sake of royal self-esteem. In the 1560s, a massive revolt erupted among the war prisoners taken to Ava. Other resistance was less flamboyant but equally effective. People bribed the military recruiting agents, melted into the monkhood, or fled into the forests. Rulers struggled to raise armies on their former scale. Cities invested in brick walls, wider moats, and defensive cannon which cancelled out the besiegers' advantages. In the 1590s and early 1600s, a succession of sieges failed, and mutinous armies dissolved into the countryside.

THE AGE OF COMMERCE

Peace brought prosperity. In the early seventeenth century, Ayutthaya revived. After Naresuan's conquests, the city ruled an inner core (*ratchathani*) in the heart of the Chaophraya delta. Ranged around were many 'great cities' (*mahanakhon*), controlled by their own ruling families but unquestionably emboxed within Ayutthaya's sphere of influence. These included the old northern cities, ports around the head of the gulf, the portage route across to the upper western coast of the peninsula, and border posts commanding the main routes to east (Khorat) and west (Kanchanaburi). Further out was a ring of tributaries whose attachment was more fitful and compromised by competing attachment to other powers. These included the port cities down the peninsula which simultaneously looked southwards to the Malay world; and the interior states of Khmer, Lao, Lanna, and Shan which balanced Ayutthaya against Vietnam, China, or Burma.

Ayutthaya again prospered as an entrepot between east and west. To the east, Tokugawa Japan conditionally opened up to trade. To the west, the Safavid and Mughal empires became rich markets and producers of fine goods. The portage route under Ayutthaya's control gained in attraction for Asian traders after the Dutch dominated the more southerly route through the Melaka Straits. Ayutthaya grew into perhaps the largest city in Southeast Asia, and certainly one of its most cosmopolitan. The city was ringed by settlements of Chinese, Viet, Cham, Mon, Portuguese, Arab, Indian, Persian, Japanese, and various Malay communities from the archipelago. The Dutch arrived in 1604, competed for a share in the trade to Japan, and added their settlement to this ring. The French and English followed later in the century.

The court made use of these peoples. It recruited Malays, Indians, Japanese, and Portuguese to serve as palace guards. It brought Chinese and Persians into the official ranks to administer trade. It hired Dutch master craftsmen to build ships, French and Italian engineers to design fortifications and waterworks, British and Indians to serve as provincial governors, and Chinese and Persians as doctors. A Japanese, a Persian, and then a Greek adventurer (Constantin Phaulcon) successively became powerful figures at court. The kings, especially Narai (r. 1656–1688), welcomed new knowledge, exchanged embassies with the Netherlands, France, and Persia, and borrowed dress and architectural styles from Persia, Europe, and China. As part of the management of such a cosmopolitan centre, the kings allowed freedom of religion, even proselytization, which impressed the Europeans (who were busily killing one another over the interpretation of Christianity at home). But this openness tempted both the French and Persians to believe they could convert the Siamese king and thus the country. This folly sparked a crisis in 1688, in which Phaulcon was killed, the French were expelled, and the British fled.

LATE AYUTTHAYA SOCIETY

Enriched by trade, guarded by mercenaries, helped by experts from all over the world, the Ayutthayan monarchy became exceptionally powerful in the seventeenth century. Through monopolies, it reserved to itself the largest share of Siam's external trade, and through other taxes it took a share of an expanding internal economy. Little was wasted on war. Much was invested in unprecedented magnificence of new palaces, new and refurbished *wat*, and showy festivals. Even the most superior French visitor, the Jesuit Guy Tachard, gulped on entering the palace's Wat Phra Si Sanphet in 1687: 'there is nothing to be seen but Gold . . . it must needs touch one to the quick to see one single Idol richer than all the Tabernacles of the Churches of Europe'.[2] The noble elite channelled their unused martial energies into elephant and tiger hunts, boat races, and martial arts displays. The court also found a new taste for gentler pursuits of courtly poetry and drama celebrating the victories and romances of kings and gods.

To dramatize and enhance its power, the monarchy was hidden, mystified, and drenched in ritual. In the 1630s, King Prasat Thong reinvented Ayutthaya's traditional links to Khmer civilization. The dynasty claimed distant roots in Angkorian Cambodia. More Brahmans were imported to elaborate court rituals. New temples were built on plans inspired by

Angkor Wat, and with strong Angkor-style identification between the king and his personal sanctuary. The palace was rebuilt several times, hiding the inner sanctum behind successive outer courtyards, higher walls, and smaller entrances. The royal body was hidden from sight, revealed to the people only on a handful of grand occasions per year, and even then officially forbidden to look upon. After seeing the court and public ritual, the republican Dutch found 'this reverence better becoming a celestial Deity, than an earthly Majesty'. But the royalist French found it rather wonderful: 'In the Indies there is no state that is more monarchical than Siam'.[3]

Late Ayutthayan society was strictly divided into a service nobility of maybe two thousand people and their families, and a mass of people bound to surrender some or all of their labour to the elite.

By the seventeenth century, the service nobility was an elaborate structure, codified in lists of official posts, each with its specific title, honorific, and rank measured in numerical units known as 'sakdina'.[4] The administration was divided into four main sections. The first looked after the palace and capital including collecting rice from the royal land, guarding the royal person, keeping the peace, running the royal household, and adjudicating disputes in the capital and the core kingdom (*ratchathani*). The second looked after military affairs, and managed relations with the outlying great cities and tributary states. The third carried out royal trade, oversaw the foreign communities, and looked after the main treasury. The fourth contained the Brahmans who took care of ritual, astrology, and record keeping.

Entry into the official ranks was a noble preserve. Families presented their sons at court, where they were enrolled as pages. Ascent up the ladder of success then depended on personal skill, family connections, and royal favour. Noble families could advance their cause by presenting the king with a daughter and hope she would gain influence in the royal bed and the intricate politics of the palace. Nobles were invested with symbols of office, mostly betel boxes of graded elaborateness of design. Senior officials might also be awarded people and maybe land or its product. They paraded through the streets displaying their betel boxes and trailed by an entourage to indicate their status. Nobles were expected to live from these grants, and from whatever income they could make through their status and office – mostly by taking a percentage of revenues collected, or charging fees for judicial work.

Over the era of warfare, all men (and some women) outside the noble ranks had been brought within systems of servitude and forced labour.

Under methods adapted from the Tai hill states, most freemen (*phrai*) were registered on a conscription roll, and placed under an overseer (*nai* or *munnai*) who was responsible for mobilization. Those who evaded this registration lost rights such as access to judicial procedure. Conscripts served on a rotational basis (alternate months, or alternating half-years). As warfare diminished, these corvée forces were transferred to other tasks such as building temples and palaces, carrying palanquins, rowing boats, or loading the trading junks. The kings and great noble-officials controlled this forced labour and sometimes competed over it. The Ayutthaya practice was replicated in other *mueang*.

War prisoners were excluded from this system, and had a status of *that*, usually translated as 'slave'. Others could sell themselves into *that* status, or be forced into it by debt or as punishment. Household heads could sell their wives and children. This slave status was hereditary. Slaves had a money valuation and were bought, sold, and redeemed. These systems of labour control were so comprehensive that European traders found it difficult to hire people unless they worked through the labour-controlling aristocracy. Even then, they occasionally found the labour supply dried up when people were needed for military expeditions or great construction projects.

Gender roles differed sharply by social status. Among ordinary people, women did at least their full share of work. Visitors ranging from Chinese in the fifteenth century to French and Persians in the seventeenth, and Englishmen in the nineteenth, noted that the women 'do most of the work' in Siam. Some attributed this to the corvée system which removed men from the household for up to half the year. Through most of the Chaophraya basin, rural households gave equal weight to their maternal and paternal bloodlines, and partitioned inheritance equally among male and female children. In the spirit religions which existed alongside Buddhism, many of the ritual specialists were women. In *Khun chang khun phaen*, an early epic which originated from oral tradition, the women have strong characters, clear economic functions, and considerable independence.

But among royalty and nobility, women were treated as assets. Patriarchs accumulated wives in order to augment the lineage. Families deployed daughters to build dynastic connections. In law, a woman was always the property of a man – first, of her father, then of her husband (marriage law was like a deed of sale from father to husband), and possibly of an owner if she were sold into slavery. Court poetry portrayed women as objects of beauty and devices in the plot, but not as agents with functions and character. In the entire Ayutthaya chronicle, there are only two prominent women: one a warrior and honorary male (Suriyothai), and the other a femme fatale whose sexuality is a threat to the dynasty (Sudachan).

In the seventeenth century, the society began to change in ways which gathered pace over the following century. The growth of a trading economy, and the decline of the military ethic, partially undermined the systems of forced labour. Many offered bribes to keep themselves off the registration rolls. Some sought less demanding patrons. Others sold themselves into slavery as a way to raise the capital for business ventures as well as gain freedom from corvée. Others entered the monkhood. Almost certainly, increasing numbers took refuge in the forests and lived beyond the reach of officialdom. By the early eighteenth century, the court found it difficult to mobilize armies of more than a few thousand. The kings issued edicts designed to improve the registration procedure, punish bribery, discourage lapse into slave status, expose fake monks, and locate people hidden under a noble's protection. But the repetition of such legislation indicates that forced labour was becoming more difficult to marshal.

The nobility also underwent change in this era. During the era of warfare, people could vault up the ladder of success through demonstrated skill in battle. After this route diminished in importance, two others were available. A few could become wealthy through the *phrakhlang*, the department overseeing trade. Many of its posts were given to foreigners, because they had the necessary skills, and because they were easier to discipline. The Thai nobles who served in the *phrakhlang* were hence rather few, but very splendid. They had the opportunity to trade, and also to demand 'presents' from foreigners trading at Ayutthaya.

The other ladder of success was through the intricate politics of royal favour within the court. This manoeuvring was constant, but peaked during times of royal succession. Those with a chance to ascend the throne had to have royal blood and preferably be closely related to the previous monarch, but there was no exact law of succession. In practice, each succession was a trial of strength, usually involving the previous king's brothers and sons. In a martial era, such a contest made sense as a way to select a warrior-king. In the more peaceable seventeenth century, the succession became an elaborate contest involving not only competing royal kin, but factions of nobles and royal guards who backed rival candidates in the hope of advancement. These contests began with a miniature civil war fought in the centre of the capital, and ended with wholesale

purges of the nobles who backed the wrong side and of male royal relatives who might want to renew the contest at some later date. Nobles
who helped to make a king could expect rewards of position, women,
wealth, and honours.

Great noble households tried to accumulate wealth and prestige over
generations. Especially in the outlying areas, they could often make their
offices virtually hereditary. At the capital they could ensure their sons entry
into the page system, proffer their daughters, and try to choose the winning
side in succession struggles. The kings, however, obstructed the growth
of such powerful households. They rotated appointments. They imposed
death duties, and administered them discriminately to disperse wealth.
They occasionally arraigned particularly tall poppies on grounds of the
bribery which was regular practice. The accused then suffered a humiliating
public execution, after which his wives and slaves were distributed to others,
and his house thrown open for public looting. European visitors noted that
the great nobles lived in splendid houses and were surrounded by hordes
of retainers, but seemed to possess almost no movable property. Diamonds
were popular because they were easy to hide.

In the early eighteenth century, however, the aristocracy became stronger,
largely because of a shift in the pattern of trade. After the crisis of
1688, British and French traders quit Ayutthaya. The Dutch remained,
but their attentions were elsewhere, and they finally departed in 1765.
Yet Ayutthaya's trade soon reoriented towards China and to a lesser
extent the Malay world to the south. China increasingly needed rice to
feed its southern peoples, and thus allowed more freedom to trade. Siam
became a favoured rice supplier. Chinese migrated to settle in Siam, with
the community estimated at 20,000 by 1735. At least two Chinese rose
to the post of *phrakhlang*. The first, according to French missionaries,
'placed his Chinese friends in the most important posts . . . with the
result that the Chinese now do all the trade of the kingdom'.[5] Some
Chinese married into the court elite. Others traded rice, manufactured
noodles, distilled liquor, and raised pigs. At least around the capital, a market economy thrived. The city's many markets were thronged with river-
boats bringing produce from the Chaophraya system. The court expanded
the coinage, passed laws to regulate commercial contracts, and invited
bids for tax-farms. Land was bought and sold. Imported cloth, crockery,
glass, and ironware found a rising market. Robbery increased. A new category of *phrai mangmi*, rich commoners, emerged. People offered bribes
to gain rank and position. At least at the capital, trade began to shake the
social order.

The succession wars became less frequent, more confined within the royal ranks, and less damaging for the nobility. A few great households managed to accumulate manpower and wealth across generations. Some were old local families, but others originated from Brahmans in the ritual department, refugee Mon generals, and Persian and Chinese traders. Gradually this aristocracy began not only to seek its own advancement, but also to try limiting the power of the monarchy. In the wake of succession struggles, some provincial nobles raised the standard of revolt, but none effectively threatened the capital. Some peasant bands, recruited probably among those who had withdrawn beyond official reach into the forests, marched boldly on the capital but were dispersed by cannon. More subtle resistance to royal power was exercised through the language of Buddhism.

BUDDHISM AND KINGSHIP

Theravada, the way of the elder, differs from other strains of Buddhism in the prime position accorded to the monk and monastic practice. The duty of the Sangha or monkhood is to preserve the *thamma* or teachings of the Buddha by adhering strictly to the *winaya* or monastic code. Some monks study the texts, preserve them by recopying, and preach their contents to the laity. Other monks exemplify the teachings by living an imitation of the Buddha's own life, gaining insight through ascetic rigour and meditation. The duty of the laity, including the ruler, is to sustain the monkhood by patronage and protection. The enthusiasm for Theravada in the Chaophraya basin, as elsewhere, stemmed especially from urban society's appreciation of its openness and inherent egalitarianism: all have the same opportunity to become a monk, to give the monkhood their patronage, and to achieve the ultimate release from the material world (*nibbana*).

In practice, this pure form of Theravada was blended with other religious practices, including roles for Hindu gods, notions of supernatural power often borrowed from tantric types of Buddhism, and folk beliefs in spirits – especially in their power to foretell and influence the future.

Southeast Asian rulers favoured the Hindu gods because of the opportunity, exemplified at Angkor, to associate the ruler with the power gods of the Hindu pantheon (Vishnu, Siva). Hence the Ayutthayan kings imported Brahmans to plan and execute royal rituals. But Hinduism developed no local following in Siam. In popular practice, Hindu gods were transformed into attendants of the Buddha or converted into local spirits (as in their popularity in spirit houses). The Brahmanical royal rituals thus had limited meaning beyond the court.

Rulers also saw opportunities to appropriate the supernatural powers muddled into Buddhist practice. They sought association with the power of local spirits, Palladian Buddha images, sacred hills and rivers, white elephants, relics of the Buddha enshrined in *chedi* reliquaries, and ascetic rishis. But often this association required the consent of the monkhood. Hence, kings and Sangha negotiated the relative roles of spiritual and political leadership. The Sangha needed the protection and patronage which rulers could provide. In return, rulers might demand administrative power over the Sangha hierarchy, and monastic approval of their rule. And in return again, monks might insist that the ruler govern well for the material and spiritual benefit of the people. During the martial era, monks criticized rulers who demanded too much tax, conscripted people during the cultivation season, seized women or property at will, killed animals for pleasure, got drunk, or otherwise set a bad example. Some major monasteries kept chronicles which judged each ruler, praising those who defended the *mueang* skilfully, ruled their people with fairness and compassion, and of course patronized the Sangha. From these delicate negotiations came the concept of the *thammaracha*, the ruler who ruled according to the *thamma* or Buddhist teachings on the model of the early Indian emperor, Ashoka. In the chronicles, the concept was exemplified by the later rulers of Sukhothai who took Thammaracha as their dynastic name.

In the seventeenth and early eighteenth centuries, there was a groundswell of Buddhist enthusiasm in Ayutthaya, probably associated with the growth of trade and a more independent aristocracy. Many new temples were built. *Wihan* (assembly halls) were enlarged to accommodate more people. The rulers invested in some of these projects, but most were the work of nobles. The seventeenth-century kings patronized Brahmanism rather more than Buddhism. Narai built or repaired very few *wat*, reduced his appearances at ceremonial events, and seemed to favour the Muslims and Christians clustered around the court. In a literary work, he challenged: 'Can monks question kings?' In the crisis of 1688, monks organized people to take up arms and prevent continued succession within the Narai line.

The king installed after this crisis was not a member of the royal clan, but had been a popular leader in the official nobility. Under this new dynasty, the patronage of Brahmans diminished, while that of the Sangha dramatically increased. King Borommakot (r. 1733–1758) and his nobles built and repaired so many temples that the skyline of Ayutthaya was totally remodelled. His personal devotion was so marked he was accorded the title of Thammaracha. His fame became such that Sri Lanka, the original home of Theravada Buddhism, sent a monastic delegation to ask for Ayutthayan monks to help revive their degraded Sangha.

The nobility acclaimed Borommakot, but also sought more power to constrain the monarchy. They adopted the Akanya Sutta, an early Buddhist text which said that monarchy evolved when the horrors of an unregulated society forced the people to band together and 'elect' the best man to be king. In their own account of the later Ayutthaya period, nobles wrote that at each succession the king was chosen by the assembly of the nobility – a record of aspiration rather than reality. The nobles and the monkhood also stressed that the king must continually prove he was the best man to rule by following the *thotsaphit ratchatham*, the ten laws of royal conduct, meaning munificence, moral living, generosity, justice, compassion, absence of bad ambition, suppression of anger, non-oppressiveness, humility, and upholding *thamma*. The Long Song Prophesy, a poetical work probably dating from this era, predicted that the city would fall if these moral rules were neglected:

> When virtues ten fall deaf on kingly ears,
> So smash the spheres; sixteen disasters smite.
> The moon, the stars, the earth and, yea, the sky
> Are knocked awry – in every realm the blight . . .
> Though *now* Ayutthaya in bliss can claim
> To shame all heaven's joys a myriad-fold,
> Yet here – behold! – are whores and sin foretold.
> Alas! Alas! Count the days 'til it shall come to pass![6]

THE FALL OF AYUTTHAYA

It indeed came to pass, in 1767, when Ayutthaya was besieged and sacked a second time by armies from the Burmese capital of Ava. The destruction was so violent that later historical writing portrayed Burma as a constant aggressor, and the defence against Burmese attacks as the central theme of Thai history. In fact, the prior round of warfare ending in the late sixteenth century had resulted in a stable settlement: Burmese influence prevailed in the interior in an arc running from Ava through the Shan States and Lanna to Lanchang and Sipsongpanna; Ayutthaya dominated the coastline from the neck of the peninsula eastward to Cambodia. Apart from some minor skirmishes, there had been almost no conflict between Siam and Burma for 150 years.

The attacks in the 1760s were not the latest episodes in an old theme. Rather, they were a huge surprise. They stemmed from the ambitions of a new Burmese dynasty to spread its influence in all directions, and they were sparked by renewed competition to control the neck of the peninsula. But unlike before, Burma had grandiose ambitions to spread its power eastwards by eliminating Ayutthaya as a rival capital.

The Burmese attack was another contest between dynasties for dominance. But over the previous 150 years of relative peace, Ayutthaya had become a wealthier and more sophisticated society. A new popular culture had emerged of ballads, dance dramas, and other performances held mostly in the *wat*. Even court poets had begun to celebrate the romance of travel and the joys of erotic love rather than victory in battle and fables about princes. Ordinary people had eased free of the ties of subordination which bound them to participate in such princely conflicts, and had not yet been captured by an *idea* which demanded their loyalty. As the Burmese armies advanced, many people around Ayutthaya avoided conscription by bribing officials. Others took refuge in the forests away from the expected passage of armies. Among the provincial lords called on for help, only a few sent troops. Cities in the path of the advancing armies concentrated on defending themselves, usually by capitulating to avoid destruction. Some people along the way were swept up into the invading armies. Others joined for the prospect of loot. The Ayutthaya nobles tried to negotiate with the advancing assailants on the basis of the same Buddhist humanism they deployed to constrain the monarchy: 'It will be like when elephants fight. The plants and grass on the ground get crushed . . . So ask your lord to ally the two countries as a single golden land . . . Both kings will gain fame for their kindness in freeing their people from worry'.[7]

The Ayutthayan rulers understood the old martial era had passed. To compensate for the lack of recruits, they had heightened the city walls, widened the moats, and bought a quantity and range of guns that astounded the Burmese when they broke open the arsenal. Behind these defences, the city could last out one campaigning season and rely on the annual monsoon floods to disperse any siege.

But the Burmese brought three armies whose combined size was much larger than any force fielded since the sixteenth century. They camped outside the city around temples built on higher ground, and thus sustained their siege over two years despite the floods. The city's supplies dwindled, and many people slipped away. The walls were breached on 7 April 1767. As the Burmese chronicle states, 'The city was then destroyed'.[8]

The Burmese aim was not to force Ayutthaya into tributary status, but to obliterate it as a rival capital by destroying not only the physical resources of the city, but also its human resources, ideological resources, and intellectual resources. Any of these which were movable were carted away to Ava, including nobles, skilled people, Buddha images, books, weapons, and (reportedly) 2000 members of the royal family. Resources that were immovable were destroyed. The walls were flattened and the arsenals trashed. The palaces and *wat* that distinguished the city as a royal and religious centre were reduced to 'heaps of ruins and ashes'.[9]

The fighting continued intermittently for forty years. The areas around Ayutthaya were heavily depopulated. The initial main Burmese attack had come through Lanna, seizing people, gold, and supplies for the campaign. Further Burmese attacks in 1772, 1774, and 1776 devastated Lanna so much that Chiang Mai was abandoned, and large areas northwards from the city were deserted. In 1785–86 the Burmese mounted another massive attack, with five armies totalling over 100,000 crossing passes along a 1000-kilometre stretch of the hills from Lanna in the north to the mid-peninsula in the south, and spreading disruption over a wide area. Phitsanulok and other northern cities were abandoned. The Burmese were finally expelled from Lanna in 1802–04, but Chiang Mai was reduced to a village, and the northward areas were not resettled fully until the 1870s. In the south, skirmishes with the Burmese continued until 1819. The first western visitor to Nakhon Si Thammarat in 1826 thought: 'It appears never to have recovered' from the Burmese wars and had 'few inhabitants, no trade and insignificant resources'.[10] Even the major central plain town of Ratchaburi, burnt down in 1767, remained deserted until 1800, and still had parts left abandoned in the 1880s.

CONCLUSION

Southeast Asia's characteristic modern landscape of tessellated paddyfields is a very misleading guide to how it was in the past. The hills and plains were covered with forest. In the seventeenth century, up to 200,000 deerskins were exported from Ayutthaya each year – an indicator of the extent of the forest and its resident game. Human settlements were scattered sparsely along the river systems. The population living within the modern boundaries of Thailand in the early nineteenth century was probably between one and two million (Chart 1).[11] As waterways were the best communication routes, the river systems came to define the cultural divisions of the region. By the sixteenth century (though exactly how long before is

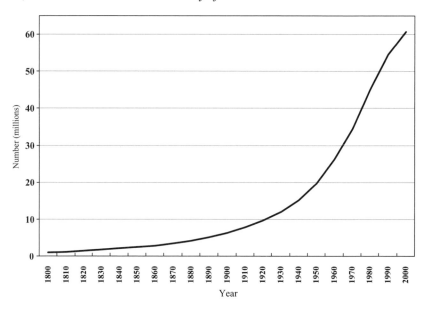

Chart 1: Estimated population in area of modern Thailand

not at all clear), Thai was the main language of the lower Chaophraya basin south of the hills. By virtue of its trading wealth, Ayutthaya became this area's dominant place. But the fragmented pattern of human settlement was reflected in the region's fragmented politics. Each locality had its own local ruler and often its own ruling practices and traditions. Ayutthaya, and rival centres, extended their influence by drawing these rulers into relationships of subordination and tribute. On the eve of Ayutthaya's 1767 destruction, the city had strong influence over the *mueang* in the lower Chaophraya system, and looser influence over Lao and Khmer rulers to the east, and over Thai-Chinese-Malay port *mueang* down the peninsula.

The premodern social structure was based on bonds of personal subordination – rice peasant to the ruler of the local *mueang, that* slave to master, commoner to conscription chief, junior noble to patron, senior noble and tributary lord to king, and king to the emperor of China. In each of these relationships, the subordinate surrendered produce (of his fields or labouring skills) or labour power in return for some measure of protection. In ordinary *mueang*, the social hierarchy was relatively shallow. But at great centres such as Ayutthaya, the king and great nobles accumulated resources through warfare and trade, and created a deep and finely graded hierarchy.

During the overall expansion of Asian commerce from the sixteenth to eighteenth century, the Ayutthaya kings amassed wealth, weapons, mercenaries, and new skills and technologies from Europe, Persia, and China. They consolidated their power locally through ritual dramas, and extended it further afield by armed expeditions, often clashing with similarly expansive rival neighbours (Ava, Cambodia, Vietnam).

By the eighteenth century, the expansion of commerce had begun to undermine royal power and militarism. An emerging aristocracy sought ways to preserve wealth across generations. Ordinary people resisted surrendering their labour and their lives. Social aspirations were expressed in the moral language of resurgent Buddhism. This faltering commitment to the old order left the city vulnerable to the unexpected and unusually fierce Burmese attack in 1767. In the short term, this event wrecked trade, dispersed wealth, and provoked a revival of militarism. But over the longer term, it paved the way for the growth of a market economy and a new social order.

2

The old order in transition, 1760s to 1860s

Although the capital was physically destroyed, Ayutthaya represented traditions of trade and rule which were not easily erased. Over the next fifteen years a new capital emerged further down the Chaophraya River located at Thonburi-Bangkok, a site with better *chaiyaphum* for trade and defence. Members of the old elite dramatized Bangkok as a revival of Ayutthaya. But in fact much was very different. This era of war extended the Siamese armies' influence farther to north, south, and east than ever before. Forced movements of people transformed the ethnic mix in the Chaophraya plain. The great noble households which survived the crisis became the dominant force in the polity.

The major change was in the economy. The trading connections with China, begun in the early eighteenth century, were resumed and reinforced. The market economy expanded rapidly in the Chaophraya plain and down the peninsula, driven largely by import of Chinese enterprise and labour. The growth of the market economy began to remake the social structure and change the mentality of the elite. The return of Europeans bringing ideas of 'progress' and threats of colonial rule prepared the ground for an era of change.

FROM AYUTTHAYA TO BANGKOK

Within a very short time, several pretenders emerged to occupy the vacancy left by the obliteration of the city and dynasty of Ayutthaya. Among these, Phaya Taksin emerged as strongest. His origins are obscure. Possibly he was the son of a Teochiu Chinese migrant gambler or trader and his Thai wife. Possibly he became a provincial cart trader, and bribed his way to governorship of the border town of Tak. He thus had no traditional claims to rule but was a leader of great charisma. He gathered around him other Chinese traders, sundry adventurers, and minor nobles. He founded a new capital at Thonburi, surrounded by a swamp that was good for defence, and opposite an old Chinese trading settlement at Bangkok. He used his Chinese connections to import rice to provision the devastated area, and then to revive trade to generate revenue. He brought back the traditions of the warrior-king and militarized society. He tattooed male wrists to facilitate conscription, and led armies by example. The ritual shrouding of the late Ayutthayan kingship was abandoned in favour of an open, personal, charismatic style resembling the *phumibun* men-of-merit who had typically led the occasional peasant revolts in Ayutthaya's hinterland.

As the Burmese threat was neutralized, people drifted back. Among the surviving nobles, few initially were prepared to serve this new and very different ruler. Later they were blocked by the adventurers whose early support for Taksin was repaid by promotion to the highest posts in both the capital and provinces. One exception was Bunma, a descendant of the foremost Mon lineage in the old nobility. He later brought his elder brother Thongduang into Taksin's inner circle. The two became Taksin's most successful generals. Thongduang was adopted as leader of the old nobles who resented their own exclusion from office, and who were disturbed by Taksin's origins, supporters, and 'abnormal' rule. They bristled when Taksin claimed to have exceptional spiritual merit, and elevated himself over the monkhood. In April 1782, they mounted a coup, executed Taksin on grounds he had become mad, purged his relatives and followers, and placed Thongduang on the throne as King Yotfa (Rama I).[1] The dynasty thus begun took its name from Thongduang's former ministerial title, Chakri.

The new regime portrayed itself as a restoration of Ayutthayan tradition in reaction against the abnormalities of Taksin's interregnum. The capital was moved across the river to Bangkok, and built on similar principles to Ayutthaya – an island created by closing a river meander with a canal. The word Ayutthaya was inscribed in the city's official name. The remains of shattered Ayutthayan monuments were brought to the city and incorporated into its new buildings. All surviving manuscripts were sought out and compiled into recensions of laws, histories, religious texts, and manuals on the practice of every aspect of government. Yotfa's coronation was delayed until it could be confidently modelled on that of Borommakot.

But this revivalism was superficial. Underneath, there were big changes.

TERRITORIAL EXPANSION

The remilitarization of society, initially for defence, resulted in an expansion of the Siamese capital's territorial influence far beyond any earlier scope.

In the north and south, Bangkok's armies pacified areas disrupted by the Burmese invasions, and settled them as tributaries. Then Bangkok's military resources were redirected eastwards.

To the south, Ayutthaya had previously imposed only loose tributary relations over ports on the peninsula. From the sixteenth century onwards, the peninsula had become more populated and more important. Malays in flight from Dutch rule in the archipelago arrived in increasing numbers. Chinese merchants fleeing legal restrictions at home settled in the ports. This increased population made it possible to exploit the peninsula's natural resources, particularly its tin deposits and its suitability for crops like pepper. Ayutthaya began to take greater interest in controlling the peninsula and its resources. It developed Nakhon Si Thammarat as its outpost. It sent navies south to impose control. But these efforts were only moderately successful until the disruptions of the Burmese invasions. In the aftermath, Taksin and Yotfa sent armies south, gained a warmer welcome from local rulers, and established Siam's influence down to the Malay states of Kedah and Trengganu.

In the north and east, the campaigns to drive back the Burmese also extended Siamese influence further than before. Chiang Mai had fallen under Burmese influence since the sixteenth century. Between the 1770s and 1804, Taksin and then Yotfa helped a local lord, Kavila, drive out the Burmese and re-establish Chiang Mai. Kavila's successors remained querulous tributaries to Bangkok. Next, Taksin took the Lao capital of Vientiane, hauling away its prince as a hostage. He also burnt the Cambodian capital to the ground, and installed a puppet ruler. Old systems of tribute collection were reimposed on these outlying areas to supply Bangkok with export goods for the China trade.

Although the Burmese threat was contained by 1804, Bangkok's military expansion continued over following decades. In the 1820s, Bangkok began to tap the resources of the Khorat Plateau which was still largely unpopulated and open for exploitation. In 1827–28, Bangkok went to war with the Lao ruler of Vientiane, Jao Anu, who competed to control this frontier region. Bangkok's armies destroyed Jao Anu's capital and dynasty much as the Burmese had set on Ayutthaya sixty years earlier. People were then resettled from across the Mekong River onto the Khorat Plateau to increase its value as a source of trade goods.

Similarly, Bangkok first extended informal control into western Cambodia, and then in 1833 the king dispatched an army to take the territory or else 'turn Cambodia into forest, only the land, the mountains, the rivers and the canals are to be left. You are to carry off Khmer families to be resettled in Thai territory, do not leave any behind. It would be good to treat Cambodia as we did Vientiane.'² Trade was redirected to Bangkok. Cardamom and other forest goods were requisitioned for export to China. People were hauled away for resettlement. Elite families were taken to Bangkok for future use as tributary rulers.

Only in the west did the Siamese armies fail. Two attempts to take Tavoy and re-establish control of the portage across the peninsula were thwarted by the Burmese. Bangkok had emboxed a new outer ring of tributary states in the south, north, and east. The chronicler of King Yotfa boasted: 'His kingdom was far more extensive than that of the former Kings of Ayutthaya'.³

This age of disorder also transformed the human geography of the Chaophraya basin. Large numbers of the former population were carried away to Burma in 1767. Many more fled during this and subsequent campaigns. One purpose of Bangkok's military expansion was to restock the population by forced resettlement. In the 1770s and 1780s, Taksin's armies captured many thousands of Lanna Yuan, Lao Wiang, Lao Phuan, Black Tai, and Khmer. The southern expeditions brought back several thousand Malays. Possibly 30,000–40,000 Mons voluntarily migrated to Siam. In the early 1800s, the Bangkok and Lanna troops went further north to seize Khoen, Lu, and Shan. After the 1827 war against Vientiane, over 150,000 were captured and some 50,000 marched down to the Chaophraya basin. In the 1830s, the Bangkok armies made six expeditions into the Lao regions, depopulating the left bank of the Mekong, and bringing back Lao Phuan from the Plain of Jars, Tai Dam from Sipsongchuthai, Khmer, and Vietnamese.

Some of these peoples were resettled around Bangkok and employed to build the new capital. Some were resettled around the central plain to increase its capacity for growing rice. Others were placed on the Khorat Plateau to collect the forest produce demanded in trade to China.

GREAT HOUSEHOLDS AND BUDDHIST KINGSHIP

The emergence of an aristocracy of great households now came to fruition.

When Ayutthaya was destroyed in 1767, 'natural governments'⁴ mushroomed in the provinces led by traders, adventurers, old nobles, and charismatic monks. Taksin crushed the local leaders who defied him, but confirmed those who gave him support, and interfered little in their affairs. With a few exceptions, the early Chakri monarchs did the same. These provincial families soon became hereditary. In Ratchaburi, for example, the Wongsarot family monopolized the governorship and other key posts for all but ten years from 1812 to 1897. Down the peninsula, two families which helped Yotfa settle the area not only retained their local governorships throughout the nineteenth century but sent their descendants to govern other towns. On the Khorat Plateau, generals from Bangkok's armies were rewarded with governorships which similarly became hereditary. Although accepting allegiance to Bangkok, in their locality these rulers acted like little monarchs – building *wat*, appointing abbots, leading rituals, appropriating manpower, and monopolizing trade. Even in a minor new *mueang* in the northeast, the ruler was a 'petty king'.[5]

At the centre, too, the great noble households consolidated their power. Both 1767 and 1782 were decisive breaks in the royal line. Yotfa made no pretence of claiming old royal blood. The new dynasty had been created by nobles who over the past century had been seeking ways to constrain the monarchy. In the symbolism of the coronation ceremony for Yotfa and his successors, the ministers had prior rights over the ministries: the king was first made into a king by the magic of the Brahmans, and then each minister presented to him the territories, people, weapons, and other equipment of his ministry.[6]

The great families which survived 1767, and especially a handful personally connected to the Chakri family, rose rapidly in the new era. A few new lineages also rose through military achievement and filled the spaces left by those killed or hauled away during the wars. Some dozen great households monopolized the powerful positions in the central administration. They intermarried with one another and the Chakri family. They participated in the revival of the commercial economy. They were not obstructed by royal antagonism. Some became almost as splendid as the ruling family itself, in particular the Bunnag family, whose roots went back to Persian immigrants in the seventeenth century, and whose leading light had been Yotfa's personal retainer in the Taksin era. In a trend that began before 1767, the provincial areas were divided under three ministries (Kalahom, Mahatthai, and Krom Tha) which became virtual sub-states with their own treasuries. The Bunnag controlled at least one and sometimes two of these across four generations. By mid-century, the two Bunnag patriarchs were popularly known by an honorific (*ong*) formerly applied to royalty.

To a new extent, the king was *primus inter pares*. Some of the features which had marked the specialness of the monarchy were now less exclusive. Great noble households patronized their own drama troupes, once a royal monopoly. Forms of dress and sumptuary display spread from royalty to a wider nobility. Popular dramas even imitated royal costumes and regalia before a ban was imposed. While Yotfa was very active in Bangkok's revival, his successor Loetla (Rama II) withdrew into a ritual role and left administration to the great nobles. Nangklao (Rama III) was active as both king and merchant, but Mongkut (Rama IV) again ceded power to the nobles, complaining occasionally how few attended either his council sessions or major royal rituals. Every succession in the nineteenth century was tense to a greater or lesser degree because of the possibility of another dynastic shift like 1767 and 1782. Approaching the last of these transitions, Mongkut worried that 'general people both native and foreigners here seem to have less pleasure on me and my descendants than their pleasure and hope on another amiable family'.[7]

The great households expanded by accumulating wives in order to produce enough talented sons to sustain the family's standing in the senior official ranks, and enough daughters to build marriage networks within the elite. The royal clan showed the way: Rama I had 42 children of twenty-eight mothers; Rama II, 73 children of forty mothers; Rama III, 51 children of thirty-seven mothers; Rama IV, 82 children of thirty-five mothers; and Rama V, 77 children of thirty-six mothers. Other great families followed suit. According to Pallegoix, a French bishop resident in Bangkok in the 1830s and 1840s, 'Several rich people have two wives: the mandarins have up to twelve, thirty, forty or more'.[8] Numbers of children were equally impressive. The founder of the Krairiksh clan had fifty. The two Bunnag brothers who dominated officialdom during the Third Reign had forty-three sons between them. Only the great households were permitted to build on land around the royal centre, and these settlements became like small towns. The Bunnag clan, for example, was granted a large plot across the river from Sampheng. They built three *wat*, a canal, and residences for the ramifying clan. Traders and artisans settled in the area to be close to a source of power and patronage. The capital was a collection of such townships.

The pre-1767 trend towards Buddhist kingship was now realized. Brahmanism was not rejected; court ceremonies were retained and the site of the new capital was dubbed Rattanakosin, Indra's jewel, or Krungthep, city of angels (only foreigners used the old village name, Bangkok). The monarchy was again hidden and mystified. But royal legitimacy did not appeal to any identity between king and god. Rather, the king claimed to be a Bodhisatta, a spiritually superhuman being who had accumulated great merit over previous lives, been reincarnated in order to rule with righteousness, and would become a Buddha in the future. The king's legitimacy depended not on blood or dynastic line (which had been broken) but on 'ties of incarnation'[9] to the great lineage of Buddhas through history. Yotfa had the Singhalese Mahavamsa chronicle that encapsulated this philosophy translated into Thai.

In the chronicles written in this era, Borommakot was idealized as the model king, and other late Ayutthayan monarchs condemned as poor rulers, poor Buddhists, and poor warriors. The new Bangkok monarchy was celebrated as defenders of Buddhism against the destructive (though Buddhist) Burmese. The conquests of Lao and Khmer territories were justified as saving these peoples from less perfectly Buddhist governance.

Under this theory, the main purpose of kingship was to assist the people to ascend the spiritual ladder towards the ultimate goal of nirvana, the release from worldly suffering. The king thus had not only to build *wat* and protect Buddhism from enemies, but also to undertake other 'royal duties'. Most of all, he had to prevent the decline and eventual eclipse of Buddhism as foretold in the texts, especially by periodically purifying the Sangha, and making corrected recensions of the texts. Yotfa passed laws to rectify the lapses in monastic discipline during Taksin's reign. He assembled a council of senior monks to compile a recension of the Tripitaka, the fundamental texts of Buddhism, and commissioned two new versions of the *Traiphum* cosmology.

So that people should not practise Buddhism ritualistically but 'understand the Thai meaning of each precept', Yotfa founded a school to re-educate monks, and had several Pali texts translated into Thai. Edicts banned cock-fighting and other 'sinful' pursuits because, as the law's preamble explained, 'the king is intent on promoting Buddhism for the happiness and well-being of the people'. Officials were ordered to live according to a moral code modelled on monastic discipline. The walls of *wat* were painted with murals teaching Buddhist lessons, often based on the *jataka* tales which showed how the Buddha achieved spiritual perfection over his five hundred incarnations before achieving enlightenment. Most popular was the Vessantara Jataka about the last of these incarnations, a tale teaching the virtue of selflessness. The king sponsored annual chanting of this story – first, in the *wat* housing the kingdom's Palladian image, the Emerald Buddha, and later all over the kingdom. This ceremony taught moral values while also dramatizing the king's authority as a Bodhisatta.

EXPANDING MARKET ECONOMY

Taksin encouraged Chinese immigration to revive the economy. Yotfa, whose mother was 'a beautiful daughter of a very rich Chinese family' in Ayutthaya, continued the policy. Through the early nineteenth century, the inflow of Chinese migrants increased. Because Bangkok never recovered control of the portage route over the neck of the peninsula, trade was mainly to the east, and especially with China. By the time Europeans visited the new capital in the 1820s, they found the river crammed with junks. They estimated that the Chinese formed the majority of the city population, which may have reflected their prominence if not their true proportion. By 1835, the Chinese settlement at Sampheng had become a thriving market stretching two miles along a brick-paved road:

It includes dry-good shops, hard-ware shops, black-smiths shops, carpenter shops, coopers shops, gamblers shops, groceries and houses of ill fame, fruit stalls, vegetable stalls, fish stalls, fowl stalls, pork stalls, druggist store and dram shops.[10]

The early arrivals were mostly entrepreneurs associated with the growing rice trade from Siam to China. In their wake came larger numbers escaping poverty and social disorder in southern China. Around 7000 arrived each year in the 1820s, rising to 14,000 by 1870. About half returned home after a few years, but those remaining to settle accumulated to around 300,000 by the 1850s. Many worked initially as 'coolie' labour in the port and elsewhere in the city. Some took up land on the fringes of the delta to grow vegetables for supplying the city. Around 1810, some began planting sugarcane, which by mid-century had become a boom crop and Bangkok's biggest export. Some filtered up the waterways to towns where they became shopkeepers, traders moving local produce to Bangkok, and owners of sugar factories, distilleries, brick kilns, boatyards, tobacco factories, sawmills, and metalworks. Around the gulf and down the peninsula, the port towns were dominated by Chinese, some of whom spread inland to plant rubber, grow pepper, and mine tin. The Chinese were the pioneers of a market economy. In Sawankhalok, the pottery gambling chips brought by the Hokkien Chinese became the first local currency.

In 1830, the British envoy John Crawfurd called migrants 'the most valuable importation from China into Siam'.[11] Government appreciated their value. It excused them from corvée, which would disrupt their trading activity, and instead levied a triennial head tax. It imposed taxes on their enterprises, and gradually found this a better way to raise government revenues than royal trading monopolies. It gradually abandoned trade monopolies, and hired more and more of the Chinese entrepreneurs as tax-farmers.

While exports included the forest goods which had always been the staple of the eastern trade, by the 1820s they had expanded to rice, sugar, dried fish and meats, tin utensils, cloth, oils, and dyes – things that had to be grown or made, often by the immigrant Chinese, but increasingly by others as well. Gradually over time, more people lived more of their lives in the market economy rather than within the old structure of labour indenture and royal service. In Nidhi Eoseewong's description, the society became more 'bourgeois',[12] especially at the capital.

JAO SUA

A handful of Chinese families prospered on royal patronage. In the early nineteenth century, these *jao sua* or merchant lords acted as traders on behalf of the king and senior courtiers. From the 1830s onwards, they secured the most valuable tax-farms levied on birds' nests from the coastal islands, and on liquor, opium, and gambling in the towns. The kings gave them official posts and noble titles which added to their status. The most brilliant became *choduek*, the titular head of the capital's Chinese community. A few of these outstanding families had arrived during the Ayutthaya period. The forebears of the Krairiksh family had come as junk traders in the mid-eighteenth century, served as King Taksin's envoys to China, and become royal traders in the early nineteenth century. Many others arrived in the period of expanding Siam–China trade in the early nineteenth century. Several of the most prominent families were Hokkien, while others were Teochiu or Hakka.

Some established dynasties. They built connections by presenting daughters to courtiers, to their peer families in Bangkok, and to their trading partners in China and elsewhere. In the early nineteenth century, some were able to pass not only their business but also their official title onto their heirs. The head of the Chotikapukkana family rose from the royal junk trade to become *choduek* in the 1850s, and was followed by two of his descendants over the next half-century. The *jao sua* served the king in various ways other than trade. The Chotikapukkana family imported items like purpose-made porcelain for the palace, and acted as judges in the special court established to settle disputes involving the Chinese. Some went farther into the traditional bureaucracy. The founder of the Kalyanamit family became minister in charge of the corvée registers, and rose to the highest rank of *chaophraya* in the 1850s. Two of his descendants secured the same title and prominence later in the century. Thian Chotikasathian, another royal junk trader and *choduek*, was drafted to help King Chulalongkorn establish his modern finance office, and his son accompanied the king on his 1872 trip to India (see next chapter).

These established Chinese families levered themselves up the social ladder by connections at court. Even the greatest *jao sua* still sought a formal patronage bond with senior members of the royal family. They propitiated these patrons with presents, and were rewarded with titles of progressively higher rank. Several daughters of *jao sua* were among the 242 wives and consorts in Nangklao's palace. King Chulalongkorn (Rama V) was specially struck by a daughter of the leading Phisolyabut family, and asked to take her into the royal household. With this precedent established, over the next few years two of the king's close relatives also took Phisolyabut consorts. Other *jao sua* families made equally splendid alliances.

These families became fabulously wealthy. The Chotikapukkana residence nestled in a 100-rai park on the river bank. The kings drew on this wealth to embellish the capital. Under royal encouragement, leading merchants funded the construction and repair of Thai Buddhist temples as well as Chinese shrines. They were coaxed into digging canals to serve as highways for trade. In the later era of enthusiasm for 'progress', their patronage was diverted to hospitals and schools.

Through the first half of the century, and particularly in the Third Reign (1824–1851), the enormous role of the Chinese in the new capital was reflected in fashion and style. Chinese crockery and stone images, used as ballast on junks, decorated many of the city's new temples. Chinese slippers and jackets were common items of court dress. Chinese furniture was imported to embellish *wat* and great homes. Translations of Chinese classics were fashionable reading, especially *Sam kok*, the Three Kingdoms. The trader-king Nangklao built Buddhist *wat* using Chinese designs, artisans, and materials; dragons replaced Thai *naga* on the roofline, while cranes, chrysanthemums, and scenes from Chinese legends replaced the usual Thai iconography inside. This style was dubbed the 'royal model'. As the junk trade dwindled after 1840 in the face of European competition, Nangklao constructed a riverside *wat* in the shape of a junk as a memorial to the junk's role in building the new capital. His successor, Mongkut, had his portrait painted in the robes of a Chinese emperor, and built a Chinese-style pleasure garden at the royal retreat of Bang Pa-in.

Established *jao sua* also took enthusiastically to Thai culture. Most took a Thai wife, and often several, although they might also have other households back in China. They patronized Thai Buddhist *wat*, and appropriated the traditional marks of high status. Luang Aphaiwanit, who made his fortune from a birds' nest tax-farm and property development, lavished money on a traditional Thai orchestra and drama troupe which he apparently treated with aristocratic presumption; the gossips said he 'had a whole drama troupe of wives'.[13]

The *jao sua* were a small and glittering elite, but their trading success and their social adjustments were reproduced in more modest ways among the tens of thousands of Chinese who settled in Bangkok and provincial towns. By long residence, marriage, royal recognition, and cultural adjustments, the *lukjin* or descendants of Chinese immigrants could easily blend into Siamese society. In 1884, a Frenchman described the phases of this process:

The Chinese of pure blood is everywhere recognizable by his narrow eyes, high cheek-bones, his generally slender features, his traditional costume. Speaking the language with difficulty, he lets the soft letters of the Siamese alphabets slip away. In a group nearby, dressed in wide pants, with their slim figures, white skin, and pleasant physical features are the sons and grandsons of the first settlers. They are the first fruits of mixed-marriages with indigenous women. They are still more like their father than mother, above all from the moral point of view. They have inherited the difficulty of pronouncing the 'r'. They have made only one concession to the country in which they were born, that of swapping the blue smock for the *pha hom*, a piece of cotton with which the indigenous people cover their shoulders and busts . . . Even more numerous are the descendents of the third and fourth generations . . . They have finally rejected the wide floating pants to take up the loincloth, and if they still preserve the pig-tail . . . it is now their maternal upbringing that predominates. The soil that has witnessed their birth will count them as its own children. From now on it will be their homeland.[14]

PROGRESS

The growth of the market economy and the emergence of new social groups threw up new ideas and mentalities. Since late Ayutthaya, the few involved in the economy of international commerce had been open to new ideas coming from east or west. In early Bangkok, both commerce and this new mentality spread to a wider group. More people came to value literacy and learning. A new popular literature, which flourished as the city began to prosper in the 1820s, reflected new values. Heroes included ordinary people, not just the princes and gods which dominated Ayutthayan works. They were not so constricted by birth and fate, but had the ability to make their own lives. Romantic love was portrayed as more personal, and less constrained by family, tradition, and status. High birth and martial talent were not the only routes to glory; money was also a means of mobility. The defining genre of the era was the *nirat*, poems relating a journey, which allowed authors to describe the widening horizons and fascinating changes of their own society rather than an imaginary world of gods and kings. Sunthon Phu, the outstanding poet of the era, was fascinated by ports filled with 'junks laden to the gunwales with varieties of wealth', by markets where 'Chinese, New Chinese, and rich Thai set up shops', by the new urban cacophony of 'a dozen languages competing', and by the new social landscape in which 'people change ranks, their names go up too; potters, scribes, cutters, carvers, masons'. He also noted rather ruefully how the power of money was changing the social order:

> At Bang Luang on the small canal, many Chinese are selling pigs.
> Their wives are so young, fair, pretty, and rich it makes me feel shy and small.
> Thai men like me who asked for their hand would be blocked as if by iron bars.
> But if you have money like these Chinese, the bars just melt.[15]

Sunthon Phu also wrote picaresque epics which mischievously mocked the old order by inverting its literary conventions, and which became highly popular.

The murals of the capital's *wat* increasingly portrayed the city itself, capturing the busy-ness of daily life as the background of scenes from the Buddha's life, and occasionally including views of the city, landmarks such as the river, characteristic architecture such as the Chinese shophouse, and even records of historic events (Figure 1).

This new urban society was open to new ideas brought by the *farang* (foreigners, westerners) who reappeared in Bangkok in the 1810s – first, a Portuguese consul, then some official envoys, missionaries, and a resident merchant, Robert Hunter, from 1824. The leaders of commercial Bangkok, clustered around the court, welcomed western innovations which had direct importance for their business. They adopted new methods of accounting and navigation. They built themselves copies of the more efficient western sloops. In 1824, the future King Mongkut withdrew into a *wat*, perhaps to avoid a succession battle with his brother, King Nangklao, Rama III. Along with another brother, Chuthamani, and a handful of young courtiers, Mongkut cultivated relations with westerners, especially the more reasonable of the missionaries. Through these contacts, members of Mongkut's group were coached in English and other western languages, learnt printing, and imported books. They became fascinated by gadgets,

Figure 1: Everyday realism enters into *wat* murals. Painted at Wat Phra Kaeo, Bangkok, in the early nineteenth century.

by the technology of steam power, and by the mathematical precision of astronomy.

The Bunnag were similarly fascinated. When the palace governess, Anna Leonowens, visited their mansion in 1862, she was struck by its westernized sophistication:

His Excellency's residence abounded within in carvings and gildings, elegant in design and color, that blended and harmonized in pleasing effects with the luxurious draperies that hung in rich folds from the windows. We moved softly, as the interpreter led us through a suite of spacious saloons, disposed in ascending tiers, and all carpeted, candelabraed, and appointed in the most costly European fashion . . . On every side my eyes were delighted with rare vases, jewelled cups and boxes, burnished chalices, dainty statuettes, – *objets de virtu*, Oriental and European, antique and modern, blending the old barbaric splendors with the graces of the younger arts.[16]

But the westerners represented not only new opportunities but also new threats. In the early nineteenth century, the momentum of British expansion in India began to spill out towards Southeast Asia. Britain established bases in Penang and Singapore, and began to develop the tin industry and its diplomatic influence up the peninsula. By 1820, Britain had collided with Siam's influence in the peninsula and begun negotiating a border agreement. Separately, British Indian forces intruded into Burma, and fought a bitter war in 1826 which gave them control of Arakan and the Mon coastline. Siam initially welcomed the defeat of its old nemesis, and considered allying with the British to regain control of the neck of the peninsula. But ultimately the Siamese court understood that the British defeat of Burma was a momentous change. In particular, it signalled a military revolution, consisting of lightweight repeating guns; metal gunboats which could threaten a riverside city with impunity; and a huge supply of Indian sepoys for sacrifice in combat. None of these innovations could be replicated by Siam.

The defeat of Burma also confirmed the westerners' appetite for territory. A Siamese official accused the first British visitor in 1823 of coming 'to view the Empire of Siam, previous to the English fitting out an expedition of ships of war to come and conquer'.[17] On his deathbed in 1851, Nangklao predicted: 'There will be no more wars with Vietnam and Burma. We will have them only with the West.'[18] When later a first Prussian ship arrived in Bangkok, King Mongkut asked its captain point-blank whether Prussia was seeking colonies, as 'The foreigners keep extending their influence until entire empires belong to them'.[19]

Another threat was opium. Following their success selling the drug in China, British traders sought markets among Chinese populations elsewhere. The first western trader to visit Bangkok in 1821 was carrying opium. Missionaries in the 1830s travelled from Singapore on vessels stuffed with it. In 1839, the government passed an edict banning opium import and sale, but the profit outweighed the risk. The government was concerned not only because of the human impact and the fear the habit would spread into the Thai population, but also because opium made some people hugely wealthy, and because many social disorders began from gang wars over this valuable trade.

From the viewpoint of the Siamese elite, the attractions of 'progress' and the threat of colonialism were unhappily intertwined. They understood that the new westerners had a sense of their own superiority, and believed this superiority justified them in seizing territory in order to confer 'progress' and bring 'benighted' peoples into the modern world. By their own accounts, the early British official visitors acted towards Siamese officials with as much arrogance as they could muster. Crawfurd wrote in 1822 that two gun-brigs 'would destroy the capital, without possibility of resistance from this vain but weak people'.[20] Missionaries such as David Abeel, who arrived in the 1830s, wrote accounts of Siam as a land benighted by slavery, opium, gambling, idolatry, despotism, and 'shameless indecency of language and dress'. He described slaves 'toiling in fetters, as though the clank of their chains was music to the ears of their cruel lords', and summed up: 'The picture of the condition, moral and political, of Siam is a dark one'.[21] Only a little more moderately, the first popular account of Siam by F. A. Neale published in 1852 described the Siamese as 'at best semi-barbarous . . . an oppressed and cringing people . . . wrapped in the grossest ignorance and superstition, and lost to all sentiment of moral virtue'. Neale also drew the obvious colonialist conclusion:

Under a better sway, what country in the East would rival Siam: rich in its soil and productions, possessed of valuable mines and gums, spices and pepper, the best and cheapest rice and sugars, and the land absolutely encumbered with the most luscious fruits in the world . . . Few countries are richer than Siam as regards produce suited for and sought after in European markets, and few countries afford a wider field for the acquisition of wealth . . . it would be much lamented that any other European power should forestall us in seizing such an advantageous opportunity.[22]

The westerners were also inquisitive. All the official missions collected information on history, trade goods, military capability, and political conditions. In 1824, James Low of the Madras Light Infantry presented his superiors with a map of 'Siam Camboja & Laos' which gained him a reward of 2000 Spanish dollars. In 1833 a trader, D. E. Malloch, sent to the British authorities in Bengal a list of Siamese places with population numbers, probably copied somehow from the official rolls. In the mid-1830s, British officers trekked from British Burma up through Lanna and the Shan States to Sipsongpanna. They presented themselves as commercial agents, but they also mapped the routes, took notes on the local economy, counted the cannon around the palaces, and enquired everywhere about local politics. The subjects of all this inquisitiveness were apprehensive about its purpose. The expeditions into the interior set off a bush telegraph of rumours about British colonial ambitions. In 1858, Mongkut remarked: 'A great number of Englishmen have been and are now residing in this country. They seem to have an accurate knowledge of everything that is to be known here.'[23]

The Siamese court's first response to the westerners was to keep them at arm's length. From the 1820s, it signed trade agreements which changed nothing of significance. Robert Hunter was the only trader to set up shop in Bangkok. He soon fell into the traditional role of supplying the court with weapons and luxuries, and acting as a go-between with other foreigners. Like similar predecessors, he was thrown out in 1844 when he had become too powerful.

Mongkut's entourage and other groups in the elite were fascinated by the westerners' idea of material 'progress', but appalled by Christianity, and irritated by the westerners' claim that their material and moral progress were interrelated. The strategy of Mongkut's group was to split the material from the moral. One of the group, Chaophraya Thiphakorawong, wrote articles in the fledgling Thai press, collected in 1867 as *Sadaeng kitjanukit* (A miscellany), one of the first printed Thai books. He explicitly rejected the traditional Buddhist cosmology and urged children to learn modern science and accept a scientific view of the physical world. This group also understood they had to abandon the Buddhist conception of time as repeated cycles of decay. Mongkut embraced the idea that people were not bound by fate but were capable of improving the world, and thus history was possible. He began to research and write Siam's history. Thiphakorawong penned a new version of the royal chronicles which described kings making history rather than reacting to omens and fate.

This group also debated fiercely with their missionary friends, and put their conclusions in print. The second half of Thiphakorawong's book for children advised readers to reject Christianity. He argued that every religion, including Christianity and Buddhism, tended to incorporate miracles and magic from folk beliefs. But, once these were removed, Buddhism's reasoned precepts were more in line with a rational, scientific mentality than the will of Christianity's god ('a foolish religion'[24]).

While in the monkhood between 1824 and 1851, Mongkut formed the Thammayut sect, partly to cleanse Buddhism of the elements which attracted *farang* criticism, partly as an extension of Rama I's ambition to create a Buddhism with more moral authority to order society. The new sect adopted a stricter code of conduct based on a Mon text, rejected the use of *jataka* tales for teaching and preaching, down-played the significance of texts based on traditional cosmology (especially the *Traiphum*), and avoided practices adopted from Brahmanism or spirit worship. The sect was small – 150 monks when Mongkut ascended the throne in 1851 – but influential owing to its royal origins.

SERVITUDE AND FREE LABOUR

By the early nineteenth century, two societies based on different principles had come to coexist in Bangkok and its hinterland.

On the one hand, the old Ayutthayan society of personal bonds, formal hierarchies, and unfree labour had been substantially revived. During forty years of war and disorder, old systems of labour control had been reimposed. Every *phrai* freeman was legally bound to a *munnai* overseer. Through to the 1840s, conscripted armies were used on the eastern expeditions. The largest armies sent to Cambodia possibly conscripted a tenth of able-bodied male labour from the lower Chaophraya basin and Khorat Plateau. Conscript labour was also used for the upkeep of royalty and nobility, the construction and maintenance of the capital, and collection of goods for the export trade. At the capital, much of the official nobility was engaged in marshalling and directing these resources of unfree labour.

In provincial areas, servitude was even more marked. The first European observers in these areas reported that 50 to 90 per cent of people were in some form of 'slavery'. Many were originally war captives, or people hauled away during military campaigns in the south and east. Some were imported: the law had a special category for unfree labour purchased 'on board a junk'.[25] In the outer regions, some people made a living by raiding hill villages and other remote settlements to kidnap people for sale in the towns and lowlands. Others fell into servitude as punishment for crime, or as a result of debt. Some sold themselves into servitude or, more often, sold their children, other kin, or other subordinates. An 1805 law prevented anyone selling their siblings or grandchildren, but other transactions were legal. The law codes laid down a price scale based on age, gender, and other conditions. Slave status was hereditary.

Many war captives were settled as farmers. The less fortunate were used for hard manual labour on public works. Those kidnapped from the hills were often sold to officials as personal retainers. Some were hired out by their masters, especially as porters, caravan drovers, and mahouts. Others were used to work the land of their patrons. Both slaves and freemen were vulnerable to various forms of coercion. In the south, peasants complained that the local nobles imposed arbitrary taxes, seized their produce, and dragooned them for forced labour. Those who resisted were bound in shackles and 'squeezed to death',[26] or sometimes left in the sun to die.

On the other hand, a new market society was emerging in parallel. Initially, most of the labour and entrepreneurship was supplied by the immigrant Chinese. But as market society gathered momentum, it involved others too. Farmers in the central plain grew some rice for export or for supplying the growing non-agricultural population. Some also grew sugarcane for the Chinese mills, felled timber for the boatyards, or made craft products for a rising market. More nobles became involved as entrepreneurs, some independently and some as partners or patrons of the Chinese. Some great households, especially those clustered around the *phrakhlang*, and pre-eminently the Bunnag, acquired a wide range of commercial interests including export, import, and plantations.

Increasingly these different economies and their respective elites became rivals for resources, especially supplies of labour. By the 1820s, the price of slaves had begun to rise far above the official scales. The king and traditional nobles strove to maintain labour supplies in traditional ways. The court poured out a stream of laws to enforce old obligations, but the repetitive nature of this legislation suggests it was ineffective. King and nobles also competed among themselves over diminishing supplies. The king reduced the annual corvée requirement. Nobles offered competitive inducements. Laws laid down punishments for poaching labour. Mongkut ordered a registration of royal *phrai* in 1855 and was dismayed by the low number. Bangkok's military expansion faltered from the late 1840s in part because the armies fielded were much smaller than earlier.

Some people were able to escape forced labour in various ways. Some melted away to *song*, fugitive villages in the forests and remote areas. The court occasionally sent out expeditions to round them up, but more often contacted them to buy forest goods for the export trade. Some sought the protection of undemanding patrons. Others simply bribed officials to be reclassified in the registers. In one local register from 1867, three-fifths of the adult males were exempt from corvée as officials, monks, slaves, disabled, destitute, mentally ill, or possessed by evil spirits. By Prince Damrong's estimate in the 1870s, four-fifths of males evaded the corvée.

Those members of the elite engaged in the market economy encouraged the development of more free or semi-free labour. From the 1830s, people began to commute their annual corvée obligation into a money payment. By the 1840s, so many took this option that government had to use hired Chinese labour rather than corvée for public works. By the 1850s, the returns from commutation had become the largest item of royal revenue. Nobles with commercial interests urged Mongkut to abolish conscription. Around the capital, debt slavery rose steeply. The resident French Bishop Pallegoix estimated that 'at least a third of the population' held this status.[27] By selling themselves into slavery, freemen could raise some capital and escape corvée obligation. Some debt slaves repaid their creditor in labour, while others worked in the market economy and repaid in cash. Ironically, this massive expansion of 'slavery' in and around the capital was a way of releasing labour from traditional servitude for use in the market economy.

Gender relations also began to reflect this division within society. In the new market society, the position of women as the legal property of men faced challenge. *Suphasit son ying* (Sayings for ladies), a mid-nineteenth century manual probably authored by Sunthon Phu, differed from earlier such manuals which taught wives how to minister submissively to their husbands. It recognized that more upper-class women wanted a say in selecting a husband, and advised them how to choose wisely. It instructed them in how to contribute to the family business activity which was increasingly important for women of this class. The manual suggests that many women were not quite as dependent as the law implied. Perhaps for this reason, in 1868 Mongkut abolished a husband's right to sell his wife or her children without her permission because 'the stipulation treats a woman as if she were a water buffalo'.[28]

But while Mongkut accommodated new attitudes in market society, at the same time he strengthened the rights of traditional upper-class families to treat women as assets. He ruled that it was acceptable for women of low or middle class to choose a husband, but not those of high birth because their choice might affect the prestige of the family. The 1868 amendment specifically noted that a man could still purchase a slave as a wife and resell her later. Specifically among families with over 400 sakdina, Mongkut strengthened the father's legal authority over wives and daughters. In the same vein, Thiphakorawong, one of the foremost advocates of 'progress', wrote a defence of polygamy. The deployment of daughters was still critical to the influence of the great households.

Approaching mid-century, there was growing tension within the elite over the linked issues of the economy, social order, and handling of the west. Traditionalists wanted to keep the west at arm's length, and preserve the old social order, especially traditional controls on unfree labour. Under King Nangklao, this faction remained strong. The king shifted from royal trading monopolies to tax-farming, but refused westerners' entreaties for more liberal trading. He relied heavily on traditional conscription for his eastern campaigns.

Reformers believed that more western trade, freer labour, and access to new technologies would stimulate economic growth to the benefit of both government revenues and private fortunes. The leaders of reform were the patriarchs of the Bunnag household, and the group of aristocratic intellectuals around Prince Mongkut. In 1842, Britain humbled China in the Opium Wars, showing the consequences of defying British demands for 'free trade'. The impact of the war ruined the Siam–China junk trade, and persuaded Siam to look to westerners for a substitute. The British victory also meant that both India and China, sources of so much of Siam's old culture, had fallen under western domination. Increasingly, the elite's gaze swivelled westwards.

In 1851, the Bunnag manoeuvred Mongkut's succession to the throne. Members of the reform faction were rewarded with promotions and increased power. They argued that it was senseless to continue defending the junk trade by differential duties in the face of the economic superiority of western shipping. They also urged that earlier attempts to block opium imports had only created super-profits and gang wars. In 1855, Mongkut invited John Bowring, the governor of Britain's opium capital of Hong Kong, to negotiate a trade treaty. This treaty abolished the remnants of royal monopolies, equalized the dues on western and Chinese shipping, granted extraterritorial rights to British citizens, and allowed the British to import opium for sale through a government monopoly. Bowring promoted his career by claiming a victory for the principle of free trade. The court made the opium monopoly into the single largest source of revenue.

The treaty marked Siam's reorientation away from China, which had been the focus over the prior 150 years, and towards the west.

CONCLUSION

The long wars against Burma in the late eighteenth century initially froze the trends of social and economic change, and brought back the traditions of militarism and control of people. But from the early nineteenth century, the pace of change resumed. The aristocracy now became much more dominant. In the capital and provinces they established virtually hereditary shares in the practice of government and its profits. The monarchs were reduced to a more limited role.

With growing Chinese trade and immigration, the market economy expanded in the Chaophraya heartland and down the peninsula. Under its impact, the social order began to shift. More people slid free of old systems of labour control. A new cadre of great Chinese *jao sua* families joined the ranks of the elite. Within old elite families, more turned to enterprise. Mentalities changed in parallel.

The return of westerners brought apprehension about colonial designs, but also intrigue about their science, gadgets, and ideas of progress. By mid-century, reformers within the elite wanted to turn to the west, increase Siam's trade, and free more labour. The enthronement of Mongkut by the Bunnag in 1851, and the Bowring treaty four years later, signalled the reformers' rising influence.

After the treaty increased Siam's exposure to the west, the critical issue for the elite changed: how to reform the polity to cope with the social changes of the market economy and the threat of colonialism.

3

Reforms, 1850s to 1910s

At the end of the nineteenth century, Siam was remade as a nation-state. The 'nation' constructed by this process was novel. The areas collected within the borders had very different histories, languages, religious cultures, and traditions. The Thai language seems to have been spoken in the lower Chaophraya system and down the upper peninsula, but in practice local dialects varied greatly, and the languages of Bangkok and Chiang Mai were mutually unintelligible. Over the prior century, the expansion of Bangkok's political influence, the influx of war captives, and Chinese immigration had added to the social variety. The fragmentation of the administration gave scope for local difference.

The ideas of nation, unified nation-state, nationality, national identity, and centralized nation-governing bureaucracy were imposed from above. They were adapted from European models, and adopted in part to parry the threat of colonial takeover. But they were taken up also to replace old systems of rule and social control which had become less effective as a result of social change and which could not satisfy the new demands of the market economy.

THE DECLINE OF THE TRADITIONAL POLITY

By the mid-nineteenth century, the combination of military expansion and the rising commercial economy had changed the demography of the core kingdom in ways which undermined the traditional political order based on personal ties.

By the 1850s, there were around 300,000 resident Chinese many of whom had immigrated over the prior two generations. The government initially tried to manage them by the traditional method of absorbing their community leaders into the bureaucracy, and making these leaders responsible for their conduct and welfare. But this method did not fit the new facts. The Chinese did not form a 'community' with established leaders who could be

47

co-opted by the court. They were too many, too varied, too mobile, and too scattered for this old technique to work. In the port, rice mills, sugar factories, and tin mines, they worked together in bigger concentrations than ever seen before. Many were far from Bangkok and difficult to control, particularly in the expanding tin mines down the peninsula. Occasionally they ran riot. Several times in the 1840s and 1870s, troops had to be sent to the sugar tracts east of Bangkok to restore order. The southern town of Ranong was 'almost lost to the government' during a miners' riot in the 1870s. When a gunboat was sent to restore order, the mob reacted by burning and looting Phuket. The ability of striking workers to paralyse the Bangkok port gave the rulers nightmares about a Chinese takeover of the city. In 1889, rival Chinese gangs fought a pitched battle in the centre of the capital for three days.

As with immigrants everywhere, the Chinese formed self-help and self-defence societies. The authorities saw these as *angyi* or *samakhom lap*, secret societies – a term that betrayed their trepidation. The government feared these organizations were smuggling opium, distilling local liquor, and running gambling rackets. They were also armed. Attempts to police illegal opium trading and illegal distilling were occasionally defied by gunfire and even cannon. While Chuang Bunnag was dominant in the government at mid-century, he adopted a policy of *liang angyi*, 'nurturing the secret societies' and entrusting them to keep the peace.

Besides the Chinese, many other people had escaped the old systems of personal control. Some were drawn off to a new agrarian frontier, especially to grow rice for feeding the growing urban population, for export to China, and for supplies for the armies on campaign. In the 1830s, canals were built east and west from Bangkok to serve as highways for trade and military movements. These canals drained areas of swamp which were immediately settled by people seeking rice land.

This new frontier allowed peasant settlers to flee beyond the reach of labour controls and policing. For the most part, the government made no objection, while gradually increasing the range of taxes on production, commerce, and entertainments. But from mid-century, it became worried about 'banditry' in the rural areas, and over following decades this worry expanded into an obsession. Some of the bandits were peasants who had suffered a bad harvest or other misfortune. Some were running opium, liquor, and gambling rackets. Some were professional cattle rustlers. Some were just *nakleng*, local toughs who defended their village against predators, including moneylenders and tax collectors. These bandits ambushed convoys carrying tax returns back to Bangkok, looted government granaries, and seized land. Some became instant folk heroes, celebrated in ballads for their defiance of authority. In some places, peasants copied the example of the *angyi* to form associations for the same mix of self-protection and defiance of the law. Farther afield, in the Lao areas brought under Bangkok influence since the late eighteenth century, people were occasionally attracted to the support of *phumibun*, men-of-merit who promised to turn the world upside down and usher in a millenarian age of justice and plenty.

The 1855 Bowring treaty, and parallel agreements concluded with other western nations soon after, further stimulated the market economy, and increased the strain on the old administrative system in a specific way. They gave extraterritorial rights to foreign citizens, especially the right to be tried by their consuls rather than Siamese courts. Traders who arrived from British Burma or French Indochina sometimes used this protection to defy Siamese officials, avoid taxation, and engage in illegal businesses. Some Chinese merchants secured *protégé* status, or allied themselves with foreign *protégés* to avoid law and control. Other Chinese converted to Roman Catholicism as another way to appeal for colonial protection. Siamese official attempts to suppress these activities threatened to create the flashpoint for a typical colonial 'incident'.

In addition, the demands on government became more complex as the economy changed. 'Every day', an official order noted, 'the number of court cases increases, because people are trading and dealing with each other more and more'.[1] The provinces, according to one European visitor, were full of 'unsatisfied litigants, unsettled claims, and untried prisoners'.[2]

While Mongkut's intellectual interests leaned towards the west, his approach to managing the increasingly disorderly kingdom was very traditional. He revived a great deal of royal ritual which had been neglected since the fall of Ayutthaya, including the annual festival of the great swing. He travelled to upcountry centres where he gave funds for the repair and upkeep of prominent *wat* which were adopted as 'royal temples'. He enforced the biennial ritual of allegiance in which the provincial ruler and officials gathered, often at the royal *wat*, and drank the water of allegiance while facing towards the capital. To fortify the capital against enemies, he built six new forts, but also created a new city pillar, cast a new horoscope for the country, and invented Sayam Thewathirat, a protective spirit for the kingdom. Traditionally, most villages and *mueang* had such spirits as a focus of unity and identity, but not the domain of a king. When the ruins of Angkor were rediscovered, Mongkut sent an expedition to dismantle one of its temples to be reassembled in Bangkok and add to the capital's sacred power, but had to abandon the idea because the temples were too large and the Siamese party was attacked.

Mongkut also issued large numbers of decrees and royal proclamations which were not administrative orders but statements of principle intended to guide the actions of officials and people – somewhat in the style of Chinese imperial rule. Several of these orders were attempts to increase the specialness of monarchy and its distance from the rest of society. He laid down rules on the use of *rachasap*, the heavily Khmer-derived language for use in addressing the king; forbade personal descriptions of the king; outlawed the adoption of consorts with a rural background; and ordered the use of regnal years for the calendar. He laid down a very precise hierarchy within the royal family based on age, the status of the mother, and genealogical distance from the reigning king, along with titles that publicised this fine gradation. He changed inheritance laws to limit the extent to which polygamy might disperse family wealth, especially in the royal family. His own historical sketches, and the chronicles revised in his reign, tried to prove that legitimate patrilineal succession was the norm in Thai history. He laid down forms of address for every level of the social hierarchy from king to slave. He forbade commoners who acquired a *wat* education from getting posts in the major ministries as these were reserved for 'men of good family and background, the sons of nobles'.[3] By using various traditional ways, Mongkut strove for a more hierarchically ordered kingdom under a more elevated monarchy.

In other ways Mongkut turned towards the west. He sent a tribute mission to China to ask formal confirmation of the succession in the usual way, but after the mission was waylaid by rebels, he did not repeat the attempt and later ridiculed the whole idea. In 1857 he sent a deputation of twenty-seven people to Britain to collect information on science, transport, and political institutions. From 1860, he hired westerners as government advisers, and set about bringing 'progress' to Siam. He tried to centralize tax revenues; issued codes of governance for the rulers of provinces and tributary states; encouraged citizens to make judicial appeals to the king; and imagined himself as a *phramahakasat*, great king, ruling over an *ekkarat*, a unified and independent kingdom. He told Anna Leonowens, the governess hired to teach English and western manners to his sons, he would 'doubtless without hesitation, abolish slavery . . . for the distinguishing of my reign'.[4] In practice, the king's powers were circumscribed by the power of the great noble families, and the limited scope of the administrative machinery. Mongkut's reign was a time of transition, suspended between different eras and different worlds (Figure 2).

Figure 2: 'King Mongkut between different worlds: (left) in full Siamese regalia, photographed by Francis Chit in 1864; (right) imagined by an unknown artist in the robes of the Chinese emperor; (bottom) sketched among the palace women by the party of the Comte de Beauvoir visiting in 1866.

The old administrative system based on personalized ties was increasingly ineffective. More people were free of the ties that bound them to the state. The elite's efforts at mobilizing Buddhism as a basis of social discipline, and strengthening traditional hierarchies, were only partially effective. Rulers extracting revenue from the rising commercial economy, as well as entrepreneurs extracting profits, wanted new methods to discipline people, mobilize resources, and protect wealth.

ADMINISTERING A COUNTRY

King Chulalongkorn succeeded his father, Mongkut, in 1868, and over his 42-year reign the old political order was replaced by the model of the nation-state.

On accession, Chulalongkorn was aged 15. During his minority, he travelled to see 'progress' at first hand in the colonial territories of Singapore, Java, Malaya, Burma, and India for 'selecting what may be safe models for the future prosperity of this country'.[5] He sent twenty minor royalty for education in Singapore. He had several European constitutions translated into Thai and was most impressed by the French Code Napoleon. On reaching his majority he pledged to rule 'so that the royal family, officials and people may continually develop'.[6] Within a month, he set up a new central treasury, and appointed a Council of State and Privy Council packed with royal relatives. Soon after, he announced a reform programme, 'What the Council should do and what it should abolish'. Among the practices earmarked for abolition were corvée, slavery, and gambling. Among the innovations were reform of the law courts; creation of a salaried bureaucracy, police, and army; and development of agriculture and education.

For the reformers, ending labour controls was the priority. Partly this was to thwart colonial criticism; Anna Leonowens made herself famous by portraying the Siamese elite cloaked in 'the darkness of error, superstition, slavery, and death'.[7] Partly it was to increase the availability of labour for the market economy. While regent during Chulalongkorn's minority, the Bunnag patriarch, Chuang, had drawn up proposals for ending slavery either by taxing it out of existence or by outright abolition. The traditionalists blocked these proposals which threatened the foundations of their economic and social status. To soothe this group, the king proposed to abolish only certain kinds of slavery and in a gradual way. By an order passed in August 1874, anyone born a hereditary slave from 1868 onwards would gain liberty on reaching 21, and anyone else born after 1868 could not sell himself or be sold into slavery after reaching 21. This still left existing debt slaves, war captives, the sale of children into slavery, and the corvée system untouched. Reformers such as Chuang had hoped for something more decisive but probably accepted the necessary political compromise.

The labour reforms found the king and the trader nobles in the same camp. But financial and judicial reforms drove a rift between the king on one side, and Chuang and other senior nobles on the other. Chulalongkorn announced the establishment of a Finance Office to take control of all the tax-farms, currently scattered across seventeen treasuries. He also announced a new court to take over some of the cases similarly scattered across courts under various ministries. Such centralization would undercut the income and authority of the great nobles, and augment the power of the crown. Chuang and other patriarchs objected strongly. They engineered a coup threat (the 'Front Palace Crisis' of December 1874) which persuaded the king to back down and proceed more slowly.

As a result of royal polygamy, Chulalongkorn had many brothers and half-brothers. He gathered together a group of them along with younger members of some great households including Bunnag, Saeng-Xuto, and Amatyakun. They called themselves 'Young Siam', implicitly defining their opponents as 'Old Siam' and part of the past. They debated 'progress' and 'reform'. Chulalongkorn absorbed them into experiments in western-style bureaucratic and military organization inside the royal household.

Over the next decade, as each noble patriarch died or retired, Chulalongkorn moved that patriarch's tax-farms under the Finance Office, and inserted an ally into the vacant post. In 1885, he placed his brother Narathip in charge of the office, and over the next three years gained the main liquor, opium, and gambling revenues from Bunnag hands. Revenue flow under royal command rose from 1.6 million baht in 1874 to 57 million baht in 1906–07. This was the seed capital of absolutism.

One of the first investments made with this money was in military power. During the regency, Chulalongkorn created inside the palace a new royal guard of 500 men, organized and trained on the model of an English infantry regiment, equipped with the latest western arms, recruited mainly from the nobility, and paid regular salaries – the first officials to enjoy this privilege. In the late 1870s, the learning from this experiment was transferred to the *thahan na*, a regiment guarding the capital. The old levies were released. New men were recruited for a five-year tour of duty with pay. Europeans helped with training. Modern rifles were purchased. An impressive barracks was built beside the palace (later converted into the Ministry of Defence). The force was small – around 4400 men – but enough to chase after bandits, intimidate the secret societies, and police the capital at important times.

This force was critical for Young Siam's major project – a new centralized pyramid of bureaucratic administration, replacing the local lords. On Chulalongkorn's accession, Bangkok's political hinterland was a patchwork of *mueang* tied to different ministries by varying systems (Map 3).[8] 'Inner' *mueang* supposedly had Bangkok-style tax systems, conscription, and appointed officials, though in practice many governors were effectively hereditary. 'Intermediate' *mueang* were ruled by local lords sending dues of forest goods, while tributaries sent only symbolic tribute.

The pioneer case for centralization was the former tributary state of Lanna (Chiang Mai). The inroads of British timber companies into the northern forests threatened to become a spearhead of colonial intrusion. They also entangled the Lanna rulers in court cases and debts which gave Chulalongkorn his opportunity. He bailed out the debts, took charge of negotiating an Anglo-Siamese treaty in 1874 to constrain the colonial loggers, and sent a commissioner to oversee the tributary state's government. The commissioner arrived in Chiang Mai at the head of a column of troops from the new paid and permanent force. The king instructed the commissioner (a half-brother): 'We have no thought of removing the court and tributary status, but we want to seize the real power . . . you must achieve this by wisdom more than by force, without letting the Lao[9] feel they are being squeezed'.[10] The commissioner gradually introduced Bangkok-style taxes, appointed local officials, and took charge of the timber concessions. The local nobles complained that Lanna was being 'picked to the bone' and some officials raised a revolt. The commissioner soothed the nobles with fancy titles and large allowances, but gradually distanced them from the administration, diverted the tax revenues to the Bangkok treasury, and established a pyramidal bureaucracy down to the local level.

The resulting structure looked uncannily like the colonial government of a British Indian district. It became the model. Commissioners were sent to other frontier states – Luang Prabang, Nong Khai, Khorat, Ubon, and Phuket – backed up with troop columns which remained to serve as garrisons. Local rulers were left as figureheads, but on death were replaced by a Bangkok appointee, often a royal relative. In 1893, Chulalongkorn appointed perhaps his favourite half-brother, Damrong Rajanuphap, to head a new Ministry of Interior which adapted this system for use in the inner provinces. The old semi-hereditary governing families of these provinces were superseded by central appointees in the same way. In 1899, the new structure was formalized in legislation. By 1914, the Ministry of

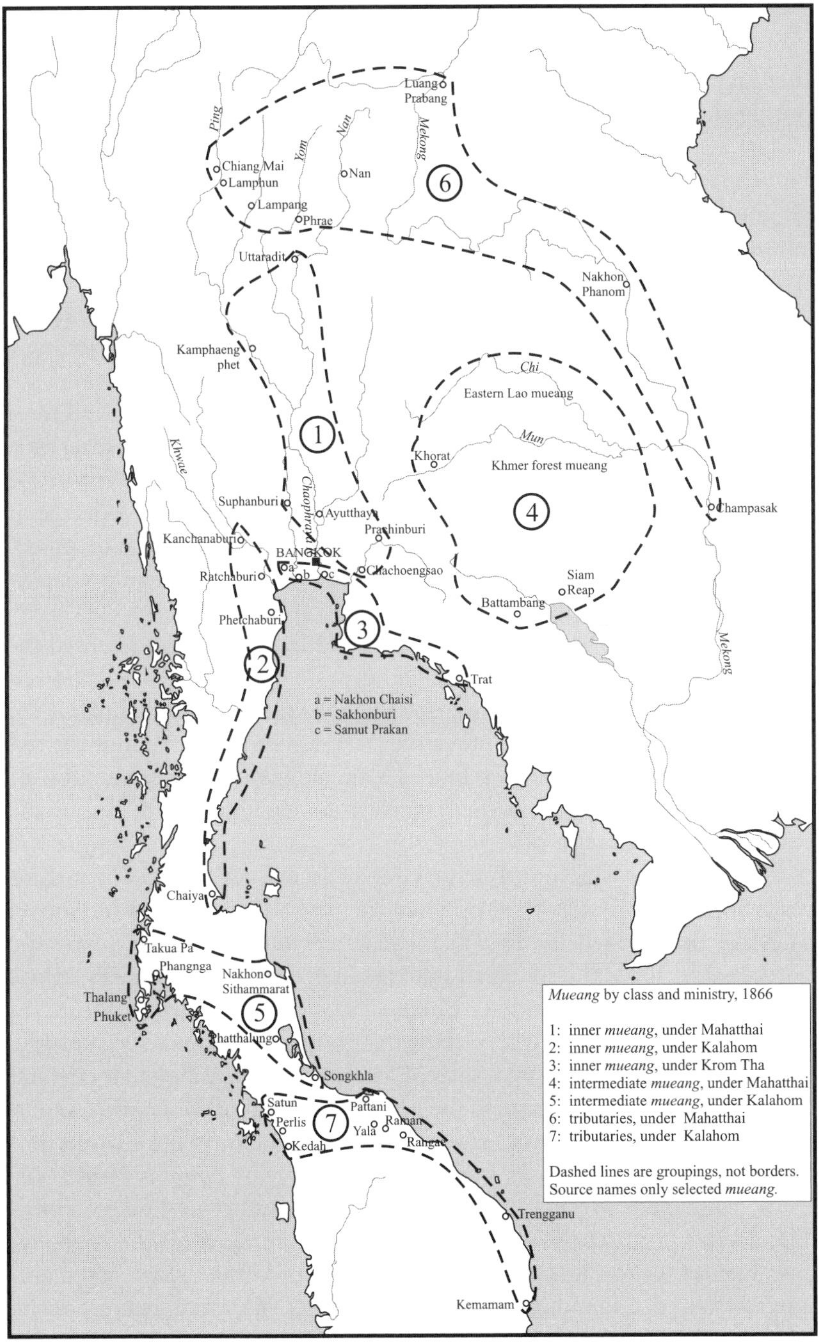
Luang Prabang
Ping
Nan
Yom
Mekong
Chiang Mai
Lamphun
Nan
6
Lampang
Phrae
Uttaradit
Nakhon Phanom
Kamphaeng phet
Chi
Eastern Lao mueang
1
Mun
Khwae
Khorat
Khmer forest mueang
Chaophraya
Suphanburi
Ayutthaya
4
Champasak
Prachinburi
Kanchanaburi
BANGKOK
a
b
c
Chachoengsao
Ratchaburi
Siam Reap
Battambang
Phetchaburi
3
2
Mekong
Trat
a = Nakhon Chaisi
b = Sakhonburi
c = Samut Prakan
Chaiya
Takua Pa
Phangnga
Nakhon Sithammarat
Thalang
Phuket
5
Phatthalung
Songkhla
Satun
Pattani
Perlis
7
Yala
Raman
Kedah
Rangae
Trengganu
Kemamam
Mueang by class and ministry, 1866
1: inner *mueang*, under Mahatthai
2: inner *mueang*, under Kalahom
3: inner *mueang*, under Krom Tha
4: intermediate *mueang*, under Mahatthai
5: intermediate *mueang*, under Kalahom
6: tributaries, under Mahatthai
7: tributaries, under Kalahom
Dashed lines are groupings, not borders.
Source names only selected *mueang*.

Map 3: Political geography on the eve of reform

Interior had appointed 3000 officials to the provinces. Many of the old people and old practices were still in place, but they were now technically part of a single bureaucratic pyramid extending down from the ministry. From 1902 officials were paid salaries from the centre, rather than living off the local profits of their office. Previously, provincial governors had administered from their house or compound. Now new official enclaves were built in the provincial centres, rather on the model of a colonial cantonment, with offices, a jail, and housing for officials, all intended to impress through scale and standard design. Damrong christened the new system *thesaphiban*, control over territory.

Judicial reform followed a similar centralizing pattern. In 1892, all cases in the capital were transferred from courts under various ministries to a new unified structure. Beginning in 1902, commissioners were sent to the provinces to reorganize their courts under a single hierarchy. A decree of 1908 formally brought all courts under the Justice Ministry. Court procedure was changed to resemble western practice, formalized in a code in 1908.

In the inner areas, there was little reaction. Many old nobles resented the loss of revenue and power, but usually they were not dislodged but allowed to retire gracefully. Their sons were encouraged to enter the schools which were the portal into the new bureaucracy. This new generation of the old central elite seems to have embraced Chulalongkorn's interpretation of 'progress' as a way to retain their status in a changing world. But at the periphery, there were revolts.

In 1895, villages in Khon Kaen revolted and excluded officials for three years. In 1889–90, some 3000 opposed the new administration in Chiang Mai. In 1901, 2500 rebels joined a millenarian revolt in the Ubon area of the northeast. In 1902, the southern border states threatened to revolt, rebels took over the northern state of Phrae, and smaller incidents occurred in Lampang and Lamphun. Many of these outbursts were directed against the new taxes. Some were led by displaced local officials and abetted by the old rulers. In Lanna, rebels attacked the new government offices, and vowed to drive out the Siamese officials and Chinese tax-farmers. In both Lanna and Isan, these revolts drew on a tradition of uprisings by *phumibun*, men-of-merit, who could overthrow the social order and usher in a better world. The northeastern rebels sacked the town of Khemmarat on the Mekong, and then set off towards the provincial capital of Ubon. Their stated aim was 'to establish a kingdom which was not under either the Siamese or the French'.[11]

Initially these revolts caught the government off balance. But rebels armed with local weapons and trusting in the power of sacred water to

Figure 3: Siamese nobility on the eve of the west. Mom Rachotai, early student of the missionaries, envoy to London, and author, c. 1860s. His dress and props are of various Asian origins – Thai, Chinese, Persian, Indian, Arab – only the books are western.

guarantee invulnerability were no match for Gatling guns and cannon. In the northeast, troops claimed to kill 200 rebels without incurring a single casualty. In Lanna, thirteen leaders were captured, pilloried for three days, and then executed. In the south, the ruler of the Malay Muslim state of Pattani was thrown into jail for two years. The revolts petered away in the face of these shows of force, but they had delivered a shock to Chulalongkorn and his court. Especially in Lanna, the implementation of the new administration ground to a halt for three years.

SCRAMBLING BOUNDARIES

In parallel with this transition to a new form of administration, the old political geography based on *mueang*, emboxment, and personal relations between rulers was replaced by a model based on territory and borders. In Thongchai Winichakul's famous coining, Siam gained a 'geo-body'.[12]

In the old political system, there were no boundaries as lines on maps or along the ground. Two *mueang* occasionally marked their frontier by a cairn, *chedi*, or customs post along the route connecting the two centres. Most *mueang* were separated by large and mostly empty tracts of forest, such as the hill ranges dividing Siam from Burma, and these tracts 'belonged to no-one'. Rulers liked to see frontiers not as barriers but, rather, as 'silver and gold roads of trade and friendship', channels for possible expansion of their trade and influence. In peripheral areas, local rulers might be tributary to two or more overlords, and these arrangements could shift with circumstance.

Once Britain became a neighbour to the south and west in the 1820s, it asked Siam to define their mutual borders. At first the Siamese court found this perplexing and rather irritating, and only reluctantly complied.

From the 1860s, colonial pressure became more complex. The British nibbled away at the southern border, and in 1852–53 grabbed another chunk of Burma. The French pressed inwards from the east, taking Saigon and then imposing a protectorate over Cambodia in 1863. Siam rushed to sign a treaty agreeing the protectorate was shared, and rationalized that this was simply an extension of Cambodia's former tributary submission jointly to Vietnam and Siam. But the French wanted more. French colonial dreams alternated between hopes of finding a northward route from Indochina into China, and consolation of forging westwards across mainland Southeast Asia. After the Garnier-Lagrée expedition of 1866–67 showed the Mekong River was not navigable up to China, one of the French men-on-the-spot declared: 'Our desire is to bring into being that French empire dreamed of by some of us, which must extend from Kwang Tung and Yunnan all the way to the vicinity of Bangkok'.[13] The French also introduced another western concept – the idea of historical claims to sovereignty over territory. They began looking for documents which showed that Vietnam (and hence its successor, France) had better claims to many of the peripheral territories lying between Hanoi–Saigon and Bangkok.

At the same time, western business interests began to arrive in Siam. British timber companies cut their way through Burmese forests, and arrived in Lanna. Tin-mining firms overflowed northwards from British Malaya. Both gained concessions from Siam's local tributaries. At Bangkok, western speculators floated schemes for cutting a canal across the peninsula, mining various metals, and building far-flung networks of railways reflecting grand imperial ambitions. For Siam, defined borders had become a good defensive idea. In 1880, Siam hired a British surveyor, James McCarthy, from India, and sent him off to map the frontiers, especially in the far northeast. Along with McCarthy went columns of troops, supposedly tasked to suppress 'Ho' bands, probably refugees from the Taiping rebellion in southwestern China. The troops' real job was to strengthen claims to the territory behind the mapped line by planting Siamese white-elephant flags, handing out Siamese titles to local chiefs, building stockades, and sometimes tattooing men for corvée. McCarthy's map, published in 1887, showed a border running southwards from Sipsongpanna along the Annamite hills into Cambodia (Map 4). In Thongchai's phrase, this map was 'the encoding of desire'.[14]

The southern and western borders with British territory were agreed relatively easily in 1894 and 1909 by sharing out local polities which had previously been tributary to both sides. France was more difficult. It responded with its own maps, historical claims based on local documents, and troop columns sent to occupy the peripheral areas. The issue was settled not by maps or historical precedent but by force. In 1893, France annexed the east bank of the Mekong southwards from the Chinese border. To oppose them, Siam attempted to raise 180,000 troops, the biggest military mobilization for over a century, but could find only a fraction of this number. Units clashed with the French near the Mekong River. In response, the French sailed two gunboats up the Chaophraya River and anchored off the French embassy. They demanded an indemnity and Siamese evacuation from the east bank of the Mekong. When the government demurred, the French blockaded the port, demanded a 25-kilometre demilitarized zone on the west bank of the river, and *protégé* status for Vietnamese, Lao, and Khmer in Siam.

This Paknam Incident resulted in a treaty which drew the boundary between Siam and French Indochina along the Mekong River, subtracting

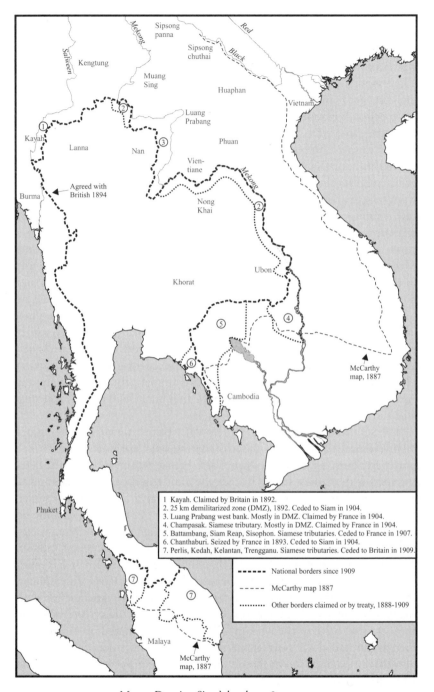

Map 4: Drawing Siam's borders, 1892–1909

Within the map image:

Saween

Mekong

Sipsong
panna

Red

Kengtung

Sipsong
chuthai

Black

Muang
Sing

Huaphan

Vietnam

Luang
Prabang

①

②

③

Kayah

Lanna

Nan

Phuan

Vien-
tiane

Mekong

Agreed with
British 1894

Burma

Nong
Khai

②

Ubon

Khorat

④

⑤

⑥

McCarthy
map, 1887

Cambodia

Phuket

1 Kayah. Claimed by Britain in 1892.
2. 25 km demilitarized zone (DMZ), 1892. Ceded to Siam in 1904.
3. Luang Prabang west bank. Mostly in DMZ. Claimed by France in 1904.
4. Champasak. Siamese tributary. Mostly in DMZ. Claimed by France in 1904.
5. Battambang, Siam Reap, Sisophon. Siamese tributaries. Ceded to France in 1907.
6. Chanthaburi. Seized by France in 1893. Ceded to Siam in 1904.
7. Perlis, Kedah, Kelantan, Trengganu. Siamese tributaries. Ceded to Britain in 1909.

━ ━ ━ ━   National borders since 1909

‐ ‐ ‐ ‐   McCarthy map 1887

· · · · · · ·   Other borders claimed or by treaty, 1888-1909

⑦

⑦

Malaya

McCarthy
map, 1887

the Lao states of Luang Prabang and Vientiane, the northern Khmer territories, and much of Sipsongpanna and Sipsongchuthai from the ambitions coded on the McCarthy map. The British blocked the idea of a French protectorate over Siam. But the two countries informally and secretly agreed that Siam should eventually be reduced to the Chaophraya basin, ceding the eastward territories to France and the peninsula southward to Britain. The French and British men-on-the-spot began manoeuvres to achieve this result. But after 1900, the home governments quashed these colonial ambitions and rivalries for the sake of alliance in Europe against the growing threat of Germany. Treaties concluded between 1902 and 1909 fixed the borders at their present positions. Siam had become a defined, bounded country. Many states along the peripheral areas had disappeared. According to the western theory which Siam was embracing, the capital of Bangkok enjoyed unique and undivided sovereignty across the territory inside this new boundary.

MAKING CITIZENS

In parallel, all the various categories of slaves and bondsmen with personal ties to a patron or overseer were transformed into citizens with a theoretically direct relationship to the state.

In 1897 Chulalongkorn took another step to end forced labour by ruling that nobody born from then onwards could sell himself or be sold into slavery. Only a few ageing debt slaves and war captives now remained (until final abolition in 1912). Abolishing corvée was more complicated because it affected the army, which was needed to protect the mapping parties, skirmish with the French, hunt down bandits, guard against Chinese riots, and suppress the peripheral rebels. Through the late 1870s and early 1880s, Chulalongkorn found ways to convert some people from noble to royal service. Then in 1887, another half-brother was placed in charge of a new Defence Ministry, and instructed to plan a conscript standing army.

Many in the court disagreed with this project. They argued that Siam could not hope to compete with a European army, and should not provoke the Europeans by trying. But Chulalongkorn insisted that a standing army was one of the attributes of a modern nation. Besides, the real need was not external, against the colonialists, but internal – imposing Bangkok authority on the area inside the new borders, and bringing all people under the king.

Several of Chulalongkorn's sons had been sent to military academies in Europe. When the first of these returned in 1897, he was entrusted with planning a new army. The difficulty of suppressing the provincial revolts over 1899–1902 further convinced Chulalongkorn and dispersed most of the opposition: 'Conscription is a necessity. If we fail to introduce it, that would be tantamount to throwing Phayap [Lanna] away.'[15] Conscription was hurriedly implemented in three provinces to complete the suppression of revolts, and then introduced universally by 1905. Commutation dues were replaced by a universal poll tax (extended to include the Chinese and other foreigners in 1909). Military expenditure rose from 1 million baht in 1898 to 13 million in 1909–10, when Siam had a standing army of 20,000 and a navy of 5000, with over 50,000 in their combined reserves.

All men were now the king's men. Almost everyone now stood in the same relationship to the state for tax and military service. In parallel, they were also reinvented as members of the same race.

MAKING THAI

The return of the westerners in the early nineteenth century, and the involvement of Siam in a network of treaties, began a debate about the nature of the people inhabiting Siam and their relations to others. The conventional yardstick used to differentiate peoples was language. Foreigners as a category were called the people of the 'twelve languages' or 'forty languages'. In the 1830s, these were partially catalogued in a display at Bangkok's Wat Pho, with twenty-seven different peoples each portrayed on a door panel and described in an accompanying poem. These pictures and poems brought in the idea that different peoples not only spoke different languages but *looked* distinctive – both in physical features and dress. The poems also occasionally mentioned that some peoples had special character traits. The Thai were portrayed as part of this catalogue:

> The Siamese, handsome as if shaped by heaven,
> Dwells in the prosperous and glorious city of Ayutthaya.
> Look! He exudes power and inspires awe across the world.
> His upper cloth is woven with silver and gold thread.
> The lower cloth, boldly patterned, is smartly held by a silk sash.
> The effect is gracefully beautiful, gloriously powerful, perfectly
>   resplendent.[16]

This description clearly made no attempt to encompass all the people within Siam. The poem described a noble, and made a claim for the Thai elite to count among those peoples with power over others.

The ruling elite might be conceived as 'Thai', but at this period the court still celebrated the great ethnic variety of peoples within the country. The king's rule extended over all those who, in the royal rhetoric, had 'sought the royal protection'. In dealing with foreigners, the state called itself Siam. Mongkut signed himself as *Krung Sayam* and Chulalongkorn as *Sayamin* (Siam + Indra). In keeping with the principle of emboxment, Siam could mean either the capital or the larger unit emboxed by the capital's influence. The outer areas were defined according to their linguistic–ethnic identity as the 'eastern Lao', 'northwestern Lao', 'Khmer', and 'Malay' or 'Khaek' states, emphasizing Siam's imperial reach over other peoples. During his 1872 visit to India, Chulalongkorn described himself as 'King of Siam and Sovereign of Laos and Malay'.[17]

Europe had evolved the idea that a nation was the political expression of a 'race'. From the 1880s, the French used this idea as part of their aggression against Siam. They argued that the Lao, though related linguistically to the Thai, qualified as a distinct race. Meanwhile, the Siamese were not a proper race because they had become too intermixed with the Chinese. Hence, the true Siamese were a minority within their country, and in fact a 'Lilliputian oligarchy' dominating subject peoples.[18] In this discourse, the French colonial seizure of Siam would mean liberation of the majority of its people. In the treaty following the 1893 Paknam Incident, France went some way to realizing this idea through the clause allowing former inhabitants of Indochina now in Siam to claim French protection. The French aggressively expanded the range of people who could qualify as *protégés*, beginning from descendants of peoples moved across the Mekong since 1828, and widening to include all claiming Khmer or Lao descent, and even many Chinese who had sought colonial protection for commercial advantage. The Thai court was horrified. Some wondered whether the king might be Khmer enough to qualify for French *protégé* status. Many people registered themselves as *protégés* to escape corvée. French entrepreneurs planned enclave businesses using *protégé* labour.

The Siamese court learnt how to use this discourse of race. In the late nineteenth century, it evolved the word *chat*, which originally meant birth, origin, or a cycle of rebirth, to express ideas corresponding to race. To define the Thai race, two overlapping definitions were used in parallel. First, the old way of defining people by language was adapted so that speakers of other Tai languages could be claimed as Thai. Commissioners sent to the periphery were instructed to persuade the local lords that 'Thai and Lao are of the same *chat* and speak the same language within a single kingdom'. Damrong claimed that 'all these people call themselves by different names . . . such as *chao sayam, lao, shan, lue, ho* . . . in fact all are Thai ethnic groups (*chon chat thai*). They speak Thai and every one of them hold that they themselves are Thai.'[19] Second, all those living within the borders and hence subjects of the king were defined as Thai. As the Bangkok commissioner in Lampang told a public dinner: 'the distinction between Siamese and Lao no longer exists – we are all subjects of His Majesty'.[20] In a border dispute with the British in 1885, Chulalongkorn blended these two definitions together: 'The Thai, the Lao, and the Shan all consider themselves peoples of the same race. They all respect me as their supreme sovereign, the protector of their well-being.'[21]

Similar ideas were written into the first textbooks for the new schools (see below). Nation was a cultural community founded primarily on language: 'We are of the same nation and speak the same language, so how can we not love each other more than we love other people who belong to other nations and speak other languages?'[22] This cultural community was also formed by a common religion (Buddhism) and common history. At the same time, nation was a political concept, demanding its members' loyalty and self-sacrifice.

At the turn of the century, Bangkok changed the geographical vocabulary to reflect this new idea. The new territorial provinces formed from 1899 were no longer named as Lao, Malay, or whatever, but given Sanskritic names, some of which identified provinces as the northern, eastern, and so on, parts of the kingdom. Damrong explained this was because their inhabitants 'were really of the Thai race', and the new names reflected the existence of 'a united Thai kingdom'.[23]

In Thai versions of treaties from 1902, the country was no longer called Siam but *prathet thai* or *ratcha-anajak thai*, the country or kingdom of the Thai. All people within the kingdom were defined as *sanchat thai*, translated in the English versions of the treaties as 'of Thai nationality'. To bring the legal position into line with this new match between territory and nationality, Siam insisted the colonial powers give up the extraterritorial rights of the *protégés* as part of the border treaties. To achieve this, the government ceded considerable territory in recompense. In 1907, Siam abandoned its claims to the northwestern Khmer provinces (Siam Reap, Battambang, and Sisophon) in return for French agreement to give up extraterritoriality. In 1909, the four Malay states of Kedah, Kelantan, Trengganu, and Perlis were ceded to Britain in return for the same concession (see Map 4).

The Siamese court had adopted a new term, *prathetchat* or *chatprathet*, which matched the compound form of 'nation-state' and had some of its strength and confusion. On the one hand, Thai was now simply the definition of all those who lived within the Thai kingdom; this idea was codified in the Nationality Act of 1913, under which all born inside the borders could claim the nationality. On the other hand, this definition also laid claim to represent a social reality of people unified by language and perhaps by ethnic origin.

While this unified Thai-ness was presented to foreigners, internally the court retained some subtle differentiation. Commissioners sent to the periphery were told to emphasize the common identity of Lao and Siamese when talking to foreigners, but to retain some of the old Thai–Lao difference in private. The description of Siam sent to the international exhibition at St Louis in 1904 catalogued the 'great Thai race' into three parts: the original and more sophisticated 'Siamese or Thai'; then the Shan or Lao 'neighbouring races'; and finally others such as Khmer, Malay, and Burmese who were 'originally . . . prisoners of war' but had 'intermarried with the Siamese and all speak the Siamese language'.[24] School textbooks distinguished between those who spoke 'proper' cultivated Thai and others who were encouraged to improve themselves in order to qualify fully as members of the nation.

The elite began to define a more complex sociology of those who were now defined as the Thai nation. Mongkut had travelled upcountry both while a monk and later when king. Chulalongkorn travelled much more, pretending to be incognito and revelling in being recognized. Damrong, and other officials engaged in mapping the new administration onto the territory, travelled even more. Like the *farang* travellers earlier, Damrong and others took notes on what they saw. From the 1880s, they began to write studies describing and classifying the variety of peoples found in the new nation-state.

These studies stratified people into three broad bands. At the bottom were the hill peoples. An army general engaged on mapping and protecting the new borders described them as living in the jungle; strange, wild, dirty, and half-naked; and beyond civilization or any hope of progress. Next came the agricultural people of the lowland. Damrong described them as more familiar, more docile, and clearly engaged in production which was useful for the economy, yet still simple in their ways, and superstitious in their beliefs. At the top were the princes and senior officials of the elite. They aspired to be *siwilai*, a Thai-ification of 'civilized' which expressed the desire to 'progress' on the model of the west, and thus qualify to dominate other peoples within and beyond the country's borders. The 'Thai race' was both united and divided.

MAKING BETTER CITIZENS

The new nation-state assumed the authority to discipline the peoples of such different backgrounds and mentalities enclosed within the borders. The new army was used almost totally to impose order inside the country; Chulalongkorn called the detachments sent against the northern rebels 'an army of occupation'.[25] A new police force was also formed, originally to control the Chinese 'secret societies' when the government resolved to close down the gambling dens in the early years of the twentieth century. A jail was a standard part of each province's headquarters.

Prince Ratchaburi, another of Chulalongkorn's sons, returned from Oxford with a law degree and was assigned to create a judicial system. He favoured a common-law approach but was overruled on grounds that foreigners would be more impressed by a codified roman law. A criminal code was completed in 1908. Ratchaburi also wanted the judiciary to be truly separate from the bureaucracy. Again he was overruled. Chulalongkorn had seen colonial systems which combined judiciary and bureaucracy for tighter control.

The nation-state was thus equipped with instruments of coercion. For the longer term, however, people had to be moulded into good citizens of the nation.

The aspiration, evident since early Bangkok, to draw on Buddhism to educate and discipline society was adapted for the framework of the nation-state. Mongkut and Chulalongkorn appointed a series of royal family members as the supreme patriarch of the Sangha. From 1874, these were members of Mongkut's reformed Thammayut sect. In 1893, Chulalongkorn entrusted Vachirayan, another half-brother, Thammayut monk, and future supreme patriarch, to head a new Buddhist Academy to improve the training of monks. Then in 1898, Chulalongkorn moved Vachirayan to develop primary education by expanding the traditional system of schooling in the *wat*. Vachirayan began by sending out Thammayut monks to survey the provinces. Their reports showed how varied were the peoples and religious practices in the regions now enclosed within the borders of Siam. Local *wat* had their own texts and traditions. Provincial monks worked in the fields, participated in village festivals, preached using homely folk tales, and had limited knowledge of canonical texts. On receiving these reports, Chulalongkorn diverted Vachirayan to the task of unifying and disciplining the monkhood. The resulting Sangha Act of 1902 arrayed all monks in a hierarchy stretching down from the king and supreme patriarch. Monks learnt from a standard syllabus, qualified by centrally administered examinations, and preached from approved texts. New *wat* were encouraged to conform to a standard design. Vachirayan gently coaxed Lanna monks to abandon their very established local traditions, and gathered well-known monks from the truculent northeast and distant south into the Thammayut order. Vachirayan hoped that Buddhism would be 'a tight binding between the government and the people'.[26]

Vachirayan then returned to training monks and producing standard textbooks for the new primary education. All children were to be taught the Central Thai language, Buddhism, and arithmetic. In 1921, primary education was made compulsory. Funds were sparse but by the mid-1920s, 40 per cent of children aged 7–14 attended the schools.

One of the subjects of the standard curriculum was proper behaviour. In the 1900s, Chaophraya Phrasadet composed a textbook for this discipline. He had been one of the early descendants of noble families to enter the new schools, had undergone ordination in the Thammayut order at Wat Boworniwet, and then served as Damrong's secretary. His *Sombat khong phu di* (The qualities of gentlefolk) instructed a generation of the newly educated to be neat, well-mannered, respectful, likeable, dignified, pleasing to the eye, good-natured, selfless, trustworthy, and free of vice – the code of behaviour of an ideal bureaucrat. Phrasadet rose to head the Civil Service School. His text began a tradition of state manuals for the instruction of children and citizens.

Progress required a large and healthy population, and thus the new state became concerned about the health of its citizens. The first hospital was founded in 1888 (Sirirat) and a medical school in 1890. After a succession of plague outbreaks between 1904 and 1906, the government issued public health regulations designed to prevent and contain both plague and cholera. It also began to designate *sukhaphiban*, sanitary districts, charged with maintaining public hygiene. To gather the information base for these policies, an Act in 1917 mandated regular population censuses, and registration of births, deaths, and residence.

MODERN, MAGNIFICENT MONARCHY

In parallel with this remaking of the polity and the people, the monarchy was transformed.

First, it acquired a new financial base. The Privy Purse was originally established to use the profits of royal trading to pay the royal household. It was expanded to finance overseas education for royal and noble scions, and then expanded again as the Privy Purse Bureau (PPB) in 1890 as the palace's investment arm. Between 5 and 20 per cent of government revenues was channelled to the PPB. Some was used to enter the expanding rice economy by investments in rice mills. Some went to property development, building shophouses along new roads in the expanding city, and markets in the up-country centres. By 1910, the PPB was the country's largest property holder. Some went into company investments, often in joint venture with foreign partners, in railways, tramways, electricity, banking, cement, coalmining, and steam navigation.

Next, royalty expanded its role in the government. Previously, royal relatives had been excluded from senior official posts. Now they dominated them. When Chulalongkorn formed a council of twelve ministers in 1892, nine were his brothers and half-brothers. He sent his four eldest sons overseas for education in 1885, and drafted them and other royal cousins into senior military and official posts when they returned from the mid-1890s onwards.

Royalty had a privileged place in the new schools founded to train people for official careers. In 1881, Damrong founded Suan Kulap School specifically to educate civil servants. It admitted 'only the sons of princes and the highest nobles'. After several commoners enrolled, the fees were raised 'to prevent common people from attending the school'. The King's School, founded in 1897 to prepare students to study overseas, was similarly restrictive. Damrong hoped to limit recruitment to the upper ranks of the expanding bureaucracy to 'those who are high born (*phu di*) or who are .acceptable because of wealth'.[27] The Civil Service School founded in 1899 initially attracted few from the nobility so it was renamed the Royal Pages School to increase its cachet. The Military Academy founded in 1897 was officially restricted to those of royal or noble birth. In 1906 the birth restrictions were tightened, and in 1909 an elite stream was created for sons of the highest families. In 1910, every military officer ranked lieutenant general or above was a member of the royal family.

For other senior posts, foreign advisers were favoured. From 1860, a handful were hired for technical skills. After the 1893 Paknam crisis, the numbers increased within four years to fifty-eight British, twenty-two Germans, twenty-two Danes, nine Belgians, eight Italians, and twenty others. These advisers not only brought expertise, particularly in international finance, but also helped in dealing with the threats from the colonial powers. Chulalongkorn noted that 'to employ foreigners is like having ready-made textbooks'.[28]

In broader ways, the court associated itself more and more with Europe as the source of power and knowledge. In the 1870s, male fashion in the court began to copy western fashions of longer hair, moustaches, hose, and shoes. By the 1890s this had extended to trousers, tailored suits, hats, and dress uniforms for ceremonial occasions. When the king visited Europe, *Tailor and Cutter* magazine declared that he 'looks just like an English gentleman'.[29] In the 1870s, Chulalongkorn built a new throne hall with an Italianate design, but topped it with a Siamese roof to please traditionalists. In 1907, this compromise was surpassed by the stridently classical Ananta Samakhom throne hall built with Carrera marble, Milan granite, German copper, and Viennese ceramics. The building dominated the entrance to a new royal quarter to the north of the old city, housing a European-style palace complex and other mansions built for other members of the royal clan. King and nobles imported European bric-a-brac to embellish these new homes.

In 1897, Chulalongkorn travelled to Europe. In part, this was shrewd diplomacy following the Paknam Incident of 1893. The French colonial minister immediately understood the significance: 'it will give the impression that the kingdom of Siam, whose sovereign has been received in the manner due to a European head of state, is a civilized country which should be treated like a European power'.[30] In part, it was a way for the king to see *siwilai* for himself at first hand. In part, it portrayed the king to his subjects as a new kind of sovereign who moved among the world's royal elite.

This new westernized monarchy became more public. In early Bangkok, pellet-archers still went ahead of royal processions to prevent people viewing the royal body. After an archer injured a woman late in the Third Reign, they were limited to 'threatening persons showing disrespect'. Mongkut stopped the whole practice and welcomed spectators at his royal rituals and provincial tours. Chulalongkorn exposed the royal body and its image much more. He delighted in being photographed, painted, and sculpted. He allowed his image to be reproduced on coins, stamps, mementoes, and postcards. He rode around Bangkok in an open landau and later an automobile (Figure 4). From 1899, he mingled among a select crowd at an annual fair at Wat Benjamabophit. In 1908 a statue of Chulalongkorn astride a horse was unveiled in front of the new Italianate throne hall. Cast in Paris and portraying the king in western military attire, the image was the first use of statuary outside a religious context, and a massive statement of the royal presence in the capital.

In the latter part of the reign, this open and modern monarchy was presented to the public in grand spectacles. The city was remodelled around the turn of the century by two avenues inspired by the Champs Elysées, and named Ratchadamnoen, the royal way. They were used for magnificent

Figure 4: King Chulalongkorn, modern and revealed. Probably in the Dusit quarter in the early 1900s.

processions on the occasion of the king's return from a second trip to Europe in 1907, and on the fortieth anniversary of his reign a year later. Both these events were themed as celebrations of the 'progress' achieved during the reign. Government departments built ceremonial arches and parade floats to dramatize advances in agriculture, health, taxation, railways, telegraphy, and electricity generation. Three years later, Chulalongkorn's son and successor, Vajiravudh, held a second coronation, attended by royalty from Britain, Russia, Greece, Sweden, Denmark, and Japan. The event lasted thirteen days, accompanied by a popular fair, and used up 8 per cent of the national budget.

Several reforms were designed to secure and dramatize the continuity of the Chakri dynasty. Mongkut had stated that 'the king is a human' and that 'attributing kingship to divine power detracts from the merit and capabilities of the man'. But the transmission of these capabilities, he insisted, was carried in the royal blood. A king was 'someone of good birth based on former lives of excellence on both sides [that is, both maternal and paternal]'.[31] Mongkut finessed the succession by giving his favoured son, Chulalongkorn, an unquestionably higher title than any rival, and rewarding Chuang Bunnag for overseeing the process. Chulalongkorn adapted western practice to ensure dynastic continuity. He abolished the concept of the Front Palace and introduced the idea of nominating an heir. He then rewrote the Palatine Law, basing the succession on European-style primogeniture modified to accommodate polygamy. In 1916, his successor, Vajiravudh, further emphasized continuity by retrospectively renaming all the Chakri kings as Ramathibodi (usually shortened to Rama) in a numbered sequence – Rama I, II, III, and so on. Portraits were made of each, relying on memory for the early monarchs.

Chulalongkorn chose all his seven major wives from among half-sisters and cousins, thus restricting his descent within bloodlines extending from the Chakri founder. He rebased the calendar to begin from the foundation of Bangkok and the Chakri dynasty, and created public holidays celebrating the dynasty's foundation and the king's birthday.

Over the last quarter of the nineteenth century, the monarchy gained financial security, dynastic continuity, and a dominant role in the new government. It made itself into a symbol of the 'progress' associated with the dominant west and the modern world. In the architecture and theatre of the new capital, the monarchy had a dominating presence. Adapting from the Code Napoleon, Chulalongkorn defined the absolute royal power:

The king rules absolutely at his own royal desire. There is nothing greater than this. The king has absolute power as 1) ruler over the realm and refuge for the people; 2) the source of justice; 3) the source of rank and status; 4) commander of the armed forces who relieves the people's suffering by waging war or conducting friendly relations with other countries. The king does no wrong. There is no power that can judge or punish him.[32]

DRAMA, ARCHITECTURE, AND HISTORY

While displaying admiration for the west, the elite also felt that Siam needed a distinctive heritage as part of its qualification as a nation-state. Since the start of the Bangkok period, the court had put efforts into retrieving and sustaining the court culture of the late Ayutthaya era, especially drama performances based on stories from the Ramakian (an adaptation of the Indian Ramayana) and the Inao tales (originally from Indonesia). It was *de rigueur* for each monarch to compose dramas based on episodes from these works. During the reigns of Mongkut and Chulalongkorn, classical forms of performance, which had gone out of fashion since the fall of Ayutthaya, were self-consciously revived – especially the *khon* masked drama – and modernized by adding some western stagecraft. There was also revival of the Ayutthaya court fashion for composing verse in complex metres on mythological themes often drawn from Sanskrit literature. Mongkut and his successors liked to rename places with words from Sanskrit or Pali as these seemed more cultured, euphonious, and *siwilai* than the Thai or Lao of the common people.

This mix of revivalism and westernization appeared in architecture. The Royal Pages School (later Vajiravudh College) was built in 1910 on the model of an English public school, but self-consciously Thai in the buildings' style and decoration. Wat Benjamabophit, the most prominent *wat* built in this era, was an idealized rendering of traditional Thai architecture, with touches of European inspiration in the walls of Carrera marble and the stained-glass windows of Gothic inspiration. The murals were designed by a Thai prince on traditional lines, then executed by an Italian in Renaissance style.

The court also adopted new cultural practice in the spirit of the age, especially social science which reflected the belief in humanity's ability to change the world. Apart from the interest in anthropology noted above, the most popular and important genre was history.

Mongkut understood the importance of history in this era fascinated by the idea of progress. He travelled to historical sites, collected historical sources, and compiled a tentative *Short History of Siam*. Chulalongkorn included a celebration of Siamese history as part of the festivals which marked the climax of his reign. The event was staged in 1907 in the ruins of the old capital of Ayutthaya. Chulalongkorn had just returned from his second tour of Europe's historic capitals. In his speech at this event he noted that well-established countries 'uphold that the history of one's nation and country is an important matter to be known clearly and accurately through study and teaching. It is a discipline for evaluating ideas and actions as right or wrong, good or bad, as a means to inculcate love of one's nation and land.'[33] He found that established countries had compiled their histories back at least a thousand years, and he announced the foundation of an Antiquarian Society dedicated to compiling such a history for Siam. The following year, his son Vajiravudh visited Sukhothai, carrying the text of an inscription found by Mongkut and dated to 1292. He matched monuments mentioned in the text with ruins found on the ground (Figure 5). He published his account of the visit 'to make the Thai more aware that our Thai race is deep-rooted and is not a race of jungle-folk or, as the English say, uncivilized'.[34] Vajiravudh and Damrong established Sukhothai as 'the first capital of the Thai', and the beginning of an unbroken sequence down though Ayutthaya to Thonburi/Bangkok.

In 1915, Damrong squabbled with Vajiravudh and quit the Interior Ministry. He was already engaged in historical research and thereafter it would

Figure 5: Monarchy mobilizing history. Prince Vajiravudh examines archaeological finds in 1907.

engage all his energy. After helping to create the nation as an administrative unit, he now gave it a history. Over the next two decades he produced over fifty studies, including texts, travelogues, and anthropological studies, but overwhelmingly historical works. In 1920 he published the book best known as *Thai rop phama*, the Thai wars with the Burmese. It was an immediate success and remains Thailand's most famous history book. It portrays the Burmese as the ever-hostile Other who give definition to Siam as a nation. It pushes the nation back into the past in a series of wars lasting over 400 years. It places the king at the centre of the story, and highlights Naresuan and Yotfa as the heroic defenders of national independence. It lingers on the two sackings of Ayutthaya in 1569 and 1767 as the great national disasters brought about by national disunity, especially within the nobility. It introduces ordinary people into the national story in the tale of Bang Rajan, a village which fought bravely and hopelessly against the Burmese in 1767, with no help from the capital yet inspired by a natural loyalty and marshalled by a solitary Buddhist monk.

Damrong defined the national character of the Thai as seen through history as 'devoted to national freedom, non-violent, and skilled in compromising different interests'.[35] Because of these qualities, people of many races had become 'Siamese' by showing loyalty to the king and adopting the Thai language.

COMMONER INTELLECTUALS

The court dominated the opportunities for modern education, overseas contact, and illustrious careers. But it could not totally monopolize them. A small number of talented commoners were able to participate. They were also fascinated by the western concept of progress, but took away rather different inspiration compared to the leaders of the court. Although their numbers were few, through the new medium of printing they gained an audience. Missionaries had introduced Thai printing in the 1830s. Initially it was monopolized by church and court, but by the 1880s was available to others.

Kulap Kritsanon was the son of a Siam-born Chinese married to the daughter of a minor official. He was educated at *wat* schools and then, because his talent attracted attention and patronage, by tutors on the fringes of the court. He worked fifteen years in *farang* companies, travelling around Asia, acquiring western languages, and falling in love with books. He settled back to Bangkok in the 1880s and was one of the first to start an independent press. He made good enough contacts at court to borrow manuscripts from the palace libraries and had them surreptitiously copied and later printed. He started a journal (*Sayam praphet*), which gained a circulation of 1500, for articles on history and culture which he conjured out of his purloined texts, and his own essays on recent historical events. Eventually he was prosecuted, ostensibly for adding his own amendments and inventions into the original texts, but equally for his effrontery in publishing knowledge which was formerly the secret property of the palace.

Thianwan Wannapho also attracted the court's anger. His parents were commoners with a remote claim to noble ancestry. Like Kulap he was educated in the *wat* and on the fringes of the court. He started trading on the Chaophraya River, and later ranged further afield to Singapore, but returned to study English and law. He made a reputation as a lawyer for defending the poor, and for openly criticizing the exploitation and corruption of the ruling elite. He was cautioned against such outspokenness, and then jailed for life in 1882 for a technical infringement of legal practice. He was released after sixteen years, and walked from the jail with a sheaf of writings. He began a journal which railed against forced labour, polygamy, the government's patronage of gambling, and the lack of political representation. Most of all, he questioned why politics was the exclusive preserve of the court. He was fascinated by Japan's success in not only resisting colonialism but also in emulating the western pursuit of 'progress'. He argued that Japan was successful because its self-strengthening was truly a national movement, whereas in Siam the court elite was deliberately exclusive.

Another commoner intellectual, Thim Sukkhayang, came from a family of raft traders. He was educated in the *wat* and gained the patronage of a high-ranking official. In 1878 he published a *nirat* about a military expedition to the northeastern frontier region. The poem charged Chuang Bunnag, who had planned the expedition, with incompetence resulting in military failure and high loss of life. It portrayed ordinary people as victims of the incompetence and corruption of the noble elite. The court ruled that 'the content of the poem was too much for a *nirat*',[36] and after a summary trial Thim was jailed and the book destroyed.

Kulap, Thianwan, and Thim came from ordinary backgrounds. Their education came from traditional *wat* schools, patronage at the fringes of the court, and contact with *farang* through involvement in the trading economy. With the foundation of new schools from the 1880s onwards, more commoners wormed their way into elite education. Despite the court's wish to restrict education to the high-born, their need for educated people to staff the new administration was greater. Many royal and noble children found the new schooling demeaning or too difficult. Chulalongkorn constantly hectored and threatened them to participate, but with mixed results. Prosperous Chinese and other commoner families, however, welcomed the new opportunities. The law, military, and civil service schools soon had large proportions of commoners whose parents were ready to pay the discriminatory fees. While some commoner recruits ascended quickly in their careers, more often they were leapfrogged by those with higher birth and better connections. Especially in the military, no commoners ascended to the highest ranks, but they dominated the middle officer cadre.

Both Thianwan and Kulap *farang*ized their names by adding initials (T. S. R. Wannapho, K. S. R. Kulap). Like the court intellectuals, they were fascinated by the idea of people making history, by the concept of the nation-state, and by 'progress'. But where the court thinkers distilled from these ideas a new concept of absolute kingship defending the integrity of the nation and leading the way to progress, the commoner intellectuals were inspired by the ideal of a nation in which hierarchies and exclusions were abolished so that all the citizens could contribute to its progress. Their ideas became the inspiration for a following generation who found that entering a service career was an education in modern knowledge and traditional hierarchy – a potent combination.

THE LIMITS OF *SIWILAI*

Within the elite, there was debate on what reforms were needed to manage the west. In 1884, as the French took Indochina and the British fought their way into Upper Burma, Chulalongkorn asked Prisdang, his cousin at the head of the Paris legation, how Siam's independence could be preserved. Three other half-brothers of Chulalongkorn in Europe at the time were among the eleven signatories of the reply in January 1885. The danger to Siam, they argued, arose from the west's belief in its own mission to 'bring progress and *civilization* so mankind everywhere is equally content'. A western power would justify seizing a country which failed to provide progress, justice, free trade, protection for foreign nationals – 'in sum, the ability to govern and develop the country'. They advised:

To resolve this problem, Siam must be accepted and respected by the Western powers as a civilized nation . . . According to European belief, in order for a government to maintain justice it must be based on popular consensus . . . No nation in Europe can believe that Siam maintains justice since everything is decided by the king.[37]

The memorial recommended cabinet government, paid bureaucracy based on merit, equality before the law, an end to corruption, and freedom of speech. Most of all, it proposed a constitution, 'so that people, feeling that repression and injustice is at an end, will love the country, and realize that Siam belongs to its citizens'. The memorialists' model was Japan, the Asian country which had begun to emulate the west.

The memorial defined the point where Chulalongkorn's admiration of Europe ended. In his replies, the king argued that Siam's political tradition was different. European monarchs had practised absolutism, triggering efforts to control them with parliaments and constitutions. But the Siamese king ruled according to Buddhist morality. Hence:

In Siam there has never been such a political event where the people were against the king. Contrary to what happened in Europe, Siamese kings have led the people so that both they and the country might be prosperous and happy . . . the people would never be pleased to have Western institutions. They have more faith in the king than in any members of parliament, because they believe that the king more than anybody else practises justice and loves the people.[38]

Chulalongkorn stressed that he had only just won power from 'conservative ministers', that there were 'no suitable and able people' to man a parliament, and that 'reform' required undivided authority.

Courtiers reinforced this argument by reviving old royal theory and restating it in the new language of nation and state. Phraya Phatsakorawong, a Bunnag and one of the two non-royals among the senior ministers, restated the idea prevalent from at least Borommakot's time that the original king was chosen spontaneously by the people for his moral goodness: 'our ancestors came together to form a *chat*. This gathering chose from one family a capable man to be the leader of the *chat* . . . This had not been brought about by the opinion of the majority; rather it had been through the leader's own authority.' Another western-educated official portrayed resistance against the French as the defence of Buddhism and urged: 'We must be united to struggle against the royal foe in order to repay our gratitude to the king; we must defend Buddhism from being trampled by the impious; we must . . . preserve the freedom and independence of *chat thai*'.[39]

The Paknam Incident of 1893 dramatically increased the elite's fear of a colonial takeover. Chulalongkorn repeatedly stressed the mystical importance of *chat*, and the overriding duty of the citizens to have *samakkhi*, unity, to defend it. In this era, the dissident Kulap was prosecuted, and Prisdang, the royal cousin who headed the 1885 memorial, was disgraced and went into exile. In 1904, Chulalongkorn stated that the king was the embodiment of the nation, that Siam needed 'unity around the middle path of the king', and that a parliament would only lead to 'additional divisions and conflicts'.

At the very end of Chulalongkorn's reign and thereafter, Damrong redefined the nature of Siamese kingship in a series of speeches and studies. In the past, the king provided protection which allowed the people to pursue the Buddhist path towards *nibbana*. Now the king's role was to bring progress. Both Mongkut and Chulalongkorn had travelled round the country like monks on *thudong* (pilgrimage) to know the people's problems. All the king's actions were devoted to improving the people's well-being. 'The Thai way of government is like a father over a son, as is called in English *paternal government*.' The result was a king 'of the people' and 'for the people', who derived his power from the people's love. Damrong claimed that the new exposure of the royal body, especially through the massive equestrian statue and the innovation of allowing mourners to pay respects to Chulalongkorn's corpse, created a new closeness so that 'people began to have a feeling of love, which had not been felt for a king for a long time. After his death, people were truly sorrowful.'[40]

This style of kingship, Damrong implied, was intrinsic to the Chakri dynasty. His historical studies showed that (non-Chakri) Taksin had failed as a king, as a patron of traditional arts, and as a leader of Buddhism because he did not belong to this tradition. Damrong subtly edited the chronicles of the early Chakri reigns so that it appeared this style of kingship had been practised from the start of the dynasty. He argued that members of the royal family dominated the government because they were educated in statecraft, were devoted to an ideal of service which won popular respect, and were hence able to will their status to their heirs. Damrong's portrayal of royal rule implied that constitutional rule was unnecessary, and any departure from Chakri dominance would be a regression. 'If there is no king', Damrong wrote into the chronicle of Chulalongkorn's reign, 'the land will fall into disorder'.[41]

CONCLUSION

The last quarter of the nineteenth century saw massive changes arising from the social strains of the market economy, the new 'bourgeois' mentality of the elite, and the threats and opportunities of contact with the west. Siam avoided colonial rule. In part, this was due to geography and timing: Siam became a buffer between French and British ambitions as the era of colonial land-grabbing came to an end. In part, it was because the Ayutthayan-era practice of absorbing foreigners into the government could be adapted into a semi-colonial compromise. In part, the Siamese elite embraced the ideas of progress and history, and the technologies of mapping, colonial bureaucracy, law codes, and military conscription.

In the traditional framework, the king's power extended over all 'who sought the royal protection'. The duties of the royal state were to provide shelter against external enemies, and allay internal disorder by policing and by settling disputes. The relations which structured the state were all personal ties – the *phrai*'s subordination to a *nai*, the patron–client links within the official bureaucracy, the fealty of a subordinate ruler or provincial *jao* to the king, expressed in ritual displays such as drinking the water of allegiance. Tax revenues, forced labour, and exotic goods flowed up this personalized pyramid to support and glorify the upper levels. People transacted with the court on a limited range of matters (tax, corvée, dispute settlement), and mostly through intermediaries such as the tax-farmer and local recruiting agent.

The new political unit was defined by a territorial boundary. All those enclosed within the boundary, and granted 'nationality', were members of the nation and subjects of the state. The duty of the state was not only to provide protection but also to achieve 'progress'. To that end it built telegraphs and railways, organized religion and education to improve the citizen's mentality, and patronized public health to improve the citizen's physical capability. This extended purpose of the state legitimized an enlarged interference in the life of the citizen. People dealt with centrally appointed officials who taxed, counted, taught, policed, recruited, examined, and much besides. They were submitted to programmes of religious instruction, schooling, and education in citizenship.

In practice, the scope of this new Leviathan was initially limited by funds and human resources to the major towns. Besides, old structures and ideas lingered. Personal connections and family networks remained important both inside and outside the new bureaucracy. Old attitudes of dominance based on social rank were reproduced in the relations between bureaucrat and peasant. But all such survivals now had to compromise with the power vested in the state. The principles were laid, and the reach of the state gradually expanded over future decades. The process was far from smooth. Throughout Chulalongkorn's reign, there were rumours of coups in the capital by both traditionalists and disappointed reformers. Some parts of the Sangha showed quiet displeasure at trends of secularization and westernization. In the outer territories, some resistance continued after the turn-of-century revolts. In Lanna, Khruba Siwichai led opposition to the centralization and standardization of the Sangha down to the 1920s. But most resistance was passive – exploiting the lacunae of an uncompleted nation-state.

The people were bystanders at the creation of the Siamese nation-state. The territory of Siam was defined as a residual of colonial expansion. The nation was imagined to fit this space and encompass whoever was inside it. The administrative structure was adapted from colonial practice and imposed from above. The creation of the nation and nation-state went hand-in-hand with an increase in royal power and a reconceptualization of the monarchy's ideological foundations. The nation was conceived, not as an expression of its people in all their variety, but as a mystical unity symbolized by the ruler – an absolutist nation.

4

Peasants, merchants, and officials, 1870s to 1930s

The nation-state was new. So too were its citizens, as a result of two sweeping social changes. Beginning in the early nineteenth century, the landscape and society of the lower Chaophraya basin was transformed by a frontier movement of peasant colonization. Uniquely in Asia, new land was being opened up faster than population growth from the mid-nineteenth century right through to the 1970s. As a result of political decisions in the late nineteenth century, this frontier society was characterized not by landlords but by peasant smallholders. Until urbanization accelerated in the last quarter of the twentieth century, this smallholder peasant society represented four-fifths of the population, and the main driving force of the economy.

Much of the urban population was also new, especially in the capital city of Bangkok. Continuous immigration from southern China made Chinese a dominant element in the city's economic life. Western merchants and advisers formed a new semi-colonial segment of the elite. A fledgling commoner middle class began to form around the city's new role as capital of a nation-state.

TRANSFORMING THE RURAL LANDSCAPE AND SOCIETY

Europeans who visited Siam in the 1820s thought much of the Chaophraya delta was a 'wilderness'. Plains of scrub forest inhabited by wild elephants merged near the coasts and rivers into marshes dense with reeds and teeming with crocodiles. Settlements clung to the banks of the main rivers. Even along the Chaophraya River from its estuary past Bangkok and into the upper delta, most of these banks looked 'deserted' and densely wooded (Figure 6). In the Ayutthaya era, the only extensive tract of rice cultivation had been the narrow corridor of floodplain running south from Chainat in the centre of the delta. Here farmers grew floating rice on the annual monsoon flooding. Even after the economic expansion and exports to China in the early nineteenth century, rice cultivation was still largely confined

Figure 6: Before the rice frontier. As sketched by Henri Mouhot in 1858, the banks of the
Chaophraya River were still dense jungle.

to this tract. Around 1850, three-quarters of the delta's land area was still
unused, and the total population of the Chaophraya delta region (or 'central
plain') was probably around 500,000 people.

On average each year over the next century, another 7000 households
settled in the delta region and brought an additional 200,000 rai (32,000 ha)
of land under the plough. By 1950, the triangle from the head of the delta
to the coastal salt flats 250 kilometres to the south had become a lattice of
canals with almost every square inch of land under cultivation.

The transformation of the delta landscape began in the early nineteenth
century when immigrant Chinese brought expertise in growing vegetables,
pepper, sugar, and other crops. From the 1810s, more Thai began to slip
away from traditional controls to this agrarian frontier. At first they grew
mainly sugarcane but in the 1870s sugar exports collapsed because beet-
sugar in Europe and Dutch colonial sugarcane production in Java were
more cost-efficient. From then, rice became the major crop and major
export. The growth of cities and plantation populations in colonial Asia

created a rapidly growing demand for food. The cheaper freight costs of western steamers made it more economic to transport such bulky crops. Rice exports averaged around 100,000 tons a year in the 1860s, and five times that amount by the turn of the twentieth century.

The early expansion of frontier settlement took place along the raised areas at the eastern and western fringes of the delta, and along canals built as highways across the delta in the 1820s and 1830s. From the 1860s, the king seized on canal building as a way to create landholdings as support for the rapidly growing number of royal kin. The king cut several new canals, and parcelled out the land along the banks, mainly to royal relatives. Big noble households copied the strategy. The Bunnag built a major canal to the west, and several other big households invested in smaller projects. In the 1890s, the royal-related Sanitwong family launched the largest of these projects to drain 1.5 million rai of the Rangsit area to the northeast of the capital. The king took a share. In these canal projects, the banks were allotted in large plots of 1500 to 3000 rai apiece, often worked by the nobles' supplies of tied labour. People migrated, especially from the Khorat Plateau, to work as tenants and labourers in these new rice lands.

The government passed a land law which granted full property rights based on a cadastral survey and title deeds. Land prices in the Rangsit project jumped from 5 baht per rai in 1892 to 37.5 baht in 1904. Several royal relatives petitioned to launch yet more such canal schemes. One of Chulalongkorn's half-brothers noted that 'of all the enterprises in which Thai of good positions can at the present invest their money, it is difficult to find any as promising as trading in land, and of the various types of land none is as profitable as rentable rice land'.[1]

But this trend towards landlordism collapsed around the turn of the century. Sugarcane lent itself to large-scale plantations, but paddy was more suited to smallholder cultivation. The settlers who moved into the canal tracts were used to having occupancy rights and not used to landlordism. Many new landlords had no experience of managing land. By the 1890s in the Rangsit tract, 'there is a dispute about almost every holding'.[2] Communities organized local *nakleng* toughs to keep rent and tax collectors out of the village. In reply, landlords hired bands 'armed with guns, cutlasses and other arms' to drive settlers off the land.[3] The Rangsit project office had to be defended by gun emplacements.

The king decided to halt the development of a landed nobility. In the 1870s, as he began to attack other bases of the power of the great households, Chulalongkorn instructed officials to allot land on new canal projects to peasant families, and to reclaim land which big landlords failed to cultivate. He refused permission for new canal projects – first, those planned by other noble households, and then after 1900 those planned by royal kin as well.

Peasant colonization had already begun to expand in areas away from the canal tracts. From the 1880s, as more people escaped from labour bondage, the pace increased. No attempt was made to extend the new land property titling to these areas. Instead, officials evolved a practical system of allowing settlers to *jap jong*, stake a claim to empty land, and gain a certificate of occupancy right as long as they brought the land into cultivation.

The task of draining the swamps for cultivation was removed from private enterprise. A Dutchman, van der Heide, was hired to prepare a massive drainage and irrigation scheme covering the whole delta. His 1902 plan was shelved on grounds of cost, but the government's Irrigation Department launched smaller schemes which gradually over following decades covered the whole delta with a lattice of canals. Settlements followed the engineers, putting 10 million rai (1.6 million ha) under paddy in half a century.

The first phase of expansion was confined to the Chaophraya delta. After railways were built to Khorat in 1900, Chiang Mai in 1921, and Khon Kaen in 1933, export demand sparked colonization around these railheads, bringing an additional 180,000 rai under paddy each year. As around Bangkok, some land was acquired by landlords. In the northern valleys, the old ruling families grabbed land to compensate for their loss of control over the state revenues and forests. Some drove peasants off the land by releasing rampaging elephants or spreading rumours of witchcraft. Some built irrigation systems to bring new land into cultivation. Around the railheads in the south and northeast, old ruling families, village chiefs, and a few successful merchants and tax-farmers acquired large landholdings by similar strategies.

But most of the expansion was carried ahead by peasant settlers released from labour bondage. Above Chiang Mai, they repopulated areas abandoned in the eighteenth century. In the northeast, they spread along the Chi-Mun river system. In the south, they cleared the broad basins between the mountains and the east coast of the peninsula. By 1937, only a quarter of land in the central plain was under landlords and the remainder occupied by smallholders. In the north, the landlord proportion was a fifth, and in the northeast insignificant.

The rice frontier created a small landlord elite, but its main effect was to turn the new citizens of the Siamese nation into peasant smallholders.

SMALLHOLDER SOCIETY

The rice frontier changed not only the landscape, but also the social geography. Previously, most people lived clustered close to a *mueang* centre. Now they spread across the landscape as villages sprang up along the waterways throughout the paddy tracts. People also became more mobile. In the early years of the frontier, settlers came from all directions. One village was settled first by migrants from the hills, then by another group from upland plains, and later by people from coastal areas down the peninsula. For security, households often moved and settled in groups, generally related by kin. Many households moved several times in one generation. The practice of the monkhood changed in response to this new social geography: some monks left urban *wat* and circulated around the countryside, staying only for the annual rains retreat in a fixed place. As villages became more permanent and well-off, they built a *wat* and invited these itinerant monks to stay.

Although most villages were newly established, that did not mean they lacked a heritage or distinctive culture. Indeed, the strength of village culture arose from its ability to survive such disruptions through communal cooperation. Most villages had a tutelary spirit, usually the ancestor-founder, often represented by a post, rock, or tree at the centre of the settlement. Spirit rituals encouraged cooperation, disciplined dissidence, and promoted the unity and independence of the community. As early travellers into the rural hinterland found, the first reaction of villagers to the approach of anything that might be official was to flee into the forests to avoid being conscripted for forced labour.

Villages on the rice frontier had a degree of economic independence also. Farmers worked with simple tools fashioned themselves from wood, with a little help from a local blacksmith. Cattle bought from pedlars were the only major investment. Most farmers broadcast rather than transplanted paddy, and chose varieties which could grow quickly during the rising annual flood. Use of fertilizer was almost unknown. The yield per rai of this simple regime was very low. But, because of subtropical conditions, the natural fertility of river silt, and plentiful land, the yield *per person* in the Chaophraya delta was higher than anywhere in Asia, even intensively cultivated Japan.

The natural environment also supplied other foods (fish, vegetables, fruit), the raw materials for tools and housing, herbs for medicine, and household fuel. The seasonal rhythm of monsoon paddy cultivation co-existed easily with a regime of supplementary hunting and gathering for these items. Production was organized on a household basis, with traditions of exchanging labour, especially for harvesting and house building. These communal projects were also excuses for festivity, and occasions for courting.

Men and women shared work on the land, including ploughing (Figure 7). During the agricultural off-season, villagers took surplus and specialist products to trade with neighbouring villages and across the ecological boundaries between hills, plains, and coast. Many of these petty traders were women. So too were most of the barge-owners who transported rice along the waterways. In the nineteenth century, female slaves commanded a higher price than males because 'the woman is decidedly as a worker worth more than the man'.[4]

The production system was highly geared to self-reliance. Visiting the far northeast in 1906, Damrong exclaimed: 'Villagers around here make all their own food and scarcely have to buy a single thing . . . Nobody is slave and nobody master . . . nobody accumulates but you cannot call them poor because they feed themselves happily and contentedly'.[5] In 1930–31, a Harvard economist, Carle Zimmerman, conducted the first quantitative survey of Siam's agriculture. Everywhere, he found, farmers produced first for their own family needs and sold only what surplus that remained. According to the local saying, the household waited until it saw the yield of the current harvest before selling off the surplus of the previous one. Food security was priority. Beyond the immediate vicinity of the major towns and railheads, the agrarian economy was 'near the state of self-sufficient'.[6]

At the same time, these smallholder householders were linked to the international rice market, but rather remotely. Throughout the delta, there was no significant road. The rivers and canals were the only highways. The international rice demand was conveyed into the villages by petty traders, mostly Chinese, who paddled up the waterways to buy the surplus crop and arrange to transport it downriver by barge. Rice mills appeared on the banks of the Chaophraya around Bangkok, at the railheads, and at junctions of the waterway system.

By the early twentieth century, paddy had become the major export crop and the major source (indirectly[7]) of the government's tax revenue. The government, rice millers, and traders were interested in driving the frontier ahead, and increasing the volume of paddy extracted from it. But their efforts were limited. The government set up a new land tax in the 1900s, and for two decades land and poll taxes levied on the peasantry were a significant part of revenues. But peasants gradually learnt how to blunt the

Femmes de la race laotienne, vivant près de Petchaburi. — Dessin de E. Bocourt d'après une photographie.

Figure 7: Working women. Descendants of Lao forced migrants in Phetchaburi. Engraving based on a photograph, possibly by John Thomson who visited this area in 1865–66.

land tax demand by petitioning for remissions on grounds of poor harvest, and winning the sympathy of local officials. Siam failed to copy the colonial systems of land revenue administration which forced peasants to increase both production and revenue. In the 1929 depression, the government was flooded with petitions for remission. It cut the land tax, never fully restored it, and finally abandoned both the land and poll taxes in 1938.

Despite the rhetoric of 'progress', the government did almost nothing to promote agriculture. In the early twentieth century, some in the elite pointed out that the citizens of the Siamese nation were overwhelmingly peasants, and that hence the progress of the nation revolved around the development of agriculture. In 1907, Dilok Nabarath, a son of King Chulalongkorn, completed a doctorate in Germany about Siamese agriculture. 'It is odd', he began the work, 'that no monograph exists about agriculture in Siam, which has always been an agrarian state'. He concluded that 'until recent times the farming population has hardly enjoyed any government support', and then of very limited extent.[8] He advocated education for farmers, transport networks, rural credit institutions, and research on agricultural technology. In 1911, Phraya Suriyanuwat, a former minister of finance, wrote *Sapphasat*, the first Thai treatise on economics, which also urged: 'The progress of Siam is ever more dependent on paddy cultivation. Whether Siam will grow quickly or slowly is dependent on the benefits farmers will receive.'[9]

But, in the early twentieth century, the government gave agriculture a low priority behind railway building for defence, magnificent royal construction, and projects of nation-building. Dilok was considered 'half-witted' by his fellow princes for his enthusiasm for agricultural improvement; he committed suicide in 1913. King Vajiravudh reacted angrily against *Sapphasat*'s argument that Siam's peasantry was poor and deserved help: 'I am able to attest that no other country has fewer poor or needy people than Siam'.[10] He had both *Sapphasat* and the study of economics banned to prevent such ideas spreading.

The government also gave little help to the rice traders who had an interest in driving increased production. In his 1930–31 survey, Zimmerman was surprised to find that credit was insignificant. Farmers borrowed only for special occasions or disasters, not in the ordinary course of cultivation. Most loans came from neighbours. Only in the more commercialized areas were Chinese shopkeepers and paddy traders giving larger loans. When the depression hit, the government feared bad debts would result in foreclosure, landlessness, and social disorder. But the lack of land titling prevented this. The occupancy titles were not technically transferable. They were traded easily within the local community, but an outsider could get no legal help to enforce title in the face of local opposition. Traders might lend on mortgage, but found it difficult to foreclose for non-payment. In the 1929 depression and other downturns, peasants suffered hardship but did not lose their land. Instead, the traders and millers often went broke.

The traders had to tempt smallholder families into the market with consumer goods – salted pork, dried fish, cloth, and household wares. But the villagers' needs were limited. Until the Second World War, even in the areas most involved in the paddy export market, many households continued to weave cloth, at least for use in special occasions. Much local trade continued on a barter basis at occasional markets. Items like carts and metal tools were made in the village by part-time specialists. In local folklore, the Chinese trader and shopkeeper became a focus of resentment for profiteering. But there was equally a recognition of mutual dependence. Nowhere did this resentment become violent, even during the market strains of the depression and the Second World War.

Thus the smallholders of the paddy tracts were drawn into the commercial rice economy only slowly and imperfectly. Gradually, more places became better connected to the market by improvements in transport, and more households made a greater commitment to the market. From the 1930s, transplanting began to replace broadcast in many areas, yields-per-rai rose, and households had a larger surplus to sell. Exports peaked on the eve of the Second World War at around 1.5 million tons, triple the volume at the start of the century.

Some of the big landlords were unable to manage tenant demands and market swings, and their estates were broken up. Yet in the 1920s in the old canal tracts there were still 127 landlords owning an average of 3000 rai apiece, including the Sanitwong family, the crown, and some other noble lineages. But outside these limited landlord tracts, this was a smallholder society with families owning plots of 25–40 rai which they could operate with their own labour, growing rice for family consumption and a surplus for sale.

PORT CITY IN THE COLONIAL ERA

By the First World War, Bangkok and its hinterland of paddy tracts and teak forests were integrated into the economy of an Asia dominated by colonial powers, especially Britain. Three-quarters of Bangkok's exports consisted of rice, and three-quarters of that was carried by British or German ships to the British ports of Hong Kong and Singapore.

What had struck visitors to Bangkok in the mid-nineteenth century was how *rural* the city seemed. A 'wide expanse of paddy fields' stretched almost up to the palace walls; a 'shady wilderness' was found just behind the bustling Sampheng market; and the whole city seemed like 'a grove interspersed with houses, pagodas, palaces'.[11]

In 1856, only a few months after the signing of the Bowring treaty, the British-owned Borneo Company set up shop in Bangkok. Yet colonial trade developed slowly. Initially, Borneo did little more than export pepper from Chanthaburi. In 1858 an American firm built a steam-powered rice mill, and in 1862 a British firm built a steam-powered sugar mill. Increasing trade caused a shortage of currency, so the government legalized the use of Mexican dollars and began minting silver baht in 1860. A decade later, more firms arrived, mostly branches of companies from colonial India or Java. By 1880 there were twelve rice mills, and the number expanded to reach eighty-four by 1925. As the junks faded from the scene, British and German steamship firms dominated shipping. In the 1880s, British timber firms moved into Lanna and began to float logs down the Chaophraya river system. In 1889, the Borneo Company entered the teak business, and over the next ten years, British-owned sawmills clustered at the northern fringe of the capital.

In 1890, H. Warrington Smyth arrived in Bangkok, expecting to find the elegant city described by earlier visitors:

But where was the Bangkok I had read of – that Venice of the East delighting the soul with its gilded palaces and gorgeous temples? Before us lay but an eastern Rotterdam; mud banks, wharfs and jetties, unlovely rice mills belching smoke, houses gaunt on crooked wooden piles, dykes and ditches on either hand, steam launches by the dozen, crowded rows of native rice boats, lines of tall-masted junk-rigged lighters, and last, most imposing, towering even above the ugly chimneys of the mills, British steamers and Norwegian and Swedish barques and ships.[12]

Once the teak and rice businesses were established in the 1880s, western bankers, managing agencies, retailers, and various service industries arrived to service a growing *farang* community, and to supply a taste for western products pioneered by the court. As Smyth noted:

In the tennis, cricket, dinners, and club life which centred around it, [Bangkok] was very much like any other settlement of the kind, except for its more cosmopolitan character. At one table would be seated Danes, Germans, Italians, Dutch, Belgians, Americans, and Britishers . . .[13]

This cosmopolitanness reflected the fact that Siam was increasingly part of the colonial economy but not a colonial subject dominated by a single master. This fact circumscribed the expansion of western business. In the teak industry, the government allowed western firms to dominate, but drew a perimeter around the area of logging concessions and restricted the extent of expansion. Western tin-mining firms overflowed from Malaya into southern Siam, but the government refused to extend the new railway network across to the western coast where the best deposits were, and most colonial tin firms concentrated on Malaya. The rubber industry also extended northwards from Malaya into southern Siam, but the government was reluctant to grant the large land concessions which western planters wanted. Railway promoters besieged the Siamese government with plans to build ambitious regional networks reflecting French and British commercial and imperial dreams, but the government prevaricated and then built its own system designed for its own strategic concerns. Imperial adventurers who wanted to cut a canal across the peninsula on the model of Suez or Panama were courteously humoured.

By 1914, total western investments in Siam were estimated at US$65 million, less than half the amount in Indochina, one-third in Malaya, and one-tenth in the Netherlands Indies.

Although this colonial economy was modest, it helped to undermine the *jao sua*, the great Chinese commercial families. Their traditional sources of income disappeared in stages over the late nineteenth century. The junk trade declined steeply after 1855. Most tax-farms were replaced by bureaucratic collection. Rivalry for the remaining tax-farms on opium, liquor, and gambling increased to the point that margins were thin and disastrous losses common. In 1906, the government also started to close down these tax-farms.

The westward gaze of the court undermined the *jao sua* in other ways. The elite bought their status-defining clothes and trinkets from the western importers and emporiums, and no longer relied on the great *jao sua* to bring valuable items from China. The government hired western advisers rather than calling on Chinese with mandarin skills.

Some of the great *jao sua* households reacted by moving into the booming rice trade, timber, shipping, and other ventures. The Chotikapukkana family built a modern rice mill and exported high-quality rice to Europe. Two other great *jao sua* lineages were among the pioneers of rice milling. Others bought land, built shophouses, ran markets, and benefited from rising property values as more immigrants crowded into the areas of Chinese settlement. The Phisolyabut family won a concession to dig the Sathorn canal on the southern edge of the city and to develop plots alongside for the colonial-style mansions coming into vogue for Europeans and the local elite.

In the 1890s, some of the great old *jao sua* households jointly resolved to set up banks and shipping companies. In part, they were seeking new opportunities to replace the tax-farms. In part, they were motivated by rising Chinese nationalism and wanted to outdo the Europeans. But they lacked the expertise required for these novel ventures, and failed to provide enough capital to survive the ensuing price war with European firms. In addition, a series of poor harvests in 1904–08 meant that for several years very little rice could be exported, and rice mills were without profit. The banks which financed them went bust. The ambitious shipping venture fell into debt and was sold in China. Many great households went down, including the Phisanbut who had established the pioneer Chinese-owned rice mill, and the Phisolyabut who had had a 40 per cent share of the rice business before this crisis.

Some well-connected families appealed to the king for help. The Privy Purse Bureau had the unique advantage of accumulating its capital from tax returns. It formed the Siam Commercial Bank, which was strong enough to weather this crisis. It made loans to both aristocratic and *jao sua* entrepreneurs. Several of the *jao sua* households survived a little longer on these loans, but then lost the property accumulated over several generations – including rice mills, shophouse developments, and paddy tracts in Rangsit – under foreclosure by the Privy Purse Bureau or its Siam Commercial Bank.

Following this crisis, none of the great Bangkok *jao sua* dynasties of the nineteenth century survived as leading entrepreneurs in the twentieth. These crises rippled down through the lower levels of the commercial pyramid, as a Bangkok poet, Nai But, noted:

> In Sampheng, shops line the road so neatly.
> When profits are good, the heart blooms.
> But the bankrupt ones are closed,
> A notice of forced sale pasted on the door,
> An Indian standing guard.
> Pity the owners whose assets were seized
> Because they had no patron to fall back on.[14]

RICE TRADE AND EARLY MANUFACTURING

While the great *jao sua* households were wrecked, a new business community developed over the late nineteenth and early twentieth centuries, mainly among Chinese migrants who had arrived after 1850.

Driven by poverty and disorder in southern China, the annual immigrant flow rose steadily. By the 1880s there were regular steamship services between Bangkok and the southern Chinese ports, and a regular supply of the poor and desperate ready to make the unpleasant trip. Between 1882 and 1910, one million immigrated of whom 370,000 remained permanently. After this surge, almost half of Bangkok's population was Chinese. Around three-fifths were Teochiu, followed by Hakka and Hainanese.

Although western firms dominated the first phase of the rice trade, this domination did not last. Former junk traders and tax-farmers discovered it was not difficult to buy the machinery and hire a Scottish or German engineer to run it. After some of the *jao sua* showed the way, more recent migrants followed. One of the most successful, Akorn Teng, had arrived in 1842, worked first as a coolie, opened a shop, and then made a good marriage which enabled him to become a middle-ranking tax-farmer in the north. From the 1880s he invested the proceeds in five rice mills, a sawmill, and a dockyard. His son went on to invest in banks, shipping, and rubber in the early 1900s and was reckoned one of the leaders of the business community. By 1912, there were fifty rice mills owned by Chinese, and by 1925, only one of the eighty-four rice mills was western-owned.

Akorn Teng and others outcompeted the Europeans because they had direct links to the upcountry networks of Chinese traders who bought paddy from the farmers, because they could better manage the labour force of Chinese coolies, and because they developed trading networks in the markets around the region. Indeed, for some, like the successful Wanglee family, Bangkok was simply one part of a regional network. By 1870, this Teochiu family had developed a coastal trading network based in Canton and connecting Hong Kong, Singapore, Bangkok, and Saigon. A son of the family, Tan Chi Huang, settled in Bangkok in 1871, married into one of the old *jao sua* households (Posyanon), established a rice mill with modern machinery, and exported rice to the family's network around the region. Over the following years, the business expanded to four rice mills, cloth import, insurance, shipping, and property development.

Several new entrepreneurs prospered quickly on the expanding rice trade, but also collapsed precipitously on the fluctuations in demand and exchange rates during a highly unstable period in the international economy. Akorn Teng's family, which had joined in the doomed banking and shipping ventures of the *jao sua*, was crippled by the 1904–08 crisis, survived in a reduced state, and finally collapsed in a similar crisis on the price swings after the First World War.

But those who did survive these swings emerged stronger. Some survived because they were part of strong regional networks. Others emerged from the lower ranks of rice traders as the *jao sua* firms disintegrated, and responded successfully to the volatility of the international market by building integrated businesses, and networks of mutual cooperation.

The Wanglee family, with its extensive regional network, was the most successful. From the First World War onwards, it dealt with the fluctuations in the international market by forming its own bank to handle exchange and remittance, and its own insurance agency. A new wave of rice millers followed the same pattern. Ma Tong Jeng had arrived as a coolie in the late nineteenth century. He worked as assistant to a German engineer building and maintaining rice-mill machinery, and accumulated the skills and capital to open one of the largest rice mills in 1917. His son, Ma Bulakun, added another large mill in the 1920s, a bank, an insurance company, a shipping business, and a network of companies in Hong Kong and Singapore. The Lamsam family shifted from timber into the rice trade on the same integrated pattern in the 1920s. After the depression, a 'Big Five' of families (Wanglee, Lamsam, Bulakun, Bulasuk, Iamsuri) controlled over half the rice trade. These families tightened links by exchanging marriage partners, crossing the usual boundaries of dialect groups. They also established a rice-millers' association to control prices.

By the 1920s, both western and Chinese firms had decided that Bangkok was now large enough to support local manufacture of matches, nails, soap, fireworks, patent medicines, tobacco, oil, textiles, paper, bricks, fireworks, shoes, furniture, and services such as power, water, and transport. A few of the successful early entrepreneurs were among the descendants of the old *jao sua* families who had gained access to education, and who had a first-hand view of the consumption patterns of the new bureaucratic elite. Nai Boonrawd squeezed into one of the first palace schools, then worked for Akorn Teng's rice-mill business and a colonial timber firm before starting his own timber trading business. After a trip to Europe, he tried importing cars, running river ferries, and founding an air service before hitting on the idea of a brewery, finally opened in 1933. One of Boonrawd's distant cousins, Nai Lert, began as a clerk in a western firm, and then imported sewing machines and cars. From there he started a bus service, and put the profits into land development. Other new entrepreneurs came from the same milieu of recent immigrants as the big rice merchants. Mangkorn Samsen had been a rice miller before moving into the manufacture of coconut oil and sugar. Koson Huntrakun had been a market owner before establishing one of the first ice factories.

To man the port, rice mills, factories, and new public utilities, Bangkok acquired a large working population. By the 1910s, the rice mills alone employed 10,000–20,000, and altogether the 'coolie' workforce approached 100,000, around a quarter of the city's population. The vast majority was still Chinese, though more Thai were recruited after the decline of labour bondage and the appearance of government enterprises like the railways. Working and living conditions were poor. Many took refuge in opium, though they had never taken the drug before coming to Siam. Occasionally, workers protested against their conditions. In 1888 dock workers paralysed the port. Rice-mill workers struck in 1889 and 1892. The government sent troops to disperse the strikers with gunfire, and deported the leaders. In 1897, it passed a law to register the *angyi* secret societies believed to be involved in labour organization, and in 1905 formed a special police unit which gained a reputation for heavy-handed policing of Chinese working-class districts. In 1910, the city's Chinese workers went on a mass strike, partly in protest at the rise in taxation after the Chinese were assimilated into the poll tax system.

With the accumulated immigration over the previous half-century, Bangkok's Chinese community in the inter-war period was large and complex. Over time, some chose to merge into Thai society. Earlier, Chinese were legally differentiated: they were excused corvée, paid a triennial tax, and were expected to wear a pigtail. But corvée ended in 1905 and the triennial tax was abolished in 1909. After the 1911 revolution in China, the pigtail became a symbol of backwardness, and most Chinese cut them off. Western-style clothing provided an ethnically neutral alternative to Thai or Chinese traditional styles. The poet Nai But observed Sampheng in the early twentieth century:

> The small road is crowded with *Jek*[15] and Thai
> Walking so mixed together they cannot avoid colliding.
> *Jek* mixed up with Thai beyond recognition,
> Who is who, it's confused and uncertain.
> In modern times the place is messed up.
> Chinese cut off their pigtails and become Thai, beyond detection
> Resulting in the abnormality
> That people can chop and change *chat*. Amazing.[16]

But others valued their Chinese identity. With more women joining the migration stream (one-fifth by the 1920s), more married within the Chinese community. Many business families sent their sons back to China for education, partly to imbue them with the culture, but mostly to equip them with Chinese literacy. In Siam and around the region, Chinese was the language of business, especially for documents. When after 1913 they had to adopt a Thai surname, several took a form which deliberately preserved their Chinese clan (*sae*) name.[17]

From the early years of the twentieth century, the merchant community began to build an infrastructure of institutions to support urban life and business. The Cantonese formed a speech-group association in 1877, and were followed by the other dialect groups in the early 1900s. In 1908 a Chinese Chamber of Commerce was formed which soon became the official mouthpiece of Chinese business. The first Chinese school was founded in the early years of the century, and the number had expanded to 271 by 1933. The first Chinese newspaper was published in 1905. Hospitals, funerary associations, and other self-help societies appeared from the 1910s. The leading entrepreneurs were the main sponsors and office-holders.

The court's increasing infatuation with the west on the one hand, and the growing wealth, independence, and organization among the Bangkok Chinese on the other, changed old relations of patronage. A member of the ruling elite commented on these changes in 1916:

In the old days, the Chinese . . . always visited princes and nobles, or high officials, and were very close to the Thais . . . Now they are different . . . they see no need to visit or please anyone. They come in to pursue large businesses, investing in rice mills and trading firms with thousands or millions of baht, without having to have connections with anyone.[18]

THE SOCIETY OF A NATIONAL CAPITAL

From the start of the twentieth century, the city and its society were reshaped by its new role as capital of a nation-state. Under the new centralized structure, revenues flowed into the ministries located in the capital, and power flowed outwards. The number of salaried officials grew from 12,000 in 1890 to 80,000 in 1919. In 1916 the Civil Service School was combined with other institutions into Chulalongkorn University, which became the main avenue into the senior bureaucracy. New government offices were built around the fringes of the old city centre. Units of the new standing army were stationed farther out. Areas close to these offices and camps developed into new residential colonies for middle-ranked officials, and for a large ancillary trading and service community.

The senior bureaucracy was the elite of this new government city. At its core were members of the royal and noble families who were cajoled by Chulalongkorn into adopting official careers. In effect, official salaries became the solution to the problem of supporting the rapidly spreading pyramid of the royal clan. In this era, senior official salaries were enough to support a whole household, while old habits of living off the profits of office also lingered. Provincial rulers and great families were also urged to send their sons to the new schools and colleges, as part of cementing their loyalty to the new nation-state.

Several of the great *jao sua* households escaped decline by clambering onto this new ladder of success. Some sent their sons to English-language schools in British Singapore or Penang. Some entered new mission schools. Others used cash and connections to gain their sons' places in the schools established to educate the high-born. A descendant of the Luang Aphai-wanit family became the only commoner at one of the palace schools and then studied with American missionaries. His English skill gained him a job at the Borneo Company and then an interpreter's post in the new Police Department. He rose to head the department, and his descendants in the Chatikavanich family followed illustrious careers in the modern bureaucracy and professions.

Recruitment and promotion within the traditional bureaucracy had depended on personal patronage. This pattern remained in the reformed structure. Junior officials attached themselves to great figures in the ministries, and ascended by a mixture of talent, personal services, and politicking. Titles and ranks continued to define and publicize hierarchy. Members of the royal family prefixed their names with distinctive titles showing their distance from the throne. All officials above clerical level received an official title and rank (Chaophraya, Phraya, and so on) modelled on Ayutthayan practice. An Act in 1913 ordered everyone to have a surname. Members of the royal family were reserved names with the suffix na Krungthep (later changed to na Ayutthaya), which resembled Lord Such *of Somewhere* in European noble titles. Provincial ruling families petitioned for a similar form identifying their place of origin (na Ranong, na Songkhla, na Chiangmai). Other great families, including ennobled Chinese tax-farmers, converted the traditional title of the current or former household head into their surname. King Vajiravudh delighted in inventing elegant Sanskritic surnames for other petitioners from the great households. These titles and special surnames publicized the hierarchical structure of the new bureaucracy as effectively as the royal-bestowed betel boxes which nobles had carried as marks of their rank in the past.

Beyond these great lineages, the city began to develop an embryo middle class of lesser bureaucrats, teachers, lawyers, managers, and other functionaries of the nation-state and commercial economy. Very few were able to rise upwards from the peasantry. Mostly this new commoner middle class developed from the minor officialdom and market society of the provincial centres.

A few succeeded as compradores, agents who liaised between a European firm and its local customers or partners. The first compradores came from the colonial ports where they had already equipped themselves with the English language. Later, members of Bangkok-settled families got the needed education. Saeng Vejjajiva came from a family operating junks along the eastern gulf. When steamers put the junks out of business, the family placed Saeng in a missionary school, from where he was employed by the leading European firm, East Asiatic.

Others found an upward route through companies formed by the royal family in association with westerners. Thian Hee Sarasin was the son of a traditional Chinese doctor and pharmacist who immigrated early in the nineteenth century. His talent gained him patronage of a leading aristocrat and American missionaries who sent him to study medicine in New York. On return, he was employed to introduce hygiene and medical care to the army. He rose to a high official rank, and also served as a director of several royal-invested companies. His sons were distributed among commercial and bureaucratic careers.

Others found a place in the expanding bureaucracy. Three men who later rose to political prominence illustrate the pattern. Pridi Banomyong came from a mixed Thai-Chinese family in Ayutthaya. The family was well connected in the local nobility, but Pridi's particular branch were market traders, and his father had (rather unsuccessfully) ventured into the rice economy by taking up land on the northern edge of the Rangsit project. Pridi went to *wat* schools in Ayutthaya and Bangkok, and then, through the influence of an uncle, progressed to the prestigious Suan Kulap School and the Justice Ministry's Law School. He was a brilliant student, won a ministry scholarship to study in France, and returned with a doctorate to teach in the Law School and work in the law drafting department. Wichit Wathakan's early career was similar. He was born in Uthai Thani to a family of petty traders who were Chinese by origin but now Thai by practice. He studied at local *wat* schools and then, through the help of a distant relative in the monkhood, at Wat Mahathat school in Bangkok, where his talent gained him an appointment as a teacher. He taught himself English and French, gained a menial clerk's post in the Foreign Ministry, then performed well in the foreign service exams and was appointed to the legation in Paris. Army recruits came from similar origins. Plaek Phibunsongkhram's family had an orchard to the north of Bangkok. He went to *wat* schools, and found a family connection to gain admission to the infantry cadet school. From there he progressed to the Military Staff College where he graduated top and won a scholarship to the French Military Academy.

Others stepped onto the same education ladder, but then diverged to other new careers. Kulap Saipradit was the son of a railway clerk. He studied in the *wat* and at the army cadet school, before gaining admission to the prestigious Thepsirin School. He entered the bureaucracy, but found it difficult to rise without the right family connections. He turned to English teaching and translation before making his name as a journalist and creative writer.

These new men came from a mix of backgrounds – urban and rural, Chinese and Thai, mercantile and official. They rose on new educational opportunities provided by the foreigners and the government. They tended to identify themselves as a part of a new society, defined by their talent and education, rather than by reference to their origins. In their passage through the elite schools, and their work in government offices, they rubbed shoulders with the privileged nobility and were sometimes acutely aware of the role of hierarchy. They were few in number, yet a powerful new element in urban society.

BANGKOK IN THE EARLY TWENTIETH CENTURY

As the capital of the new centralized government and as the funnel for rice and teak exports, Bangkok totally dominated the nation's urban population. Bangkok grew from maybe 100,000 people in 1850 to around 360,000 in the 1910s, twelve times the size of the next largest city.[19] The city also moved from water to land. In the 1850s, most people still lived on or over the water, and almost all traffic was water-borne as the land routes were generally too muddy to be passable. The first road was built in 1857, but in 1890 there was still only nine miles. By 1900, however, a rapidly expanding road network was lined by the palaces and mansions of the bureaucracy, and the shophouses of the mercantile Chinese.

Over the same period, urban dress also changed. In the early nineteenth century, the Chinese usually wore loose-fitting pyjamas, but most Thai and others wore only a wrap-around lower cloth, with some women adding a second cloth loosely draped over their upper body. Early European envoys were shocked to meet even royalty attired thus, and confessed their frank surprise to find that people attired in such a 'semi-barbarous' fashion were intelligent. The elite responded to the link between clothing and civilization implied in such *farang* attitudes. Mongkut ordered people attending court

Figure 8: Late nineteenth-century photo of streetside gambling. Girls still keep their hair short. Clothing is still loose wraps, not tailoring.

to wear an upper cloth in order to be more *siwilai*. By the Fifth Reign, both men and women in the court clothed their full body with mainly tailored garments. The new bureaucrats, often working with European advisers, affected a colonial style of cotton shirt and trousers. So did employees of *farang* companies. These elite styles were quickly adapted by other levels of urban society. Male labourers remained bare-chested, but others wore a tied upper cloth, tailored shirt, or jacket in public (Figure 8). By the early twentieth century, urban Siam was fully clothed.

The city had changed from a rather traditional 'fort and port' into the capital of a new nation-state, and the centre of a booming rice and teak export trade. The landscape of the city reflected these two sides of its divided character.

The areas to the north and west were the headquarters of the royal-focused nation-state. As the central state's revenues increased from the 1880s, new roads were cut leading north and west from the traditional royal centre on Rattanakosin Island. These roads were lined with the palaces of the expanding royal clan, and the mansions of other great households which dominated the new bureaucracy. At Dusit on the outer rim of this northeastern corner of the city, the royal family developed a modern palace complex, including both traditional teak buildings and European suburban villas. Around this complex spread the offices housing the expanding bureaucracy, camps for the garrisons of the standing army, *wat*, and schools.

The mercantile part of the city clustered on the river to the south. The river frontage itself was lined with monuments to colonial commerce – western embassies, the Oriental Hotel, and the mills, godowns, and offices of western firms like East Asiatic, Louis Leonowens, and the Borneo Company. Behind this river front to the east was Bangrak, the main European quarter, centred on New Road, built in the 1860s for westerners to reside, stroll, and drive their carriages. Here were the 'foreign legations and the majority of the banks and offices of the Western business people'.[20] Here too were emporiums, dispensaries, the racecourse, Bangrak market which sold beef, lamb, and European vegetables, and Bangkok United Club, 'the hub around which social foreign Bangkok gyrates'.[21]

Equally prominent along the waterfront were the distinctive mansions of the Chinese merchant princes, often built in a large compound to house different branches of the joint family, and often with a mill or warehouse on one side, and a Chinese shrine on the other. Even more prominent were the rice mills, with their distinctive large warehouses and tall chimneys belching black smoke from burning rice husk. The early mills were situated on the city outskirts. But, by the First World War, they had spread through the centre of the city on the western bank, and their chimneys vied with *wat* towers and palace spires in dominating the central city's skyline.

Back from the river on both sides stretched the settlements of the expanding Chinese community, with Hokkien favouring the western Thonburi side, and Teochiu more on the east. The early market area of Sampheng had sprawled south and east in a cluster of streets and markets with different specializations, all marked by the characteristic two-storey shophouse in which the family lived above and worked below. These areas were littered not only with Chinese shrines but also with Buddhist *wat* as these communities honoured the traditions of their places both of origin and adoption.

Visitors to Bangkok celebrated its cosmopolitan population: 'The crowds which throng the streets are composed of Siamese, Chinese, Malays, Tamils, Bengalis, Madrassis, Pathans . . . Burmese, Ceylonese, Javanese,

Cambodians, Annamites, Laos, Shans, and Mohns'.[22] But the first city census of any detail and reliability in 1883 showed that Siamese and Chinese together contributed 97 per cent of the total, and other populations were tiny. This census counted Chinese as a quarter of the population, rather less than the half that many visitors estimated. Partly this was because the census incorporated the still agricultural outskirts, but partly because many *lukjin* – and many descendants of Malay, Lao, and Khmer war-prisoners – by now considered themselves 'Thai'. Occupations were clearly divided. The Chinese dominated commerce (three-fifths of all in this occupation), and commerce dominated the Chinese (three-fifths of all Chinese households). Most of the city population of Siamese was engaged in agriculture, general labour, or earmarked as on corvée duty. The Siamese absolutely dominated official posts, but again this was an ethnic simplification induced by the new idea of nationality; the middle and lower officials of the tax department in the 1900s in fact included 'people of many races and tongues. There were Thais, Chinese, Japanese, Europeans, Indians, Sinhalese, Malays, Malay-Chinese and half castes.'[23]

Gender roles differed sharply by social status. Within all the elite cultures of the city, males were dominant. The traditional bureaucracy, shaped by its warrior role, had been exclusively male, and this principle was carried over into its modern reincarnation. Chinese migration into Siam was almost exclusively male until the 1910s, and the typical entrepreneurial family was a pure patriarchy. Equally, there was not a single woman among the western business leaders photographed for the early commercial gazetteers.

For both the bureaucrat and Chinese commercial families, women were an instrument of dynasty building and diplomacy. They produced the sons needed to sustain the family's next generation, and they bridged connections to patrons and partners. Chinese patriarchs often had several wives – in Siam, in their Chinese place of origin, and perhaps also in other regional ports where they traded.

Within these patriarchal structures, women were far from powerless. Inside the palace, some women had substantive roles, including looking after treasuries. Chulalongkorn's correspondence shows how much he valued the opinions of his favourite queen, Saowapha, whom he designated as regent on his second departure for Europe. The most famous fictional account of an aristocratic dynasty, Kukrit Pramoj's *Si phaendin* (Four reigns, 1950), makes a woman the axis around which the household and the plot revolve. Under law, money and property gifted to a bride at marriage remained hers alone, and some wives used this capital for their own business. Among the

Chinese, female poker and mahjong circles often brokered the marriage alliances which cemented commercial ties. Moreover, despite polygamy, families sometimes failed to maintain a continuous male line. Cholera took its toll – the hot months were known as the 'cholera season' – and recently arrived Chinese who had perhaps not developed any resistance seemed especially vulnerable. Some Chinese patriarchs *chose* to will at least some property to daughters, partly in honour of local Thai custom, partly because the sons might move elsewhere within the family's regional network, while daughters were likely to stay put. In one of the greatest *jao sua* households of the nineteenth century, the family property passed down the female line. Several Chinese matriarchs became property developers and owners of pawnshops.

But among the working population, the female role was much different. They worked. They dominated the street and canal markets to the extent that the government appointed women as market overseers. They planted rice and vegetables on the city outskirts. They laboured in the factories and public utilities. As Smyth noted, 'the energy and capacity so conspicuous in the women of Siam . . . makes them the workers and the business people of the country'.[24]

This combination of elite male dominance and a culture of female labour was the setting for a thriving sex industry. The port and the Sampheng market area, home to many single immigrant males, housed many tea houses and brothels. The government included them among the services subject to tax-farms. In the late nineteenth century, women were imported from Japan to supplement the local supply. Aristocratic men, who once acquired women through the system of personal slavery, turned to commercial sources. The expansion in higher education, bureaucracy, and professions in Bangkok created another concentration of males and new techniques of trading sex. In the early twentieth century, street prostitution flourished. 'No matter where you go in Bangkok', wrote a newspaper correspondent, 'you cannot avoid coming across these women'.[25] In 1908, the government passed an Act to regulate brothels as part of its growing interest in public health, but the illegal trade far outweighed the regulated segment. The new cinemas served a secondary function as pick-up sites. By the 1920s Bangkok had both exclusive clubs and street shows with erotic entertainment. In the early Thai talkie film, *Long thang* (Gone astray, 1932), a man abandons his wife and wallows in the city's demi-monde until penury forces him back to home and morality. An observer warned that 'Bangkok will become like Paris'.[26]

CONCLUSION

The release of forced labour and the integration of the economy with colonial enterprise accelerated changes in the economy, society, and landscape.

Between the mid-nineteenth century and the early twentieth, Siam became a nation of smallholder peasants. The Chaophraya delta was converted
from 'wilderness' into a patchwork of paddyfields. Unfree labour became
frontier smallholders. But while the rice frontier supported the majority of
the population and drove the national economy, it also drew the peasantry
away into the villages, remote from the political life of the nation.

Over the second half of the nineteenth century, the conversion of the
traditional 'fort and port' city into a colonial port and national capital
brought into being new social forces. The great families of the service
bureaucracy, and the great families of the junk-trading and tax-farming *jao
sua*, were converted into the new bureaucratic elite of the royalist nation-
state. A new entrepreneurial elite of Chinese origins emerged in the late
nineteenth century, and consolidated in the early twentieth. Often the
families were part of regional networks. They retained links back to their
birthplace, especially for education. They increasingly brought their wives
from China. Their businesses were not dependent on royal favour, and they
were not tied by titles and patronage to the court and Siamese elite. With
growing wealth and numbers, they built a new community infrastructure
of associations, schools, and welfare groups.

The freeing of labour and the economic transformation of the city created a new working class. As education, bureaucracy, and modern business
expanded, a small but important commoner middle class began to form.
Its members were often drawn from the mixed Thai-Chinese society of the
provincial towns. They were remote from the traditions of the old court,
and were self-consciously pioneers of a new urban life and culture.

In the early decades of the twentieth century, these new urban social
forces challenged the absolutist conceptions of the nation and nation-state.

5

Nationalisms, 1910s to 1940s

In the latter part of his reign, Chulalongkorn and his supporters repeatedly justified the creation of a strong state and its absolutist management on grounds of the need for Siam to progress and be a significant country in the world. This formulation marks the start of one of the two recurring visions in modern Thai politics. The same idea, adapted to changing international and local contexts, would reappear over decades to come. The Chulalongkorn era had also created the key vocabulary of this theme, particularly the notion of *samakkhi*, unity, and its highly masculine and militaristic imagery exemplified by Chulalongkorn's equestrian statue, and Damrong's account of Thai history as a series of wars.

An opposing vision took shape in the early twentieth century, in the new urban society created by colonial commerce and by the nation-state itself. Old relationships of patronage were replaced by contracts in the marketplace. People evolved new ideas on man and society by reflecting on their own status as independent merchants and professionals, and by grabbing the increasing opportunities to compare Siam to an outside world undergoing tumultuous change. The new men and women of early twentieth-century Siam took up the ideas of nation, state, and progress, and recast them. They challenged the definition of the nation as those loyal to the king. They demanded that 'progress' be more widely shared. They redefined the purpose of the nation-state as the well-being of the nation's members.

In 1932, absolute monarchy was overthrown in a revolution whose inspiration came from these ideas and whose force came from the standing army created in Chulalongkorn's reforms. But attempts to redefine the nation were complicated by the status of Siam's large Chinese population, and attempts to reorient the state were complicated by Siam's gradual absorption into a clash of nationalisms on a world scale.

ABSOLUTISM DEFIANT

Despite his own opposition to any qualification of royal power, Chulalongkorn told ministers shortly before his death in 1910, 'I entrust onto my son Vajiravudh . . . that upon his accession to the throne he will give to them a parliament and constitution'.[1]

From age 12 to 22, Vajiravudh had been educated in England. He was an aesthete with interests in literature, history, and especially drama. He translated Shakespeare and Gilbert and Sullivan, built a playhouse, and wrote 180 plays and countless essays. He was homosexual and brought favourites first into the palace entourage and later into official positions. He continued Chulalongkorn's enthusiasm for royal display by holding a glorious coronation, and building three pleasure palaces on the seashore. He also continued the enthusiasm for military pursuits by forming the *Sua pa* (Wild Tiger) Corps as a royal guard and as a vehicle to display loyalty to the throne. He fell deeply into debt, forcing the ministers reluctantly to allow him to raise a foreign loan to prevent bankruptcy proceedings. His actions deeply upset many conservative courtiers. His reign saw at least two attempts at a military coup, and possibly one projected palace revolution.

Vajiravudh rejected his father's suggestion about parliament and constitution. On accession he noted that 'things of benefit to Europeans might be evil to us'.[2] His first list of ministers included ten royal relatives and only one other. But several were later replaced by noble and commoner favourites, angering the court conservatives.

Vajiravudh was aware that some nobles wanted to reverse the extreme royal centralization of the previous reign. He was also aware that others beyond these privileged circles were critical of absolutism (see below). He gave lectures to bureaucrats, and contributed articles to the press, presenting his view of the nation and nationalism. He theorized that humans who came together in society chose a king to overcome their mutual disagreements. From that point forward, the power of the king was absolute and unchallengeable. Succession continued in one lineage for stability. A state was like a body in which all the parts had a certain role. The king was the brain. The other parts should not question the orders of the brain, but obey them:

We are all in one boat. The duty of all is to help paddle. If we don't paddle and only sit back all the time, the dead weight in the boat will slow us down. Each person must decide whether to paddle and not argue with the helmsman.[3]

Nationalism and royalism were identical: 'loyalty to the king is identical with loving the nation because the king is the representative of the nation'. The duty of the ordinary people was only to be unified, obedient, and grateful, to the point of self-sacrifice: 'When our country faces danger, anyone not prepared to sacrifice his life for the country should cease to be a Thai'.[4] He urged the Siamese to unite in the defence of 'Nation, Religion and King'. The phrase was adapted from 'God, King, and Country', with the difference that the three parts were the same rather than different. The king was the political embodiment of a nation of Buddhists, and the protector of both nation and religion. The phrase wrapped a very traditional concept of royal power in the modern language of the nation. In 1917, a new tricolour national flag was designed for a Thai contingent sent to fight on the Allied side in Europe. Vajiravudh noted that the blue, white, and red not only matched the colours used in flags of the other allies, but also represented the elements of his nationalist trinity: white for Buddhism, blue for the monarch, and red for the blood Thai people should be prepared to sacrifice in defence of the nation.

CREATING A PUBLIC SPHERE

This duty of passive acceptance held scant appeal for men and women making new lives by personal achievement. The world outside Siam was changing rapidly. Many of the dynasties with whom the Chakri hobnobbed during the *fin de siècle* went into oblivion or retreat after the First World War. More Thai had a chance to view other societies and compare them to Siam. Small but growing numbers travelled abroad. Others could observe Bangkok's foreign enclave. Rather more became literate and created a growing readership for books and journals. Newspapers were brought from Singapore and Penang. Translations of western novels and romances became popular from the 1880s onwards. Cinema extended this opportunity to eavesdrop on other cultures and ways of life beyond the literate. The first commercial film was screened in 1897, and screenings became regular and popular by 1910.

Local production of newspapers and magazines proliferated from the 1890s. The first journals circulated only a few hundred copies. By 1901–06 Thianwan's journal had a print-run of a thousand. In the mid-1920s popular journals had a circulation of 5000. By 1927 there were 127 printing presses and fourteen publishers. Bookshops were 'filled with so many strange new publications'.[5] Original Thai short stories appeared in the early 1920s and then a flood of pioneer novels at the end of the decade. The first full-length commercial Thai silent film was produced in 1927 and commanded an audience of 12,000 in its first four days.

The recurrent themes which attracted both authors and audiences were about the ability of people to make their own lives, and about the corruption and unfairness of absolutist society.

Several writers took up the new enthusiasm for history but challenged the royalist claim that kings alone were the prime movers of history. Some great families compiled their own histories. K. S. R. Kulap made a living for a time as a jobbing genealogist. Monks wrote spiritual autobiographies. Some of the new entrepreneurs wrote accounts of their commercial success (Nai Boonrawd and Koson Huntrakun). Sometimes these works explicitly challenged the royal monopoly on making history. The author of a military history pointed out that kings had been able to defend the country in the past only 'because of the ordinary people who belonged to the same nation as the king and were patriotic'. One author compiled histories of all the ministers of the Bangkok period to show that 'the kings could not have delivered protection and progress without ministers' help'.[6] All these works showed how their subjects contributed to national 'progress'.

Many stories vaunted talent over birth. One of the first full-length novels, Kulap Saipradit's *Luk phu chai* (A real man, 1928), told the story of a carpenter's son who rose through his own talent to become a leading judge. Kulap's subsequent novel, *Songkhram chiwit* (The war of life, 1932), contained a tirade against inequalities of wealth and privilege: 'Siam doesn't encourage people to have faith in opportunity. Siam only curses people who do wrong.'[7] The first hit novel, Akat Damkoeng's *Lakhon haeng chiwit* (Circus of life, 1929), introduced a theme, later repeated many times, of a new man venturing overseas and thus gaining the perspective to criticize Siam and become committed to social change.

Both male and female authors focused on the practice of polygamy as something unfair to women, symbolic of Siam's backwardness in international perspective, and contributory to the culture of prostitution. Essayists and writers idealized a society in which talent was rewarded, and gender relations were made more equal through female education, monogamy, romantic love, and sexual reciprocity. Elite women rebelled against and campaigned against Mongkut's law under which families of high sakdina could legally dictate their daughters' marriage partner. The pioneer silent film *Nangsao suwan* (Miss Golden) in 1923 dealt with the issue of marriage across class barriers. In *Romaen son rueang jing* (Romance concealed in a true story), Dokmaisot, a leading female story writer, showed women how they could turn an indulgent, old-style man into both a good husband and ideal citizen by abandoning the traditionally passive feminine role.

Kulap Saipradit popularized a term, *manutsayatham*, humanitarianism or a belief in people, which summed up the sentiments of the new commoner writers and readers.

Journalism developed in this same milieu. From the 1890s onwards, a new press carried a discourse in opposition to the royal view of the nation and nationalism. In 1917, one publication described itself for the first time as a 'political newspaper'. The first political daily appeared in 1922.

Some of these papers criticized Vajiravudh's profligacy and idiosyncrasies. Vajiravudh engaged them in literary debate, and in 1912 purchased one of the papers (*Phim thai*) as a mouthpiece. He argued that *khon samai mai* (modern people) or *khon sot* (shortened from 'sophisticated') with their overseas education had become 'half-Thai' and 'clap traps', and that the import of western ideas (especially democracy) would not work. In 1916, the king withdrew from the public debate and chose repression. He had a tough press law drafted in 1917, but hesitated for fear of foreign reactions and instead used security laws to close several papers. In 1923 he finally passed a stringent press law and prosecuted scores of Bangkok publishers for libel, sedition, and lese-majesty. Eight printing presses were seized and seventeen papers closed. But by this time a public sphere was well established.

REJECTING ABSOLUTISM

Through the 1920s, journalists moved beyond personal criticism to a broader rejection of absolutism and the royal interpretation of nationalism, on various grounds.

First, they captured the discourse of progress and *siwilai*. They redefined progress as a situation in which 'human beings have a better and happier life . . . as a result of their own efforts'. They redefined *siwilai* as people 'who behave nobly . . . and contribute to the country's progress'.[8]

If such national progress was the goal of the nation-state, asked the new political journalists, why then was Siam so poor in comparison not only to Europe but also to an Asian country, Japan. Some attributed this to the strict division into rulers and ruled, which allowed a privileged minority to 'farm on the backs of the people' (Figure 9). The elite was reluctant to develop education, particularly for women or the poor, because it believed 'education creates unrest' and wanted to protect the economic advantages of 'less than half a percent of the population'.[9] An open society profited from the talents of all its members, but absolutism condemned Siam to rule by a few, selected by birth rather than talent: 'There are both clever men and stupid men among the royalty . . . People have become more conscious that birth does not indicate human goodness'.[10] According to Kulap Saipradit:

If we leave things like this, these big people (*phu yai*) will always make blunders, and little people (*phu noi*) who have the right wisdom and capability will not have a say. In the end this may lead the country to ruin. Or at the very least, we will not progress in line with neighbouring countries.[11]

Second, absolutism fostered corruption and inefficiency. The cartoons that became a prominent feature of this journalism featured nobles and bureaucrats stuffing their pockets with money or running off with bags of loot. The court was 'a giant leech, draining blood from the provinces, leaving the principal producers of the nation's wealth to live in the forests'.[12] A middle-ranking military official argued: 'The national income was used to feed many people who actually did not work. In addition, the national decay and the inefficiency in the administration was due to the fact that there were many incompetent men in high positions.'[13]

Third, absolutism promoted foreign interests above national interests. The royal elite had become fascinated with things *farang*. It fostered profligate consumption of foreign goods to the detriment of the economy. The absolutist government had accepted unequal treaties which allowed foreigners to dominate the economy.

Royal nationalism contended that the king alone could lead the nation to progress. The new men turned this argument on its head. One summed up: 'the absolute monarchy was the cause of this injustice. Nothing could be done to solve these problems, so long as the king had absolute power.'[14]

Within this general framework, specific groups within the new urban society had a specific agenda. Businessmen wanted to use the nation-state to promote the growth of domestic capitalism. They blamed the absolutist regime for concluding the unequal treaties and popularizing foreign products, with the result that Thai were 'becoming the slaves of foreigners in their own home'.[15] They wanted the government to erect tariffs and provide cheap capital so that 'Siam would have more established industries, Thai and Chinese labourers would have employment, and Siam could produce for self consumption without having to rely on imports'.[16]

Commoner bureaucrats wanted advancement based on merit. They found that appointments, promotions, and salaries depended on birth, on connections, and on loyalty to the throne. They pressed for competitive examinations, standardized salaries, and promotion by seniority and

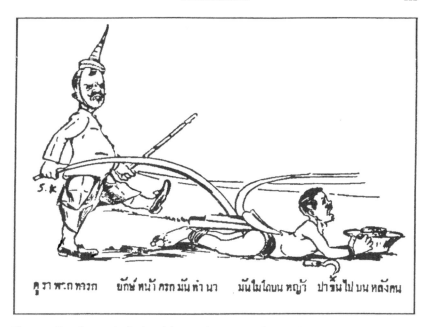

Figure 9: Farming on the backs of the people. Cartoon from *Si krung* newspaper, 4 August 1931. The caption translates as: 'Cruel-faced giants don't plough the fields but on the backs of the people'.

merit – summarized as *lak wicha*, the principle of law and rationality. Vajiravudh replied that Siam's bureaucracy was based on *lak ratchakan*, the principle of service to the king. Not until 1928 were the rules and practices of the bureaucracy formalized by legislation.

Urban labour also expressed its demands in the language of nationalism. In 1922–23, tramway workers went on strike for better wages. Labour leaders portrayed the strike as a blow against the tramway company's foreign owners and noble shareholders 'by labourers who are attempting to make a cruel employer realize that the Thai are not slaves and that the Thai nation must be free'.[17]

Perhaps the most significant centre of dissent was among the new men in the recently created standing army. In 1912, the government uncovered a plot among junior army officers to overthrow the absolute monarchy. Three thousand were possibly involved. Leaders had been recruiting support by highlighting the abuses of absolutist power, such as sycophancy, luxurious personal spending, and arbitrary seizures of land. They disliked Vajiravudh's *Sua pa* corps and had been provoked by public flogging of military officers at royal command. They complained that 'individuals who are determined to work hard tend to have no chance to show their capability, because *phu yai* do not support them'. They believed Siam's progress required a change of government, comparable to the Meiji period in Japan. Their programme included a constitution, but was otherwise vague. They had no leaning to representative government, believing 'the people in our country Siam still know very little about civilization and are very ignorant'. They proposed to change the formula of 'nation, religion, and king' into 'nation, religion, and people'. Twenty-three were jailed for twenty years. All but two were from commoner backgrounds, and the two most senior were medically trained.[18]

Vajiravudh died in 1925. His successor, Prajadhipok (Rama VII), removed Vajiravudh's favourites from office and announced his government was contemplating reforms in taxation, economic policy, the bureaucracy, and the structure of government in order 'to do something at once to gain the confidence of the people'.[19] The press became optimistic. But, in practice, Prajadhipok focused on soothing the divisions inside the court, and finding 'some sort of guarantee . . . against an unwise king'.[20] He instituted a Supreme Council of State and filled it with five of the most senior members of the royal family. He set up a Privy Council and appointed forty members of the royal family or the official nobility. A Bangkok journalist responded: 'I think these people will draft laws to benefit the upper classes because all the members of the Council come from the upper classes'.[21]

Prajadhipok then considered the possibility of a constitution and a prime minister. Even though the sketched constitution unconditionally enshrined royal power, the proposal met opposition both from members of the court and from foreign advisers. Damrong, by now the senior royal adviser, felt that 'the authority and prestige of the King would suffer in the eyes of the People'.[22] Despite the growing public criticism, the monarchy clung to its paternalist ideal. In 1931 Prajadhipok told an American newspaper, 'the King is the father of his people and . . . treats them as children rather than subjects. The obedience the king receives is the obedience of love not of fear.'[23]

REDEFINING THE THAI

Historians like Damrong talked about the nation but then wrote about kings. The new urban intellectuals gave the Thai nation a presence in history.

In 1928, a mid-ranked official, Khun Wichitmatra, published *Lak thai* (Origins of the Thai). His material came largely from the Sinologist

Terrien de Lacouperie and a missionary W. C. Dodd, who had travelled in southern China and noted the large numbers of Tai language speakers. In *The Tai Race* (1923), Dodd wrote that the Tai originated in northern China before 2000 BC, moved south in seven 'great migrations', and arrived in Siam after the overthrow of their previous state of Nanchao in Yunnan. Khun Wichitmatra fashioned this into a new kind of history which centred on the Thai as a race, not just the dynasties which figured in works by Damrong. He extended Dodd's list of migrations further back into history by arguing that the Thai must have come from the Altai mountains because 'that was the birthplace of the Mongols'. He extended the history to the present, and included a map of 'lost territories' assigned by treaty to French Indochina, including all of Cambodia and Laos. His aim was to make the Thai 'count as one of the important races of the world'.[24]

Luang Wichit Wathakan returned from France in 1927 and rapidly became a prolific author, journalist, and early radio broadcaster. He reworked Khun Wichitmatra's story into his encyclopaedic *Prawatisat sakhon* (Universal history, 1929). Wichit presented the main theme of all history as a race's progress towards nationhood, and placed the Thai ethnic history alongside and on par with the stories of other races. Wichit also characterized the Thai as a martial race, symbolized by the country's axe-like shape. Wichit Wathakan's *Prawatisat sakhon* became the first non-fiction best-seller. Khun Wichitmatra's *Lak thai* was awarded a prize by the National Academy.

Other writers wanted to refashion the Thai language as a 'fundamental ingredient of Thai-ness' and 'source of national life and tradition'. They criticized the growing use of English words; the government's 'addiction to Sanskrit' for coining new words; the court's use of long titles which 'slow the development of the nation;' and the court's specialized vocabulary of *rachasap* based on Khmer. These imports were 'threats to independence' and inappropriate 'for the free peoples of Siam'. These critics wanted to simplify the language, in particular by discarding the large number of pronouns which identified social status and were 'a source of national division' and 'breach of democratic principles'. A nine-part essay in the press in 1929 was headlined, 'The existence of the Thai nation depends on the Thai language'.[25]

The commoner nationalists shifted the meaning of a nation from the people enclosed within the national territory and bound by loyalty to the sovereign, to a community defined by ethnic origins, a long and unique history, and a common language.

LUKJIN IN A WORLD OF NATIONS

The rising discourses of nation and nationalism complicated the position of Siam's population of Chinese origins.

In the new world of nations, belonging and identity, like borders, had become more precise. In 1909, China passed a law granting Chinese nationality to those born of Chinese fathers. In 1913, Siam passed a law granting Siamese nationality both to those born of Thai fathers and to those born within the national boundary. This latter provision opened up a route for descendants of Chinese migrants to 'become Thai'. But China's law meant that Chinese in Thailand could claim dual nationality, and hence promised to add another dimension to the issue of extraterritoriality.

This mattered because the nation had new political meanings. In 1908, the Chinese leader Sun Yat Sen visited Bangkok to raise funds for his attempt to overthrow the Chinese empire and form a new Chinese nation-state. He got enthusiastic support. Sun's Kuomintang (KMT) provided funding for Bangkok's fledgling Chinese press, which in return propagated his nationalist and revolutionary ideas. The government became nervous about the involvement of Siam-resident Chinese in the politics of China, and even more nervous that republican and revolutionary ideas would excite aspirations for change in Siam. Their fears were justified. Around this time, Pridi Banomyong, the future leader of Siam's 1932 revolution, got his first political inspiration listening to a KMT propagandist in his local market. The 1912 military officers plot (noted above) occurred four months after Sun's overthrow of the Manchu dynasty in 1911.

The court's fears were heightened by the sheer size of the population of 'new' Chinese following the late nineteenth-century surge of immigration, and their economic domination of Bangkok as both capital and labour. After the June 1910 Chinese strike paralysed Bangkok business for three days, Chulalongkorn warned: 'We must be careful. Their influence is tremendous.'[26] Chinese immigration surged again in the 1920s, to its highest ever level, adding another half-a-million 'new' Chinese to Siam's population between the two world wars.

The court's attitude to the Chinese was also influenced by its bias towards the west. Since their return to Siam in the 1820s, westerners (especially British) had seen the Chinese as rivals for trade and for cultural dominance. In the age of high imperialism at the end of the nineteenth century, the west revelled in portraying China as a civilization in terminal decline. The Siamese elite, anxious to be *siwilai*, followed this lead. Borrowing from the anti-semitism which flourished among European aristocracies in the early twentieth century, Vajiravudh labelled the Chinese as 'The Jews of the East'. In the 1913 pamphlet of that title, he accused the Chinese of refusing to be assimilated into Siamese society, being politically disloyal, expecting undue privileges, worshipping wealth as a god, and being parasites on the economy 'like so many vampires who steadily suck dry an unfortunate victim's life-blood'.[27]

In other writings, Vajiravudh differentiated between the Chinese who settled down and 'became Thai' like the ennobled *jao sua* and market gardeners, and those whose commitment to Siam was more short-term like the coolie labourers. Government policy followed this class-based divide. Labour agitators were jailed and deported, while businessmen were left alone. The KMT, though illegal like any political organization, flourished, especially among prominent businessmen. The Chinese Chamber of Commerce acted as its front. Some of its leaders sheltered behind extraterritoriality. Siew Hut Seng, who headed both the KMT and Chinese Chamber, was born in Siam but acquired British protection through his father, a Hokkien from Melaka who had become a successful rice miller in Siam. By 1928, the KMT had an estimated 20,000 members in Siam.

In 1924 a radical wing formed within the Siamese KMT. Partly, this reflected the rise of a communist wing in China's KMT. Partly, it indicated the development of an independent urban intelligentsia in Siam; many of the activists were teachers in Chinese schools and journalists in Bangkok's Chinese-language press. When Chiang Kai Shek purged the communist wing from the KMT in Shanghai in 1927, many activists took refuge in Southeast Asia, including Siam. In the same year, King Prajadhipok included the Chinese among nine 'Problems of Siam' identified at the start of his reign. He noted the surge in numbers of Chinese immigrants. He grumbled that Chinese in Siam 'determined to remain Chinese' and that 'new and dangerous ideas are coming in from China'.[28]

In May 1928, a Japanese army killed and wounded 5000 in a clash with a KMT force at Jinan on China's Shandong peninsula, provoking a surge of Chinese nationalist feeling. Leaders of the Bangkok Chinese organized a boycott of Japanese goods which rapidly halved imports from Japan into Siam. The government moved to restrict the spread of revolutionary ideas into the broader population. It began to arrest communists after their pamphlets called for an uprising of Siamese workers and peasants. It banned the republican writings of Sun Yat Sen which a *lukjin* businessman had translated into Thai. But it still avoided provoking the business community. It refused to suppress the boycott of Japanese goods, and made little use of new powers to restrict immigration after the Chinese Chamber protested against them.

This Chinese nationalism existed uneasily alongside Thai nationalism. On the one hand, many well-established Chinese became involved in Siam's growing nationalism. They reacted angrily against Vajiravudh's attempts to stir up animosity against 'fellow citizens of Chinese descent'. They supported the Siamese nationalist press. They appended Thai surnames to their Chinese names, and formed the *Samoson jin sayam*, the association of Siam-Chinese, to emphasize their identification with Thai nationalism. In the early 1930s, they pinned hopes on political change in Siam.

But on the other hand, some Thai nationalist ideologues had begun to imagine a Thai people for whom the Chinese were an enemy. They accused foreign merchants, both Chinese and colonial, of 'sucking Thai blood to the marrow'. They argued that the flood of Chinese migrants made it 'impossible for Thai labourers to find employment in their own home'.[29] They demanded a programme of import controls, immigration restrictions, state funds for industry, and help for Thais to find employment. One newspaper called itself *Thai tae* (true Thai).

THE 1932 REVOLUTION

On 5 February 1927, seven men met in Paris and over the next five days plotted a revolution in Siam. They included three students at military colleges (including Plaek Phibunsongkhram), a law student (Pridi Banomyong), a science student, a London barrister, and a deputy at the Siamese mission in Paris. They called themselves the *Khana ratsadon* or People's Party, using the word for 'people' which the Bangkok press favoured as the opposite of 'rulers'.

The intellectual leader of the group was the brilliant law student, Pridi Banomyong, then 27 years old (Figure 10). From his studies in the French legal tradition, he saw the importance of placing the king within the law under a constitution. From studies in political economy, he adopted the idea prevalent in post-war Europe that the state was a powerful instrument to bring about economic growth and greater equity. At the Paris meeting, the group adopted two aims: first, to convert the absolute monarchy into a constitutional monarchy; second, to use the state to achieve economic and social progress through a six-point programme which summarized themes developed in the Bangkok press over the previous decade – true independence, public safety, economic planning, equal rights (with no exceptions for royalty), liberty for all, and universal education.

The seven recruited secretly among other students in Europe, and then in Siam after their return over the next few years. Their most important

Figure 10: Revolutionaries in Paris, c. 1927. From left: Khuang Aphaiwong (future prime minister), Pridi Banomyong, Thaep Aphaiwong, Luang Wichit Wathakan.

converts were a group of senior military officers, who mostly came from commoner background and who had earlier studied in European military academies (especially in Germany). The leader of this group, Phraya Phahon Phonphayuhasena, explained that he joined because of 'the birth of the feeling that in the government at that time high officials and princes acted according to their whim and were not willing to pay heed to smaller people'.[30]

Over the late 1920s, the focus of the press changed from criticism of absolutism's failings to proposals for its replacement. More articles explained to readers the meaning of a constitution, and the benefits of parliamentary rule. A few advocated republicanism. Underground communist groups distributed pamphlets about revolution. With the world sliding into economic depression in 1929, criticism of the absolutist government reached a peak. In response to business petitions for government to aid the economy, Prajadhipok wondered sarcastically if they wanted 'the government to make a Five-Year Plan like Soviet Russia'.[31] In 1927, his government had made teaching economics a criminal offence.

The government struggled to balance the budget by retrenching more officials, cutting spending on education, and raising taxes on salary earners. Investigations uncovered corruption in several departments, but punishments were limited to minor officials. The government refused to abandon the gold standard which, critics argued, inflated the value of the baht and prejudiced Siam's rice exports – further evidence of Siam's subordination to the foreigner. Prajadhipok told military officers in February 1932:

The financial war is a very hard one indeed. Even experts contradict one another until they become hoarse . . . I have never experienced such a hardship; therefore if I have made a mistake I really deserve to be excused by the officials and people of Siam.[32]

Resentment spread to senior levels of the bureaucracy. The government reacted by drafting an anti-Bolshevik bill, but then modifying it to combat a wider range of dissident opinions. Serious offences incurred the death penalty. More papers were closed. Some journalists were intimidated with threats or violence. Immigration laws were used to deport many critics.

By early 1932, the government was bombarded with petitions from farmers and businessmen demanding new economic policies; the press and magazines were full of articles discussing reasons for the progress and decline of nations; and the coffee houses hummed with rumours of a political coup. A royal relative and minister suggested the king should adapt Mussolini's plan of pro-Fascism education to rebuild support for absolutism, but Prajadhipok counselled that 'fathers of schoolchildren now like badmouthing the king so much it has become a habit', with the result that 'the former popularity and credibility of the king is, I think, beyond revival'.[33]

By June 1932, the People's Party had around a hundred members, just over half in the military. In the space of three hours on the morning of 24 June 1932, this small group of conspirators captured the commander of the royal guard, arrested about forty members of the royal family and their aides, and announced that the absolute monarchy had been overthrown. The extent of resentment against absolutism ensured the coup's success.

People queued up to join the People's Party. Business and labour groups welcomed the event. Messages of support flooded in from the provinces. Opposition was insignificant. There was only one minor shooting incident, and no deaths. Pridi circulated a manifesto which justified the revolution on the grounds of economic nationalism, social justice, humanism, and the rule of law:

> The King maintains his power above the law as before. He appoints court relatives and toadies without merit or knowledge to important positions, without listening to the voice of the people. He allows officials to use the power of their office dishonestly, taking bribes in government construction and purchasing . . . He elevates those of royal blood (*phuak jao*) to have special rights more than the people. He governs without principle . . . The government of the King above the law is unable to find solutions and bring about recovery . . . The government of the King has treated the people as slaves . . . and as animals. It has not considered them as human beings.[34]

The Cabinet of princes was dismissed. Around a hundred royal family members and royalists were purged from the military and senior bureaucracy. On 27 June, the People's Party promulgated a constitution which began, 'The supreme power in the country belongs to the people', and which created government by an assembly and a 'committee of the people'.

The apparent ease of the takeover was deceptive. On the night of 24 June, the king and his entourage debated 'whether to agree to the demands of the People's Party or resist'.[35] Military members of the entourage wanted to bring upcountry troops to besiege the city. The king vetoed any action which might cause bloodshed, and decided to cooperate with the People's Party. But the royalists also founded an organization dedicated to regaining control. They spread rumours that the revolution was a 'communist' plot. They visited western legations to petition for foreign powers to intervene against this 'communist' menace. The former police chief funded rickshaw drivers to strike and create disorder in the capital.

The People's Party barricaded their office, took to carrying side arms, and proceeded cautiously. They apologized to the king for the demagoguery of Pridi's manifesto. They agreed to the king's suggestion that the constitution was only provisional and that he should participate in drafting a permanent version. They included twenty-five senior officials in the 70-member provisional Assembly, and invited eight senior officials to form the first government. As its head they chose Phraya Manopakon (Mano) Nithithada, who had been one of the few non-royal members of the Privy Council, and whose wife had been a lady-in-waiting to the queen. The 'permanent' constitution appeared to grant more power to the king, and its promulgation on 10 December 1932 was stage-managed as a gift from the throne.

Behind this façade, the following three years saw a protracted struggle between the old order and the new. This struggle revolved around two related issues: property, and the constitutional power of the king.

The Bangkok press claimed that 'the property of each and every member of our royalty exceeds the capital stock of Siam'.[36] It urged the new government to strip the royal and other aristocratic families of their land, and use this wealth to bail out the depressed economy. The government did not follow this suggestion, but prepared a bill for estate and death duties, while Pridi drafted an 'Outline Economic Plan' whose main proposal was a voluntary nationalization of all land.

These moves frightened the royal family. Prajadhipok wrote to a relative: 'I'd like to have a real go at them (the People's Party) but I'm somewhat afraid the princes would come off badly . . . We're thinking of so many different plans of action'.[37] The king responded to Pridi's Outline Economic Plan with a long, dismissive essay equating Pridi with Stalin. During the drafting of the 'permanent' constitution, the king insisted that the monarch should appoint half the Assembly and have a veto over legislation, but Pridi successfully resisted these proposals. The king then worked on Mano and the other senior officials in the government to break with the coup group. Mano persuaded the Cabinet to reject Pridi's plan, and sent troops to intimidate the Assembly to do likewise. When the Assembly refused to comply, Mano dismissed it on grounds that the plan betrayed 'a communistic tendency . . . contrary to the Thai tradition'.[38] Pridi was hustled into exile, and his supporters removed from the Cabinet. Two royalist generals were elevated to senior posts, and young People's Party military officers were dispersed to the provinces. An Anti-Communist Act was rapidly passed, defining communism as any theory which 'rests upon the total or partial abolition of private property'.

But Mano's victory was short-lived. A month later in June 1933, the young military officers in the People's Party staged another coup, dismissed the Mano government, and purged several more royalists from the army. They again drafted senior officials into a new Cabinet, but chose with more care. They recalled Pridi from exile. The royalists again spread rumours of social disorder and foreign intervention. In October, a group of royalist officers, several of whom had been purged from the army by the People's Party a few months earlier, staged an armed counter-revolt under the leadership of Prince Boworadet, Prajadhipok's cousin and a pre-1932 minister of war. The group aimed to bring nine upcountry garrisons to besiege the city, but only three moved to the city's northern outskirts while the others prevaricated. The city garrisons held firm to the People's Party. Businesses and organizations offered money and volunteer services to help the defence.

Neither side much wanted a shooting war, and most of the salvoes were propaganda. The People's Party put out radio broadcasts and leaflets damning the Boworadet forces as 'rebels' and 'bandits'. In reply, the besiegers dropped leaflets on the city from aeroplanes, accusing the People's Party of restraining the king. After an artillery exchange, the besiegers retreated to Khorat. A few days later, the leaders fled, mostly to Saigon. Twenty-three lives had been lost. The People's Party arrested the remnants and eventually jailed 230 people. Two retired senior military officers were tried and executed. A royal prince was sentenced to life imprisonment. Over the next two years, there were two more attempted counter-coups. After the first, two royal family members and thirteen others were jailed.

The king sailed to the south as the Boworadet revolt began. He gave no open support, but in the aftermath called for an amnesty. The People's Party believed he helped in both planning and financing. After long negotiations, the king agreed to return to Bangkok, but left within three months on the pretext of seeking medical treatment in Europe. While abroad, he refused to sign legislation passed by the government, including a bill which he believed would transfer control of the Privy Purse to the government and subject the king to inheritance tax, and a new penal code which reduced the royal prerogative. In response to entreaties for his return, he demanded large changes in the constitution to enhance the power of the throne, including a legislative veto. In March 1935, while still in Europe, he announced his abdication. The government decided that the legitimate successor was one of Prajadhipok's nephews, the 10-year-old Prince Ananda Mahidol, then at school in Switzerland. For the next sixteen years, Thailand had no resident, reigning monarch.

PROGRESS AND LEGITIMACY

The defeat of the Boworadet revolt ended the period of open struggle. The People's Party now had to demonstrate that its post-absolutist order could satisfy the aspirations of a changing society.

Over the 1930s the People's Party divided into two groups, roughly identified with the civilian and military members and their respective leaders, Pridi Banomyong and Plaek Phibunsongkhram (Phibun). The two groups had different views on the role and purpose of the state which they had wrestled from the royalist grip.

Pridi's thinking was formed by the French liberal tradition with a tinge of European socialism. The role of the state was to provide a framework within which individuals could 'develop to their utmost capability'. That required the rule of law, a judicial system, help for the economy, and systems for education and health. Pridi attracted support among businessmen, labour leaders, and upcountry politicians who had high expectations of a more liberal state. Phibun and the military group, by contrast, tended to see the state as an expression of the popular will, with the duty to change the individual by education, legal enactments, and cultural management. Despite this contrast, the two groups cooperated reasonably well, in common fear of a royalist counter-revolution, until the Second World War.

For the Pridi group, the 'progress' which the state had responsibility to achieve included economic progress. Against the background of the depression, traders, entrepreneurs, and farmers bombarded the new government with petitions for help. Governments around the world were drawn to intervene in their economies to combat the depression. Over the next few years, seven full economic plans were drafted and submitted to the new government, and several other proposals presented in the press.

The Outline Economic Plan which Pridi presented in 1933 had two main proposals. First, land would be sold to the state, which would raise its productivity by applying better technology, while all farmers would become salaried civil servants. Second, the state would start industrial and commercial enterprises to replace imports, using capital raised through taxation and through loans from a new national bank. These measures would meet the aspirations for Siam to 'progress' economically and draw the mass of the people out of poverty. They would also undermine the economic base which the royal family and some aristocratic allies had created over the past generation by using political power to acquire land and by using tax revenues to fund capital investments.

After the political crisis of 1933, this plan was quietly forgotten. Following Prajadhipok's abdication in 1935, the Privy Purse was divided into Prajadhipok's personal property and the Crown Property Bureau which was taken under the Finance Ministry. But proposals to seize, purchase, or deplete aristocratic assets by taxation were shelved. Through the mid-1930s, economic ministers proposed schemes to help peasants survive the depression by forming cooperatives and promoting new sources of employment. But the political will and administrative machinery to implement such schemes were lacking.

The Pridi group concentrated on other forms of progress. Pridi completed the preparation of a modern law code, a project begun in the early 1900s but constantly delayed. The new code removed legal bases of aristocratic privilege, withdrew legal recognition of polygamy, and cancelled the requirement for parental consent of marriage partners. The People's Party government increased investment in education, raising the number of primary school pupils from 0.7 to 1.7 million over 1931–39. Pridi spearheaded the foundation of a second university, named the University of Moral and Political Sciences (Thammasat), designed to train a new kind of bureaucrat for the post-absolutist age. The government also expanded local government, and increased spending on roads, hospitals, and electricity generation.

In 1935, Pridi travelled to London to negotiate lower interest rates for Siam's foreign loans, and to initiate talks to renegotiate the mid-nineteenth-century treaties which restricted Siam's fiscal autonomy and granted extraterritorial rights to western nations. These treaties were all revised over 1937–38, after which Siam increased tariffs to protect local industries.

Pridi's civilian wing thus made modest steps towards its new definition of 'progress'. But its attempts to legitimize the new regime through popular representation were much shakier. Under the 'permanent' constitution promulgated in December 1932, half of the single-chamber Assembly was elected, and the other half appointed. The Cabinet was theoretically responsible to this Assembly but could always dominate by manipulating the appointed half. In early 1933, a royalist group attempted to form a political party, but the king refused permission and attempted to outlaw all political parties, including the People's Party. Later, MPs tabled several bills to allow political parties, but the government blocked them in fear they would facilitate a royalist comeback. On the eve of the 1932 coup, the People's Party leaders had sworn an oath of solidarity and, despite internal factionalism, negotiated each of nine changes of leadership between then and 1941 by internal debate behind closed doors.

Many groups which had enthusiastically supported the 1932 revolution became disappointed. Some businessmen were appointed to the Assembly and won the right to form a Board of Trade, but failed to convince the government to give more solid support to domestic entrepreneurs. Leaders of the Chinese community were distressed by signs of Thai ethnic nationalism, including regulations to restrict Chinese schools. Labour leaders were allowed to form the first labour associations, but when they lent support to a strike in the rice mills, the leaders were arrested and the associations suppressed. Dissident journalists who had helped to nurture the political atmosphere in which the 1932 revolution took place fared little better. Between June and December 1932, ten newspapers were closed by government order, and more closures followed in 1933 and 1934, while government funds were used to support papers friendly to the People's Party. In 1933, 2000 monks from twelve provinces supported a petition for Sangha reform, but leaders of the movement were accused of rebellion and forcibly disrobed. In the wake of the Boworadet revolt, the government passed an Act for the Preservation of the Constitution under which suspected dissidents could be imprisoned or exiled to the provinces without trial.

Pridi hoped to make nation and constitution a new focus of public loyalty. He spoke on radio, urging people to love the nation and preserve the constitution because it 'fuses us all together as one unity'.[39] A Constitution Association was formed in late 1933. Monks and teachers were recruited to explain the importance of the constitution to the people. Miniatures of the constitution were distributed to all provinces and honoured on the newly designated Constitution Day (10 December) in the same manner as a Buddhist image. Constitution Day was gradually elevated into the premier national holiday of the year, with parades, art contests, dances, and a Miss Siam national beauty contest organized by the Interior Ministry to find 'a symbol of the goodness of our race'.[40] In 1939, a Constitution Monument was completed. It was conspicuously the largest monument in the city, designed with symbols of Thai tradition, and placed in the middle of Chulalongkorn's 'royal way'.

RISE OF THE MILITARY

The young military officers who controlled the firepower gradually came to dominate the People's Party. The original revolution, the second coup of June 1933, and the suppression of the Boworadet revolt depended on the ability of a small group of officers commanding the city's battalions. After the Boworadet revolt, the minister of defence argued that 'keeping the peace' had become the 'single most important problem' and hence soldiers 'who existed for the nation alone' had to be at the centre of politics.[41] Despite financial stringency, the military demanded increased funds, secured 26 per cent of the national budget from 1933 to 1937, and doubled the number of military personnel.

Within this young military group, Phibun emerged as the leader and became minister of defence in early 1934. He argued that Siam possessed four basic political institutions – monarchy, parliament, bureaucracy, and military – of which only the military was 'abiding and permanent'. The parliament, by contrast, could be 'abolished through various events and causes'.[42] The army set up its own radio stations which broadcast Phibun's slogan: 'Your country is your house, the army is its fence'. Without the military, Phibun stated, Siam would be 'effaced from the world'. His Defence Ministry commissioned a cinema film, *Luat thahan thai* (Blood of the Thai military, 1935), in which Siam is attacked by an anonymous foreign power, and the heroes and heroines abandon their romances to defend the nation.

Phibun and his group were attracted to other states which were rising on the basis of a strong, militarized version of nationalism. In 1933, Phibun had contacted the Japanese legation for assistance in the event the western powers intervened in Siam. Over subsequent years, this contact developed into broader sympathy and cooperation. In 1935, a Japan–Siam Association was formed, including several of Phibun's group. In 1934, he inaugurated Yuwachon, a militarized youth movement modelled on the officer training corps found in the UK and US. After he had sent one of his group who was half-German and German-trained to study the rise of the Nazi party in Germany, Yuwachon became more like the Hitler Youth.

In December 1938, Phibun took over as prime minister. Since 1935, he had been the target of at least three assassination attempts, one of which aimed to kill the whole Cabinet. According to a royal insider, one attempt was 'brilliant in its conception . . . and very nearly succeeded'.[43] A month after becoming premier, Phibun claimed to have uncovered a major restorationist plot. He ordered the arrest of seventy people, including the conservative old guard in the People's Party and leading royalists. After trial by a special court, fifteen were executed, two were exiled, and another three (including the senior royal family member, Prince Rangsit) were condemned to death but reprieved and imprisoned along with nineteen others. The lengthy court proceedings were published as a condemnation of royal conspiracy. The government successfully sued Prajadhipok for transferring 4.2 million baht from the Privy Purse to his private accounts overseas. It seized his palace, banned his picture from public display, and disbanded the Ministry of the Royal Household. Many remaining royalists left the country.

Phibun appointed himself head of the army and minister of defence, interior, and (later) foreign affairs. The rest of the Cabinet was packed with military men, and the military subvention rose to 33 per cent of the total budget. When a group of provincial (mostly northeastern) MPs protested strongly against the increase in the military budget and other aspects of military aggrandizement, Phibun dissolved the Assembly. When the opponents were returned in the following election and threatened to vote down the budget, he began to bypass the Assembly and rule by decree. In 1940, shortly before the Assembly was due to become wholly elective, he rammed through an amendment to extend the appointed half for another decade (up to 1953).

Phibun awarded himself the rank of field marshal, which had previously been held only by the monarch. Early in 1942, he started to have himself referred to publicly as 'The Leader' (*than phu nam*), and to plaster the daily press with slogans such as 'Our nation's security depends on believing in our leader'. He commanded that his picture should be displayed in every home. He passed a series of authoritarian laws, including a press Act and an emergency decree which allowed almost unlimited arrest. Critics suggested that Phibun's model was Mussolini, and that he was elevating himself into a presidential or even royal role. Phibun explained: 'The campaign is meant to demonstrate that we, the whole nation, can act as one person'.[44]

MOULDING POST-ABSOLUTIST CULTURE

Phibun and Luang Wichit Wathakan set out to create a new culture for post-absolutist Siam by using the power of the state.

As noted earlier, Wichit was a quintessential example of the new men of the 1920s who rose from commoner obscurity through talent and access to education. He served abroad in the foreign service and saw Siam in international perspective. After his return in the late 1920s, he quickly made his name as a writer, publicist on the new medium of radio, and ardent advocate of nationalism.

He was also a traditionalist who saw the monarchy as an essential part of the Thai nation. He was acquainted with the Pridi group in Paris but was not drafted into the early People's Party, probably because of his royalist sympathies. Over 1932–33 he served as a publicist for the royalist counter-revolutionary party, but gradually shifted his allegiance. He showed his skill as a political publicist in preparing the People's Party's propaganda during the Boworadet revolt. From 1934 onwards, he became a strong ally of Phibun. The combination of his extraordinary flair for popular culture, his official position, and Phibun's backing gave him the opportunity to shape a new version of Siam as a nation in history.

Wichit was appointed head of a new Fine Arts Department, established to help mould the public culture of the post-absolutist era. After the abdication, the department inherited musicians, craftsmen, and performers from the palace, and used them to create a new national theatre troupe. Wichit wrote plays for the troupe which used traditional historical themes but a dramatic presentation which was more western than royal-traditional. These plays popularized a new style of *phleng sakhon* (international song) which blended elements of traditional singing into a western format of the popular song.

Wichit believed in 'human revolution', the potential for people to change themselves and thus the world. He wrote manuals of self-improvement, including *Brain, The Power of Thought*, and *The Power of Determination*, which guided people to be modern and successful. He idealized the Sukhothai era as the exemplar of Siamese civilization not, as Vajiravudh had done, because of its form of kingship, but because of its perfect expression of the freedom-loving character of the Thai. Freedom was important because it gave opportunities for all to contribute their talents to the nation. Sukhothai, in Wichit's version, was so creative in art and language, and so productive in material life, because people had the freedom to produce. Indeed, Sukhothai was proof that 'free enterprise has been part of Thailand's philosophy for many generations'.[45] After the Sukhothai highpoint, Siamese civilization declined in the Ayutthaya period because of the adoption of Khmer practices such as slavery and divine kingship.

In Wichit's view, history was made by great personal achievements. One of his first works on return to Siam in the late 1920s was an essay on *Mahaburut* (Great men, 1928), with capsule biographies of Napoleon, Bismarck, Disraeli, Gladstone, Okubo Toshimichi (of the Meiji Restoration), and Mussolini. Four years later he wrote another laudatory study of Mussolini. These figures were heroic because of their service to the nation. 'Man instinctively loves his fellow men, his friends, his family, and his compatriots', Wichit wrote, and hence 'the division of humanity into nations is correct according to natural law'. Man's duty was 'to uphold the importance of the nation; think of the nation and not individual or sectional benefit in any endeavour; preserve the nation; and unify it through integration'.[46] Wichit wrote plays identifying King Naresuan and King Taksin as great men who defended Siam from its enemy neighbour, Burma. But such heroism was not reserved for kings. In his most popular play of the 1930s, *Luat suphan* (Blood of Suphanburi, 1936), the heroine is an ordinary young woman who rouses other ordinary people to oppose a Burmese invasion. The Thai were a martial people, including the women. Another Wichit play, *Suk thalang* (Battle of Thalang), celebrated two sisters who defended Phuket against the Burmese. Corrado Feroci, an Italian sculptor trained in the monumental classicism favoured by Mussolini and now working for Wichit's Fine Arts Department, depicted similar ideas on the Constitution Monument (Figure 11), a statue of Thao Suranari, the legendary female

Figure 11: The nation free and militant. Bas-reliefs prepared under the supervision of
Corrado Feroci on the Constitution Monument (1939) introduce ordinary people into
official iconography, but with the prime role for soldiers.

defender of Khorat against the Lao in 1828, and another statue depicting
the villagers of Bang Rajan who defied the Burmese in 1767.

Wichit further elaborated the Thai national character as constructive,
detailed, aesthetical, and martial. Through this martial prowess, the T(h)ai
had become the dominant power in Suwannaphum, the golden peninsula.
Also as a result of its advanced civilization, 'Siam has become the heart of the
Golden Peninsula, like Athens was the heart of Greece' and thus other races
had 'come to settle . . . within the boundaries of Siam'.[47] In his 1937 play,

Ratchamanu, a military commander during Naresuan's reign announced that the Khmer were 'Thais like us' but had somehow become separated; 'all of us on the Golden Peninsula are the same . . . [but] the Siamese Thais are the elder brothers'.[48] *Chaoying saenwi* (Princess of Saenwi) dramatized the common ethnicity of the Shan and Thai. *Mahadevi* (1938) imagined a sixteenth-century queen of Lanna helping to unify her country with Siam.

For Wichit, the Thai were, as the Nationality Law prescribed, those born in Siam and hence ethnically diverse. But in his songs, like '*Luat thai*' (Thai blood), they were also mystically united into 'one unified stream of blood which must never be broken into many streams'.[49] The national anthem, rescripted in this era, contained the same sentiment: 'we are all of the Thai blood-flesh-lineage-race'.

Wichit took little interest in the mass. He believed they remained poor because they were too 'lazy' to achieve his 'human revolution'. He argued that the constitution guaranteed justice without any need for mass participation. Only states where the mass was highly educated qualified for democracy. Political parties were like 'the brains of the nation'. He cited Aristotle for the assertion that, 'From birth, some people are marked out to rule others, and some to be ruled'.[50]

Because he chose forms like theatre, song, cinema, and radio which reached beyond the boundaries of high literacy, and because his works were absorbed into the curricula of the expanding education system, Wichit's influence was broad, deep, and lasting.

A WORLD OF RIVAL NATIONALISMS

In September 1937, Japanese troops invaded Manchuria. In April 1938, Hitler launched the *Anschluss* into Austria. From this point, Siam's emergent nationalisms – Pridi's liberal version, Phibun's militaristic one, and the *lukjin* affection for their place of origin – were bound up with the clash of nationalisms on a world scale.

The Japanese invasion of China provoked another wave of nationalist feeling among the Siam Chinese, and a renewed upsurge of organizations and newspapers. Rival KMT factions, the Communist Party in Siam, and other Chinese groups cooperated to sell war bonds, dispatch rice and other supplies to the KMT forces, send 2000 volunteers to fight alongside them, and reinstitute a boycott of Japanese goods. Merchants who imported Japanese goods were blackmailed into making donations. Sixty-one were killed for failing to comply.

The People's Party had hitherto acted carefully towards both China and the local Chinese. It had placed some restrictions on Chinese schools but then revoked them when the Chinese Chamber complained. It welcomed a Kuomintang goodwill mission in 1936. Wichit inserted a song on 'Chinese-Thai unity' in his 1937 play on King Taksin. But the 1937 boycott again drew the government's attention to the powerful Chinese grip over commercial activity, and hence the economy's vulnerability to an external political issue. It also raised the issue of Chinese loyalties in the event of a war of competing nationalisms, and the possibility that Siam would get dragged into the Japan–China war as an enemy of Japan. The deaths of several prominent merchants in the boycott campaign, and of others by freelance gangsterism, rekindled fears about the Chinese secret societies.

In July 1938, Wichit Wathakan gave a speech reviving Vajiravudh's comparison between the Siamese Chinese and the European Jews. He added that the Jews had no homeland, whereas 'the Chinese cannot be compared to them; they come to work here but send money back to their country; so we can say that the Chinese are worse than the Jews'.[51] He wrote another play, *Nanchao* (1939), portraying the Chinese driving the Thai out of their earlier homeland.

The government doubled the immigration fee and closed two banks engaged in remittance to China. It cracked down on the *angyi*, businessmen, and political activists engaged in the boycott and fund-raising. Hundreds were arrested and deported. All but one Chinese newspaper ceased publication. Regulations on Chinese schools were tightened, resulting in all but two closing down.

The government also launched a programme to create 'a Thai economy for the Thai people'. This was partly preparation for a possible war, partly an attempt to compete against western and Chinese firms through state enterprises, and partly aid for the 'Thai' peasants who formed the mass of the population. In the mid-1930s, the Defence Ministry began setting up companies to make Siam more self-reliant in strategic industries such as oil supply and textiles. As the prospects of a widespread nationalist war heightened, this war-style economy was expanded. In 1938, when the Chinese boycotted Japanese trade, the government set up the Thai Rice Company. The economic minister explained that it was dangerous for 'the country's most important product to be totally in the hands of foreigners', meaning merchants of Chinese origin. Phibun added that 'rice is the backbone of the people . . . but people are poor because they are squeezed by middlemen'.[52] The Thai Rice Company leased existing mills and eventually took control of 70–80 per cent of the rice trade. The government also set up a pyramid of companies to distribute imports and other consumer goods from the capital down to local markets.

In 1939, the government imposed monopolies on tobacco and salt; reserved several occupations and businesses for Thai citizens, including driving taxis, slaughtering pigs, fishing, planting rubber, and selling petrol; imposed an alien registration fee of 4 baht; and in other ways shifted the tax burden onto commerce through levies on shops, signboards, and income, and increased rates on opium and gambling. In 1941, the government drew up a National Industrial Plan under which the Defence Ministry ventured into more strategically important industries, including mining, tanning, sugar, shipping, tobacco, rubber, salt, fisheries, and (!) the manufacture of playing cards. Most of these were existing factories commandeered from (usually Chinese) private entrepreneurs.

Since the mid-1930s, two commissions had been appointed to consider what to do about the question of nationality for the large numbers of Chinese who had arrived in recent decades. A few first-generation immigrants had petitioned to adopt Thai nationality but there was no mechanism. In April 1939, a law was passed enabling people to change their nationality to Thai as long as they disclaimed any loyalty to China and proved their loyalty to Siam by speaking the language, changing their names, and educating their children at Thai schools. In the first year, only 104 passed these rigorous checks, but they were an important group. Virtually all were wealthy merchants, mine owners, and industrialists. Their change of nationality provided the government with a group of 'Thai' entrepreneurs to help run the proliferation of new state enterprises. Ma Bulakun (who in fact transferred from English nationality acquired in Hong Kong) ran the government's rice trading company. Wilat Osathanon, son-in-law of the late KMT leader Siew Hut Seng, and Julin Lamsam, member of one of the biggest rice-trading families, helped run the government's wholesale and retail network. Under the cover of Thai nationalism and war, the rising commoner politics and rising *lukjin* business cautiously linked hands.

THE GREAT THAI EMPIRE AND THE NEW THAILAND

Soon after 1932, some of the military wing in the People's Party made plans to reclaim the 'lost territories' assigned to other states by the treaties of the 1900s. In 1935, Bangkok's envoy in Paris referred to 'the Siamese Alsace-Lorraine'.[53] In 1935–36, the Ministry of Defence published a series of maps which depicted Khun Wichitmatra's story of Thai migrations, and which showed the imagined boundaries of Thai kingdoms from the Nanchao era to Bangkok. One map showed the 'full' extent of Siam and seven pieces of territory 'lost' to Burma and the colonial powers between the late eighteenth century and 1909.

After the *Anschluss*, a military lecturer claimed that the Burmese, Annamese, Khmer, and Malay were all of 'original Thai stock' and should be united with Siam. In 1939, the École Française d'Extrême-Orient presented Wichit Wathakan with a map showing Tai-speaking peoples scattered across Southeast Asia and southern China. He exclaimed: 'If we could recover the lost territories, we would be a great power . . . Before long we could be a country of around 9 million square kilometres with a population of 60 million'.[54] He began campaigning for the return of the 'lost territories', particularly parts of Cambodia and Laos. He travelled to the Mekong border and had the That Phanom shrine, one of the sacred centres of the Lao world, heightened by 30 metres so it would be more visible from the eastern bank in French Laos.

The government distributed the map showing the 'lost territories' to schools. Army radio advocated building a *maha anajak thai* (great Thai empire) on Hitler's model. Newspaper articles and street demonstrations helped to fan popular irredentism. Wichit reasoned: 'When the present war was over, there would be no small nations in the world; all would be merged into big ones. So there are only two ways left for us to choose, either become a Power or be swallowed up by some other Power.'[55] Phibun agreed: 'If you don't want to be scum you have to be a Great Power'.[56]

In 1939, the government issued seven *ratthaniyom*, often translated as 'cultural mandates' but better rendered as 'state edicts'. Over the following four years, the series was extended to twelve, and strengthened by other Acts and rulings. In part, these were attempts to strengthen Siam in the context of a global war which the country could not avoid. But more basically they showed the Phibun regime's faith in the ability of the strong state to remake the nation and its culture from above.

The first theme of these measures was to move Siam finally away from its royalist past. The first edict, issued on 24 June 1939, changed the country's name from Siam to Thailand on grounds that 'We are of the Thai race, but . . . the name Siam does not correspond to our race'.[57] A later edict abolished the use of official titles from the absolutist era. The anniversary of the 1932 revolution (24 June) was designated as National Day in 1938, and subsequently elevated as the premier annual holiday, marked by military and cultural displays. In 1942, Phibun passed a Sangha Act which removed the royalist Thammayut sect from its privileged position, and shifted authority away from the royally appointed supreme patriarch to councils of elders.

The second theme of these measures was 'to make Thai people truly Thai'. One edict explained: 'We must remember there are many new Thai. Now we have Thailand, we can mix the true Thai together with the new Thai to work together in friendship for the united nation.'[58] This meant applying pressure and providing facilitation for Chinese and other non-Thai to speak and act in ways which confirmed their membership of the national community. An edict prescribed rituals for honouring national symbols such as the flag and anthem. Everyone was urged to learn and speak the Thai dialect of the central region. To make this 'easier to read and easier to write', a government commission modified the language with a simplified alphabet, regular phonetic spelling, unique pronouns which ignored distinction of gender and status, and standard versions for greeting (*sawatdi*) and other common usages. In 1942, a National Culture Commission was established to define and disseminate Thai culture.

A third theme was unity. People were no longer to be described as 'northern Thai', 'northeastern Thai', and so on, but henceforth were simply *chao thai*. Another committee scanned popular songs and removed mentions of 'Lao', 'Ngiew' (Shan), and other non-Thai ethnic descriptors.

A fourth theme of the state edicts was progress. Thai were urged to help the economy in various ways, such as being self-reliant and buying Thai goods. Standards of dress, public conduct, and social life were prescribed to remove any justification for outsiders to treat Thailand as uncivilized. Contests were arranged to promote 'modern' dress (Figure 12). Thai were urged to conduct themselves with decorum in public places, including queuing in an orderly way, and refraining from making graffiti. Some western habits were advised, including using forks and spoons, wearing hats, and kissing one's wife before leaving the house. One edict prescribed a timetable for people to divide their day between work, eating, leisure, and sleep.

Since progress was dependent on the number and health of the population, Phibun aimed to increase the population to 40 million and to make people stronger and healthier. A National Nutrition Project had been launched in 1938. The doctor in charge wrote: 'In revolutionary times, there should also be a revolution in people's food and eating'.[59] People were encouraged to eat more protein. Exercise was included in the school curriculum, and more funds were devoted to medicine and hygiene. The edicts prescribed public education on nutrition. A mother's day was designated to revere and encourage motherhood. A Ministry of Public Health was formed in 1942.

Figure 12: Miss Afternoon Wear. Winner of the contest for afternoon wear and special occasions, probably 1941–42, as part of Phibun's campaign of modernization.

A final theme was national security. The second of the edicts defined treasonous and anti-national activities. The whole programme was publicized on radio in dialogues between Nai Man and Nai Khong, whose two names joined formed *mankhong*, security. Slogans included 'Hats lead nation to power'.

The whole project, as Phibun explained, was launched because 'government is forced to reform and reconstruct the various aspects of society, especially its culture, which here signifies growth and beauty, orderliness, progress and uniformity, and the morality of the nation'.[60] In 1944, the government defined a 14-point Code of National Bravery based on the *bushido* code of Japanese warriors, which Wichit and several others had openly admired for some time. It began by stating that 'the Thai love their nation more than their own lives', and went on to define the Thai as martial, Buddhist, industrious, peace-loving, self-reliant, aspiring for progress, and loyal to their leader.

THE SECOND WORLD WAR

The Phibun group had cultivated strong links with Japan over the 1930s, yet his government's major aim was to keep Thailand out of a war between the great powers by balancing between the Allied and Axis camps. After Paris fell and Japanese forces invaded Indochina, however, Phibun took the opportunity in January 1941 to send troops across the border to seize parts of French Cambodia. The armed clashes with the French were indecisive, but Phibun's government declared victory, held parades, and began building a Victory Monument (with more heroic sculptures by Feroci). The Japanese stepped in to broker an agreement which ceded two chunks of territory to Thailand (Map 5). Phibun was now indebted to Japan. When he was informed that the Japanese would land troops in Thailand to attack the British in Malaya and Burma, he urged the Cabinet to comply in order to regain more 'lost territory'. The Japanese troops landed on 8 December 1941. The government initially agreed to allow safe passage, and then in January formally declared war on Britain and the US. Phibun told Cabinet: 'We should not let them [Japan] build Asia alone . . . They will appreciate us . . . Speaking plainly among the Thai, it is about time to declare war with the winner'.[61] In May, with Japanese blessing, a Thai army marched north to seize territory in Burma's Shan States.

Phibun imagined Thailand serving as Japan's partner in ridding Asia of western colonialism. Wichit, elevated to foreign minister, dreamed of 'raising our country to be the cultural centre of southern Asia'.[62] But the

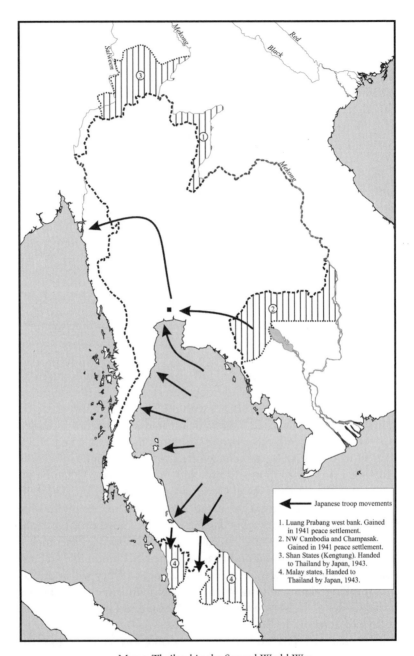

Map 5: Thailand in the Second World War

Japanese troop movements

1. Luang Prabang west bank. Gained
   in 1941 peace settlement.
2. NW Cambodia and Champasak.
   Gained in 1941 peace settlement.
3. Shan States (Kengtung). Handed
   to Thailand by Japan, 1943.
4. Malay states. Handed to
   Thailand by Japan, 1943.

reality was that the Japanese treated Thailand as an occupied state, Japanese troops looked down on the Thai as inferior, and the Japanese government ravaged the Thai economy for war supplies. By mid-1943, Thai leaders were aware that the tide of war had turned against Japan, and they began easing away from the relationship. To strengthen the faltering ties, the Japanese prime minister visited Bangkok and formally confirmed Thai control of four Malay and two Shan states. But Phibun pointedly refused to attend the Greater East Asian Conference in Tokyo in November 1943, and sent messengers through China to make contact with the Allies. He told one of his military commanders: 'which side do you think will lose this war? That side is our enemy.'[63] The government began to provide the Allies with intelligence, and laid plans for resisting the Japanese.

The war had widened the rift between the military members of the People's Party who were attracted by the militarized states of the Axis, and many civilian members who had been educated in France or England and sympathized with the Allies. After the Japanese invasion, the civilian leader, Pridi, had been kicked out of the Cabinet and become regent. He began to organize a resistance group which made contact with the Allies through China in mid-1943. In parallel, students and other Thai in the US and Britain formed resistance groups and offered their services to the Allied armies. The group in the US was led by the ambassador to the US and minor royal family member Seni Pramoj. By early 1944, these various networks, known collectively as Seri Thai (Free Thai), came together. Men and equipment were parachuted into Thailand to organize resistance. Both Pridi's undercover group and Phibun's government secretly lent assistance.

In July 1944, the Pridi group manoeuvred Phibun out of power to improve the chances of negotiating with the Allies to avoid being treated as an enemy. Seri Thai wanted to launch a rising against the Japanese to show its bona fides, but the Allies discouraged any such move, and only a few sabotage operations had been completed when the war ended. The British wanted to punish and dominate Thailand in the aftermath, particularly in order to secure Thailand's rice supplies for the devastated colonial territories. The US, however, was opposed to any return of colonial influence and made it clear Thailand would be treated 'as an enemy-occupied country'. To strengthen this US support, Pridi invited Seni Pramoj to return from the US to become prime minister and front the peace negotiations. Eventually, the British were satisfied with an indemnity paid in rice, and the US insisted that Thailand's borders were returned to their pre-war positions.

CONCLUSION

The creators of a new public sphere in the early twentieth century founded the second of Siam's major visions about the uses of the nation-state. Whereas the royalist reformers of the Fifth Reign argued the need for a strong, dictatorial state to enable Siam to survive and be important in the world, the commoner nationalists contended that the main purpose of the nation-state was the well-being of the nation's people. This meant economic progress to benefit more members of the nation through agriculture, industry, and an end to exploitation by both the old elite and the colonialists. It also meant more public services, including education, health, and communications. Most of all it meant new institutions, the rule of law, and especially a constitution as tools to limit or block old forms of power and to create new ones.

This vision consciously set itself apart from the masculine imagery of the strong-state version. Journalists skewered polygamy as the epitome of the old order. The novels and stories of the era are full of strong heroines. The 1932 constitution granted the franchise equally to men and women. Even Wichit built several of his plays around heroines, and conjured women out of Thai history for immortalization in statuary – though these women were rather martial.

But this second vision proved very vulnerable. The main protagonists of the 1932 revolution were servants of the nation-state with great faith in its capacity to effect social and economic transformation from above. They doubted the existence of any mass base which would rise to defend them in the face of a royalist counter-revolution. With growing influence from contemporary fascist models, Phibun's military wing projected the ideal of a strong military leadership leading a united orderly society to modernize and expand in order to survive in a world of clashing nationalisms. They created a modified and more powerful version of the strong-state tradition minus only the monarchy.

By 1945, the economy was wrecked by Japan's wartime demands; Bangkok was subjected to over 4000 Allied bombing raids, resulting in evacuation of 60 per cent of the population; Japan, the exemplar of Asian 'progress', had been defeated; and Thailand's leaders were scrambling to deny the recent past in order to preserve independence at the peace negotiations. Temporarily at least, the ideal of a strong state was discredited. Many of Phibun's innovations were scrapped – the edicts on dress and social conduct, the language reforms, and the bushido-type code. Even the country's name was temporarily reversed to Siam in September 1945 (for three years, but only in foreign-language usage).

But many of Phibun and Wichit's innovations lasted because they commanded wide acceptance in the new urban society. Wichit invented the Thai, not simply as the citizens of a certain state but also as people with a history and 'national character'. He offered guidance on how new urban Thai could become modern citizens of the world. He helped new bureaucrats imagine themselves as a paternal elite which 'relieved the sufferings and increased the well-being' of a backward and passive peasantry.

Phibun and Wichit built their version of the nation on the foundations laid by Chulalongkorn, Damrong, and Vajiravudh, rather than digging those foundations up and building anew. They continued to imagine the Thai as a *race* with martial characteristics, threatened by bad neighbours and great powers, rescued by unifying around a strong leader, and dedicated to the pursuit of progress. They placed the monarch within a constitution, but never seriously threatened to move towards republicanism. They continued to treat the mass of the people as bystanders at a politics carried out by palace coup and intrigue.

These were still the politics of a national capital city in an overwhelmingly peasant society. The royalists, the military party, and the businessmen and professionals clustered around Pridi were elite groups vying for influence over the new central machinery of the nation-state. But the Second World War made two changes which brought this political era to an end. First, it created a war economy with deeper government involvement, and with fluctuations which affected more of the population. The economic crisis after the war brought mass distress and mass political mobilization. Second, the war drew Thailand deeper into a complex international politics involving Japan, China, and the western powers, especially the US. This shift was permanent. The aftermath of the war saw competitive attempts to build transnational empires around rival communist and capitalist visions of the state's potential to lead economic and political development. The struggles to define the Thai nation and control the Thai state were now skewed to the pattern of this Cold War.

6

The American era and development,
1940s to 1960s

After the Second World War, the US became a new foreign patron, more intrusive than anything Siam had experienced in the colonial era. While Britain had focused on its colonies and never taken more than peripheral interest in Siam, the US seized on Thailand as an ally and base for opposing the spread of communism in Asia. To build Thailand's capability for this role, the US helped to revive and strengthen the military rule which had faltered at the close of the Second World War. To consolidate Thailand's membership of the 'free world' camp in the Cold War, the US promoted 'development', meaning primarily economic growth through private capitalism. To achieve 'national security', US funding helped to push the mechanisms of the nation-state more deeply into society than before.

Under this regime, a new elite emerged consisting of ruling generals, senior bureaucrats, and the heads of new business conglomerates. Strengthened by the ideology of development and unconstrained by democracy, business was able to exploit both people and natural resources on a new scale. The countryside was transformed again, by driving the agrarian frontier through the upland forests, and subjecting the smallholder decisively to the market. Against this backdrop, the old Thai social order faded into history.

FROM WAR TO CIVIL WAR

The aftermath of the war was a period of great economic disruption and political tumult. Phibun's fall in late 1944 propelled Pridi back into the limelight. He returned to his task of founding democracy through constitutional engineering, overseeing passage of a constitution in 1946 which finally created a fully elective legislature. Remnants of the civilian wing of the People's Party, and more recent recruits to the Seri Thai resistance, formed political parties in his support. He began to purge the army of

Phibun's militarists, and to restrict military involvement in politics by law. He recognized that urban labour had become important as a result of state-led industrialization, and supported legislation for labour rights and labour protection. He also gave support to anti-colonial struggles in neighbouring territories. In Pridi's vision, Thailand could play a special role as agent and exemplar in the creation of a new post-colonial, democratic Southeast Asia.

But other forces did not share this vision. The power which the military had built over the previous decade was not easily doused. The army which had invaded the Shan States in 1942 returned home full of resentment at the lack of support for its withdrawal, and the sacrifice of its territorial gains. The generals looked with distaste and envy at some of the new businessmen and politicians who wanted to profit from the close nexus of power and profit established since 1932.

The royalists also returned to the scene. Ironically, it was Pridi, the anti-royalist ideologue of 1932, who paved the way. Kicked upstairs to be regent from 1942, he enjoyed good relations with some of the royal family, especially Prajadhipok's widow, Rambhai Bharni. As a key leader of Seri Thai, he moved closely with some royal kin who joined Seri Thai in Britain. From 1944, he brought back the royalists, possibly as a political counterweight to Phibun and the army. He granted amnesty to sixty-one political prisoners, mainly the royalists jailed by Phibun, and posthumously restored honours Phibun stripped from Prajadhipok. In September 1945, he invited Seni Pramoj to return from the US to become prime minister, and in December he encouraged King Ananda Mahidol to return temporarily to celebrate his twentieth birthday. Many other royalist exiles returned around the same time, and others emerged from self-imposed silence. One noted they were still 'frightened . . . because they think their property might be confiscated', and 'the extremists among them still hope against hope for a restoration of the Absolute Monarchy as a means of restoring their own lost privileges'.[1] Seni Pramoj and his businessman-aesthete brother Kukrit formed the Democrat Party which opposed Pridi in the Assembly. As Seni noted, despite Pridi's pro-royalist tilt, 'We could never get over the suspicion that Pridi was a Communist'.[2]

The elite contest between militarists, royalists, and pro-Pridi liberals over control of the new nation-state was broadened by urban forces stirred up by the war and the economic dislocation. Japan's forced 'loans' from Thailand had undermined the currency and provoked inflation of over 1000 per cent since 1938. Many officials, whose salaries had not kept pace, were tempted to live off corruption, and many other people off crime. With the disruption of trade, everyday goods were in short supply. Political organization among workers, built by both the Seri Thai resistance and the communists during the war, overflowed into a surge of mass politics with street demonstrations and unionization. In 1945, workers went on strike in rice mills, docks, cement works, oil refineries, and timber yards. The Association of United Workers of Thailand was founded in 1947 and had 60,000 members two years later. As a result of the Allied arms drops, and the disarming of the occupying Japanese, the country was awash with arms and 'Buying arms in Thailand was as easy as buying beer'.[3]

The elite leaderships experimented with manipulating these new mass politics. Pridi's group supported labour organizations and used government funds to sponsor mass demonstrations. Militarists teamed up with fledgling bankers to hire communist intellectuals to run newspapers which lambasted their opponents. This confused period climaxed on 6 June 1946, when the young King Ananda Mahidol was found dead in the palace from a gunshot wound. The case has never been properly explained. Royalist politicians, especially Kukrit and Seni Pramoj, tried to pin the blame on Pridi. Three palace aides, one of whom was an associate of Pridi, were arrested and eventually executed. The police chief who conducted the investigation was a brother-in-law of the Pramoj brothers. He was later found to have bribed witnesses to implicate Pridi. Ananda Mahidol's younger brother was elevated to the throne as King Bhumibol Adulyadej, and returned to Switzerland to complete his education.

On 8 November 1947, the military seized power by coup. Phibun was the figurehead, but the coup was plotted among veterans of the 1942 Shan States campaign – especially the expedition head, General Phin Choonhavan, and his aide and son-in-law Phao Siyanon – with firepower from Colonel Sarit Thanarat who controlled men and tanks in the capital. Phin claimed that Pridi's Seri Thai forces were about to launch a republican revolt. The coup group announced that they acted 'to uphold the honour of the army', to clarify the royal 'assassination plot', and to install a government 'which will respect the principles of Nation, Religion and King' – a conscious revival of Vajiravudh's royal-nationalist formula.[4] The British ambassador reported that the coup was 'a right-wing movement supported by the royal family'.[5] The regent (Prince Rangsit) endorsed the coup within twenty-four hours. Two weeks later the king sent from Switzerland a message stating that 'those who were involved in this operation do not desire power for their own good, but aim only to strengthen the new government which will administer for the prosperity of the nation'.[6]

For the next five years, the coup group and Pridi's supporters waged a low-key civil war. After the coup, Pridi and a few others narrowly escaped overseas. The coup group purged the army of Seri Thai men, and replaced Pridi's men on the boards of state enterprises and banks. In 1948, several northeastern supporters of Pridi were arrested and accused of plotting a rebellion, but subsequently released. In February 1949, Pridi returned to Bangkok and attempted to seize power with the help of the Seri Thai arms cache. Sarit again showed the importance of the city garrisons, bombarding Pridi's forces inside the Grand Palace (hence the 'Palace Rebellion'). Pridi fled once again, this time finally. A month later, three pro-Pridi MPs and one associate were shot while in police custody. Another pro-Pridi MP was shot a month later after surrendering to the police. In June 1951, some remaining Pridi supporters in the navy attempted a coup by seizing Phibun during the ceremony to accept a vessel donated by the US (the 'Manhattan Coup'). Phibun's lieutenants bombed the navy's flagship to the bottom of the Chaophraya River. The fact that Phibun was aboard and had to swim ashore emphasized that power now lay with Sarit and Phao, rather than the figurehead. They proceeded to dismember the navy. The Pridi group had lost to the gun.

After the 1947 coup, the royalist Democrat Party dominated the Cabinet, while the generals held power in the background. But the royalists and generals shared no common platform beyond opposition to Pridi and political liberalization. The royalists wished to revive something of the old political and social order. Phibun saw himself as the custodian of a new, modern nation. For four years, the two groups fenced over appointments and positions. When the government rejected Phao's claims to become police chief, Phao challenged the Democrat interior minister to a duel. In 1951, the Democrats prepared a new constitution which greatly increased the king's formal powers: he appointed the Senate, directly controlled the armed forces, had power to veto legislation, could dismiss any minister, issue decrees, and reform the constitution. The generals appealed to the young king completing his education in Europe to moderate these provisions. When these appeals failed, they took another course. On 26 November 1951, on the eve of the king's return to Thailand to reign, they executed another coup (the Silent or Radio Coup), pushed the Democrats aside, and scrapped this constitution. They brought back a slightly modified version of the 1932 constitution, and formed a Cabinet with nineteen of the total twenty-five from the military. The regent refused to approve the new charter but was simply ignored. Subsequent elections and appointments created a military-dominated parliament. The royalists had been demoted to junior partners in the ruling alliance. The military was in command for the next two decades.

The main justification given for the Silent Coup was that communists were infiltrating the parliament and Cabinet. This vocabulary signified a momentous change. The local battle over the control of the Thai state was being absorbed within a worldwide ideological struggle.

AMERICAN PATRONAGE, ANTI-COMMUNISM, AND MILITARISM

In the 1945–46 peace negotiations, the US became Siam's protector, warding off any extension of British colonial influence. Initially, the US was interested in Thailand as part of a regional plan for rebuilding Japan's economy. With the explosion of leftist anticolonialism in neighbouring countries in 1947–48, the 'loss' of China to communist revolution in 1949, and the commitment of US troops in Korea in 1950, the US grew steadily more interested in Thailand as an ally and base for the prosecution of the Cold War to stem the spread of communism in Asia.

After the 1947 coup, Phibun asked the US for arms and dollars to strengthen the army. But the US still viewed Phibun as a wartime enemy. Over the next two years, however, the US need for friends increased, while Phibun and his allies became practised at espousing anti-communist and anti-Chinese sentiments to appeal for patronage. In September 1949, following Mao Zedong's revolution in China, the US made US$75 million available for supporting allies in Asia, 'such as Thailand', and released £43.7 million which Japan owed Thailand for wartime purchases. In March 1950, the Phibun government, under strong US urging, officially endorsed the French puppet, anti-communist emperor Bao Dai in Vietnam and was rewarded with US$15 million of the US funds. In July 1950, Thailand became the first Asian country to offer troops and supplies for the US campaign in Korea. Phibun told parliament that, 'by sending just a small number of troops as a token of our friendship, we will get various things in return'.[7] A month later, the US provided another US$10 million in economic aid, the World Bank gave a US$25 million loan, and the arms supplies started arriving.

The US was still concerned that the Phibun government's support for anti-communism was lukewarm, and repeatedly urged an internal crackdown. The US even tried to manufacture the evidence to justify fiercer action. Believing that the *Communist Manifesto* had not yet been translated into Thai, the American embassy provided a grant for an American linguist,

William Gedney, and a rising Marxist poet and intellectual, Jit Phumisak, to remedy this defect; but the project was never completed.

The military rulers were not concerned about Thailand's left. Phibun told parliament in 1949 that 'there is now no communist unrest in Thailand'.[8] While the US viewed Asia through the ideological spectacles of the Cold War, Phibun and other Thai leaders were more concerned with the longer-term complexity of their relationship to the big neighbour, China, and the existence of a large Chinese community in Thailand. Phibun was reluctant to provoke any retaliation from China. But he increasingly valued US support, and saw the chance to use repression against other enemies such as the Pridi remnants and opponents in the local Chinese community.

The unification of China in 1949 prompted another wave of nationalist feeling among Thailand's Chinese. The use of Chinese names came back into vogue. Enrolment in Chinese schools soared to 175,000, ten times the number before Phibun imposed restrictions in the late 1930s. Remittances to China increased. At the same time, conflict between the KMT and communists intermittently erupted in battles on Bangkok streets. As in the late 1930s, this surge of Chinese nationalism and disorder provoked government efforts at control. Since the Phibun government perceived 'communism' as largely a Chinese problem, the crackdown on communism and suppression of the Chinese were interlocked.

From late 1950, the government began to harass the press, deport Chinese involved in political activity, smash labour organizations, and use the military and Sangha for anti-communist propaganda. On 10 November 1952, under heavy US pressure, the government moved decisively against the local left. It arrested members of a small remnant group of leftists and Pridi supporters suspected of plotting a coup. It struck at members of the Peace Movement, a Stockholm-based campaign against nuclear weapons which Beijing patronized to bring international pressure against US military action in China and Korea. The local branch included not only some communist party members but also independent leftists like the writer Kulap Saipradit. Over a thousand were arrested, mostly Chinese who were deported, but also sundry enemies of the regime including Thammasat student activists, and Pridi's wife and son.

A new anti-communist law, phrased widely enough to target any dissent, was rushed through three readings in one day. Thirty-seven Thai citizens were jailed, including Kulap and other journalists, the president of the leftist labour federation, and several members of the Communist Party of Thailand (CPT). The main leftist newspapers and bookshops were closed down. In December 1952, another prominent pro-Pridi MP and four other men were strangled, burnt, and buried by Phao's police. In March 1953, a leftist newspaper publisher was shot on his honeymoon. In 1954, another pro-Pridi MP was strangled and dumped in the Chaophraya River tied to a concrete post. Phao gave the police a motto: 'There is nothing under the sun that the Thai police cannot do'.

The government reimposed strict restrictions on Chinese schools, resulting in enrolment dropping by two-thirds. It also increased the alien tax a hundred times to 400 baht, curbed remittances, reintroduced laws reserving occupations for Thai nationals, changed the Nationality Law to impede naturalization, and banned Chinese opera shows in Bangkok.

The US was now impressed. In July 1953, the US National Security Council proposed developing Thailand as an 'anti-communist bastion' in order to 'extend US influence – and local acceptance of it – throughout the whole of Southeast Asia'.[9] After the French defeat in Indochina in 1954, the US organized the Southeast Asia Treaty Organization (SEATO) and committed itself to defend Thailand. The US began to build strategic roads through the northeast, upgrade ports and airfields for military use, and launch a programme of psychological warfare aimed at both peasants and officials.

Thailand had become a US client-state under military rule. But the result was a severe division within Thailand's ruling junta – between army and police.

Beginning in January 1951, the US sent twenty-eight arms shipments with enough equipment for nine army battalions. By 1953, US military aid was equivalent to two-and-a-half times the Thai military budget. With command of this patronage, Sarit Thanarat was able to strengthen his grip on the army. He brought all the troops in Bangkok under his old unit, the First Division of the First Army, staffed with his loyal subordinates. In 1954 he became army chief.

Simultaneously, the CIA began to arm the police. These efforts began from a covert and failed attempt in 1950–51 to sponsor a counter-revolutionary expedition from the northern Thai hills into southern China. The CIA formed close links with the police chief, Phao, and subsequently provided him with tanks, armoured cars, aircraft, helicopters, speedboats, and training by 200 CIA advisers. The police became virtually a rival army. Sarit and Phao were soon locked in competition. Their manpower was roughly equal: 48,000 police and 45,000 in the army. They vied to take over the lucrative monopolies and business patronage originally developed by the Pridi group. They both visited the US in 1954, and returned with aid commitments of US$25 million (Sarit) and US$37 million (Phao). They competed to control the opium trade, and in 1950 came close to fighting a battle over the crop. They jockeyed with one another for political succession. In 1955, Phao asked the US to back him in a coup against Phibun but was declined. Phibun survived by mediating these conflicts. The US increasingly supported him.

Phibun returned to the 1932 group's mission of building the nation-state as the caretaker of the people's welfare and the focus of their loyalty. But the project was no longer pursued by edicts designed to change people's behaviour, but rather through the state's adoption of traditional forms of rule. The government became a public patron of Buddhism. It restored 5535 *wat* and built some new ones. Phibun visited major *wat* during his provincial tours, and presented them with donations and Buddha images. The government also sponsored dance troupes, and undertook restoration of major historical sites, beginning with Phimai, Ayutthaya, and Chiang Saen. A National Culture Council was formed in 1948 and converted to a ministry in 1952. Wichit Wathakan produced a string of plays on the theme 'Power and Glory', celebrating Ramkhamhaeng of Sukhothai and other figures in Thai history. Dreams of a Thai empire were quietly dropped. 'If we can build nationalism in people's hearts', wrote Wichit, 'in the same way that communists make people believe in communism like a religion, we don't need to worry that the country will fall to communism'.[10]

Phibun wished to limit the expansion of royalism. He banned the king from touring outside the capital. The palace resented the obvious attempt to extend state patronage into cultural areas formerly monopolized by royalty. In 1957, Phibun oversaw a grandiose celebration of the 2500th anniversary of the Buddhist era. The king ducked his allotted role on grounds of illness.

In 1955, Phibun announced that he would 'restore democracy' to counter the growing financial and military power of Sarit and Phao. He lifted the ban on political parties, eased press censorship, promised to release political prisoners, cancelled many restrictions on the Chinese, allowed a public 'Hyde Park' for speechifying, passed a Labour Act legalizing unions, and scheduled elections for 1957. In the face of opposition from the palace, he passed a law imposing a 50-rai ceiling on landholdings. He also (less successfully) launched a campaign to suppress opium, and demanded that ministers drop their business involvements. On the pattern of his wartime diplomacy, he tried to gain some independence from the US patrons by reopening links with China. A secret mission went to meet Mao in Beijing and agreed to 'normalize relations in the long run'. Restrictions on trade and travel were eased, and several leftists and leaders of Bangkok's Chinese community visited Beijing.

The US initially welcomed Phibun's support for democracy. But the US need for a client-state and its support for Thai democracy were at cross-purposes. Once press controls were relaxed, the Bangkok newspapers voiced strong resentment of the growing US role in Thailand, and enthusiastic support for the resurgence of China. Left-wing parties reappeared. In the approach to the 1957 elections, the parties and papers representing both Phao-Phibun (now allied) and Sarit opportunistically espoused these anti-American and pro-Chinese sentiments. The launch of the film *The King and I* in the US attracted a barrage of press ridicule.[11] Phao and Phibun won at the 1957 polls, but Sarit accused them of chicanery and suggested the US was complicit. On 18 September 1957, showing yet again the strategic importance of the First Army, Sarit executed a coup, sending Phibun and Phao into exile. The US feared its decade of investment in Thailand might be forfeit. They had long written off Sarit as a corrupt and drunken libertine. In the 1957 election campaign, his press had been the most virulently anti-American. During the coup, his troops came close to attacking the CIA office because of its association with his rival, Phao.

But Sarit needed continued US patronage to retain control over the army. As an olive branch, he appointed as prime minister Pote Sarasin who was US-educated, a former ambassador to the US, and currently secretary-general of SEATO. Elections in December created a parliament with many leftists which Sarit found difficult to control, even with generous use of bribes. In early 1958, Sarit went to the US for medical treatment and held consultations with Eisenhower and Dulles. On 20 October 1958, he carried out a second coup, declared martial law, annulled parliament, discarded the constitution, banned political parties, and arrested hundreds of politicians, journalists, intellectuals, and activists. The US cheered and granted US$20 million in economic aid. The State Department memorialized that this was not a coup but 'an orderly attempt by the present ruling group to solidify its position'.[12] Sarit called it a 'revolution'.

Sarit now unified the armed forces. Units and hardware were removed from the police and placed under the army. Sarit's old subordinates in the First Division moved into the command of the army and into the Cabinet. Future American funding was channelled through the army.

Sarit's consolidation of power and crackdown on left and liberal dissent in 1958 made the US more confident about Thailand as a base. The outbreak of civil war in Laos in 1960 made Thailand a frontline state in US thinking. In 1962, the US committed to defending it against communist attack, stationed the Seventh Fleet in the Gulf of Thailand, and moved 10,000 troops to Thailand. These were shortly removed, but returned in 1964, and were steadily augmented until Thailand was host to 45,000 US army and airforce personnel in 1969. The first air strike on North Vietnam was flown from Thailand in December 1964. Three-quarters of the bomb tonnage dropped on North Vietnam and Laos in 1965–68 was flown out of seven US bases in eastern Thailand. Thai troops were secretly hired as virtual mercenaries to fight in Laos from 1960. Some 11,000 Thai troops went to fight alongside the US in South Vietnam in 1967.

From 1962, the US poured money into the Border Patrol Police and counter-insurgency operations inside Thailand. US military aid quadrupled over the 1960s and peaked in 1972 at US$123 million. Economic aid grew in parallel to peak at the same level, with much of it channelled to the police and military programmes. With US backing and with state power, the Thai military budget increased even faster, from around US$20 million a year in the 1950s to around US$250 million a year in the early 1970s. Dollars consolidated Thailand's militarized state.

The US built an imposing new embassy in Bangkok, and sent a prominent Second World War soldier, 'Wild Bill' Donovan, to serve as ambassador. After the US located the SEATO headquarters in Bangkok, several UN bodies, international organizations, and American foundations followed this lead. Bangkok's *farang* population increased rapidly. Unlike in the colonial period, when this population was very varied, now it was distinctly American. Bangkok was chosen for the GIs' R&R ('rest and recreation') tours, with 45,000 visiting by 1967 (Figure 13). New Phetchaburi Road became an 'American strip' lined with bars, nightclubs, brothels, and massage parlours. Similar clusters mushroomed around the US air bases. The sex industry was not new; the public garishness was.

Estimates of the number of prostitutes in Bangkok ranged up to 300,000. The interior minister, General Praphat Charusathian, wanted even more because they attracted tourists and boosted the economy. Until the late 1950s, Thailand had no organized tourism industry, only 871 tourist-standard rooms, and only 40,000 foreign visitors a year. In 1959, a tourist authority was formed as part of development planning. In the early 1960s, a new runway was built at Don Muang airport to accommodate jets. Total foreign visitors grew rapidly to over 600,000 by 1970, when tourism was ranked as the fifth largest earner of foreign exchange. The largest group of visitors was American. The mid-1960s saw a frenzy of hotel building which added over 7000 rooms.

The city changed in shape, style, and tastes. New suburbs clustered around the schools, shops, cinemas, and clubs catering for westerners. Elite Thai families were attracted to the same areas because of their perceived status and their rising property values. Foreign goods – and especially American brand names – acquired new status value. The American era

Figure 13: Really R&R. American servicemen leap ashore into the arms of Pattaya's
Hawaiians.

redefined what was modern and aspirational, especially for the urban middle
class.

DEVELOPMENT AND CAPITAL

The US set out to develop a free-market economy to cement Thailand into
the US camp of the Cold War.

President Truman introduced the word 'development' in his inaugural
speech in 1947. Sarit understood its role as a key concept of the US global
mission, and as a new and powerful justification for the power of the nation-
state – 'progress' translated for the American era. His regime converted the
new Thai coining, *phatthana*, into its watchword: 'Our important task in
this revolutionary era is development which includes economic development, educational development, administrative development, and everything else'. Sarit popularized slogans such as: 'Work is money. Money is
work. This brings happiness.'[13]

Sarit welcomed a World Bank mission to Thailand after his first coup.
Its report was transformed into Thailand's first five-year development plan,
launched in 1961. The plan condemned the state-led development policies

pursued since the late 1930s and announced: 'The key note of the public development programme is, therefore, the encouragement of economic growth in the private sector'.[14]

The US helped to set up a new bureaucratic infrastructure for promoting development – a planning board, budget bureau, investment promotion machinery, and restructured central bank. US advisers arrived to help run them. Sarit also scrapped Phibun's labour legislation and initially suppressed labour politics completely. But US advisers counselled a more subtle approach. Sarit's government instituted many new regulations governing urban labour, and established a labour bureaucracy to administer them.

The first Thai recruits to the new technocracy had often been educated in the old world. But the US began to create a new generation of technocrats who shared an American viewpoint. Several senior officials were taken to the US for training. Around 1500 went on Fulbright or similar grants between 1951 and 1985. The numbers attending US higher education rose from a few hundred in the 1950s to 7000 by the early 1980s.

The early economic plans had three aims: intensify exploitation of Thailand's natural resources to deliver growth; transfer some of the resulting surplus for investment in the urban economy; and facilitate foreign investment to acquire technology. US firms were allowed 100 per cent ownership, while other foreign investors were limited to a minority share. US firms began to set up in Thailand from the late 1950s, but the volume of US investment was modest – confined mostly to mining and petroleum firms, a few consumer businesses like Coca-Cola, and projects directly connected to the war in Indochina. For most US capital, Thailand was too remote, unknown, and risky. The main beneficiaries of this capital-friendly development strategy were the Thai-Chinese entrepreneurial groups which had risen since the 1930s.

The emergence of new business groups had begun tentatively before the Second World War. The 'Big Five' rice traders built integrated trading businesses, and a handful of long-settled Chinese families ventured into manufacturing. These groups developed relationships with the new post-1932 politicians that enabled them to survive and strengthen through the turmoil of the war and its aftermath.

The process of accumulation quickened from the war years. Many businesses suffered in the war economy, but a few profited spectacularly. Some Chinese entrepreneurs refused to cooperate with the Japanese because of their invasion of China, but others were tempted by the profits and grateful for the relaxation of Phibun's anti-Chinese constraints. The Japanese military worked directly through the Chinese Chamber of Commerce to secure wartime supplies. Some firms did very well. A handful of shophouse scrap-metal dealers, for example, were boosted by the extraordinary demand for scarce metal. After the war, one of them (Phonprapha) progressed to importing and then manufacturing Japanese cars; another became Thailand's largest steel maker (Sahaviriya); and a third developed expertise in making sugar-crushing machinery, and became a major sugar miller (Asdathon). In 1945, one prominent businessman was shot dead in the street, probably in resentment against wartime profiteering.

The forced withdrawal of European firms provided another source of opportunity, especially in banking. Chin Sophonpanich was a shophouse trader who shuttled between Bangkok and China. In 1944–45, he was part of a syndicate which had suddenly found the capital funds for a whole range of new ventures, including gold trading, liquor, cinemas, match manufacture, and banking. He helped to set up systems of currency exchange and remittance to replace the services of the departed European banks. In 1944, Chin's group founded the Bangkok Bank, one of seven banks formed around the armistice.

The economic pace slowed in the post-war disorder, but then quickened with the pan-Asian Korean War boom of 1950–52, and the growing US economic patronage of Thailand. The new banks became central to an emerging business class. After the Chinese revolution in 1949, their main remittance business dwindled, and they refocused on the domestic economy. Through the 1950s, they formed upcountry branch networks which collected the savings of farmers and local traders. They used the proceeds to invest directly in new business opportunities, and also to loan to associated families. They developed Asian regional networks, which collected trading information. Along with other entrepreneurs, they made friends with the generals who came to power in 1947, and hence gained protection and also access to profitable business opportunities. Bangkok Bank took off after the generals found government funds to help it over a liquidity crisis. The Phonprapha car import business prospered after the government bought its buses and ordained that all taxis should be Nissan. The Techaphaibun built a liquor empire from distilleries which the government sold off cheap.

The banking families and their associates took the lion's share of the succession of new opportunities which appeared in the era of US-directed 'development'. The policy to develop agricultural exports and drive the agrarian frontier through the uplands (see below) created new opportunities in crop processing and export. The Wanglee rice-trading family became one of the biggest exporters of upland crops. The Chiaravanon family, which had begun importing Chinese seeds in the pre-war period, built mills to convert the new crops into animal feed, and then developed an integrated chicken farming business which became the country's largest business empire, Charoen Pokphand (CP).

By the 1960s, demand from the growing urban economy, and government policy to replace imports with domestic manufacture, created a new range of manufacturing opportunities. Families which had once been importers now invited their foreign partners to invest in local factories to overcome import barriers. In 1962, the Phonprapha family persuaded Nissan to set up a car assembly plant, followed by another for Yamaha motorcycles two years later. The Sahaviriya, former scrap-metal dealers, started making nails and barbed wire, expanded to construction steel in the late 1960s, and then took a Japanese partner for more complex products. In 1960, the Chokewatana family, which had begun importing Japanese products during the war, persuaded the Japanese Lion group to join in production of toothpaste and detergent, and added other similar ventures to its Sahapat consumer goods empire through the 1960s.

Demand for services soon followed. The Chirathiwat family had pioneered modern retail development since the late 1940s, but took off after opening its Silom Central department store in 1968, catering for a new enthusiasm for western goods in the era of American patronage. The Omphut family, which had earlier owned liquor shops and agencies, invested in a string of massage parlours, cinemas, hotels, and restaurants to cater for a new demand for entertainment among American visitors and local patrons. The family later transferred the proceeds into retail (the Mall group) and banking (Bank of Asia).

A few of these rising entrepreneurial families had roots back in the late nineteenth-century boom in rice, timber, and regional trading (for example, Lamsam and Wanglee). Most, however, had arrived, usually with nothing more than the proverbial 'one pillow and one mat', in the inter-war period when immigration surged as China's economic and political crisis deepened. After the 1949 Chinese revolution, the route back to the mainland home was closed. Families concentrated on building their family and business futures in Thailand. They prospered by exploiting their own family labour, saving hard, reinvesting heavily in their businesses, prioritizing their children's education, developing family networks, and drawing on political contacts.

Around thirty family groups dominated this era through their privileged access to capital and political favours. They became business conglomerates by diversifying into property, hotels, hospitals, finance, insurance, and other ventures to provide occupations for sons (and sometimes daughters). Leading lights of these families took prominent roles in speech-group and welfare associations. They exchanged marriage partners, crossing old boundaries of clan and dialect. They invested in one another's ventures to share profit and risk. The thirteen banks, which persuaded the government to ban new entries and exclude foreign competition, towered above them all. Their deposits grew at an average 20 per cent a year for twenty years (the 1960s and 1970s). The four largest accounted for most of this growth, and each had hundreds of subsidiary companies, many accommodating the ruling generals on their boards. Below this elite sprawled a mass of smaller shophouse family enterprises with similar origins and aspirations.

In 1966, the American scholar, Fred Riggs, described the new Thai-Chinese business elite as 'pariah entrepreneurs',[15] condemned by their ethnic origins to low social status and political subordination to the bureaucrats and generals. In fact, the situation was more complex and less rigid than this judgement suggests. The legal framework for incorporation into the nation-state was now fixed. Children born in Thailand (that is, second generation) qualified for nationality, and their children (third generation) gained full civic rights, including voting, entry to parliament, and service in the armed forces. Some distinguished long-settled Chinese families, who had roots in the nineteenth century or earlier, were by now firmly embedded in the 'traditional' elite. They intermarried with royal-related families, and supplied some of the most prominent civilian and military officials, professionals, educators, and technocrats. They also sometimes acted as brokers for the new men of the Chinese community. The Sarasin family, for example, had become one of the most prominent bureaucratic families in the post-war era. Yet Pote Sarasin also acted as patron of one of the most remarkable new entrepreneurs, Charoen Siriwattanapakdi, who rose from humble origins to dominate the liquor business. Pote invested in Charoen's businesses, guaranteed his loans, and helped him to acquire the status equal to his rising wealth. Similarly, Anand Panyarachun, who was descended from one of the great Hokkien families of the late nineteenth century via an alliance with a prominent Mon family, started his career on a classic pattern of European education and the foreign service, but then joined one of the major conglomerates, and became an important figure in the diplomacy between government and big business.

The new business elite families overcame all difficulties through money and political connections. For the mass of recent immigrants, the nationality issue was more vexed. Although the route back to China was closed in 1949, hopes that this might be temporary faded slowly. Families naturally retained pride in their culture, and attachment to the language and customs they knew. The protagonist of a 1969 novel on Bangkok's Thai-Chinese said: 'We shall remain Chinese wherever we find ourselves'.[16] The language of everyday business, especially in the vast mass of shophouse family firms, remained Chinese, especially Teochiu.

The state's insistence that the immigrant Chinese merge themselves into the nation, particularly by adopting the Thai language and displaying political loyalty, was rooted in the ideology of a unified, imagined 'Thai culture'. In the short term, the delay in granting full civic rights, and the occasional public attacks on the Chinese, helped bureaucrats and generals to extract gatekeeping fees and to resist pressure for political participation. The post-1949 identification of 'China' with 'communism' added another dimension which the US patrons encouraged. But this situation could only be temporary. As a result of inter-war immigration, the Chinese and their *lukjin* descendants dominated the urban population. Promotion of urban-biased economic development made them wealthy. Eventually, numbers and money would have political impact.

THE UPLANDS FRONTIER

> In 1961 Headman Li banged the drum, and the villagers came to the meeting.
> 'I Headman Li will now inform you what this meeting is all about;
> The authorities have ordered all villagers to raise ducks and *sukon*'.
> Grandpa Si with the shaky head asked: 'What's this *sukon*?'
> Headman Li answered like a shot,
> 'A *sukon*, yes, it's just an ordinary puppy, a puppy, an ordinary puppy'.

The joke in this hugely popular song turned around the word *sukon*. It means 'pig', but is a fancy Sanskritized word found mainly in official reports and dictionaries. The song satirized the 1960s' passion for 'development' under which officials from a remote, urban culture began telling villagers what to do.

The second transformation of Thailand's rural landscape and society began after the Second World War. After a century of the rice frontier, land in the Chaophraya delta and other smaller rice-bowls was fully occupied. Moreover, with better food, no warfare, and some control of epidemic diseases, population growth had spurted up to 3 per cent a year by the 1950s. Under these pressures, the frontier moved beyond the rivers and coastal areas into the upland plains.

Most of the area beyond the river valleys was still covered by forest. Malaria and other diseases were still a deterrent to settlement. Most of those who died building the Japanese railway in the western forests during the Second World War were taken by fever. The upper slopes of the hills were inhabited by hill peoples, including Karen, Hmong, Yao, Muser, and Akha. More trickled in, particularly in flight from the turmoil in southern China. From the Second World War onwards, these areas were connected to the international drug trade, enabling hill communities to obtain a cash income from opium cultivation. Loggers trawled the forests for valuable timber.

Between the highlands and the floodplains were large areas of undulating upland plains. The largest expanse was in the northeast, the Khorat Plateau, covering almost a third of the country's territory. Other areas were found on the fringes of the river systems. Three changes begun in the 1950s pushed the frontier out of the lowlands and into the upland forests. First, the Malaria Eradication Programme reduced malaria deaths from 206 per 100,000 in 1949 to 2 per 100,000 in 1987. Second, the US sponsored the construction of highways as part of its war campaign in Indochina, beginning with the Mitraphap (Friendship) highway cut from Bangkok into the northeast in 1955–57. Third, the new development strategy prioritized more intensive use of Thailand's natural resources. Dams were built for power and irrigation. Mines and agribusinesses were granted government promotion subsidies. Restrictions on logging were removed to supply match, paper, construction, and other industries.

In the Chaophraya delta, the spearhead of the frontier had been the canal-digger's hoe. In the uplands, it was the logger's saw. Trees were felled for roads, dams, mines, US air bases, or just for the timber itself. Some of the large numbers of workers hired on these projects settled on their outskirts, and cleared further areas for cultivation. Over a decade or so, many places went through three waves of settlement. First came the loggers, along with early settlers who practised shifting cultivation and then moved on, following the logging parties. Next came lowland farmers, sometimes commuting between their lowland paddy-farm, and an upland plot which could be worked in a different season. The third wave brought the landless poor, squeezed out of the valleys by population pressure. Often they were trucked in by a new breed of agrarian entrepreneurs who hired them tractors to plough the land, lent them money to plant the crop, and took away the produce. These entrepreneurs worked in turn for export agents, sugar mills, tobacco-curing yards, oil pressers, rubber packers, feedmills, and canneries which sprang up in boom towns throughout the uplands zone.

Borne along by these powerful forces, the frontier moved through the upland forests like a firestorm. In forty years, Thailand's cultivated area tripled. Almost all the additional area was in the uplands. About half was planted to rice, and the rest to a wide range of cash crops. Sugar plantations again appeared on the raised areas around the rim of the Chaophraya delta. Rubber trees and oil palms were planted on the slopes of the hills running down the peninsula. Pineapple fields nibbled into the western forests. Cattle ranches spread along the escarpment between the central plain and the Khorat Plateau. Tobacco fields appeared around the northern valleys.

But some land soon proved unsuitable for such crops. The virgin fertility was quickly lost. Rainfall was too unreliable. Soil eroded from the slopes, and subsoil moisture disappeared once too many trees were removed. Underground saline deposits were leached upwards by irrigation. Over large areas, only maize and cassava could survive in these harsh conditions. These two crops came to occupy half the total area of this upland cash-crop expansion. They were sold to feedmills and other starch producers. The typical farmer on the uplands frontier owned a 25-rai rolling plot, growing rain-fed rice in the hollows and maize or cassava on the slopes. Between the 1950s and 1970s, another 70,000 of such farms occupying an additional 2 million rai appeared each year.

These farms were hacked out of the forest, which had covered two-thirds of the country at the time of the Second World War but only one-third just thirty years later. The government tacitly encouraged this destruction because the export of these new crops drove the expansion in the national economy. When communist rebellion began to spread through the forests in the mid-1960s, the government encouraged clearing even more to deny cover to the rebels. It built military roads into the forests, and shepherded pioneer settlements along them. It burnt areas around the rebel bases. It handed out concessions to loggers who were supposed to clear areas and then reforest them. By 1986, these concessions covered half the country. In the mid-1970s, forest was disappearing at the rate of almost 600,000 rai a year.

At first, this frontier ran ahead of any government control. Force rather than law decided possession of land or settlement of disputes. But, by the 1960s, the government had become concerned about the spread of communist bases, and suspected that the lawlessness not only facilitated the rebels' activities but also encouraged settler communities to support them. Backed by US aid funds, government offices moved into the uplands zone. In the vanguard were the special police and army units engaged in counter-insurgency. They were followed by schools, and then a range of offices set up to dispense aid funds in an attempt to win the 'hearts and minds' of the peasants. They built village roads, sank wells, connected up electricity, and provided disaster relief.

The society which developed in these upland conditions was very different from that of the paddy tracts where communities were oriented to subsistence, sold a surplus, and were gradually drawn deeper into the market economy. While some of the new upland villages were settled by kin groups, most were a mix of people coming from all directions. In the early stages of the upland expansion, many moved out from the old paddy tracts, especially into the northeast. Later, many northeasterners moved south to open up new tracts in the coastal basins down the peninsula. Some evolved communal institutions to cope with the harsh environment, but most did not.

Few upland farmers were self-reliant. For cash-crop cultivation they needed to buy seeds, fertilizers, and pesticides, and perhaps hire equipment for land preparation and harvesting. Many producing vegetables, sugar, or poultry were tied into contract farming schemes where they supplied little more than the labour. Those growing tobacco, rubber, or oil palms were often obliged to sell to a sole local purchaser. Maize and cassava farmers worked on annual advances from the local trader. Only a minority of the households had enough paddy land for subsistence, and the unreliability of the rainfall meant that subsistence was never assured. Upland households were bound to the market to sell their produce and buy their staple. The local economy was geared around flows of inputs, credit, and government patronage into the village from outside, and flows of cash crops outwards.

Upland areas developed a distinct elite of people who straddled these inward and outward flows. These included the crop trader who often doubled as a moneylender and was likely to be someone of Chinese origin with connections to the local town and beyond. It might also include loggers with links to nearby sawmills, and owners of the trucks and buses that connected the locality to the outside world. It also included the local police chief, army commander, and district officer who wielded the government's power and dispensed the government's patronage. The post of *kamnan*, the head of a group of villages, became central to these networks of commerce and officialdom, and rivalry for the post was often fierce. This local elite was usually overwhelmingly male, and ritually bound together by a drinking circle. By pooling their commercial and official power, they could further profit from illegal businesses and official chicanery: illegal logging would go unnoticed, land titles be generated in the paperwork, smuggling proceed unimpeded.

Most settlers arrived poor and remained so. The nation's first count in 1962–63 found over three-quarters of rural households in the northeast living below a poverty line. By 1988, the proportion had fallen, but only to around a half. Few had a full land title. The government failed to extend the titling system into the upland tracts, so most had only an occupancy certificate. In 1964, the government resolved to preserve 40 per cent of the country as forest, and began mapping areas in which people would not be allowed to settle. This mapping exercise ran in parallel with the rapid destruction and settlement of these same forest areas. By 1974, perhaps 5–6 million people were living inside the official 'forest' and were considered 'squatters' who did not qualify for any land deed at all. By the early 1990s, the number had risen to 10–12 million, over a third of the whole rural population.

PEASANTS INTO THE MARKET

Development also transformed the old paddy tracts. After 1945, international agencies were interested in expanding Thailand's rice surplus to help feed the war-torn countries of Asia immediately, and the growing population of Asia in the longer term. Van der Heide's 1902 plan to regularize the water supply of the whole Chaophraya delta was revived and updated with international expertise and sponsorship. The Chainat dam at the head of the delta was completed in 1957, and two more dams on the upper tributaries added over the next decade. These dams lessened the risk of seasonal flooding or scarcity. The rivers and an extended canal network spread the flow from the dams more evenly across the whole delta zone.

The initial impact of this big investment was disappointing. But the 1960s 'Green Revolution', sparked by research on rice technology in the Philippines, combined with greater water security to bring big changes. New paddy seeds adapted to Thai conditions were developed and distributed in the 1960s. Fertilizer and pesticide use rapidly increased. Two-wheeled tractors, developed in China and known as 'iron buffalo', were locally produced and rapidly replaced their four-legged counterpart. The dams spread the water supply over a long period, the new seeds ripened more quickly, and the iron buffaloes shortened the time for land preparation. Favoured areas, especially around the top and sides of the Chaophraya delta, could now grow two or three crops of rice a year.

On a lesser scale, government water projects brought the same benefits to other established paddy tracts. The Mae Teng project extended the same principle of stable water supply to the Chiang Mai valley. Dams on the upper tributaries of the Chaophraya created more secure water supplies along valleys which had been highly prone to seasonal flooding. Barrages improved the usability of the water along the Mun-Chi river system of the northeast. Smaller projects were built in the rice-bowls down the peninsula coasts.

With these innovations, paddy yields-per-rai in the central plain doubled in thirty years. Rice exports surged again, making Thailand the world's largest rice exporter. People benefited. The proportion of households below the poverty line in the central region fell from two-fifths in 1962–63 to just one-eighth only thirteen years later.

In the mid-1970s, a Japanese anthropologist returned to a village in the upper delta which he had first studied a decade earlier. Then, it had been a recent frontier settlement of smallholder farms using exchange labour and traditional technology. He was amazed by the change over the intervening handful of years. Bullocks had disappeared, replaced by small tractors. Exchange labour had collapsed, and professional agents now managed people in labour gangs. Traditional rice varieties had been replaced by the new Green Revolution seeds nourished with fertilizer and chemicals. Most of all, the anthropologist noted the mental change. Villagers who had described the local rituals to him only a decade ago now exclaimed that 'the rice spirit is no match for chemical fertilizer'.[17]

This anthropologist, along with many others, feared that this rapid commercialization, combined with the pressure on land, would break the society apart. In other countries, the Green Revolution favoured the big farmers, and many predicted a similar result in Thailand. But the Chaophraya delta's experience was subtly different.

There were no scale barriers preventing the Chaophraya delta smallholders gaining access to the new technology. With land pressure, farms became smaller – the old 25-rai average was reduced to around 19 rai. But smallholders could compensate by investing in more productive technology, or tapping a growing market for rented land. There was another spurt of mobility as families shifted around the delta in search of new opportunities, now framed not by access to land but by access to inputs, water, and markets. The smallholders did not disappear. Indeed, their numbers increased markedly. But they were now more conclusively transformed into market-oriented farmers, supplementing their family resources of knowledge and labour with purchased technology, wage labour, and rented land.

A few entrepreneurial farmers played the market to amass large land-holdings. But at the same time, some of the old noble landlords took the opportunity of rising land prices to liquidate their holdings. The concentration of landholding increased only marginally, and the large proportion of land worked by owner-occupiers barely changed.

At the social base, the number of households with no land or too little land slowly increased. By the 1970s, about a fifth of households in the central plain and in the northern valleys were landless, and around another tenth were land-poor. Many, particularly in the north, survived by share-cropping. The rest worked mainly as wage labour.

The big change was that smallholder households now dealt with and depended on commercial markets much more than before. They hired tractors to level or raise their land to take best advantage of the secure water supply. They bought high-yielding seeds, fertilizer, and chemicals. They invested in iron buffaloes and water pumps. Some switched from rice to fruit, vegetables, and other higher-value crops. Many now grew high-yielding varieties of rice which did not suit local tastes. More households bought their staple food from the market. Weaving and other crafts withered away, and the number of shops and occasional markets increased. To increase rural credit, in 1966 the government created an agricultural bank (BAAC) which by 1979 was advancing 19 billion baht a year. In 1975, the government forced the commercial banks to direct at least 5 per cent of their lending to agriculture.

Smallholders also dealt more with the government. As in the uplands, schools, police, and district offices spread into the countryside. Unlike in the uplands, the government opened land offices and began to give full land titles. Water had earlier been a gift of nature, but, as the saying came to be, 'nowadays water has a master'. Farmers often had to negotiate with officials to get their share.

Also as in the uplands, an elite appeared which handled these relations with the commercial and official worlds beyond the village. As a popular song joked, a few seemed to monopolize a whole range of new business opportunities:

> Talking of riches, none equals me.
> All over Suphan I'm known as the big millionaire.
> Even my thousands of cattle have their teeth capped with gold.
> I've a rice mill, a construction store, a pottery, an ice factory, a
> brewery.

I've just built an iron works, gambling joint, upholstery, and several
   funeral parlours.
But I stay clear of the police station.[18]

The subject of this song was female – quite common in the delta where
the traders and rice barge-owners had often been women. But generally
within rural society, the position of women had declined over the past
century. After corvée ended and settled agriculture spread, men took the
leading role in agricultural work. As contacts with the (male) merchant and
(male) official increased, men displaced women from their roles in trade.
Local spirit worship, often led by female experts, gradually but incompletely
ceded space to Buddhism with its exclusively male monkhood.

   Almost everywhere, communal practices of exchange labour faded away.
Villagers might still cooperate strongly for managing irrigation, festivals,
and the local *wat*, but increasingly they dealt with state and market as
individuals.

VILLAGE AND CITY

The era of development prompted rural migration into the city. For over
a century, the open land frontier had drawn people away from the city.
Most labour for the rice mills, sawmills, port, and other enterprises which
boomed in the colonial era came from Chinese migration. Because of high
natural productivity and expanding supplies of land, rural wages were high,
creating little incentive to look for work in the city.

   From the 1920s, some villagers were pushed to the city by bad seasons and
periodic slumps in the international rice trade. In 1949, immigration from
China was effectively stopped. Over the next two decades, urban growth
on the one hand, and growing demographic pressure and exhaustion of
land in the Chaophraya delta on the other, widened the gap between urban
and rural wages. More rural people were drawn to work in the city. Road
construction and new bus services made such moves easier. In the 1960s,
Bangkok's population spurted from 1.8 to 3 million people. The growth
of the city not only created factory work but also jobs as drivers, house
servants, shop and restaurant workers, and construction labourers. The
arrival of US troops and the use of Thailand for 'rest and recreation' from
the Vietnam war boosted the sex industry. From the early 1970s, labour
contractors conveyed people to work overseas, especially in the Middle
East.

A complex pattern of migration was established which continued over decades to come. Teenagers left the village to complete their education, to make some money, or just to have some fun and broader experience. Some stayed in the city only a few years, but others remained permanently, or returned to the village only at retirement. Meanwhile there were also many shorter-term moves. Most farming depended on the monsoon rains and hence lasted only half the year. Some people sought work elsewhere for the other half. Others shuttled back and forth between planting and harvest. By the late 1970s, 1.5 million people were moving between village and city in these seasonal flows. At first, most of the migrants came from the central plain because of proximity and because of the land crisis. By the 1970s, northeasterners had also begun to join the flow, particularly on a seasonal basis. The migration stream contained almost as many women as men.

This passage from village to city was reflected in *luk thung* (literally, 'child of the field') music which boomed in the 1960s and 1970s. The music was rooted in folk styles from the central region where most of the migrants originated. But the boom was created by the development of a national radio network in the 1960s, the construction of roads which conveyed touring roadshows around the villages, and the development of audio-tapes. To succeed, singers had to have an authentic rural background. The female star, Phumphuang Duangjan, had been a child labourer on sugar plantations. The male star, Sayan Sanya, had been a rice farmer:

> I studied only to fourth grade.
> I travelled from Don Chedi, Suphanburi, in the forest.
> Singer Sayan Sanya, a rural lad,
> I gambled my life with my songs.

The songs convey the excitement and the heartache of leaving the village for the city. Many songs described new urban lives as truck drivers, waitresses, bus conductors, factory hands, and sex workers. They lamented the crop failures, natural disasters, and general poverty that had forced them to migrate. They warned other migrants that city people would look down on them with comments like 'the poor are smelly'. They cautioned migrant girls about predatory urban men. Several songs emphasized that the city sojourn was a temporary life-stage, and that the singer intended to return as soon as possible to the village. The singer of 'I won't forget Isan' explained to his girlfriend left behind:

> I have to go though I miss you all the time.
> If I save enough I would ask for your hand.

> I'm poor and that's why I have to leave you
> To find money in Bangkok.
> Please wait until I save enough.

The sheer energy of *luk thung* celebrated the excitement of experiencing the city. But the content of the songs emphasized the difficulties, and the desire to retain contact with the village. Many songs returned to the theme of remembering the peace of the village, the warmth of the family, and the boyfriend or girlfriend left behind. Phumphuang sang:

> Mum and dad, help me, or else I'm dead this time.
> My youth and beauty ruined because of a city slicker's sweet talk.
> Mum and dad, help me to go back home.

THE PASSING OF SAKDINA

The old elite of great households was not destroyed after 1932, but its role and significance changed. For sixteen years there was no resident king to serve as the ritual focus of the old order. Many royal family members were purged from the top ranks of military and civilian officialdom. The Ayutthayan-era ranks and job-names were discontinued from 1932 and banned in 1941 (though some, including Phibun and Wichit, converted the latter into a personal name). People in the bureaucracy were now known by a name which recognized their individuality and their family, rather than their rank and position as granted by the king. The education of new officials, especially at Thammasat University, stressed service to the state rather than to the monarchy. The great inflation of the Second World War decimated the real value of official salaries, eroding the overall cachet of bureaucratic office. Yet this transformation was far from complete. The conventional term for bureaucrat remained *kha ratchakan*, the servant of the king.

The great households which had been the foundations of the old elite changed in character. Chulalongkorn was the last king to practise and hence endorse polygamy. Vajiravudh had only one wife and one daughter at the very end of his reign. King Prajadhipok had only one wife, Queen Rambhai Bharni, and no children. The 1935 legal code recognized only one marital partner. Many elite men still practised polygamy but increasingly by taking minor wives in serial sequence or in separate domiciles. Many elite children rebelled against parental control over their choice of marriage partners. Great households could no longer build influence through strategic webs of polygamous marriage connections. Once the great households lost this ability, and their privileged grip on high office, they began to disintegrate. Kukrit Pramoj's hugely popular novel *Si phaendin* (Four reigns, 1950) traced the fragmentation of one fictional aristocratic family as the members of its new generation are drawn off to varied careers, rival political ideas, and diverse marriage partners (*farang*, Chinese). The bombing of the family house in 1944 symbolizes the household's final disintegration.

The state ceased to act as a mechanism for the old elite's financial support and accumulation. Allowances to the sprawling royal clan ended in 1932. Other great households lost sinecures. The crown's landed property and investments, mostly accumulated in the Fifth Reign, were managed by the Crown Property Bureau, rather like a foundation. Other great families fell back on the land and other assets they had been able to accumulate over the previous half-century. Urban land, in particular, inflated in value and sustained many families. But other assets lost value because of changing fashions and the great wartime inflation. And the culture of polygamy, which had once built the great households, now divided and dissipated their assets by inheritance. A popular memoir described how Queen Rambhai Bharni and a chance co-inheritor divided up Prajadhipok's personal assets by drawing lots over the land deeds, then sharing out the movables in the grounds of Sukhothai Palace, with many items auctioned immediately to Chinese dealers or pilfered later because of neglect.[19]

Education was a more secure support for the descendants of the old households. Chulalongkorn had encouraged his kin and other aristocrats to invest in education so their sons could contribute to progress. The culture of sending sons overseas for education, preferably to Europe, had taken strong root among the elite. In the post-1945 era, many descendants of the royal clan and great households had outstanding careers as professionals, educators, technocrats, scientists, and artists.

A handful with royal or noble blood were drawn to the People's Party from conviction, and had political careers after 1932, especially Wan Waithayakon who became an envoy and virtual foreign minister. Even after many exiles returned at the end of the Second World War, very few gained political prominence. The Pramoj brothers, Seni and Kukrit, were the outstanding exceptions. The revival of the monarchy in the post-war era (see next chapter) focused very much on the immediate royal family. Personal titles which indicated royal family membership (prince, MC, MR, ML) remained in use and carried social cachet. But the driving forces of society and politics were now the new generals, businessmen, and technocrats.

CONCLUSION

The Second World War proved to be a boundary between eras. The memory of an absolute monarchy faded. The great households disintegrated. The old colonial powers retreated. The liberal nationalist ideas of the 1920s and 1930s were first pushed aside by the militaristic nationalism of the wartime era, then crushed by the anti-communist fervour in the aftermath.

After the war, the US recruited Thailand as ally and base for prosecuting the Cold War in Asia. The colonial concept of 'progress' and its local interpretation as the cultivation of a new national citizen was replaced by the concept of 'development' and its more precise focus on economic development through private enterprise. 'Development' released the potential of the urban society imported from southern China over the past century – and especially the large chunk which had arrived in the last surge of immigration in the inter-war period. Entrepreneur families grabbed opportunities created by the collapse of the old colonial economy in wartime, and were then boosted by the money flows, ideological commitment, bureaucratic infrastructure, and political links of the era of US patronage. From the late 1950s, the Thai economy grew at a sustained average of 7 per cent a year, one of the fastest rates in the developing world.

This growth came from more intensive exploitation of natural resources and people. Another surge of the agrarian frontier completed the transformation of the natural landscape of forest into a zone of intensive agricultural exploitation. Peasant smallholders were bound much more firmly into the market, and subject more to governmental instruction and patronage. Increasing numbers were squeezed out of the villages to work in the factories and service establishments of the expanding neo-colonial city.

In the American era, Thailand became a subject of academic study. By avoiding colonial rule, it had not had such full attention earlier. American academics portrayed a society where passivity and paternalism were traditional. Sociologists discovered that Thai society was 'loosely structured', meaning it lacked institutions and traditions for collective action. Anthropologists explained that Theravada Buddhism concentrated people's minds on merit in future lives, not the present day. Riggs argued that the 'bureaucratic polity', meaning the absence of democratic politics, resulted in large part because Chinese businessmen had to depend on bureaucratic patronage. Historians reproduced Damrong's story of a singular and dominant monarchical tradition stretching back through Ayutthaya to a Sukhothai 'golden age'. There were also dissenters who examined the diverse cultures of outlying regions, the little traditions of resistance and revolt, and the rise of militarism. But the mainstream of American scholarship provided reassurance that the current military dictatorship, perched over a passive society and legitimized by monarchy, was a natural outcome of Thailand's history, sociology, and culture, and was unlikely to be threatened.

Yet the results of Thailand's insertion into the ideological contest of the Cold War were complex. In Thailand, the US underwrote dictatorship, but at home it exemplified ideals of liberalism and republicanism which were experienced by more and more Thai visiting the US as students or absorbing its cultural output in literature, song, and film. Opposition to neo-colonialism, military dictatorship, and rapid capitalist exploitation also looked for inspiration both backwards into Thailand's pre-American past and outwards to America's Cold War rivals. The crucible for this conflicting mix of new ideas was a new generation of students.

7

Ideologies, 1940s to 1970s

The era of development incorporated more people more firmly into the national market economy. The era of 'national security' brought more people more firmly under the direction of the nation-state. Armed with new funds and technologies, the nation-state extended its power deeper into society, and farther into the villages and hills. Struggles to control and direct the nation-state now affected the lives and commanded the interest of larger numbers of the nation's citizens.

In the late 1950s, the US brought together the military, businessmen, and royalists – the three forces that had tussled since 1932 – in a powerful alliance. Together they resurrected and embellished the vision of a dictatorial strong state, demanding unity in order to achieve development and to fight off an external enemy – in this era, 'communism'. But the alliance's strength was undermined by the generals' abuse of power and their obvious subordination to American policy. Opposition to the intensity of capitalist exploitation grew. Protests emerged against American domination. Communists launched a guerrilla war which attracted the support of old intellectuals, young activists, and exploited peasants. Students became the channel through which radical, liberal, nationalist, Buddhist, and other discourses were focused against militarism, dictatorship, and unrestrained capitalism.

MILITARY POLITY

Sarit Thanarat was typical of the military strongmen who flourished under US patronage all over the world during the Cold War (Figure 14). He came from an ordinary family in the provincial northeast, and had his education and career entirely within the army. He made himself prime minister, supreme commander, head of the army, director of the police, and minister of development. He espoused the military virtues of discipline, unity, and strong leadership – including summary executions of arsonists and other criminals.

His rise realigned the military against the constitutional project begun in 1932. He argued that constitutions had failed because they were a western import and unsuited to Thai conditions. He justified rule by soldiers on the precise grounds that soldiers had no need to court popular favour: 'We work with honesty, scholastic competence, and just decision-making which is not under the influence of any private party and does not have to demonstrate personal heroism for purpose of future elections'.[1] He projected himself as a *pho khun*, a paternal ruler in the legendary mode of the Sukhothai kings. He argued that this was 'Thai-style democracy', sanctioned by tradition. He suppressed all opposition on grounds of the threat of 'communism'. When he died in 1963 (cirrhosis of the liver brought on by heavy drinking), his subordinates from the First Army took over as if by military promotion. Thanom Kittikhachon became prime minister and defence minister, with Praphat Charusathian as deputy prime minister and minister of interior.

The generals focused on dividing up the spoils of the massive dollar inflows and the resulting increase in government budgets and business profits. They formed companies to supply goods and services to government agencies, particularly construction, insurance, and import. They participated in the exploitation of natural resources, particularly logging which began with clearances for dams and roads, and climaxed in schemes to level whole forests to deny base areas to communist guerrillas. They shared out land opened up by new roads; when he died, Sarit's estate included over 22,000 rai. They took cuts on arms purchases. They exploited the US presence: an air vice-marshal ran the travel agency handling the R&R programme for US servicemen, and an airforce general ran the transport company ferrying military cargo. They continued to patronize major business families in return for shares and directorships. Sarit sat on twenty-two company boards and Praphat on forty-four.

The military officer elite became somewhat like a ruling caste, distinguished by its unique dress and rituals, vaunting its own purity, and claiming extensive privileges. Generals took over executive posts in state enterprises, and honorary posts in sports and social organizations. By their own machismo and corruption, they relegitimized old-fashioned male privileges and habits of exploiting political power for personal gain. Sarit appropriated women as kings once had, with a special interest in beauty queens. After his death, his assets were estimated at 2.8 billion baht. Virtually all

Figure 14: Sarit on tour in the hill villages of Mae Hong Son, c. 1962.

had been accumulated while he was prime minister, and the amount represented around 30 per cent of the total capital budget for that period. The government eventually seized 604 million as illegally acquired. Over fifty consorts and their children emerged to claim part of the remainder. Journalists gleefully paraded their numbers, their photographs, and their life-stories. The collapse of his successors' regime in 1973 also resulted in the seizure of 600 million baht of illegally acquired assets. The behaviour of this ruling caste was echoed through society. Beauty contests proliferated. The sex industry boomed. Corruption increased. Poh Intharapalit and other authors wrote hugely popular serialized fiction about swaggering bandit chiefs and superheroic crimebusters.

Military rule reproduced 'strongmen' at other levels of society. In the provincial areas, such figures had begun to emerge since the early twentieth century with the growth of a market economy without strong administration or the rule of law. From the 1950s, these *nakleng* (tough guys) or *pho liang* (patrons) became more prominent. They made money from the expanding cash-crop trade, from logging, from government construction contracts, and from local monopolies like liquor distribution concessions. Particularly around the US bases, they made fortunes from the businesses which flourish around the margins of a war – drugs, gambling, girls, gun-running, and smuggling. The new wave of officials appointed into the provinces often found they had to work with these figures rather than against them. In return, the generals made the officials their local partners in logging, construction, and other ventures. Occasionally, Sarit and his successors vowed to eliminate these tall poppies, but truly only those unwilling to cooperate.

EXTENDING THE NATION-STATE

Justified by 'national security', US aid funds and rising tax revenues underwrote a major expansion in the bureaucracy. The number of civilian officials increased. Many new 'development' departments appeared. Spurred by the US patrons' need to understand the country, the government increased its investment in data-gathering of all kinds.

All these new activities were built around the old colonial-style, centralized system of provincial governors and district officers under the Interior Ministry. New clusters of government officers dominated the landscape of the provincial towns. Their size and distinctive, standardized style signified both the centralized unity of the government, and its difference from local culture. The uniforms of local officials emphasized the same features. Many new administrative districts were created, pushing the government deeper into the countryside. Some provincial areas, particularly on the expanding uplands agrarian frontier, had previously been run by the local mafia rather than the government. In 1959, Sarit established control over Chonburi by a virtual military invasion, arresting hundreds of gunmen and local bosses.

The government loomed much larger in the life of ordinary citizens, especially beyond the provincial centres where the government had previously been virtually non-existent. The government supplied more public goods, including health services, seeds and fertilizer, birth control devices, irrigation, household water supplies, and all-weather roads. It imposed more restrictions on citizens, such as rights of access to forests and other natural resources. The personal ID card and house registration document became increasingly important as the basic documents of citizenship required for any transaction with officialdom.

The increased funding from the US made possible some of the projects of national discipline that had been conceived during the Chulalongkorn reforms but never fully realized. Primary schooling was now pushed out beyond the district towns into the villages and hills. New school buildings, again in a distinctive and standardized style, stood out among village houses as much as the government complexes in the towns. To enter these special places, schoolchildren donned a uniform, again a mark of difference and standardization. Primary education focused first and foremost on the Thai language, which for most children outside the central region was different from the language spoken at home. Other primary subjects were history and social studies, which meant indoctrination in the national ideology of nation, religion, and king. School texts encouraged children to 'buy Thai goods; love Thailand and love to be a Thai; live a Thai life, speak Thai, and esteem Thai culture'.[2]

Buddhism became more closely associated with this extension of the scope and reach of the government. Renewed efforts were made to replace *wat* texts written in local scripts and embodying local traditions with documents issued from the centre. Particularly in the northeast, which was becoming identified as most susceptible to communism because of its poverty and its proximity to Indochina, renewed efforts were made to recruit villagers into the monkhood. In 1964, the government's religious affairs department, headed by an army colonel, launched the *thammathut* (ambassadors of *thamma*) programme to send monks to tour the remote northeast. They were instructed not only to preach Buddhism, but also to organize villagers in development projects, explain about laws, and discourage communism. Locally famous monks were absorbed into the Thammayut sect.

These programmes went much further in trying to realize the Chulalongkorn-era ambition to create the 'unity' of a 'Thai nation'. In particular, they tried to impose 'unity' on parts of Thailand where linguistic, religious, and cultural traditions differed from the imagined national standard. These differences had been present ever since diverse areas were collected within the first national boundaries, but they became more apparent as the government intruded more deeply. Resistance to the spread of government was often expressed in terms of the defence of local identity and practice. The government perceived such resistance as a special threat to 'national security' because these remote communities had historical and cultural links which flowed across the borders drawn at the turn of the twentieth century, and often into areas already engaged in communist revolt. Three regions were critical.

The northeast or Isan contained a third of Thailand's population. Most spoke a dialect of Lao, while many along the southern border spoke Khmer or Kui. Poor soil, a harsh climate, and the nature of its agrarian colonization meant the region had far more in poverty than other areas. Since 1932, political leaders of the region had opposed the increasing centralization of power in Bangkok, and petitioned for resources to counter the region's disadvantages. In the late 1940s, some northeastern leaders hoped that national borders would be redrawn as part of the process of decolonization, uniting Isan with other Lao-speaking areas. Northeastern leaders were regularly jailed or killed in the bouts of repression that followed each advance of military power. In 1959, Sila Wongsin, a religious adept and traditional healer, set up an independent village 'realm' in Khorat. Troops attacked the village, and Sila was publicly executed. Two former MPs formed a Northeastern Party committed to socialism, and demanded more development funds for the region. Sarit accused the leaders of advocating communism and separatism. Khrong Chandawong, a peasant turned teacher who gained a large following for his ideas on socialism and self-reliance, was jailed for five years and then publicly executed in his home town in Sakon Nakhon (Figure 15).

In the four southernmost provinces, a majority of people practised Islam and spoke a Malay dialect. Since the 1930s, the Phibun governments had tried to impose Thai language and Thai dress, and to close down local community schools and Islamic courts. Resistance was led by religious leaders who took their inspiration from contemporary anti-colonial movements in the Islamic world. Some appealed to the colonial British in Malaya for help. Some petitioned for a federal structure that would allow them to preserve the area's distinctive culture within Thailand. The most prominent of these

Figure 15: The execution of Khrong Chandawong and Thongphan Suthimat, by Sarit's
personal order, on 31 May 1961 in a field near Sakon Nakhon.

leaders, Haji Sulong Tomina, was charged with treason in 1948, prompting
a revolt in Pattani, Yala, and Narathiwat in which hundreds died over six
months. Haji Sulong was jailed and then probably assassinated by Phao's
police in 1954. Teachers led resistance by founding *pondok* schools which
taught in local dialect and according to Islamic principles, while community leaders like Haji Sulong's son were elected MPs and raised Muslim
demands in parliament. As in the northeast, Sarit accused them of plotting
a separatist revolt and threw the leaders into jail. After release, they and
many others fled into Malaysia. Underground organizations were formed
to support Islam and socialism. In Pattani, which had been the centre of

a Muslim Sultanate for over three centuries before 1900, a movement appeared in 1968, headed by a former local aristocrat educated in south Asia, and dedicated to creating an independent Islamic state.

The northern hills were inhabited by around a quarter of a million hill peoples, mostly practising shifting cultivation in the forests. Since the 1940s, several had begun growing opium for international trade. In 1959, the government set out a plan to stop opium growing, stabilize shifting farmers, recruit hill peoples 'to maintain the security of national frontiers', and in other ways make them 'contribute to national development'.[3] Teachers were posted into the hills to transform them into Thai-speaking loyal citizens, and monks were sent under a *thammajarik* programme to convert them to Buddhism. In parallel with these efforts, millenarian ideas spread about the coming of a 'Hmong King' who would bring prosperity and justice. In 1967–68, a full-scale Hmong rebellion spread across four provinces of the north. The army reacted by bombing and napalming hill villages.

Equipped with bigger budgets and better means of communication, the militarized nation-state believed it could realize the imagined unity of a homogenous nation of Thai-speaking, loyal, development-pursuing Buddhist peasants throughout the area enclosed within the national borders. Many communities in areas only recently annexed to the Bangkok heartland, and even more recently subject to government control, felt they belonged to a different world from that imagined by the Thai state. They were provoked into re-examining and re-emphasizing their own very different identities.

MONARCHY RESURGENT

Sarit and the US oversaw a revival of the monarchy following its partial eclipse since 1932. Both the generals and their US patrons believed the monarchy would serve as a focus of unity, and a force for stability, while remaining susceptible to their control. The process began in earnest once Phibun was removed from power in 1957. But the roots of the revival were laid in the late 1940s.

In December 1945, Prince Dhani Nivat, former royalist minister and now one of the senior palace advisers, delivered a lecture on Siamese kingship attended by the young King Ananda Mahidol and his family. Dhani constructed a Sukhothai model of a naturally elected king who follows the ten royal virtues and 'justifies himself as the King of Righteousness'.[4] He emphasized the monarch as the protector of the people and of Buddhism. This represented a departure from the idea of the king as embodiment of the nation, as promoted from the Fifth to Seventh Reigns, and a return to the theory popular at the start of the Bangkok era.

Dhani also slated constitutions as 'a pure foreign conception', with no place in Thai tradition because the king's inherent morality and wisdom were the true source of law. He summed up: 'Our national prosperity and independence in the first 150 years of the Bangkok era (1782–1932) was the result of the wisdom and statecraft of our kings. And I cannot see how we can maintain such a state of affairs without good kings.' Another returned royalist asserted that 'representatives of the people are elected individually by certain groups of people and they do not, in fact, represent the whole people' as only the king could.[5]

Dhani noted that traditionally the conception of the monarchy was 'ever kept before the public eye in literature, in sermons, and in every other channel of publicity'. He and the other senior royalist (and regent), Prince Rangsit, orchestrated a new ritual dramatization of monarchy, and a further extension of Damrong's project of public exposure of the royal body. The first days of Ananda Mahidol's temporary return from exile were crammed with ritual performances. The remainder was peppered with staged interactions with groups of subjects – receptions for high officials, visits to military camps, meetings with Muslim and Chinese leaders, a talk on radio, and forays into the countryside to meet the people. The short visit was a prelude to the new version of monarchy, steeped in ritual but tinged with populism, sharply different from the pre-1932 model of modernity, westernization, and distance.

After Ananda Mahidol's unexplained death in 1946, the succession passed to his younger brother, Bhumibol Adulyadej, who returned to Switzerland to complete his education. He visited Thailand briefly in March–May 1950 for another flurry of ritual, including his coronation and marriage. But after Bhumibol's permanent return in 1951, the royal revival was temporarily slowed. Phibun blocked the royalist politicians' attempt to reinstate royal power through the constitution, and through the 1950s restricted the king's public duties to the rituals which established the essential specialness of the monarchy. Outside that, the king dabbled in painting, sailing, photography, and jazz.

All that changed with Sarit's coup in 1957. Initially, the king, like the Americans, had reportedly considered Sarit 'corrupt and uncouth'.[6] But Sarit belonged to a later military generation with no involvement in the revolution of 1932. During the mid-1950s, he had quietly distanced himself from Phibun's antagonism to the throne. On the eve of both his 1957 and 1958 coups, Sarit visited the king. On the day of the 1957 coup, the king named Sarit as 'Defender of the Capital', and Sarit displayed this decree as legitimation. On the following day, Sarit visited the palace, and the king issued a message of support and encouragement. After the 1958 coup, Sarit's group declared it 'firmly holds that the King and Nation are one and indivisible'.

Sarit talked of the 'Army of the King' and the 'government headed by the King'. He scrapped Phibun's land Act, which the king had opposed, and switched national day from the day of the 1932 revolution to the king's birthday. He showed he believed that power radiated downwards from the monarch, rather than upwards from the people: 'The ruler is none other than the head of that big family who must regard all the people as his own children and grandchildren'.[7] Thanat Khoman, later Sarit's foreign minister, explained:

The fundamental cause of our political instability in the past lies in the sudden transplantation of alien institutions on to our soil . . . If we look at our national history, we can see very well that this country works better and prospers under an authority, not a tyrannical authority, but a unifying authority around which all elements of the nation can rally.[8]

Sarit encouraged expansion of the royal role. In 1955, Phibun had allowed the king to make a tour to the northeast which attracted large crowds. From 1958, these tours became a regular event and took in all regions of the country. He also travelled overseas on state visits which advertised Thailand as a traditional but modernizing country cleaving to the 'free world'. The king's attention to the ritual foundations of kingship also became more public and more widely spread. He resumed the custom of presenting *kathin* robes to monks in the capital, and later beyond. He revived the glittering royal barge procession which dramatized this event. He presented Buddha images, tablets, and amulets to *wat* and offices during his provincial tours. Later, he appointed royal representatives to convey the royal *kathin* robes and the Buddha images to a wider range of places. The US contributed by reproducing pictures of the king for distribution all over the country.

In 1962, Sarit amended the Sangha Act, overthrowing Phibun's 1944 reform, returning roughly to Chulalongkorn's 1902 organization of the Sangha, and restoring Mongkut's Thammayut sect to a privileged position. Sarit had Phra Phimontham, a Mahanikai (that is, mainstream) monk who advocated a more democratic Sangha, arraigned as a communist, forcibly disrobed, and thrown into jail. The Ministry of Education was entrusted to Pin Malakun, a royal family member and enthusiastic royalist who had returned from exile in the post-war era. School textbooks were revised to emphasize the king as the focal point of the nation.

The king cultivated an interest in rural development. After his return from Europe in 1951, Prince Dhani had arranged for Phya Anuman Rajadhon to tutor him on Thai culture. Anuman was a tax official and remarkable amateur scholar who had collected folk tales, written a detailed account of the annual rural cycle of cultivation and ritual, and studied the blending of animism and Buddhism in everyday rural life. Against a background of urban growth and great rural changes, Anuman imagined a 'self-contained' village life only superficially changed by modernity:

> The important thing for all humans is the desire for happiness, fun, and comfort. To speak only of farmers, if they are not addicted to evil ways, such as gambling, they have not a little happiness, because they have few needs. It is happiness deriving from their surroundings, namely nature. When they have enough to eat and enough to use they are happy . . . I have told the life of the farmers, which is a simple, smooth life, not adventurous, not progressive, not wealthy, and not powerful. However things are, they go on like that.[9]

Around 1960, the king set up a fishery, an experimental farm, and a dairy project inside the Bangkok palace. He planned an irrigation project close to his beachfront palace in Hua Hin, and became enthusiastic about the potential for irrigation to transform small-scale farming. He recruited technical help inside the Irrigation Department, and began to identify and promote projects during his provincial tours. On trips to the north in the 1960s, he developed another interest in the hill peoples and in projects to replace opium growing by new crops (Figure 16). The queen promoted hill peoples' handicrafts.

The king's own home movies from these trips were shown on the new medium of television. Pin Malakun, who also oversaw broadcasting, recognized the potential of this material, and soon film of the king visiting the villages was regularly shown. In an axis stretching from Phya Anuman's folklore to Pin Malakun's television features, Bhumibol had become the paternal, activist king of a childlike, quiescent peasantry.

The king established a new range of gifting relationships with various social groups. In the late 1950s, he led several appeals for relief of disasters, including a major cholera epidemic. Over the following years, he also began to accept donations for funding his rural projects and other charities. Donating to the royal charities soon became a way to make merit, especially for rising businessmen keen to convert some of their new wealth into social recognition. The king had already revived royal decorations, mainly

Figure 16: The king as developer, on opium replacement and water projects, in the 1970s.

for presentation to officials. Now he multiplied the classes of decorations, and extended the catchment to include charity donors and others who performed valuable services. Similarly, the circle of people who merited royal sponsorship for weddings and funerals was widened to include a broader elite. The number of functions, ceremonies, and audiences attended by the king rose from around 100 a year in the mid-1950s to 400 a year during the Sarit regime and 600 in the early 1970s. The royal family paid special attention to their relations with the army, the senior bureaucracy, and the Buddhist establishment. But they also found occasions to interact with the business community and the growing professional middle class.

· Although the king's rural projects were in line with the Sarit government's theme of development, they pointedly focused on the small peasants and marginal peoples who were being crushed, confused, and bypassed by development in practice. Although the generals and the US sponsored the royal revival, the results differed somewhat from these patrons' intentions. The lurch to Americanization turned the monarchy into an alternative symbol of nation and tradition; the corruption of the generals and their cronies created an opportunity for the monarchy to assert a revived and modernized form of moral leadership; and the harsh results of rapid development gave the king a role as defender of the weak.

The alignment of army, palace, and business concluded by Sarit under US patronage in 1957–58 benefited all parties. The US secured a base. The monarchy revived. The generals enjoyed power and profit. Business boomed. But these gains did not come without costs, and without releasing new social forces.

THE LEFT

Before the Second World War, communist activity in Siam had been confined to Chinese groups (mainly in Bangkok) and Vietnamese groups (mainly in the northeast) acting as émigré bases promoting revolution in their home countries. A party branch was founded in the early 1930s, but only a handful of Thais were recruited. The government was relatively successful at rounding up and deporting the activists, and considered them unthreatening.

Over the 1940s, the leftist movement was transformed into something much more powerful. Many more second-generation *lukjin* Chinese were recruited through teachers in the Chinese schools, especially Xinmin school. They became more involved in radicalizing Thailand, rather than supporting a revolution in China. Anti-Japanese activists arrested in 1938 spent several years ensconced in jail in the company of royalists arrested after the failed Boworadet rebellion. In this 'jail university', the leftists taught the aristocrats political strategy, and in return were tutored in Thai language and culture.

The Communist Party of Thailand (CPT) was refounded in December 1942, and committed to a policy to drive out the 'Japanese bandits' and promote democracy. During the war, the communists organized 'welfare associations' in shipping, railways, docks, timber, and rice mills. Some groups carried out disruption and sabotage. In 1944, the CPT organized a volunteer force to lead a rising against the Japanese, cooperated with the parallel movement of the Seri Thai, and engaged in a few skirmishes before the war ended. Through such activities, Kasian Tejapira argues, in the 'dimension of cultural political imagination . . . a radical anti-Japanese Chinese nationalist could possibly turn into a radical anti-Japanese Thai nationalist'.[10] By the war's end, Thailand had a communist movement dedicated to overthrowing the local political order.

The two years following the armistice allowed the party to work in the open. Using their links with the Seri Thai, and the influence of Russia at the peace negotiations, the movement succeeded in gaining repeal of the Anti-Communist Law in October 1946. The party foreswore insurrection in favour of working through parliament and trade unions. Prasoet Sapsunthon, a Surat Thani MP who promoted the repeal, joined the party and openly proclaimed his affiliation. Against the background of post-war economic disruption, the party helped to organize labour, coordinate two large-scale strikes by rice-mill workers in 1945 and 1947, form the umbrella Association of United Workers of Thailand in April 1947, and hold the largest mass rallies to date on May Day in 1946 and 1947. The party newspaper, *Mahachon* (The masses), which had circulated underground intermittently since 1942, began to appear openly as a weekly in 1944. A communist newspaper in Chinese, *Chua-min pao*, appeared in October 1945.

Some early party members who had gone to China to fight in the revolution, returned to Thailand, including Udom Srisuwan, a Christian-educated Chinese-Shan who became *Mahachon*'s leading columnist and the party's main theoretician. Some bright provincial students, both *lukjin* and Thai, who travelled to the capital for higher education were attracted to leftist ideas. Jit Phumisak, son of an excise clerk from Prachinburi, enrolled at Chulalongkorn University in 1950, and wrote a Marxist critique of Buddhism soon after. A student committee was formed at Thammasat

University in 1953, and some of its members joined the party after Sarit's 1957 coup.

Several members of the new commoner middle class of the 1920s were drawn leftwards in this era. Supha Sirimanon, who figured among the pronationalist journalists from the late 1920s, became an intermittent aide to Pridi over the next fifteen years, and used foreign trips to acquire leftist literature. He evolved into a self-taught socialist who published one of the first Thai analyses of Marxism in 1951. The journalist and writer, Kulap Saipradit, whose fiction in the late 1920s speared the aristocracy, visited Japan in the late 1930s, took a Thammasat University law degree during the war, and began translating texts from European socialism. After spending 1948–49 in Australia, he published a flurry of short stories on class divisions in Thai society. 'Lend us a hand' illustrates the Marxist labour theory of value: 'Who builds everything? Is it money, or is it damn well labour that does the job?'[11] Some of these convert intellectuals kept aloof from the CPT. In 1949 Supha and Kulap, in cooperation with several followers of Pridi, started a journal, *Aksonsan* (The adviser), that 'did not lead people by the nose'.[12] But others went the whole way. Atsani Pholajan, member of an aristocratic family, took a law degree from Thammasat, worked as an official, wrote poems and stories for *Mahachon*, and joined the party in 1950.

From 1947 the CPT, influenced by those returning from China, began to adopt a Maoist line of rural-based revolution. In 1950, this was defined in Udom Srisuwan's *Thailand: A Semi-Colony*, which rewrote Thai history in the Marxist framework, condemned 1932 as a failure because of no mass support, and concluded that Thailand was a 'semi-feudal semi-colonial' state, similar to pre-revolutionary China. It argued that the revolution had to be pursued, as in China, by a broad coalition spearheaded by both workers and peasants.

Within this left milieu there was a strand that tried to build a bridge between Buddhism and Marxism on a common platform of social justice. Many activists were attracted by the ideas of a Buddhist thinker, Buddhadasa, who had distanced himself from the Sangha authorities at a forest temple, Wat Suan Mokh in Surat Thani, and who in the 1940s began to publish booklets arguing for a more democratic and this-worldly interpretation of the fundamental Buddhist texts. Kulap Saipradit attended Suan Mokh, wrote in Buddhadasa's journal, and summarized Buddhadasa's ideas in the left-wing Bangkok press. Samak Burawat, a London-educated geologist who translated Stalin, also taught philosophy at a Buddhist academy, attended Suan Mokh and wrote comparisons of Buddhadasa's Buddhism and

Marxism. Pridi considered forming a branch of Suan Mokh in Ayutthaya, and later from exile in China wrote a blend of Buddhism and Marxism, serialized in the Bangkok press as *The Impermanence of Society*. One of Pridi's followers returned from Beijing to found a party named after Sri Arya Mettraya, the future Buddha who ushers in a utopian age metaphorically similar to the ultimate goal of Marxism.

GUERRILLAS

In late 1948, inspired by the Chinese revolutionary movement, the CPT resolved to pursue a Maoist-style revolution by organizing the peasantry. Cadres began working in villages, particularly in the northeast where they had earlier organized anti-Japanese cells. A party congress, held secretly in Bangkok from February 1952, confirmed the strategy to 'mobilize the masses in thousands and millions, go to the countryside',[13] but with some dissenters, including Prasoet Sapsunthon. However, the Peace Movement sweep in November 1952 jailed several party activists and some of the early rural recruits in the northeast and south. Many remaining party members escaped to attend training at the Marxist-Leninist Institute in Beijing. For five years, party activity lapsed. In Beijing, Prasoet Sapsunthon argued that the rural strategy was misguided, and proposed that the party seek power through the ballot box. He was expelled from the party, and after the 1957 coup offered his services to Sarit.

Other trainees returned from Beijing in the late 1950s. A third party congress in 1961 confirmed the rural strategy ('encircling the cities from the rural areas'), adopted armed struggle, and moved the party headquarters out of the city. Several, including the ideologist Udom Srisuwan and the poet and historian Jit Phumisak, moved to the forests of the northeast.

The party began to harvest not only the urban intellectuals' increasingly bitter frustration against military dictatorship, but also the peasants' reaction against the market, and the outer regions' opposition to the imposition of the nation-state with its intrusive bureaucracy and demands for linguistic and cultural uniformity. The party formed its first base in the Phuphan area of the northeast where Khrong Chandawong had recently been executed. His daughter became a leading cadre. A second base was formed in the hills of the south, and linked with the separatism in the Muslim far south and the communist rebellion in Malaysia. A third major area formed in the north and garnered support from many hill villages, including Hmong, Yao, and Lua. With Chinese cooperation, the Voice of the People of

Thailand (VOPT) radio began to broadcast from Kunming. Supply routes were created through Laos.

The rebellion spread widely in a peasant society disrupted by the intrusion of teachers, bureaucrats, policemen, and primitive capitalism backed by a mighty foreign power. A chance encounter between a police patrol and a guerrilla band in Nakhon Phanom on 7 August 1965 began armed confrontation (the 'first shot' or 'gun firing day'). The number of clashes between guerrillas and government forces rose from around one per day in the late 1960s to a peak of around three per day in 1977. The Thai army treated communism as a foreign invasion. The US was interested in Thailand as a base for its war in Indochina and initially paid little attention to the roots of the local rebellion. The armed forces relied on military sweeps, bombing and napalming villages, and deliberate atrocities such as burning captured guerrillas alive. There was little attempt to understand the principles of Maoist guerrilla warfare, with the result that major armed assaults on CPT bases, such as at Phu Hin Rongkla and Thoeng in 1972, were military disasters. Attempts to garrison villages and organize village defence forces often failed because soldiers used the power of their uniform and guns to dominate, loot, and rape.

By 1969, the armed forces counted 'communist-infested sensitive areas' in thirty-five of the seventy-one provinces. By the mid-1970s, it estimated there were some 8000 armed guerrillas, 412 villages totally under CPT control, and 6000 villages with a total population of 4 million under some degree of CPT influence.

In 1967, the police captured some CPT members who had opposed the rural strategy, including Prasoet Sapsunthon. The Communist Suppression Operations Command (CSOC, later ISOC), set up in 1964 by the US to coordinate counter-insurgency, recruited their help to plan a more effective strategy. The CSOC began to work at village level, forming village defence organizations, and lavishing money on local development under the Accelerated Rural Development programme. But the army command resisted widespread adoption of this strategy, and used every setback as an argument for more firepower and more violence. Between 1973 and 1978, almost 6 million rai of forest was destroyed each year as the army attempted to deny the guerrillas access to forest bases. Even so, a CSOC expert concluded: 'The inescapable reality is the insurgents and communist revolutionaries . . . have grown steadily, virtually untouched, for as much as ten years . . . they are largely secure in their jungle and forest base areas where the government forces, police or military, rarely care to venture'.[14] By 1976, government estimated that

2173 guerrillas and 2642 government troops had died in 3992 clashes since 1965.

STUDENTS

The guerrilla war was just one form of opposition to military dictatorship and its US backing. Other forms of dissent developed in urban society. They too were influenced by the Cold War's worldwide polarization into left and right, and its accompanying vocabulary (communism, revolution, free world, and so on). But they were also tinged with nationalism, Buddhism, cultural defence, and the aspirations of maturing groups of businessmen and urban middle class.

The enthusiasm to 'develop' Thailand rapidly increased the numbers in higher education. Tertiary students increased from 18,000 to 100,000 over 1961–72, while growing numbers also went overseas, especially to the US. The catchment area for higher education extended beyond the old elite. Many were drawn from the provinces to the colleges in Bangkok. In the short stories through which this generation shared their experience, the central character is often a provincial boy or girl who escapes from poverty through education, but remains angry at the exploitation of others less fortunate. Any overt political activity on the campuses was rigorously suppressed. According to Sulak Sivaraksa, 'By 1957, there were no intellectuals left . . . The universities were controlled entirely by the military'.[15] But from the early 1960s, student publications began to articulate dissatisfaction. The journal, *Sangkhomsat parithat* (Social Science Review), founded by Sulak in 1963, leaned to the school which tried to merge socialism and this-worldly Buddhism. Its writers, including Sulak and Sujit Wongthet, criticised the Americanization of Thailand because of its crass materialism and its destruction of Thai culture.

By the late 1960s, this and other journals also began to carry articles from overseas students describing the intensity of the movement against the Vietnam war and the rise of leftist ideologies in the US and Europe. In the early 1970s, Thai students began to discover and translate New Left writings from Europe and the US. Young academics produced political economy analyses of modern Thai society which highlighted the poverty and exploitation of the peasantry, the dismal conditions of urban labour, and the roots of social injustice in the traditional social order. Writers from the post-war period were rediscovered and republished, including Kulap Saipradit, who had lived in exile in China since Sarit's coup, and Jit Phumisak, who had joined the CPT's rural movement in 1965 and been shot dead in Phuphan a year later. Literary circles and discussion groups mushroomed. In 1972, Thammasat students printed a pamphlet, *Phai khao* (White peril), attacking US imperialism in Thailand.

This growing readiness to criticize military dictatorship was not confined to the students. From the late 1960s, the king began to make public comment on political matters, often specifically directed at the emergent student activism. He wondered aloud about the army's use of violence, which sometimes seemed to drive villagers into the hands of the guerrillas. He criticized the army's attempts to remove settlers from the forests. He recognized that farmers were angry because they wanted to be left alone. He noted that 'foreign' communists 'incite the people into thinking that they must fight for freedom and economic liberty. This however, may be partly true since many in Thailand are poor.'[16] He began allusively to criticize capitalism for encouraging values destructive of the humanitarian empathy in Buddhism. He urged students to campaign against the corruption which flourished under dictatorship. At the same time, he advocated gradual change and denigrated the growing enthusiasm for revolutionary methods. Privately he told the British ambassador that 'students must be controlled' and that student demonstrations were 'very wrong'.[17]

In 1968, the king nudged the military government to complete the constitution promised a decade earlier and to restore an elective parliament. The 1968 constitution copied earlier military models of a parliament dominated by an appointed Senate. Despite the charter's restrictions, MPs were bolder than ever before in using parliament as a forum to critique and qualify military rule. They blocked the military budget, demanded more funds for provincial development, and exposed corruption scandals. The prime minister, Thanom Kittikhachon, seemed deeply shocked by these intrusions on the generals' power and privilege: 'Never, in my long political career, have MPs caused such trouble to government administration as in these recent times. Some of them even attacked me over my private affairs.'[18] In November 1971, Thanom executed a coup against his own government, revoked the constitution, and dissolved parliament.

Student demonstrations about the war, corruption, and other issues began tentatively in 1968. In 1972, they became better organized and more forceful. The CPT recognized the potential and began to publish leftist literature and to recruit student leaders. But leftist ideas were only one element in an ideological swirl that included democratic liberalism, Buddhist notions of justice, and nationalist opposition to exploitation by both the US and Japan. Many of the student activists came from a provincial background (especially the south), were the first members of their

Figure 17: The people arrive in Thai politics. The mass demonstration on the eve of 14 October 1973 around Democracy Monument, with the landmark 'dome' of Thammasat University, where the protest began, in the distance.

lower- or lower-middle-class families to gain higher education, and were among the brightest. Thirayuth Boonmi was the son of an army sergeant and had been placed first in the nationwide secondary school examinations. Seksan Prasertkun was son of fishing-boat builder and a brilliant political science student.

In November 1972, Thirayuth organized a ten-day protest against Japanese goods. In June 1973, the demonstrations began to focus on the issue of restoring the constitution and democracy. The generals refused to negotiate, and arrested the student leaders. Meeting in the Interior Ministry, they agreed that '2 per cent of the student population' should be 'sacrificed for the survival of the country'.[19] Publicly they claimed that the students were manipulated by 'communists'.

The press cautiously supported the students. On 13 October 1973, half a million people joined a Bangkok demonstration to demand a constitution (Figure 17), and parallel gatherings formed in major provincial towns. The generals backed down and released the student leaders, but the protest now had a momentum of its own. In the afternoon, the crowd moved towards the palace to avoid military harassment, and appealed to the king to mediate.

The student leaders extracted a promise from the generals to reintroduce a constitution within a year, and were granted an audience with the king. But the dispersal of the demonstration on the morning of 14 October 1973 deteriorated into violence. Soldiers fired into the crowd, killing 77 and wounding 857. The shedding of young blood on Bangkok streets undermined any remaining authority of the junta, and allowed the king and other military factions to demand that the 'three tyrants' (Thanom, Praphat, and Narong, Thanom's son married to Praphat's daughter) go into exile.

The king took the unprecedented step of nominating a new prime minister (Sanya Thammasak, a judge and privy councillor) and laying down the process for writing a new constitution to re-establish parliament. The final collapse of military rule catapulted students into a historic role, and elevated the king as a supra-constitutional force arbitrating the conflicts of a deeply divided nation.

RADICALS

The events of 14 October 1973 began an extraordinary period of debate, conflict, experiment, and change. The immediate aftermath of the generals' fall saw a complex interplay between students and other radical forces on the one hand, and a much more moderate agenda to found a post-military state and social order on the other.

For the next year, street protests were almost daily events. They maintained pressure on the government's procedure to restore constitutional democracy. They campaigned for ending the American use of Thailand as a base. They widened the agenda to issues of social and economic justice. The university campuses, especially Thammasat, were converted into open debating halls. Writing on Thai history, society, and culture mushroomed. Jit Phumisak's writings were republished and revered, especially his call for a politically committed literature and art, and his challenge to traditional Thai historiography which identified Siam as a feudal society and the monarchy as 'great landlords'.[20] The CPT helped to nudge the student movement leftwards.

The student protests catalysed resentments which had developed but been suppressed over the past two decades of 'development'. Labour disputes and labour resentment against institutionalized repression had increased in the late 1960s and broke out in a wave of strikes in 1972. The years 1973 and 1974 saw more strikes (501 and 357, respectively) than at any previous time, mostly for improved wages and working conditions. In mid-1974, when some 6000 textile workers in the Bangkok industrial suburbs struck against attempts to lay off workers in the face of a market downturn, students helped to organize the strike, form a new coordinating body for the labour movement, and pressure the government for labour reforms. The government responded by raising the minimum wage, arbitrating strikes, and passing a new labour law which legalized unions and created the machinery for disputes.

Starting in early 1974, peasants in the north and the upper central region agitated for higher paddy prices, controls on rents, and allocation of land to the landless. In June some two thousand travelled to Bangkok to rally. Again, the government reacted positively by establishing a price support scheme and introducing a rent control Act. But it did not have the machinery to implement these schemes. Local offices were deluged with petitions from farmers detailing how moneylenders had cheated them of their land. Farmers complained that local officials sided with the local landed and monied elite. In late 1974, they created the Peasants Federation of Thailand (PFT) which grew rapidly to branches in forty-one provinces and membership of 1.5 million. PFT leaders travelled around villages educating farmers about their rights. At a PFT rally in Bangkok in November 1974, young monks occupied the front rank. One explained, 'We take pity on the farmers who are the backbone of the country . . . Being the children of farmers, we cannot turn our backs on them when they need help'.[21] In May 1975, students, workers, and peasants announced a 'tripartite alliance' to fight for social justice, beginning with the farmers' issues.

Students felled the military dictatorship, but other forces in urban society emerged to shape the successor regime. Over the prior quarter-century, business had grown richer, more sophisticated, and more self-confident. The leading conglomerates no longer wanted to kowtow to the generals and share their profits with them. They sought more power to influence policy. A small but influential elite of technocrats wanted to divert resources away from the military towards development. Many businessmen and professionals were frightened by the polarizing logic of militarism and radicalism.

Kukrit Pramoj emerged as the representative of this reformist agenda. He was a minor member of the royal family and an enthusiastic practitioner of traditional high culture. He had been educated at Oxford and was thoroughly westernized in the style of the early twentieth-century court. But he quit a bureaucratic career to enter banking and then journalism. He moved among the new businessmen, and boasted about a Chinese element in his heritage. His business took him upcountry, and he claimed to know and understand the peasants. In 1974, he left his business career to found the Social Action Party, which attracted many big businessmen.

He was strongly attached to the traditional social order, and horrified at attempts to re-engineer society through state power from above. He was horrified too by the levelling implications of Buddhadasa's this-worldly Buddhism, and engaged the thinker in public debate on radio. He wrote a Thai adaptation of the Don Camillo stories, pitting traditional folk-ish Buddhism against communism. He supported a classic division of powers (executive, legislative, judicial) to act as a check on the abuse of authority, and saw the monarchy, equipped with both moral and constitutional power, as the surest bulwark against dictatorship. He believed the government had to redistribute income to remove the poverty which allowed communism to take root. He and his brother Seni both wrote essays idealizing the Sukhothai era as a liberal society under a paternal king. Kukrit represented a marriage of free-market capitalism, elitist democracy, exemplary monarchy, and paternalist government which appealed to many businessmen and urban middle class as a route beyond military rule.

In late 1973, the King hand-picked a National Convention that in turn elected a National Assembly to serve as an interim parliament and constitutional convention. The constitution completed in 1974 was modelled on Pridi's 1946 version, but with an appointed Senate and other checks. At elections in 1975, socialist parties won a third of the seats in the northeast but very few elsewhere. Military figures backed conservative parties like Chat Thai (Thai Nation) but had to stay in the background. Businessmen and professionals each supplied around a third of the MPs. No party dominated, and forming a coalition proved difficult. Kukrit eventually succeeded because of his personal popularity, even though his party had won only eighteen seats.

Kukrit sought to moderate the radical demands for social change, and create space for the old social elite and new business elite to negotiate a mutually acceptable accommodation, free from the polarized logic of the Cold War, the predatory designs of the generals, and the revolutionary ambitions of the radicals. Since 1968–69, the US had effectively faced defeat in Vietnam and begun to wind down its operations. Nixon had visited Beijing, and committed to removing US troops from Vietnam. Initially, this increased Thailand's importance as a base for guarding the withdrawal. US troops and aircraft were moved from Vietnam to Thailand. Thai troops joined operations in Laos and Cambodia. But resentment against the US inside Thailand increased. Kukrit opened negotiations with the US to withdraw troops. He travelled to Beijing to meet Mao Zedong and restore relations with China. He quietly withheld support from the students' attempts to build labour and peasant organizations. He launched a scheme to distribute development funds directly to the grassroots level as a way to relieve poverty and hence halt the spread of communism.

In the fledgling democratic politics, this centrist agenda commanded large support. But it was undermined by a campaign of right-wing terror.

RIGHTISTS

A right-wing reaction began in late 1974 and built over two years. Hardliners in the military, raised on Cold War ideology and US patronage, could not accept any solution other than a military defeat of the guerrilla forces. They tried to quash alternative political solutions, and branded even the military officers who supported such strategies as communist. They were increasingly alarmed by the spread of ideas and organizations which challenged the military's ideal of a controlled, orderly society – especially the PFT's ability to built a widespread peasant organization, the success of

Figure 18: In 1974, women workers at the Hara factory resisted being laid off by seizing control and running the plant as a cooperative. This poster from June 1975, amid rising right-wing violence, is headlined 'Hara workers need help'.

strikers in winning wage and other concessions, the possibility of monks lending legitimacy to popular movements, and students' adoption of Marxist ideas and vocabulary. They feared that urban protest would link with rural guerrilla forces and Indochinese revolution. They campaigned for the US troops to stay longer or hand over key weaponry. Over 1975–76, business, the palace, and a broader urban middle class abandoned the project to found parliamentary democracy and lent tacit or open support to a military solution.

In late 1974, the ISOC and the Interior Ministry supported the formation of *Nawaphon* (New *or* ninth force), a propagandist campaign to rally support for the army around the symbols of nation and monarchy. The organization convened meetings of businessmen and officials in the provincial towns and asked them, 'Do you love your King? Do you love Thailand? Do you hate communism?' By late 1975, *Nawaphon* claimed a million members. Two ISOC officers formed the *Krathing daeng* (Red Gaurs), a vigilante movement which, from early 1975, recruited vocational students and disaffected urban youth to break up demonstrations with sticks, guns, and grenades. Between April and August, seventeen leaders of the PFT were murdered (three others had been killed earlier), resulting in the collapse of the organization. After Kukrit's government quietly stepped back from earlier attempts to arbitrate industrial disputes, strikes were broken up by bombs, gunfire, gangs wielding chains, and even a fire engine driven into a crowd (Figure 18). Over nine months, 8100 workers were dismissed, mostly for strike activity, and several leaders were arrested as 'communists'.

The Village Scouts Movement had been founded in 1971 by the Border Patrol Police to combat communism through rural organization and propaganda. It conducted camps in which villagers listened to nationalist lectures, played team games, sang patriotic songs, joined in emotional pledging rituals, and were rewarded with a neckscarf and pin from the king. In early 1976, it moved its activities into Bangkok and other urban areas. In the previous April, Saigon and Phnom Penh had fallen to the communist forces, and on 2 December 1975 the Laotian monarchy had been abolished, increasing the sense of panic in the Thai elite and middle class. Over 1976, two million people, including businessmen, officials, and society wives, attended the Village Scouts recruitment sessions. It had become 'an urban-based movement funded by economically and politically nervous fractions of the middle and upper classes' which 'increasingly took on a fascist character'.[22]

From early 1976, the military propaganda and street violence were directed against the stumbling attempts to establish democracy.

Army-controlled newspapers and radio stations condemned parliament as another route to communist victory. The army chief forced Kukrit to dissolve parliament rather than take a socialist party into the coalition. A television programme fronted by an anti-communist judge, Thanin Kraivixien, attacked the 'inseparable trio of communism, student activism and progressive politics'.[23] In January, Phra Kittiwuttho, a monk associated with *Nawaphon*, proposed that the government resign and make way for a National Reform Council – essentially a coup proposed from within the monkhood. In February 1976, a US-educated lecturer heading the Socialist Party was shot dead. At the April elections, the pro-military Chat Thai Party campaigned on the slogan 'Right Kill Left'. Thirty people were killed and one leftist party office was firebombed. Kukrit was defeated at the polls, but his brother Seni became premier as head of the Democrat Party and followed a similar reformist agenda. The military and its political friends promptly manoeuvred to split Seni's party. In June, Phra Kittiwuttho said it was not sinful to kill communists: 'It is the duty of all Thai . . . It is like when we kill a fish to make curry to place in the alms bowl for a monk. There is certainly demerit in killing the fish, but when we place it in the alms bowl of a monk, we gain much greater merit.'[24] Under challenge he repeated that it was legitimate 'to kill some 50,000 people to secure and ensure the happiness of 42 million Thais'.

The military-orchestrated campaign portrayed any advocates of political or social change as 'communist', 'un-Thai', and treasonous 'enemies of nation, religion, and king'. Those trying to find a middle ground, including the Democrat government and several senior soldiers and officials, were condemned as 'communists' and often threatened with violence.

The finale only needed a trigger. In August 1976 Praphat, one of the 'three tyrants' exiled after 14 October 1973, returned to Thailand but left after students protested and two died from Red Gaur attacks. On 19 September Thanom, the former premier, returned in monk's robes and was ordained in Wat Boworniwet, the *wat* most closely associated with the palace. The king and queen visited him. Some days later, two workers putting up posters protesting at Thanom's return were lynched. A rightist newspaper carried pictures of a student dramatization of the event, and claimed one actor had been made up to look like the crown prince. An army radio station broadcast a repeated call for people to kill students in Thammasat University. Units of the Border Patrol Police were brought into the city, along with several Village Scouts and Red Gaurs. Early on 6 October 1976 they began firing rockets, hand-guns, and anti-tank missiles into Thammasat University (Figure 19). A handful of students who tried to escape were brutally lynched, raped,

Figure 19: A wounded student inside Thammasat University after it was invaded by armed forces on 6 October 1976.

or burnt alive outside the university. Officially, forty-three students were killed, and two policemen. Over 3000 were arrested on the day, and some 5000 later. That evening an army faction took power by coup. The television presenter and anti-communist judge, Thanin Kraivixien, became prime minister and announced a twelve-year hiatus before the return of constitutional democracy. Books were banned and burned, journals closed, publishers harassed, and political meetings outlawed.

As the violence had grown over the previous eighteen months, several student, worker, and peasant activists had already left the city for the CPT camps in the jungle. Now another 3000 joined them for mixed reasons of political conviction and self-preservation. Others fled abroad.

RESOLUTION

With 6 October 1976, the military and its allies had shot and bombed urban radicalism into submission. But the awfulness of the Thammasat massacre was a profound social shock which ensured it marked a new beginning as well as a terrible conclusion.

The US had lost the wars in Indochina – both to the guerrillas on the ground, and to the protesters at home and around the world. Over 1975–76, its troops left Thailand. As a parting present, the US gave a large dollop of military aid and continued smaller subsidies for several years. But the Thai army was now on its own. Through its control over the state, it was able to triple the defence budget over the next six years, and never faced the anticipated retaliation from the Indochinese states. But the Thai army had been swollen, corrupted, factionalized, and politicized by its massive US patronage and its involvement in an ideological war. Over the next decade, military factions fought over both the spoils of power and the direction of policy. Between 1977 and 1980, there were three more coups, one unsuccessful (in 1977) and the two others resulting in successive generals becoming prime minister. For all its own propaganda, the military was no basis for political stability.

The flight from urban repression swelled the number of armed guerrillas to a peak of 10,000 in 1979. The number of clashes also rose, with deaths rising over 1000 a year between 1977 and 1979. But the students who entered the jungle chafed under CPT discipline. Seksan Prasertkun complained that they 'had to fight for democracy all over again in the jungle'.[25] After their experience against military power and middle-class panic in the city, they doubted whether the CPT's Maoist strategy of 'village surrounding city' would ever succeed in Thailand. Emerging awareness of Cambodia's bloody experience under the Khmer Rouge further undermined enthusiasm for rural-based revolution. Moreover, in 1978–79, the communist states fell to fighting among themselves. Vietnam invaded Cambodia, and China responded by attacking Vietnam. The CPT split into pro-China and pro-Vietnam factions. The support and supply routes for the CPT's jungle campaign were undermined. The VOPT radio station in Kunming was closed.

In these circumstances, the centrist agenda, which had failed in 1974–76, re-emerged with both civilian and military support. The suffocatingly anti-communist regime installed in October 1976 was overthrown by the army after one year, and the timetable for restoring constitutional democracy shortened. The new government under General Kriangsak Chomanand returned to Kukrit's policy of normalizing relations with China, and bargaining for the withdrawal of Chinese support for the CPT. Advocates of a combined military and political strategy against the local guerrillas gained influence within the army. General Prem Tinsulanond, who applied the methods in the northeast, rose to army head and defence minister in 1979, and prime minister in 1980. With continued help from USAID, money

Figure 20: Supporters of the CPT surrender their weapons to the army in a ceremony at Umphang in December 1982.

was poured into schemes of rural development, while the army battered the remaining communist bases, and offered amnesty to defectors. Most of the students left the jungle between 1979 and 1981. Orphaned by their former international patrons, most CPT armed units emerged from the jungles and surrendered their arms over 1982–83 (Figure 20). The remnants of the CPT were arrested when they attempted to hold a congress in 1987. The people's war was over.

CONCLUSION

By the late 1940s, the aspirations for the nation-state held by the old aristocrats, officials, generals, and new businessmen in Thailand's narrow political elite were divided into two broad camps. One side upheld the ideal of a diverse, liberal, fair, and egalitarian nation achieved by the rule of law, a constitutional framework, and democratic representation. The other upheld the ideal of a strong and paternal state with the duty to protect, discipline, and educate its citizens within a hierarchic social order.

Over the next three decades, this division was absorbed within and eclipsed by the worldwide division of the Cold War. The US patronage of Thailand accelerated the development of a capitalist economy, strengthened military dictatorship, revived the role of the monarchy, and extended the reach of the state deeper into society. The resulting disruption combined with the spread of Marxist ideology to create an opposition of intellectuals, students, peasants, workers, and peripheral communities opposed to capitalism, US imperialism, and military dictatorship.

By the early 1970s, some businessmen and technocrats began to seek an escape from the polarization of dictatorship and communism. Kukrit represented a new formula of liberal capitalism, limited democracy, and state paternalism held together by the moral leadership of the monarchy, and dispensing with both US patronage and military rule. This vision was suppressed in the polarization of 1975–76, but re-emerged in the shocked reaction to the 1976 massacre and guided a future course.

Although the student idealism of 1973 was crushed – Seksan left the jungle in 1981 with the declaration, 'I am a historical ruin' – the activists of 1973–76 went on to have a profound effect on following decades. After felling a dictatorship and taking part in a guerrilla war, they were neither victorious nor annihilated, but allowed to return to the mainstream and resume their ascent to elite positions throughout society. Along the way they broke the moulds for academic study and creative arts, challenging the American academic portrayal of Thailand, and generating a legacy of songs, short stories, critical social science, and other cultural forms which spread ideas of democracy, social justice, and Buddhist compassion more widely through society. Among the *phleng phua chiwit*, songs for life, with which bands like Caravan and Kammachon stirred the student demonstrations and then the guerrilla camps, the most famous was Caravan's *Khon kap khwai* (Man and buffalo):

> Man and man work the fields as men; man and buffalo work the
> fields as buffalo.
> Man and buffalo, the meaning is so deep, so long they have worked
> the fields,
> So long they have grappled with the toil, to their happiness and
> satisfaction.
> Let's go, let's all go, we carry the firewood and the plough to the field.
> We endure, become heavy-hearted, and inwardly the tears fall.
> Our hearts ache and our minds burn, but we are not afraid.
> This song is about dying, about the loss of being human.
> The bourgeois take our labour, divide up the classes, push the
> peasants down,
> Despise them as jungly. The effect is surely dying.

8

Globalization and mass society, 1970s onwards

The Cold War in Asia eased after the US departure from Indochina. The US remained Thailand's military patron, but at much greater distance. Thailand's orientation to a liberal market economy, established in the American era, strengthened as the socialist alternative declined on a world scale. After an initial period of economic and political adjustment to the US departure, Thailand caught the tail of an Asia-wide boom led by Japan and the East Asian 'Tiger' economies. The liberalization of first trade and then finance accelerated the pace of industrialization and urbanization, and incorporated Thailand more firmly within a global economy. The close of the Cold War also transformed neighbouring countries from enemy territory into economic hinterland – as markets, and as sources of human and natural resources. In the late 1980s, China emerged from its four decades of partial eclipse, and again became a major factor in Thailand's economy and position in the world.

The pace of economic transformation quickened over the last quarter of the twentieth century. The balance of economy and society shifted decisively from rural to urban, and from parochial to open and globalized. The peasantry declined steeply as an element in the national economy, more moderately as a factor in the demography, and very markedly in the national culture. The rural remnant became an increasingly marginalized and truculent part of a society whose dynamism was decidedly urban.

Bangkok continued to dominate urbanization, swelling to over 10 million people, and earning the title of 'the most primate city on earth', over forty times the size of the next largest place (Khorat). Business prospered. The middle class grew larger and more assertive. Millions were pulled out of the villages and across the nation's borders to swell the urban working class. Changes in literacy, mobility, and media created a new sense of a mass society whose obvious variety undermined the official discourse of the nation.

Map 6: Modern Thailand

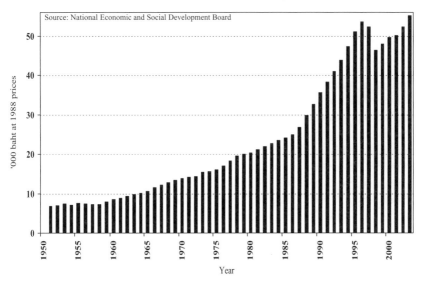

Chart 2: Real GDP per head, 1951–2003

THE URBAN BOOM

Over the last quarter of the twentieth century, Thailand experienced a rapid demographic transition. The birth rate dropped as a result of birth control campaigns, rising prosperity, and delayed child-bearing for education and careers. Annual population growth dropped from 3 per cent in the 1950s to 1 per cent in the 1990s. The bulge from the 1960s' population spurt entered the workforce in the 1970s and 1980s.

In this quarter-century, the urban economy grew faster than ever before on the foundations laid in the American period. The total size of the economy (GDP) increased fivefold and GDP per head tripled (Chart 2). Around a quarter of the working population moved out of agriculture. Bangkok grew from a city of 3 million, to an urban sprawl housing over three times that number. In 1975, only two high-rise buildings poked above the shophouses. By the 1990s, a dreamer had planned to plant the world's tallest building in Bangkok's alluvial mud.

The urban boom started slowly. The political excitement of the 1973–76 era disrupted business. After October 1976, the prime minister, Thanin, hoped the return of firm rule would also mean the return of foreign investment: 'I have a vision. It is of US dollars, Deutschmarks . . . all flying into Thailand, millions and millions of them.'[1] In fact, the dollars flew out, following the departing US military. Many US firms feared that Thailand

would fulfil the domino theory. Besides, the military which again dominated government had an anti-business streak. Military ideologists argued
that Thailand's unregulated and exploitative capitalism was responsible for
provoking people to embrace communism (see next chapter).

Though dollars flew out, yen began to fly in. Japanese investors had
come to Thailand since the late 1960s. Over the 1980s, Japanese foreign
investment exceeded that from the US by almost three times. Much of
the investment was made by Japanese trading companies in tariff-jumping
ventures to assemble automobiles and household goods from imported
components for domestic sale. Some investment went into labour-intensive
manufacturing, especially textiles, for both the local market and export. By
the early 1970s, many 'modern' goods in Bangkok stores had Japanese brand
names, not American ones. A satirical poem began:

> First thing in morning,
> Grasp White Lion toothpaste and enjoy brushing teeth;
> Then make some tea with a National electric kettle
> And smooth down hair with Tanjo pomade.
> Put on Thaitorae Tetoron clothes,
> Wear a Seiko watch when leaving home,
> Listen to government news broadcasts on a Sanyo radio,
> Drive a Toyota to pick up girlfriend.[2]

There was satire, but no protest. The students who had demonstrated
against Japanese economic power in 1972 and again during the tour of the
Japanese premier, Tanaka, in 1975 had been repressed. The Japanese government invested in cultural diplomacy. Most Japanese firms linked up with
a joint venture partner chosen from among the big domestic conglomerates, and let the partner manage local marketing, government contacts, and
public relations.

Japanese joint ventures further strengthened the leading Thai conglomerates. When democratic politics re-emerged in the late 1970s, leading
businessmen joined or supported parties, and pressed to influence policy.
In 1980, Boonchu Rojanastian, formerly managing director of Bangkok
Bank and now deputy prime minister overseeing economic policy, proposed that government and business cooperate to create 'Thailand Inc.', an
allusion to a popular book on Japan's success. Boonchu said: 'We should
run the country like a business firm'.[3] This effort failed. But business leaders
also lobbied for policies through associations of industry, commerce, and
banking. In 1981, government agreed to form an official liaison committee
between these bodies and the economic ministers. The business leaders used

this route to lessen red tape, and reduce the opportunities for bureaucratic restriction and gatekeeping. Business began reaching for political influence commensurate with its rising wealth.

Boonchu's scheme was for Thailand to follow Japan and the East Asian 'Tiger' economies in producing manufactured goods for export. From the mid-1970s, technocrats wrote the same strategy into the five-year plans. But as long as the old pattern of agricultural exports and limited protection of domestic manufacturing continued to deliver growth, vested interests were able to resist change. Even when the World Bank demanded 'structural adjustment' in the same direction in return for loans offered in the early 1980s, little of substance changed. Export manufacturing expanded, but very gradually.

The shift came in the early 1980s. Thailand's agricultural export growth faltered at the same time as US subsidies tailed away, and the second oil crisis of 1980–81 raised the cost of the country's single largest import. The government reacted initially with measures that delayed the impact of the oil crisis, while promoting tourism and labour export to the booming Middle East to earn more foreign exchange. But it was not enough. In 1983–84, the economy slumped. Debtors stopped paying their bankers. One bank crashed, and another bank and several finance companies had to be bailed out. The Finance Ministry ran out of money to service Thailand's foreign dues.

Reform-minded technocrats and business supporters seized the opportunity to switch Thailand towards export-oriented manufacturing. In November 1984, the baht was devalued by 14.7 per cent. The army chief went on television to demand the devaluation be reversed, but the technocrats held out and thereby gained greater influence. Leading businessmen supported a change of policy. The government began to revise tariffs, tax systems, and investment promotion to support export-oriented manufacturing.

One external factor completed the change. In August 1985, the US and Japan met to sort out the chaos in world currency markets after the oil crisis. Under the resulting Plaza Accords, Japan allowed the yen to rise against the dollar and dollar-linked currencies such as the baht. Over the next four years, the value of baht in terms of yen halved, and the value of Thailand's exports to Japan tripled. Thailand lurched into the 'Asian model' of export manufacturing.

The first to take advantage were local firms and established joint ventures. Banks and finance companies enthusiastically financed expansion. Exports increased by an average 24 per cent a year over 1984–89, led by garments, toys, bags, artificial flowers, and other labour-intensive products.

This local boom was soon overtaken. Japanese firms had to 'escape the rising yen!' (a Japanese slogan from this period). So too did firms from Taiwan, Korea, and Hong Kong, whose currencies were carried up in the yen's wake. From 1988, foreign investment accelerated as East Asian firms moved export-oriented manufacturing to Thailand and other low-cost sites in Southeast Asia. Some of these firms (especially Taiwanese) were in labour-intensive sectors, but increasing numbers used Thailand as part of complex multi-country systems for manufacturing technology-based goods such as integrated circuits, computer parts, electrical goods, and automobiles. By the end of the 1980s, the computer-part maker Minebea had transferred 60 per cent of its world production into Thailand and become the country's largest private employer. In 1991, the government deregulated the automotive industry, encouraging Japanese and later US firms to increase their investments. From 1990 onwards, these technology-based goods were the fastest-growing sector of exports. Between 1993 and 1996, a new Japanese factory opened in Thailand every three days.

Tourism grew over the same era. The government first promoted tourism heavily as a counter to the early 1980s slump, and then continued as falling air-flight prices increased the potential market. Beach and island resorts were created for holiday-makers from the temperate north. Thailand's religious aura attracted Asian visitors. The sex industry developed over the Vietnam war was repackaged for tourist demand. Annual arrivals grew from a few hundred thousand in the mid-1970s to 12 million at the millennium.

Thailand had very quickly ceased to be a fundamentally agrarian economy. In the early 1980s, agriculture still supplied almost half of exports. A decade later, the share was a little over a tenth.

DRAGON DAYS

The boom made urban Thailand – and especially Bangkok – a more dominant element in the economy, society, and culture. It converted businessmen into a wealthier, more socially confident, and more politically influential elite. It brought a new confidence and pride in the Chinese social origins now shared across business, bureaucracy, and the professions.

Much of the profits of the boom went to the old conglomerates which continued to diversify into new business opportunities. But financial liberalization and the sheer pace of the boom allowed others to participate. Several of the new entrepreneurs began from the provinces. The most successful of the era, Thaksin Shinawatra, came from an established business family in Chiang Mai. Thaksin rose rapidly by gaining government concessions for the new sector of telecommunications (mobile phones, satellite), and by exploiting the rising stockmarket. In five years from the late 1980s, his net worth rose to over US$2 billion. Other new families prospered in telecommunications, property, retailing, and other sectors geared to the booming home market.

The boost in the income and the economic importance of the big-business community resulted in new social and political confidence. With almost no new immigration since 1949, virtually all Thai-Chinese families had entered a third or higher generation. The children of the leading families had taken privileged routes through the education system alongside the children of the old elite. From the 1960s, intermarriages between the great business families and more established clans became more acceptable. In the prospering 1990s, they were frequent. A son of the Chirathiwat retailing family (Central) married a royal relative. The son and heir of the Sophonpanich banking family married into one of the great bureaucratic households. Prominent figures from old aristocratic families decorated the boards of large corporations. A new business press and glossy magazines glamorized corporate success. Biographies of the founders of the conglomerates were written to celebrate their success and to inspire emulation.

Business families, both large and small, put more of their children (especially, but not only, the males) through higher education and into the bureaucracy and professions. Many recruited into the growing technocracy came from these origins. Puey Ungphakon was a pioneer example. Son of an immigrant fish wholesaler, he won scholarships to study in England, and soared up the technocratic ladder to become Governor of the Bank of Thailand in 1959 at the age of 43. He founded Bank of Thailand scholarships which enabled others to follow his path. Many children of wealthy families were schooled in the US and returned to take leading roles in the technocracy, universities, and professions. The old division between Thai officialdom and Chinese business became blurred.

As urban enterprise became the driving force of the economy, intellectuals of Chinese origin demanded recognition of the Chinese role in the history which the earlier nationalists (like Wichit Wathakan) had tried to define as exclusively 'Thai'. In 1986, the historian Nidhi Eoseewong began a study of King Taksin by discussing *jek*, the pejorative word for Chinese or *lukjin*, and arguing that *jek* was part of the diversity which was the strength of Thai culture. Nidhi and Charnvit Kasetsiri showed that the founders of both the Ayutthaya and Bangkok dynasties probably had some Chinese ancestry, signifying the long and important Chinese role in Siamese history.

Nidhi described the very large role of the Chinese in the trading economy and 'bourgeois' society of early Bangkok, to emphasize how much the
Thai nationalist historians had painted out. The poet and essayist, Sujit
Wongthet, described himself in a 1987 book as *Jek pon lao*, Chinese mixed
with Lao, suggesting such mixing was typical of the true 'Thai' ancestry.

China's reopening to the world in the 1980s, and its emergence as an
economic power in the 1990s, further legitimized pride in Chinese origins.
Families travelled back to visit their birthplace and resume links with relatives. The CP conglomerate became one of the largest foreign investors in
China's opening economy, and several other Thai-Chinese firms followed
the example. Learning a Chinese language became popular for reasons
of both ethnic pride and practical business. The Chamber of Commerce
published a bilingual journal to promote Mandarin language skill. In the
mid-1980s, the government lifted a ban on electoral candidates making
appeals based on Chinese origins, following which many urban candidates
boasted of their clan (*sae*) name and their place of origin. Chitra Konun-
takiat became a media personality and best-selling author by explaining
Chinese customs, ceremonies, and culture to those whose families had
lost the memory over the past generations. Family histories of some of the
great business families became best-sellers. The cover of a 2001 compilation
entitled *Legendary Lives of the Jao Sua* displayed a golden dragon on a red
background, with the sub-title, 'from one pillow and one mat to the biggest
businesses of Thailand'.[4]

At the height of the economic boom, this reclamation of origins spread
to mass culture. A 1994 TV drama series, *Lot lai mangkon* (Through the
pattern of the dragon), traced the rise of a Chinatown street smart to the
head of a great conglomerate – a pastiche of several real dynastic histories.
A huge audience watched it, and pundits analysed its significance. Political
scientist Kasian Tejapira exclaimed: 'What a "bourgeois revolution" in Thai
entertainment culture!'[5] A string of later TV dramas dwelt on other parts
of the migrants' story, from the initial migration to the delicate topic of
links with relatives in China. From *Lot lai mangkon*, the term 'dragon' was
adopted as shorthand for Chinese entrepreneurial success, and its title song
became an unofficial anthem:

> From the Chinese land overseas
> On a small boat drifting afar,
> Penniless like a beggar . . .
> Fights the battles of the business world . . .
> Through the days and nights of struggling . . .
> Dragon begins to spread its wings,
> Pays back what it owes to this land.

In 1996, a singer who emphasized his Chineseness by dressing in pyjamas, sporting a pigtail, and calling himself Joey Boy, was hugely successful with a rap song, 'Ka ki nang' (No stranger). In the late 1990s, looks which would earlier have been called 'too Chinese' became the fashion for actors, singers, and even the winner of the Miss Thailand World contest. In a deconstruction of Thai identity unimaginable only a few years earlier, a leading businessman described his origins as '100 per cent Cantonese born in Thailand'.[6]

In the Phibun era, the government set out to 'assimilate' the immigrant Chinese into the 'Thai' nation. In a sense, the project was very successful. The Chinese learnt the Thai language, adopted new forms of behaviour, and identified themselves as citizens of the Thai nation. But at the same time they helped to mould a new urban culture which included speech, taste, and aesthetics from their own heritage. They also separated 'Thai' as a nationality from the old effort to conflate nationality, ethnic origins, and culture.

MAKING A MIDDLE CLASS

The tertiary education system had been designed to staff the expanding bureaucracy. In the 1960s, David Wilson noted – with some exaggeration – that the only educated Thai outside the ranks of officialdom were a few journalists, condemned to this trade because they failed the exams. With US patronage and encouragement, tertiary education began to expand. The first provincial universities appeared in the 1960s, the open Ramkhamhaeng University in the capital in the 1970s, and a swathe of new private and public colleges from the mid-1980s onwards. In the three decades following 1970, the numbers with tertiary education expanded twenty times up to 3.4 million. Most became not officials – the expansion of bureaucratic jobs slowed in the 1980s – but professionals, technicians, executives, and managers in the commercial economy.

Commercial salaries were much higher than official scales, and accelerated from the mid-1980s as the economy boomed. One prime use of this new wealth was to migrate away from the shophouse homes in the old city centre to new suburban 'villages'. In the late 1980s, this migration sparked a property boom in the paddyfields, swamps, and orchards on the city outskirts. This was a shift not only of location but also of culture – away from the tight inner-city neighbourhood to detached homes, and often away from an extended family to a nuclear one. The ads for the new housing projects played constantly on the theme of a 'new life' in the new location.

Consumption patterns shifted to models influenced by the west and Japan. The American period had allowed a glimpse of western lifestyles in Bangkok. Large numbers of Thai had travelled abroad for education. Reductions in tariffs as part of the economic liberalization in 1984 and more emphatically in 1991–92 cheapened the cost of imported goods. Western films increased in popularity. Satellites beamed in international news and cable television. Retailing changed to meet the new demand. The department stores which had become popular in the American era were superseded by palatial retail complexes which glamorized the act of purchase.

Gender patterns in this new middle class were complex. As among the mass of working families, the women in the new white-collar working class went to work. In the expansion of tertiary education from the 1960s, female participation initially lagged slightly behind men, but then overtook it. By the 1990s, a majority of university graduates were women. In the total labour force, numbers of male and female graduates were roughly equal. Business families often channelled their daughters into learning useful technical skills (accountancy, business administration) and let them study longer, while their brothers were taken more quickly into the family business. As a result, by the 1990s, women outnumbered men in professional and technical careers. In many new business sectors, such as finance, they had a dominant role. At one point in the late 1990s, all the deputy governors of the central bank were female. Among the big Thai-Chinese business families, some women rose to prominence from a background as property owners, and others simply by outshining their male siblings, creating a number of new female business role models, including Chanat Piyaoui of Dusit hotels and Sirilak Omphut of the Mall group.

Yet most family firms remained patriarchal. Curiously, the entertainment industry remained rather male-dominated, and the TV dramas tended to repress women by portraying them as weakly subordinate, more emotional than rational, and prone to tragedy, especially as the reward for ambition. Meanwhile, political power retained a strong male bias, from bottom to top. In 1995, only 2 per cent of village heads were female. In the bureaucracy, women were an overwhelming majority in the lower rungs, and a negligible minority at the top. The female proportion of MPs never exceeded 15 per cent. As a result, the strong patriarchal bias in the legal framework changed slowly, and women continued to be disadvantaged, especially in marital law. Men continued to acquire women as minor wives or through the sex industry, while demanding different standards from women.

LABOURING HARD

The policy shift in the early 1980s quickened the pace of urbanization. Urban labour demand grew. The multiple crises in agriculture (see below) encouraged more migration out of the villages. Between 1985 and 1995, the manufacturing labour force doubled to almost 5 million. At the height of the boom, in five out of six years running, a million people a year shifted from agriculture to an occupation in industry or services. Many still circulated between city and village for short or medium periods. But gradually more moved more permanently to the city. The catchment for urban migration spread beyond the central region, which had supplied most of the early migrants. From the mid-1980s, the majority came from the northeast, the poorest region. The second language of the city became the northeastern dialect of Lao.

During the 1973–76 political upsurge, workers secured a labour law which legalized unions and federations. After the 1976 coup, the Thanin government revoked the law, and promised foreign investors they would have no difficulty with strikes. This policy was eased in the late 1970s, but labour was still kept under control by a battery of measures. Legislation restricted unions to labour issues and outlawed political activities. As part of anti-communist strategy, the military intervened to divide worker organizations, and to coopt labour leaders with patronage ties. The government established tripartite (labour–employer–government) bodies which set minimum wage rates, and mediated labour disputes. The labour bureaucracy practised divide and rule by selective patronage. Once Thailand set out to attract foreign firms manufacturing for export, this enforced docility of labour was advertised as one of the country's attractions.

With growing labour demand and a more democratic atmosphere in the 1980s, labour organization temporarily strengthened. In 1989–90, unions won a Social Security Law providing basic medical care and life insurance. The minimum wage was raised. State enterprise unions successfully resisted proposals for privatization. But these victories were short-lived. After a military coup in 1991, the junta government banned all unions in public enterprises, halving union membership to below 5 per cent of total workers in manufacturing. A labour leader who opposed the ban disappeared without trace.

Government antagonism towards labour encouraged employers to evade labour laws. Textile, garment, and other labour-intensive industries were the first to grow in the boom. Some of the workers were gathered into factories, but many more worked at home or in small workshops under putting-out or subcontract arrangements. By the late 1980s, garment making was estimated to employ 800,000 in this way. Gem, shoe, toy, and many food industries used similar arrangements. In factory-based industries like textiles, employers hired workers as subcontractors or on short-term contracts so they could reduce their labour force easily and evade the labour laws. A 1988 survey of factories in one of Bangkok's industrial suburbs found 61 per cent of workers hired on subcontract.

The technology firms which led industrial growth from the late 1980s needed a more trained and settled workforce. Conditions in these factories were generally better than elsewhere and the work was highly prized. Yet employment conditions were still uncertain. The processes which these firms located in Thailand were mostly assembly and other labour-intensive jobs which required keen eyesight and good manual skills. Firms preferred younger workers. Few could expect to remain employed beyond the age of 40, and in some firms beyond 30. Besides, many firms were footloose. While the computer-part maker Minebea was the country's largest single employer in the early 1990s, five years later its workforce had dwindled to a tenth. Many computer disk-drive firms moved from Singapore to Thailand in the early 1990s, making the sector one of the largest employers, and then moved on to China a decade later.

With no unemployment benefit system and usually no pension scheme either, some workers retained links to their village as their main form of social security. In the 1997 economic crisis (see below), around 2 million people, or one-in-eight of the non-agricultural workforce, were laid off within a matter of months. Many relied on the village as a temporary shelter while they sought new work. But large parts of the working class had become permanently urbanized and severed from any rural base. In the crisis, they dropped into sweatshops, vending, and petty services to survive.

With the formal union movement trussed up by legislation, patronage, and bureaucratic control, a movement of informal 'labour clubs' spread through the working-class suburbs of the capital. They organized protests at the workplace level, provided mutual support, and allied with non-governmental organizations (NGOs) and activists. After a fire at the Kader toy factory in May 1993 killed 188 and injured 500, this informal movement pressured government for better regulation of health and safety at work.

Many firms preferred women workers, not only because of their skills but also because they could be paid less. From the early 1980s, three out of every five additional recruits to the manufacturing labour force were women, and by 1995 half of the total was female. In seven of the ten leading export industries, four-fifths of the workers were female. Beyond the factories, women supplied much of the other labour needed by the booming urban economy. They carried bricks on construction sites, staffed the department stores, sold noodles on the pavement, hawked T-shirts in the markets, and welcomed the tourists in the hotels and bars. By the mid-1990s, more women than men were leaving the villages in the migration streams. The birth rate fell sharply as women delayed marriage and child-bearing. The nature of the rural family changed. Young couples often left children with their grandparents in the village while they went to the city to work. In some villages of the northeast, 'There is no one left but old people and little children'.[7] A 1997 song, 'Home', told the story:

> Oh you young kids, so much suffering, not enough to eat.
> The young brides and bridegrooms have all run away to Bangkok.
> Only old folks and young kids are left behind,
> Waiting for them to come home and work on the land of their birth.[8]

Money in the pocket gave working women a new standing in the family and in village society. Festivals which used to mark the transitions in the agricultural calendar were transformed into occasions for young people to return from city jobs to visit the village, pay respects to their parents, make merit at the temple, display their prosperity, see their children, and maintain their long-term ties to family and community.

As the labour market tightened in the early 1990s, the borders were tacitly opened to admit labour migrants from neighbouring countries. By 1994, an estimated 400,000 had crossed the borders and were working in Thailand. Three years later, the number had grown to 1–3 million (nobody was quite sure), possibly 10 per cent of the total labour force. The vast majority of these came from Burma, in flight from its collapsed economy and repressive regime. Smaller numbers came from Cambodia, Laos, and China. They worked in the fishing industry – some fishing ports became Burmese enclaves – on fruit plantations, as housemaids, and in sweatshops. Much of the garment industry relocated to the Burmese border region. The government established a permit system to legitimize these migrants in 1995, made a half-hearted attempt to eject them during the 1997 crisis, and reintroduced permit systems with restrictions on areas and sectors in 2000. But only a minority registered under these schemes. Most were allowed to stay under informal arrangements negotiated in each locality. They had few civil rights and no protection. They earned around 50–60 per cent of local wage rates. Those who argued with their employers risked being beaten or killed. By the early 2000s, they had become a semi-permanent labour under-class of 2–3 million people.

The first deaths from HIV/AIDS in Thailand were recorded in the mid-1980s in the gay community. In the late 1980s, the infection rate increased rapidly by transmission through the large sex industry, especially in the north, making Thailand one of the centres of the epidemic. By the mid-1990s, 2 per cent of the sexually active population was reckoned to be HIV-positive, and AIDS had become the single largest cause of death. The government launched containment policies from 1990, and the sex industry cooperated for survival. By the mid-1990s, the rate of new infections had begun to decline, and Thailand had become a model for community-based approaches to the problem. But infection continued to spread beyond the sex industry, especially by transmission from philandering men to their wives, and among sexually active youth. By the early years of the new century, 600,000 were infected.

RURAL DECLINE

In the 1970s, analysts predicted that Thailand's peasant society would be transformed into a society of commercial farmers and landless labourers by population pressure and the power of the market, especially in advanced areas like the central region. But around 1980, the emphasis of the economy shifted away from agriculture. Industry overtook agriculture in contribution to GDP in 1984, and to exports in 1985. By 2000, agriculture supplied only 10 per cent of GDP and 7 per cent of exports. Once the economy was no longer driven by agriculture, the government's attention and private investment were redirected elsewhere. The CP agribusiness conglomerate turned to telecommunications. Sugar firms bought into hotels. Rice millers built Bangkok shopping malls.

The land crisis never materialized because people were drawn away to the city. In the central region alone, the rural labour force dropped from 3.5 million to 2.5 million over the boom decade (1985–95). To compensate for the drain of labour, farmers invested in tractors, automated harvesters, chemicals, and other aids. Growing urban demand and easy access to markets enabled the remaining farmers to move into higher-value cropping patterns. Some grew three crops of rice a year. Some abandoned paddy and planted fruit and vegetables for Bangkokians to eat. Some grew crops like babycorn to be canned for export. In the 1990s, many farmers turned their rice paddies into sea-water ponds for tiger-prawns, reaping in two years profits equivalent to a lifetime of paddy-farming, though with high risks from disease and salination of the land. For the first time in 150 years, the area planted to paddy in the Chaophraya delta shrank.

In other areas with good natural conditions and good access to booming urban markets, the same pattern was repeated. In the Chiang Mai valley, farmers turned paddy land into lychee and longan orchards for export to China. In the coastal rice-bowls down the east coast of the peninsula, more farmers took to fish and prawn farming. On the lower Mun and Chi rivers in the northeast, the saline land proved perfect for growing the jasmine rice preferred by urban consumers and overseas markets. In all these areas, smallholder family farming survived, but became much more commercialized. The younger generation of the family left for education and urban work, but with better roads and bus services, and with the relocation of industry closer to the labour supply, many could commute on a daily or weekly basis. The higher-value crops and urban incomes brought more money into the community, creating opportunities for new local businesses such as shops, auto repair, beauty parlours, and karaoke restaurants. In these advanced rural areas, villages acquired a suburban air.

Beyond these areas favoured by nature and urban access, conditions were more difficult. Farmers faced two problems. First, from the mid-1970s agricultural prices declined on a worldwide scale. If measured in terms of sacks of rice, the cost of a two-stroke motorcycle, one of the rural family's first durable purchases, increased three to five times over the next thirty years. In more remote and less fertile upland areas, it was difficult to counter this trend of falling prices by diversifying away from crops like rice, maize, and cassava whose prices were falling.

Many farmers subsided gradually deeper into debt. Between 1987 and 2000, total debt to BAAC, the government's agricultural bank, grew ten times (from 25 to 256 billion baht). The government tried to counter the price fall by crop diversification schemes, but with poor results. Some schemes failed because of harsh local conditions. Some failed because of incompetence – imported cattle breeding stock which proved to be infertile were famously dubbed 'plastic cows'. Some failed because the Agricultural Department recommended the same scheme to everybody, creating a market glut.

Some farmers reacted to the unreliability of the market by trying to withdraw from it. Local communities invented credit clubs, rice banks, buffalo banks, and environmental groups to reduce their dependence on the outside. A Chachoengsao village headman, Wibun Khemchaloem, abandoned the rice monoculture which had sunk him in debt, and devised a small mixed farm which was virtually self-sufficient. He became one of several public advocates for this strategy. In 1994, the king presented a model version of a similar mixed farm, along with a 'new theory' based on the Buddhist principles of sufficiency (*pho yu pho kin*) and self-reliance (*phung ton eng*).

This strategy was inspirational, but difficult. Many other households survived by compromising between subsistence and market. They clung onto their land and village base; still grew their own rice in spite of market logic; hunted and gathered for foods and other needs; and took part in non-market forms of local exchange. At the same time, they sent out more of their youth to earn cash from the urban economy. By the mid-1990s, almost two-thirds of farm households' total cash income was earned away from the farm (four-fifths in the northeast), including 43 per cent from wage work. The cash was used for everyday consumption, for investment in sustaining the increasingly unprofitable farm, and for education which might release the next generation from farming.

The second problem was that the booming urban economy became a competitor for the resources of land, water, and forests on which many smallholder farmers depended.

Around Bangkok, housing estates and factories sprawled across the Rangsit tract which had pioneered the rice frontier a century earlier. To the east, some of the pioneer areas of the 1950s upland expansion were buried under the Eastern Seaboard's industrial estates. In the north, resort projects sprouted on valley slopes. Land was also lost to new highways, to golf courses (over a hundred built in the boom decade), to quarries for construction materials, and especially to dams and power stations feeding the growing urban demand for power. Total cultivated area shrank by 2 per cent over the 1990s.

After the defeat of the CPT, the Forestry Department began to reassert control over the depleted forests, half of which had disappeared in thirty years. It agreed with a suggestion from some agribusinesses to grant areas of degraded forest on long-term leases at minimal rents for 'reforestation' as commercial plantations. Many businesses took this opportunity to plant large areas with trees for the pulp and paper industry, particularly eucalyptus. Adjacent villages objected because they lost usage of the forest, and because eucalyptus trees drained the local watertable. Activists discovered that politically connected firms used these provisions to take control of areas of pristine forest. Villagers in parts of the northeast attacked bulldozers clearing the land for eucalyptus, destroyed seedling nurseries, and burnt Forestry Department property.

In early 1989, a landslide on an eroded hillside in the south carried away two villages. The incident triggered the government to revoke all logging concessions and declare the forests closed. In fact, illegal logging continued. Particularly along the Burmese border, timber was felled and then transported in and out of Burma (sometimes only in the paperwork) so that it could be claimed as legal import. In many other areas, resorts continued to be built on cleared forest land. Over 1989 to 1995, another 7 million rai of forest disappeared. Villagers living in the forest adapted the idea of 'ordaining' trees by wrapping them with a yellow robe, as in the ordination of monks. In 1995, villages across the north cooperated to ordain 50 million trees to mark the king's jubilee.

Dams built for irrigation and hydropower generation also deprived villagers of land, forests, and fishing rights. The first dams had been built on the upper reaches of the Chaophraya where they flooded deep valleys in mostly unoccupied forests. But such prime sites were rapidly exhausted. By the mid-1980s, most future plans would dam rivers used by local villagers for fishing, and flood areas which already had a large settled population. Villagers affected by such schemes began to protest.

Water became another focus of competition, especially in the Chaophraya delta. Because of expanding cultivation in the north, less and less water reached the dams storing water at the head of the delta. Meanwhile, Bangkok's usage of that water increased: from 0.5 million to 7.5 million cubic metres per day between 1978 and 2000. In 1993–94, the El Niño climatic effect lessened annual rainfall, resulting in a sharp drop in water storage in the dams. The Irrigation Department issued a ban on second-crop cultivation in the Chaophraya delta. Many farmers refused to comply and fought officials trying to control the watergates. Officials began to talk about a 'water crisis' and the need to tax and regulate irrigation, especially to safeguard water supplies for the capital.

Coastal waters were another focus of competition. From the 1960s, the marine fish catch increased from 0.4 million to 3 million tons a year because of new large-scale technology and the promotion of seafood exports. Stocks began to decline steeply in the early 1990s. Small-scale fishermen were supposedly protected by a 3-kilometre exclusion zone for trawls and push-nets, but the law was poorly enforced. In the early 1990s, coastal communities petitioned authorities to enforce the law, and occasionally blockaded fishing harbours in protest.

The rapid exploitation of natural resources, begun as the foundation of 'development' in the American era, had transformed Thailand from a resource-abundant into a resource-scarce country within a single generation. While poverty diminished steadily over the long boom, the division between rich and poor grew steadily worse over four decades. Primarily this was a division between urban and rural, and especially between the capital and the periphery – in particular, the northern hills, the southern border provinces, and the resource-poor northeast.

The first NGOs were established in the late 1960s. Their progenitors were Dr Puey Ungphakon, the outstanding technocrat with an interest in social justice, and Sulak Sivaraksa, the activist-journalist and advocate of this-worldly Buddhism. In the 1976 terror, both were forced to flee overseas, permanently in the case of Puey. From the late 1970s, several of the 1973–76 veterans took up NGO work as an alternative route to social change, avoiding the political polarization and violence of 1976. In the early 1980s, a movement of 'development' monks began to apply the teaching of this-worldly Buddhism that monks should work for social improvement.

In the mid-1980s, several activists in this fledgling NGO movement began to argue that the top-down development policy adopted since the 1960s had failed to improve the lives of the majority of people; rather, it had brought great social and emotional disruption. Top-down development demanded that villagers change to a more modern, scientific, and market-rational way of operation. By contrast, the activists argued that development should be rooted in villagers' own knowledge, and should try to strengthen local culture and preserve village-style social relationships since these were inherently more humane and more in line with Buddhist values than those of urban capitalist society. Seri Phongphit, a former Catholic priest and university lecturer, said: 'Let [the people] be themselves; let them be subject to their development; give them back their power, their decision, their education, their health, their government, their values, their self-respect, [their] confidence'.[9] This approach was dubbed the 'community culture movement' and became a guiding principle for many NGOs.

In the mid-1980s, the environmental movement provided another source of support. In 1982, the government proposed to build the Nam Choan dam which would flood 223 square kilometres of one of the largest remaining forest tracts in mainland Southeast Asia. The protest brought together local villagers threatened with displacement, activists from nearby towns, Thai NGOs, journalists, academics, monks, singers, and international environmental groups. The protest forced the government to delay the project and finally cancel it in 1988. This experience founded several new NGOs, which provided a bridge between local protests, middle-class sympathizers, and the international environmental movement.

In the early 1980s during the anti-communist campaign, army patrols and vigilante networks intimidated the countryside into silence. The few who resisted this regime were quietly 'dealt with'. But over the decade, the pressure gradually lifted. A new cadre of rural leaders emerged. Some, like the Karen leader Joni Odochao, had worked with NGOs. Some were villagers who had climbed the education pyramid and returned home to become local teachers. Some had gained urban experience as migrant workers. The northeastern leader, Bamrung Kayota, had been a migrant worker and labour leader in Bangkok in the 1973–76 era.

In the early 1990s, several protests gelled into new organizations. Northeastern groups protested against failed government schemes of agricultural innovation which had left them with large debts. Other groups protested against a massive army scheme (*Kho Jo Ko*) to move 6 million 'squatters' out of 1253 'forest' areas. These two protests then joined forces to oppose a government scheme to form an Agricultural Council which would offer agribusinesses, but not small farmers, an influence over policy making. From these events came the foundation of the Small-scale Farmers of the Northeast. In parallel, protests against evictions of forest dwellers in the northern hills led to the creation of the Northern Farmers Network.

Out of these events also came a new strategy of protest. To oppose the *Kho Jo Ko* forest clearances, farmers marched towards Bangkok along the Mitraphap highway, the first of the US-financed roads built into the region three decades earlier (Figure 21). The government dispatched ministers by helicopter to negotiate an agreement by the roadside before the march descended the escarpment onto the central plain. *Kho Jo Ko* was abandoned.

Over the next three years, the northeastern groups repeated this strategy to press a slate of issues which included agrarian debt, falling crop prices, access to forests, compensation for old dam projects, and cancellation of new ones. The Northern Farmers Network led a similar march through the Chiang Mai valley on issues of land and citizens rights for hill peoples. In December 1995, a new umbrella organization was formed. The Assembly of the Poor was a loose network of local protests with no leader and only a skeletal organization of NGO 'advisers'. Its name was a deliberately accusatory polemic aimed at a prospering city. The Assembly gathered together northeastern farmers, northern hill-dwellers demanding nationality and land rights, southern fishing communities threatened by big trawlers' depletion of fish stocks, and a few urban labouring groups. In 1996, it brought thousands of protesters into the city and negotiated an agreement with the prime minister which lapsed when the government fell shortly after. In 1997, the Assembly brought more than 20,000 for a

Figure 21: Farmers walk into politics. March along the Mitraphap highway in protest at the *Kho Jo Ko* land resettlement scheme in June 1992.

sustained 99-day protest and negotiation with the government which ended with an unprecedented raft of concessions, including compensation of 4.7 billion baht for villagers displaced by dams, recognition that settlers could remain in 'forests', and review of several pending dam schemes. But the government fell at the end of the year, and its successor revoked most of the concessions.

The Assembly of the Poor was the high-profile peak of a swelling movement of rural protest. The 1997 economic crisis further stoked dissent. In 1998, crop prices fell and input prices rose as the value of the baht depreciated; remittances from the city dwindled; and many migrants were thrown back on the support of the rural household, at least temporarily between job searches. In early 1998, several rural organizations demanded relief for rural debt. Over the next two years, many farmer groups blocked roads or marched to the city to demand government intervention to support crop prices. The Assembly of the Poor demanded restoration of the dam compensation payments, and opening of the sluice gates on the Pak Mun dam, a small hydro project which had devastated the ecology and fisheries of the lower Mun River. The aggrieved fishing communities camped semi-permanently outside Government House. In the north, where the government had persisted with attempts to clear the forests by defining more areas as national parks, hill villagers protested against (often violent) attempts at eviction.

Local groups became bolder in protest at large infrastructure projects which the government planned with no local consultation and perfunctory environmental assessments. Protesters failed to halt the building of the Yadana pipeline bringing natural gas from Burma through the western forests, but blocked (at least temporarily) plans for two coal-fired power stations on the east coast of the peninsula. After the World Commission on Dams condemned the Pak Mun dam, the electricity authority abandoned other planned hydro projects. A proposed gas pipeline across the southern tip of Thailand into Malaysia provoked three violent clashes between protesters and police. In several places, villages resisted the siting of waste disposal schemes.

In sum, as the urban economy increasingly attracted investment and government attention, the likelihood of a full-blown capitalist transformation of agriculture receded. The countryside remained an economy of smallholder farms, though more tied to the market than ever before. The countryside's contribution to the economy drastically fell, but the numbers living in the villages declined more slowly – to just under half the total population at the millennium. This semi-peasant society was too varied, too fragmented, and too weighted by history to translate its numbers into equivalent power in a parliamentary democracy designed and dominated by urban interests. But from the early 1990s, rural groups were able to exploit new political spaces in media, in academic and policy debate, and on the national highways and city pavements. As one leader said: 'The power of the soldier is in his gun. The power of the businessman is in his money . . . From our experience, the power of the poor is in our feet.'[10]

The peasant had ceased to be the 'backbone of the nation', either as a producer of the national wealth, or as an imagined passive supporter of the political order. By the millennium, the government could no longer blithely expect villagers to 'sacrifice' (that is, submit) for the 'national interest', and politicians had begun to court the rural vote more systematically. This rural assertiveness provoked a sharp division in urban opinion. On the one hand, some saw the countryside as a deadweight on both economic and political progress which should be developed out of existence by education and capital. On the other hand, others believed rural communities had a right to protect their own 'way of life', were more likely to conserve the environment because they depended on it, and were curators of a culture which was more ethical, more congenial, and more truly 'Thai' than that of urban capitalism.

Over the last quarter of the twentieth century, a mass society emerged. More people were more deeply involved in a national economy. Communications shrank social space. The spread of mass media created a mirror in which the society was reflected and became more conscious of itself.

In 1975, nine-tenths of the working population had at least primary education, but only 6 per cent or just over a million people had gained secondary or higher education, which was largely designed to train offi-cials. Nothing more was deemed appropriate for a predominantly peasant society.

But the industrial boom from 1985 created a demand for people with enough basic skills for factory work. The government responded by increasing education's share of the national budget from a sixth to a quarter, adding secondary classes to more rural schools, and providing free tuition, lunches, and uniforms to reduce the cost. Over the last quarter of the twen-tieth century, the numbers with secondary or higher education multiplied almost ten times to 10 million.

This expansion created a readership for writing of all kinds. By the 1990s, even a small upcountry town had at least one shop with newspapers and magazines out the front, and a stock of several thousand pocketbooks in the back. Because publishing costs were low, these books and magazines were cheap and widely bought.

In novels and short stories, the social realism of the 1970s continued into the 1980s with a bleaker atmosphere, such as the novels of Chart Kobjitti (*Kham phiphaksa*, The judgement, 1981). More popular were the melodramas aimed at the rapidly growing middlebrow readership by writers like Tomayanti and Krisna Asokesin. In their own way, these popular family dramas and historical romances acted as a mirror for the broadening urban middle class to form an identity. In the 1990s, new writers like Prabda Yoon wrote for a young readership which had grown up in the era of globalization.

Much larger was the explosion in magazine publishing. Here the most popular genre was 'real life' magazines, including sensationalist titles like *Chiwit tong su* (Life's struggle) which featured tales of crime, love, mystery, and personal tragedy; and a feel-good type exemplified by *Khu sang khu som* (Perfect couples) which featured tales of success, happiness, and the overcoming of hardship.

Newspaper publishing surged in the 1970s. Some 177 licences were issued for dailies in 1974 alone. Some like the *The Nation* in English and *Prachathipatai* (Democracy) in Thai were breakaways from established titles and dedicated to a more aggressive and committed style of journalism. Censorship was reimposed in 1976 but eased after a year. *Matichon* was founded as a 'quality' Thai daily in 1977. In 1980, it inaugurated a weekly of news analysis that grew into a compendium of political commentary, short stories, and entertainment which was widely copied. During the post-1985 boom, Sondhi Limthongkun launched *Phujatkan* (Manager) as a business daily which combined economic news with politics, and was again copied by several other press houses. In 1991, the press successfully campaigned to revoke Thanin's Decree 42 which gave government the power to suspend publication or revoke the licences of newspapers. When the generals took power by coup in 1991 and tried to impose censorship by threat, several papers defied them. By the 1990s, dailies reached almost two-thirds of urban adults, with around half reading the popular *Thai rath* and 6–7 per cent reading the upmarket *Matichon*. A few provincial centres such as Chiang Mai had local papers, usually weekly. But essentially the press was national, issued from Bangkok, and reaching most of urban Thailand and a fifth of people in the countryside.

All other forms of publishing were overshadowed by the genre of self-help or *hao thu* (how to) manuals on all subjects but especially business success, health, and social conduct. They provided a new urban society with the guidance that neither formal education nor parents could. Many of the most popular were built around literary works, especially Chinese texts such as the *Art of War*, the exploits of the judge *Paobunjin*, and *Sam kok* or the Three Kingdoms.

In their various ways, the daily press, 'real life' magazines, melodramatic novels, and *hao thu* manuals shared the experience, fears, and aspirations of the broadening urban middle class.

THE COMING OF MASS SOCIETY: MOBILITY AND MEDIA

In 1959, the anthropologist Michael Moerman had taken two-and-a-half days by pony to reach his study village in Phayao province. A return trip in 1987 took ninety minutes by road. Four things transformed the Thai village's relations with the outside world: paved roads, tour buses, television sets, and two-stroke Japanese motorcycles (Figure 22).

The US stimulated the construction of provincial highways in the 1950s and 1960s to reach its air bases. The Thai army began to build feeder

Figure 22: Mass mobilization. Two-stroke motorcycles helped to connect rural Thailand to the market and the nation.

roads in the 1970s to have better access to the areas commanded by jungle guerrillas, and the Accelerated Rural Development programme used US aid funds to pave village roads. Local politicians with construction businesses kept up the momentum through the 1980s and 1990s. By around 1990, every village except some in the highlands was accessible by a paved road, and every provincial and most district centres were connected to the capital by an overnight bus.

Japanese firms began assembling motorcycles in Thailand after the Second World War and gradually converted to local production. By the mid-1970s, sales ran around 50,000 a year. As the economy accelerated and as migrant remittances to the villages increased, motorcycle sales rose steeply, touching 2 million a year before the 1997 crisis. Most of these were sold in the rural areas, where by the mid-1990s over three-fifths of all households owned one. With their cheap price and ability to go where there are no roads, they revolutionized rural transport – ferrying farmers to their fields, housewives to the sub-district markets, children to school, and everyone to temple festivals.

By 1980, almost every urban household had a television, but only a third of households in the countryside. Over the next decade, the Japanese government gave aid for rural electrification to promote demand for consumer durables, and the TV stations extended their coverage nationwide. Once the remittances from migrant labour increased in the late 1980s, a television set became the first purchase choice. By the mid-1990s, over 90 per cent of rural households had one.

While the government abandoned the fight to control print media, it was acutely aware of the power and rural reach of electronic media, especially television. Up to the 1990s, all four TV stations and all 400-plus radio stations were operated or licensed by the armed forces or government agencies. The content was closely controlled. The radio news was a succession of press releases by official agencies. The TV news began with the royal family and tracked down the military and political hierarchy. Prime time was reserved for locally made drama serials. Special programmes were broadcast about the monarchy, armed forces, the standard version of history, and official views of national development.

Gradually, this situation eased, albeit partially, but enough to allow these media to become more of a mirror in which the society could project itself. Around 1990, television channels moved the royal news to its own segment, and abandoned the strictly hierarchical format. More programming was subcontracted out, allowing companies like Watchdog and the Nation Group to introduce more independent political commentary and debate. Locally made drama serials grew in quality and popularity, often adapting popular melodramatic novels, and serving as a mirror for the formation of the new middle class. Every night around half of urban adults sat down to watch, and newspapers serialized the scripts for those who missed episodes. Though scattered across genres of love story, family drama, ghost story, and action drama, few scripts wavered from a focus on the new middle class. Favourite themes were the individual achieving success against adversity, the family achieving new prosperity without losing its moral compass, and the struggles against old habits of nepotism, violence, and corruption. The dramas were also a showcase for sharing tastes in dress, fashions in home design, forms of speech, and models of social behaviour.

As the rural audience widened and prospered somewhat in the 1990s, the programming tilted towards them. The TV drama, *Nai hoi thamin* (The hardy drover), was the first to present villagers as more than comic relief, and to feature urban actors struggling to approximate northeastern rural accents. More time was devoted to gameshows, often hosted by comedy troupes recruited from the low-brow nightclubs (*kafe*) catering to rural migrants. Radio DJs quietly overthrew official linguistic unity by playing and introducing songs in local dialects.

Popular music formed another social mirror. The 'songs for life' band Caravan returned from the jungle in the early 1980s. A new band, Carabao, managed to popularize the genre while retaining some of its political content. In 1984, Carabao's 'Made in Thailand' became one of the first national hit songs by poking fun at the enthusiasm for foreign goods and brand names. The central region style of *luk thung* became popular in concert tours from the 1960s onwards by reflecting the sorrows and aspirations of the rural migrant. It then gained a national audience through audio-tapes and radio. The early death of *luk thung* singer Phumphuang Duangjan in 1992 found a prime minister and a princess anxious to associate themselves with her funeral. In the 1990s, *luk thung* penetrated TV, and singers became national stars, wafted off to Tokyo and Los Angeles to entertain the Thai diaspora. The northeastern style of *mo lam* was also updated and popularized, and the Khmer border region's *kantreum*. In the 1990s, companies like Grammy began to organize these stars, as well as domesticated versions of western and Japanese pop, and to cultivate a national 'star culture' by exploiting the synergies between music, TV dramas, and product advertising.

CELEBRATING DIVERSITY

This expansion of new public spaces in print and electronic media formed a mirror in which a rapidly changing society could reflect and share tastes, social conduct, aspirations, and even political ideas. It was very much a single national mirror. Almost all of the media emanated from Bangkok, and primarily reflected city society. Hence it had a powerful influence in establishing an aspirational standard for the rest of the country. But it was also a mirror that increasingly reflected the diversity of the society.

One area where this was evident was in religion. Popular practice of Buddhism in terms of temporary ordination and attendance at the local *wat* was in decline. But other, new forms flourished, aided by the advances in media and communications. Pilgrimage tours by charter bus became popular, swelling the patronage of temples associated with famous monks, both living and dead. Several living monks acquired a national audience through radio talks, audio-tapes, or simply prominence in the national news. The differences in their style and message allowed the audience a choice. Phra Phayom Kalyano advocated a modern and rational approach to urban life. Luangta Mahabua had a reputation for ascetic practice and resulting supernatural power. Luang Pho Koon offered a talent for miracles coupled with a distinctly northeastern, levelling earthiness. Such monks attracted huge followings, and channelled large donation incomes to projects of charity and construction.

Popular religious practice had never been as controlled as the authorities might want, but now many new forms flourished in response to social change. People removed from their communities needed more individual forms of practice. Many sought ways to manage life's new uncertainties, which were no longer about the weather or epidemic disease but about business risks, marriage prospects, exam results, and social standing. Amulets became even more popular as protection against misfortune. Several magazines appeared to publicize their provenance, powers, and prices. Spirit mediums were consulted for advice on business and personal matters. Retreats and insight meditation became fashionable among the more sophisticated. Help on anything from business decisions to lottery selections was sought from Brahma images in spirit houses, shrines to the Chinese goddess of compassion, Kuan Im, a host of monks with auspicious names like Luang Pho Ngoen (Reverend Father Money), and even the spirit of the deceased country singer, Phumphuang. The equestrian statue of King Rama V in Bangkok became the centre of a votive cult, which began among middle-class Bangkokians concerned about economic and political stability but then broadened its social and geographical base to become a stop on upcountry bus tours to the capital. Buddhist *wat* which had some historical association with the Chinese in Thailand (such as Wat Phananchoeng in Ayutthaya) attracted the patronage of the urban wealthy, and began to acquire some of the functions and the atmosphere of a Chinese shrine.

Some monks attracted sect-like followings. Phra Pothirak offered a lay, urbanized version of the forest monk practice of asceticism. After the followers of his Santi Asoke movement increased and also became entwined in politics, Pothirak was forced to disrobe in 1989, and his followers mostly retreated to self-reliant rural communities. Dhammakai began from one monk's popularization of a form of insight meditation, but was then marketed to students and young professionals as a route to both worldly and spiritual success. It built by far the largest religious centre of the modern era on the outskirts of the capital, and attracted over a hundred thousand to its major events. In 1998, after followers claimed to witness a miraculous apparition in the sky, its leader was accused of using high-pressure marketing and misusing the movement's massive assets.

Although attempts to reform the Sangha organization emerged again after 2000, they seemed scarcely relevant. Conventional practices had been superseded by a 'religious market place' or, to reverse the pairing and emphasize the importance of supernatural aids for worldly success, 'a mystification, spiritualization, and enchantment of the market and capitalist enterprise'.[11]

This sense of variety was also celebrated in new versions of Thai history which emerged more in public media of magazines and pocketbooks rather than in academe. The school gathered around the *Sinlapa watthanatham* (Art and culture) magazine bypassed both the monarchical continuity and the idea of a 'Thai race' that had structured the official versions of Thai history. Instead, it adopted the modern geographical space of the nation-state and then described the variety of ethnic, social, and cultural influences which crowded its past. Sujit Wongthet, the magazine's editor, argued that the 'Thais were always here', meaning that the major 'ancestors' of the modern nation were the ancient settlers identified by new archaeology, especially in the northeast, not the Tai who migrated from the north in the standard version of Thai history. Srisak Vallibhotama, who provided much of the research background, traced Thai history as a story of widening trade networks which produced ever greater ethnic complexity which in turn demanded broader and more sophisticated political systems – with almost no role for the kings and warriors who dominated the standard interpretation. Dhida Saraya further displaced the ethnic definition of the nation by arguing that Thai was a 'civilization' characterized by its long Theravada Buddhist tradition.

The social mirror also displayed the great variety subsumed within the ethnic descriptor 'Thai'. In the protest campaigns which emerged in the 1980s, groups often drew on local identity as a source of support. The Karen in the northern hills, for example, claimed the right to remain resident in forests on grounds that they possessed special knowledge of plants and forest conservation. In the early 1990s, academics in regional universities published cultural encyclopaedias of the south and the northeast which highlighted the very different local traditions in areas which had only been attached firmly to the Thai capital in the nineteenth century. Intellectuals like Srisak highlighted the *lak lai* (diverse) origins of the people enclosed within the Thai borders by immigration and by people-raiding. Tourism encouraged the rediscovery or reinvention of local identities. A new generation of ethno-historical research began from the premise that pure Tai culture could only be found in Tai communities *outside* Thailand.

Government continued to promote 'Thai culture' through a National Culture Commission and campaigns such as the Thai Culture Promotion Year in 1994. These bodies admitted that Thai culture had been formed from many influences, but still argued that there was a coherent and unified synthesis. This consisted, on the one hand, of the high culture of Buddhism, classical arts, and courtly behaviour; and, on the other, the folk arts and close social relations of the village community.

This official royal-and-rural definition of Thai culture had increasingly less relevance to the lives and environment of the growing number of urban people, particularly those in the capital. From the American period onwards, the language of urban consumer culture (especially brand names) was English. The liberalization of markets in the 1980s, and the global revolution in communications, increased the inflow of foreign commercial products and cultural artefacts. Personal relations in everyday life, both in the open spaces of the skytrain or mega-mall and in the smaller world of the business company, diverged from the legendary closeness of the village community or the noble-bureaucratic ideals of politeness defined as proper Thai behaviour. Urban society increasingly evolved its own conventions which owed little to these supposedly 'Thai' codes of behaviour. Youth sought entertainment from Hollywood, Japanese pop, and European football. Traditional cultural performances were increasingly museumized, or reinvented for sale to tourists.

In practice, the social mirror had helped to overthrow the conceit of a single, unified, and regimented 'Thai culture' or 'Thai nation'. What remained was something more casual, and more subject to personal interpretation. Some conservatives continued to imagine 'Thai-ness' as the polite manners of the old hierarchical society. Neo-traditionalists sought it in the face-to-face traditions of a vanishing rural society. Advertisers appealing to the mass audience for beer and energy drinks identified Thai-ness with the martial spirit of Thai boxing and violent episodes from Siam's legendary history.

INTERNAL BORDERS

But the nation retained some subtle internal borders. From the American era of 'development' onwards, Thailand's rulers and the urban middle class increasingly thought of Thailand as a modern nation, enmeshed with the advanced states of the world. Those unable or unwilling to keep up with modernity risked having their membership of the nation challenged. Urban was clearly more modern than rural. Most villagers appeared to embrace development, and thus qualified as citizens of the nation, though perhaps of second-class status. Those who resisted centralized development to protect a local way of life or culture were regularly accused of being anti-national and 'un-Thai'. Most at risk were those who chose to live in remote places, especially in the hills. In the 1950s, the nationality law was amended to bring an element of discretion into the rule that anyone born within the borders qualified for Thai nationality. Ostensibly this amendment was to handle children of the refugee communities which became a constant presence over the next half-century of war and economic imbalance in the region. This discretion was used to deny full nationality to the children of hill peoples. Some were given secondary documents. Others slipped through the bureaucratic processes which conferred nationality. All suffered considerable disabilities as a result. This lack of nationality in turn justified social prejudice and governmental aggression. The massive decline in forest cover, brought about mostly by the army, government agencies, professional loggers, and lowland settlers was squarely blamed on hill peoples' shifting cultivation and opium growing. This 'crime' in turn justified denial of land and civic rights.

Another internal border marked off the Muslim population in the provinces of the far south. Despite the official policy of religious tolerance, the state remained suspicious and resentful of a community which refused to assimilate in language or religious practice. Few people from the region became teachers, bureaucrats, or soldiers. Half-hearted development funding turned the area into one of the poorest parts of the country. Lack of real tolerance for Islam or the local language in education meant that communities created their own *pondok* schools, and youth went to South Asia or the Middle East for further education. Many went to work in Malaysia, and some used the courts in Kelantan to decide issues under Islamic law. These external links reinforced the state's prejudice against this area. They also drew people from the area into contact with the changing currents of the Islamic world, especially the trend towards orthodoxy. This setting resulted in sporadic outbursts of violence – in the early 1950s, again in the 1970s, and again in 2002–04 – when local people demanded either more space for their culture within Thailand, or separation from it.

CONCLUSION

Over one generation during the last quarter of the twentieth century, Thailand's society changed with unprecedented speed. Building on the foundations of urban capitalism laid in the American era, big-business families grew not only in wealth but also in social prominence. A new white-collar middle class embraced western-influenced consumer tastes, and concepts of individualism. Capitalism drew into the city a much larger working class.

The borders of the nation were punctured by increasing flows. Total trade grew from 40 per cent of GDP in the early 1970s to 120 per cent at the millennium. Total capital flows grew from less than 1 per cent of GDP in the early 1970s to over ten times that ratio in the 1990s. Tourist arrivals swelled from a few thousand to 12 million a year. Labour flowed in from Burma and other neighbouring countries, and out from Thailand to Japan, Taiwan, and the Middle East. Information, images, and ideas arrived via satellite, TV transmission, film, and internet. The economy became more exposed to global forces, and the society to global tastes and ideas.

Equally important as globalization was the coming of mass society. Until the 1960s there were few channels through which ideas and images could be shared around. Communities were still relatively enclosed. The government was the dominant national network. From the 1970s, that changed rapidly. Paved roads, tour buses, and cheap motorcycles shrank the nation's space. National mass media created a social mirror in which the society could begin to see itself. In this mirror, the imagined unity of the nation was fragmented. The reflection revealed the variety of the society's ethnic make-up, the complexity of its history, the diversity of religious practice, and the scale of social divisions.

The boom conferred by globalization and the emergence of a national society were background for challenges to the paternalist traditions of the nation's politics.

9

Politics, 1970s onwards

The massive economic and social changes begun in the American era spilled into politics over the last quarter of the twentieth century.

After 1976, the senior bureaucracy, palace, and military still clung to the model of a passive rural society which accepted the hierarchical social and political order, and which needed to be protected against both communism and capitalism. The generals and bureaucratic elite laid plans to engineer social harmony and guide 'democracy' from above. But economically and culturally, the country was rapidly becoming more urban than rural, more dominated by business than bureaucracy, and more assertive than passive. The paternalist vision was swept away by the advance of industrialization, urbanization, globalization, and the growth of mass society.

Through the 1980s, business politicians inside the parliamentary system, and a new 'civil society' outside it, pushed the military back towards the barracks, but reluctantly, slowly, and incompletely. An attempt to halt this trend over 1991–92 proved to be a critical transition. Thereafter, the military's role declined steeply. Political spaces widened. High expectations arose for wide-reaching changes aided by the forces of globalization, and the new assertiveness in parts of mass society. The political forces which prioritized the well-being of society and nation seemed set to flourish in the broader political space. But the traditions of the strong dictatorial state had been deeply embedded. When big business felt squeezed between the forces of globalization and the growing pressures for democratization, these traditions were revived.

NATIONAL IDEOLOGY AND NATIONAL IDENTITY

The violence of October 1976 was an immense shock. It violated the official self-image of a peaceable and progressive nation. In the aftermath, the National Security Council, a policy-making body founded in the Cold War era, began to seek ways to 'create unity between the people in the nation . . . so that people are of one heart'.[1] The Council's academic advisers concluded that the old triad of 'nation, religion, and king' was no longer 'stimulating' for a society which had changed so rapidly in the previous generation. Thailand needed a 'national identity' to overcome the polarized politics of the 1970s, and a 'national ideology' which could capture aspirations for progress, as communism had done for many people in recent years.

This project concluded that the new touchstone would be 'nation, religion, monarchy, and democracy with the King as head of state'. In practice, this differed from the old formula in two ways. First, the monarchy would assume a much more prominent role as the focus of national loyalties in comparison to the other two components of the old trinity. Second, democracy was added in recognition that the 1973–76 era had revealed aspirations for liberty, participation, and self-expression which were too powerful to suppress. The 'national ideology' was not publicly promoted like Pancasila in Indonesia, but was 'an instrument of the national leaders . . . to use with the masses in order to produce change in the required direction'.[2] In the late 1970s, a National Culture Commission and National Identity Office (NIO) were established. New magazines and radio programmes were launched to implement the project.

From research, the National Security Council found that the peasantry, estimated to be 80 per cent of the population, honoured the monarchy and religion, and had no interest in politics. It concluded that they needed reasonable livelihood, and paternal officials to look after them. A book on Thailand published by the NIO in 1984 pictured Thai society as a pyramid, essentially unchanged since the Sukhothai era. At the top was the king; next came the bureaucracy created when 'the king found it impossible to manage the nation's affairs single-handedly'; and at the base were peasants living in unchanging, peaceful villages 'where democracy is practised in its purest form'.[3]

The Interior Ministry embarked on 'political education' to prepare the people for 'democracy'. Its own research studies concluded that the Thai people were not ready for democracy because of poor upbringing, an innate lack of ethics or seriousness, or simply a 'disposition to be under the command of others'. These findings justified education programmes to inculcate the national ideology and the duties of citizenship, not rights and freedoms. The NIO defined 'Thai-style democracy' as good government which respected the (undefined) rights and aspirations of the people and hence could rival communism for popular appeal. It would be achieved by 'good people', rather than by representative institutions.

The phrase 'democracy with the King as head of state' had appeared in earlier constitutions. Now it became standard. History was adjusted to reflect this close association between the monarchy and Thailand's progress towards democracy. In 1980, a statue of King Prajadhipok was completed outside the new parliament building. The project had been mooted much earlier, but funded only in the aftermath of 1976. The statue expressed in solid form a history in which Prajadhipok ushered in democracy by granting the constitution on 10 December 1932. In this revisionist version, the People's Party's revolution had been a rushed mistake which resulted in fascist militarism and communism. The statue was inscribed with words from Prajadhipok's 1935 abdication statement in which he refused to cede power 'to any individual or any group to use it in an autocratic manner'. The monarchy thus became the fount of democracy.

POLITICAL SOLDIERS AND 'PREMOCRACY', 1980–88

The military assumed the major responsibility for realizing this paternalist vision of the nation and its political future.

The coup of 6 October 1976 returned the army to power. With a record now stretching back four decades with only two short intermissions, the military domination of politics was deeply embedded. But the impact of the massive US patronage – and then its removal – was unsettling in many ways. The number of generals had rapidly increased (to over a thousand), creating intense competition at the top. From the 1930s to the 1950s, the First Army had managed politics through its ability to control the streets of Bangkok, but now there were several centres of power in the armed forces. The counter-insurgency had increased the size and status of the provincial armies, and of new technical and strategic offices at the centre (like the ISOC). In addition, fighting a political war had politicized the army, especially the middle officer cadre. In army journals, different groups debated why the army was fighting a war against its own people, and how to oppose communism by *political* means.

Politicized groups of mid-ranked officers gained influence because their direct control over men and firepower was critical in the power plays among rival generals. The *Khana thahan num*, dubbed the 'Young Turks', was a group of around ninety middle-level officers who came together in the early 1970s and became prominent in the coup politics at the end of the decade. Most had been trained by the Americans and seen combat in Vietnam. They were not only fiercely anti-communist (several were involved in the 6 October repression) but also fiercely anti-capitalist. They viewed the peasantry as 'the producers and backbone of the nation' and believed communism had prospered because 'the capitalists take too much advantage . . . these capitalists are destroying the nation, the institutions . . . destroying everything, not only causing misery for the people'.[4] They distrusted parliament because businessmen could manipulate elections. They believed the military had the right and the duty to control the state in order to manage these social divisions. They were distressed by the army's fall in status in 1973, which they attributed to corrupt relationships between businessmen and generals like Thanom and Praphat. Because of their command over Bangkok troops, they were instrumental in the successful coups of 1976 and 1977.

The *Thahan prachathippatai* or Democratic Soldiers came mostly from the ISOC or the general staff. They had been involved in devising political strategy to counter communism, and been greatly affected by working with CPT defectors such as Prasoet Sapsunthon. Like the Young Turks, they believed that the problem of communism stemmed from capitalism because 'some groups have been able to take advantage and build up monopolistic power which inflicts social injustice and material hardship on the people, creating conditions for war'.[5] Chavalit Yongchaiyudh, one of the group's leaders, argued: 'What is even worse are all the "influences" which are deep rooted in the rural society . . . if they are not happy with someone, that one may die, he may get killed'.[6]

The Young Turks revered General Prem Tinsulanond as a 'clean' soldier and helped his rise to the premiership in 1980. But Prem did not depend on them. His rise had also been overseen by King Bhumibol who saw Prem as a soldier on whom the monarchy could rely. Prem did not adhere to the Young Turks' narrow ideology but understood the need to compromise with business as one of the powerful forces in society. In 1981, he took into his Cabinet a soldier and some businessmen whom the Young Turks found objectionable. They launched a coup on 1 April (hence the April Fool's Day coup), which Prem evaded by escaping to his old garrison base at Khorat in the company of the royal family. Against this combination, the Young Turks surrendered. The leaders were jailed but only temporarily, because Prem believed they might still be a useful source of support. In 1985, they launched another failed coup attempt, after which the leaders were cashiered and the group dissolved.

The Democratic Soldiers were more pliable, and Prem drew on them to plan a 'political offensive' to mop up the remains of communism and manage the return to parliamentary democracy. This strategy was issued in 1980–82 in two orders known as 66/2523 and 60/2525. The state under military tutelage would remove the basic causes for communism and dissent:

Social injustice must be eliminated at every level, from local to national levels. Corruption and malfeasance in the bureaucracy must be decisively prevented and suppressed. All exploitation must be done away with and the security of the people's life and property provided.[7]

This would be achieved by 'cutting down the monopolistic power of the economic groups' and distributing income more evenly. As in the discussion of national ideology, the policy highlighted 'democracy' and 'popular participation in political activities', but was not committed to full popular representation. The threat of communism still gave the army a 'sacred' duty to rule.

Under Prem's leadership, this strategy of managed democracy stretched from the parliament down to the village. Under a new constitution, parliament was controlled through an appointive Senate packed with military men. With this support and quiet palace backing, Prem remained prime minister for over eight years (1980–88). Other key ministries (defence, interior, finance, foreign) were reserved for military men and a few trusted technocrats. At the same time, parliament was restored; elections were held from 1979 onwards; and other ministries were allotted to elected MPs. Some generals resigned to support Prem in parliament. This arrangement was dubbed semi-democracy or 'Premocracy'.

More government funds were invested in rural uplift to remove the rationale for communism. The Fifth Plan (1981–86) for the first time included greater social and economic equity as an objective on grounds of 'national security'. A poverty programme identified the 12,652 poorest villages (60 per cent in the northeast) and showered them with water supply, roads, schools, irrigation, electrification, and soil improvement. General Chavalit oversaw an *Isan khieo* (Green northeast) scheme under which the army built small irrigation works and other development projects. None of this stemmed the trend to growing inequality. Similarly, the avowed attempt to restrain capital came to little. The Fifth Plan vowed to break up monopolies in banking and industry, but nothing resulted.

The army oversaw a network of propaganda and surveillance, especially in the countryside. The Village Scouts were revived after a short lull. They continued to receive royal patronage, and counted 3 million members in the early 1980s. In 1978, the ISOC set up the Thai National Defence Volunteers which trained and armed around 50,000 villagers to act as informants and vigilantes. The Red Gaurs, rangers, and several other groups operated alongside. Army radio broadcast propaganda morning and evening from the loudspeakers erected at the centre of every village. Rural activists were quietly dealt with. A deputy head of the ISOC explained later how they operated in these years: 'we had a "hunting unit". It was easy. We got a list of communist leaders, then . . . bang! That's it. Then we went home and rested.'[8]

MONARCHY TRANSCENDENT

With the support of Prem and efforts of the National Identity Office, the king's public role in the polity expanded further, in three main aspects. First, in keeping with the rural emphasis and his own interests, the king concentrated increasingly on the 'royal projects' of village uplift. In 1980, the government began to contribute to these projects from the regular budget as part of the overall strategy of rural development. An office was created in the planning board. Top officials in the Irrigation Department were seconded. Six development centres were built at regional palaces. The range of activities expanded from the earlier emphasis on irrigation and hill peoples to encompass rural projects of all kinds. Pictures of the king and other royal family members engaged in these activities figured prominently in the television news.

The king championed the small farmer in the face of accelerating change and growing urbanization. In 1991, he said: 'We do not want to be one of those very advanced countries . . . because if we are a highly advanced country, there is only one way to go: backwards . . . if we use a "poor man's" method of administration, without being too dogmatic about theory, but with the spirit of unity in mind, that is, mutual tolerance, we will have more stability'.[9] In 1994, he unveiled a scheme to make small farmers totally self-reliant and independent of markets through a mixed and integrated organic farm. Queen Sirikit explained: 'Misunderstandings arise between people in rural areas and the rich, so-called civilized people in Bangkok . . . we try to fill that gap'.[10] In 1984, the National Identity Office dubbed Bhumibol the 'Farmer King' and 'Developer King'.

In the mid-1990s, the king also turned his attention to urban problems, seeking solutions to the problems of flooding in sinking Bangkok, and identifying sites for new highways to unclog the traffic. But the public projection of the king as developer in television and print still focused on his rural role, including testimonials from the beneficiaries of the royal projects.

The second role of the king was as the focus of public ceremonial on an even larger scale than before. The bicentenary of Bangkok was celebrated in 1982, complete with a glittering royal barge procession. Seven hundred years of the Sukhothai king's legendary invention of the Thai alphabet were celebrated a year later. These were followed by the king's fifth cycle (60th birthday) in 1987; the longest reigns of any Thai monarch (1988), and of any living monarch in the world (1992); the funeral of the king's mother (1995); the reign's jubilee (1996); the king's sixth cycle (72nd birthday, 1999); and the queen's (2004). The monarchy also figured strongly in the Year of Promoting Thai Culture which the NIO orchestrated in 1994. By the late 1990s, the old city on Rattanakosin Island was a site of almost constant royal celebration. The municipality drew up plans to return the area to its late eighteenth-century layout, ostensibly to promote tourism, but also to reclaim some sacred space from later intrusions such as Thammasat University with its connection to the revolution of 1932. Prostration became fashionable again in the court. Any possibility of criticism of the sort which royalty faced in the 1920s was prevented by use of lese-majesty laws.

Third, the monarchy was even more strongly associated with orthodox Buddhism. Mass television brought the main events of the royal ritual calendar into the home. The Department of Fine Arts revived interest in the *Traiphum phra ruang*, the Sukhothai-era text which justified monarchy and social hierarchy in terms of unequal religious merit. A 1983 conference discussed the text's relevance to contemporary life, government, and 'national security'. The king took an interest in the monastic lineage of Acharn Man Phurithatto, a northeastern monk who had practised intense asceticism and meditation. Acharn Man had died in 1949, and his disciples soon after claimed he had achieved the status of *arahant* or Buddhist saint. Devotees from the upper ranks of business and bureaucracy had begun to patronize his monastic lineage since the 1960s. The king invited surviving members of the lineage to Bangkok, built a retreat for them in the palace grounds, visited the Sakon Nakhon *wat* where Acharn Man had died, and presided over funerary rites for three disciples.

In 1987, a palace *Memoir* of the king published for his fifth cycle noted that, since Sukhothai, the Thai monarch had ruled 'not out of any divine right, but by the consent of his fellow peers', and hence 'a Thai King is judged by the sole criterion of how much benefit and happiness he could bring to the country'.[11] The king repeated this theory of spontaneous election in interviews with foreign journalists, suggesting: 'If the people do not want me, they can throw me out, eh?'[12]

The king's birthday speeches and other public addresses attracted more attention, and became more like sermons. They constantly returned to the theme of unity, and the need for good men to rule the country. At times he showed displeasure at the institutionalized disunity in representative democracy and political party competition: 'between these two sides there is only talk, talk, talk, talk and they argue, argue, argue'.[13] His aides and courtiers were often more explicit. Tongnoi Tongyai, a royal secretary, claimed that Thailand's constitutions were 'French in foundation and American in ideal'.[14] The National Identity Office echoed that constitutions were 'an alien concept'.[15]

In 1995, the king published his own adaptation of one of the traditional *jataka* tales about the previous lives of the Buddha. In the story, Prince Mahajanaka loses his kingdom but then regains it through a test which reveals his magical kingly power. He reigns for thousands of years but then becomes aware of the meaninglessness of wealth and retires to an ascetic life. Bhumibol changed the traditional version by inserting a didactic speech on the theme of perseverance, and by delaying Mahajanaka's retreat to asceticism until he has first weaned his people from destructive acquisitiveness through education and through sustainable development using traditional technology. Mahajanaka explains this is necessary because everyone 'from the horse handlers to the Viceroy, and especially the courtiers are all ignorant'.[16]

With the passing of his senior royal advisers (Dhani died in 1974), the king gathered a new cadre who were distinguished not by royal blood but by prominence in modern society. They included soldiers from the Cold War era (notably, Prem), technocrats who shared his view of development and society, and business leaders often from the great Thai-Chinese lineages of the late nineteenth century.

With his image of devotion to the peasantry, constant ceremonial presence, promotion as the centrepiece of national identity, and increasing longevity, the king's *barami* (charisma, innate authority) steadily increased. With his European upbringing he had begun in the style of the Fourth to Seventh Reigns as a symbol of westernized modernism. But with Dhani's initial urging and thereafter on his own, he had become more a symbol of tradition in the face of change. Under Sarit, this traditionalism had been promoted by military and business in the face of communism, with the king portrayed as the paternal ruler of a nation of loyal and untroublesome peasants. But, as communism declined and the peasantry became both smaller and more truculent, this image lost its power. The new generation of courtiers and royal supporters celebrated the monarch as a modern *thammaracha* and a moral counterweight to the excesses of military and business. A book for the 1996 jubilee, *Thailand's Guiding Light*, described the king as a 'beacon of hope . . . symbol of unity . . . pillar of stability', working to overcome 'the "forces of greed" represented by the collaboration of unscrupulous private investors, politicians, and public officials'.[17] The monarchy had been reinvented as the hope of a new urban middle class.

THE BUSINESS OF POLITICS

In their different ways, the mandarin ideologues of the NIO, the political soldiers, and the new royalists imagined the state constraining the rise of business on behalf of a bewildered peasant. Reality was rather different. Once an elective parliament was restored in 1979, businessmen jumped at the opportunity it presented them. The military's suppression of any form of political organization among peasants or workers delivered the parliament into the hands of commerce. The proportion of Assembly seats occupied by businessmen rose from one-third in 1979 to two-thirds in 1988.

Three parties dominated through the 1980s decade: Social Action, Chat Thai (Thai Nation), and the Democrats. Each was led by someone with a title signifying old forms of hierarchy: the royal-related Pramoj brothers, Kukrit and Seni, and General Chatichai Choonhavan. But the financial support and dynamism of these parties came from Bangkok's business community. Social Action attracted 'modern' businessmen, often in partnerships with western firms. Chat Thai was centred on the textile industry and other joint ventures with the Japanese. The Democrats were weighted towards agribusiness. The banks, which still dominated the business world, stayed unaligned but also unmatched in influence over all parties.

While Bangkok business initially dominated these parties, over the 1980s it was displaced by provincial business. Ninety per cent of MPs were returned by upcountry constituencies. Local business figures, borne up by the expansion of the provincial economy, gradually claimed these seats, and then also control of the main parties.

Until the 1950s, most provincial towns were administrative centres with populations of a few thousand and only petty commerce. Since the 1960s, they had been transformed – first by the rising cash-crop trade; then in some places by the US spending on its bases; then by government investments in infrastructure (roads, schools) to tie the localities more closely to the nation; and finally by rising demand for transport, retail, services, and entertainment. Some of the successful provincial entrepreneurs came from old noble and bureaucrat families. Many more were second- or third-generation Chinese immigrants. Laws and regulations imposed little restraint on business practices. The biggest profits were often made in areas which straddled the line dividing the legal and the illegal (logging), or which were clearly criminal (smuggling, illegal gambling), or which required official cooperation (contracting, land development). Because such businesses often delivered the highest profits, some of the most prominent local figures were those involved in them. They needed help from local officialdom in the form of protection from the law, advantages over competition, and assistance to overcome bureaucratic and legal barriers. They paid for this aid by sharing some of the profits with officials, but also by supporting the state's campaigns of surveillance and propaganda. Local businessmen were major supporters of the Village Scouts.

The rising provincial businessmen grew not only rich but also powerful. They developed close connections with the stratum of village-level traders, contractors, and village heads who served as the channel through which crops and other resources were siphoned out of the villages, and government schemes of patronage and propaganda imposed on them. Through cooperation with local officialdom, they had access to the semi-official armed forces which enforced the military government's policies of control. They reinvested some of their profits in local patronage – sponsoring funerals, subsidizing schools, helping out in times of sickness – which supplemented the government's sparse provision of social services. They were increasingly referred to as *itthiphon* (influence), *itthiphon meut* (dark influence), or *jao pho*. This last term originally referred to a local spirit and alluded to supernatural power to act above the law. It was also an exact translation of 'godfather' and was used for the Thai version of the Hollywood film. A police general noted: 'The structure of a godfather's power is like a pyramid. At the top is the man with influence. At the left and right bases of the pyramid are hired gunmen and officials who support the godfather.'[18] The lack of law, access to violence, and official connections were the basis of rapid primitive accumulation. They were also the basis for success in electoral politics.

At elections, ambitious new provincial businessmen used village-level networks, cash, official backing, pork-barrel offers to fund local projects, intimidation, and sometimes chicanery (ballot stuffing) to gain votes. Local electorates chose them perhaps for immediate rewards (vote-buying), perhaps because a strong, ambitious representative was more likely to bring benefits back from Bangkok to the locality. At each successive election (1979, 1983, 1986, 1988), more of the MPs were provincial businessmen. One of the most prominent was Banharn Silpa-archa, a second-generation

Chinese, raised in the market of Suphanburi. He made his first fortune by gaining a monopoly on selling chlorine for municipal water supply. He extended into construction contracting, and then into land dealing, transport, petrol stations, and other businesses in the locality. He was first elected MP in 1975, and concentrated on gaining an abnormal share of budget funds for Suphanburi. His businesses rose on the results, and the grateful citizens voted him back at every opportunity.

The provincial MPs were able to distribute budget spending away from the centre and, rather haphazardly, spread it more widely. Their role attached the provinces politically to the centre more tightly than decades of administrative plans. At the same time, parliament gave such new MPs a higher social status, broader access to business opportunities, and higher levels of protection. Laws were passed in 1979 and 1983 to force them into parties, but in reality these parties were little more than factional groupings jockeying for access to the Cabinet and government decision-making. While soldiers and technocrats monopolized the principal ministries, the business parties competed to control the lesser ones, especially those with substantial capital budgets for construction and procurement (education, transport), or those with rule-making powers which framed business opportunities (agriculture, industry). The parliament became a clearing house for business deals, especially construction contracts. Its operation reflected this commercial logic. Candidates invested heavily in elections, and then sought ways to recoup through corruption or business profits inflated by political advantages. Parties were held together by regular payments from the leader. By the 1990s, elections were preceded by a transfer season of competitive bidding. Money was occasionally distributed to influence specific parliamentary votes. Prem reshuffled the Cabinet on a roughly yearly basis, and called elections on a two-and-a-half-year rhythm, to allow competing factions to share the benefits. The system was dubbed 'money politics'.

BUSINESS AGAINST MILITARY: THE CHATICHAI CABINET, 1988–91

Over the eight years of Premocracy, the relationship between business and military soured. After Prem tamed the 'political soldiers', old-style generals rose back to prominence. With the ending of US patronage, the military relied on the national budget both for legitimate funding and secondary incomes. Its share of the total budget rose from 17 per cent in 1975 to 22 per cent a decade later. With increasing confidence from their base in parliament, business politicians wanted to divert these funds to economic growth. They also resented the generals' sinecures in the management of state enterprises and their domination of electronic media. The press began to raise questions about corrupt commissions on arms deals, and other profiteering from the generals' privileged positions in the state apparatus. From 1984, MPs launched attacks on the size and secrecy of the military budget. In 1985 and 1987, they defeated attempts by the military to extend the constitutional clauses which underpinned the military's political influence. At the 1988 election, the press and political parties launched a campaign for General Prem to retire and allow an elected MP to rise to the premiership. Prem reluctantly concurred, and Chatichai Choonhavan succeeded him.

Chatichai's career symbolized the changing foundations of power over the past generation. He had begun as a cavalry officer leading Bangkok troops in the 1947 coup. After Sarit's rise to power in 1957, he left the military and became a diplomat. He and associates in the Ratchakhru group concentrated on business interests in finance, textiles, and joint ventures with the Japanese. In 1975, they formed the Chat Thai Party. Chatichai established an electoral base in the northeastern regional centre of Khorat, where he allied with a group of local businessmen. By 1988, Chat Thai had become the most successful party at aggregating the factions of provincial businessmen.

Chatichai's Cabinet set out to transfer power from officials to elected MPs. The key ministries of defence, interior, and finance were given to elected politicians rather than technocrats or generals. Ministers removed senior officials from key bureaucratic posts and state enterprise boards, substituting more pliant candidates and intimidating officialdom to become more obedient to elected political masters. The parliament cut the military budget, demanded more transparency in its usage, and raised queries over 'irregularities' in arms purchases. The old dictatorial press law was cancelled. The National Economic and Social Development Board (NESDB) was relieved of its key role in planning development budgets and in big projects like the Eastern Seaboard scheme. Chatichai set up a think tank ('Ban Phitsanulok'), headed by his ex-activist son Kraisak and manned by young academics. This group took the initiative for making policy away from ministry technocrats. The Chatichai government represented an end to the military's post-1976 strategy of guided democracy, and a dramatic attempt to shift power away from the bureaucracy and military to the Cabinet and business.

The 'Ban Phitsanulok' policy team proposed that the government change its regional policy by 'turning battlefields into marketplaces', namely ceasing to consider the communist and ex-communist neighbours as enemies, and exploiting the opportunities in their economic liberalization. This policy resumed the attempt, begun by Kukrit in 1975, to obliterate the divisions imposed on the region by the Cold War. It rejected the military concern for security in favour of business's desire for profit. It challenged the military's ability to make foreign policy, and threatened the military's control over border zones and their lucrative trades.

The bureaucracy, and especially the military, reacted angrily against these attacks on their powers and privileges. Through the mid-1980s, a new group of officers belonging to Class Five of the military academy rose to dominate the armed services. They disdained the ideological concerns of the Young Turks or Democratic Soldiers, and represented a return to the traditions of Sarit. They claimed to be directly loyal to the king and were openly sceptical of elected politicians. They also saw no problem about becoming involved in business, and were personally wealthy from construction and other ventures. Over 1989, the Class Five military clique established a dominating position in the military hierarchy, and began manoeuvres to undermine the Chatichai Cabinet. The issue of corruption gave them a handle to build wider support for this attempt.

Elected ministers had more power over budgets than ever. With the economy hitting a heady phase of double-digit growth, the budgets were bigger. Many large projects were launched to upgrade the country's in-creasingly inadequate infrastructure of roads, ports, telecommunications, schools, and other facilities. In December 1990, Banharn, the MP who had been most successful at diverting an excess share of the national budget to his home constituency, was appointed finance minister. Some MPs began to accuse their more successful peers of malfeasance.

The rise of 'money politics' created a reaction, especially among the new urban middle class. In 1985, Bangkok elected as mayor Chamlong Srimuang, a former Young Turk turned lay ascetic, who promised to clean up corruption. In 1988, he formed the Phalang Tham (Moral power) party to take the same crusade into parliament. Over 1989–90, press attention switched from scandals over the military budget, to stories of kickbacks on infrastructure projects. The transliterated term *khorrapchan* entered the language and became a major theme of the daily press. In a deft play on the phrase *kin mueang* ('eating the state', meaning traditional remuneration from the profits of office), Chatichai's government was dubbed the 'buffet Cabinet'.

The press exposure of corruption undermined urban middle-class support for the government and made Chatichai more vulnerable to

Class Five's manoeuvres. On 23 February 1991, the generals seized Chatichai at gunpoint and declared a coup.

THE POLITICAL CRISIS OF 1991–92

The coup represented a complex transition. On the one hand, it was a step back into the past. The military was moving to protect its privileged position in the state, and its self-appointed role to guide democratic development. The Class Five generals justified the coup to stop the corruption of the elected government, and to clear up rumours of plots against members of the royal family several years earlier. They sacked parliament and formed themselves into a National Peacekeeping Council (NPKC), whose Thai name meant 'the council to preserve the peace and the orderliness of the nation'. They later formed a political party named Samakkhitham, or unity. This vocabulary restated the old military ideology of creating unity and orderliness from above. They hand-picked a body to draft a new constitution that restored the military's ability to manipulate parliament through the Senate. The senior bureaucracy quietly supported the coup because it removed the elected politicians who had aggressively encroached on its powers.

On the other hand, the coup expressed the wish of Bangkok business and the urban middle class to find a solution to the 'money politics' of the provincial business politicians. The Class Five generals established a commission which arraigned Chatichai and his colleagues on corruption charges. They also sacked parliament and picked a former foreign service official turned businessman, Anand Panyarachun, to serve as prime minister. Anand formed a Cabinet of leading technocrats which, free of parliamentary scrutiny, rapidly passed a string of liberal economic reforms. Bangkok business and the middle class were initially enthusiastic.

But ultimately these two agendas were in conflict. As with previous dictatorial cliques, the Class Five generals' wish to oversee the state could not be separated from their wish to use it for personal benefit. These generals presented a contrast to Prem's discreet, almost ascetic style. They were already rich from business and enjoyed flaunting their wealth and power. At a class reunion, one proclaimed: 'Now we control everything except the moon and the stars'. Perhaps Thailand's first internet revelation appeared to show a member of the junta cavorting with a famous former beauty queen. The generals took control of the Defence Ministry and resumed the arms purchases blocked by the Chatichai government. They also gained influence over the Communications Ministry and awarded a huge contract to the CP conglomerate for laying 3 million telephone lines, and confirmed another contract for the rising entrepreneur, Thaksin Shinawatra, to launch a satellite. The junta's own hand-picked premier, Anand, challenged the telephone contract for corrupt over-pricing and conflict of interest (a leading member of the junta was connected to the CP company through marriage). Business support for the junta slipped after foreign governments and financial experts warned foreign tourists and investors to avoid a coup-ruled country. With the added impact of the Gulf War, the growth rate slackened and the stockmarket index lurched downwards.

Against this background of waning urban support, the announcement of the military's new constitution provoked a revival of pro-democracy groups from the 1973–76 era. These came together in the Campaign for Popular Democracy (CPD), which protested against the 'despotic' provisions of the constitution draft to show that 'the army could not claim they had the full support of the country'.[19] Yet, in his birthday speech in December 1991, the king advised: 'Anything can be changed . . . if it does not work smoothly, it can be amended',[20] and the protests faded. But the respite was temporary. In early 1992, the junta cancelled the corruption proceedings against several of Chatichai's ministers, who shortly afterwards joined the Samakkhitham Party formed to support the military. At elections in March 1992, this party won the largest number of seats and prepared to form a government. After its initial candidate for premier had to withdraw under suspicion of drug trading, the junta leader General Suchinda Kraprayun stepped into the breach, contravening a public promise never to aspire to the premiership. His Cabinet was a mixture of military figures and prominent money politicians, including Banharn at the helm of the lucrative Communications Ministry. The junta had metamorphosed from the scourge of money politics into its patron.

When the CPD relaunched demonstrations in May, the urban middle class gave open support. The anti-corruption Bangkok mayor Chamlong, who had been re-elected in 1990 by a landslide, pushed himself into a leading role in the protest. On 17 May 1992, around 200,000 joined a mass demonstration in Bangkok. The press noted the large middle-class showing, dubbed it the 'mobile phone mob', and drew a contrast with the student demonstrations of the 1970s. In fact, the crowd was a cross-section of Bangkok, including many rural migrants, workers, and students. Parallel gatherings met in many provincial centres.

The NPKC junta responded with a strategic plan designed for a communist insurrection, using fully armed soldiers imported from the jungle areas on the borders. Violence continued over three nights (Figure 23). Soldiers

Figure 23: Black May. A demonstrator being beaten on Ratchadamnoen Avenue on the night of 17 May 1992.

shot into the crowd. Buildings and buses were burnt. Chamlong was arrested. Suchinda claimed the demonstration was an attack on nation, religion, and king. He said: 'They want to destroy the system of government, overthrow the constitutional monarchy, and bring in a government that will machine gun people in the streets'.[21] State-controlled television showed only property destruction by demonstrators, but CNN and the BBC broadcast footage of military violence which soon circulated locally on videotape. The press defied censorship and published full reports. On the night of 20 May, when events seemed to be moving to a bloody climax, the king summoned Chamlong and Suchinda to the palace and, in a scene broadcast on television, ordered them to stop the violence.

Suchinda's government resigned. The constitution was amended. Anand was brought back for the interim. New elections were held and a new elective Cabinet formed in September 1992.

The damage to the military's status and political role was enormous. The death toll of May 1992 was initially estimated at several hundred, but later reduced to a range of 40–60. For a short time, men in military uniform were abused in the streets and refused treatment in hospitals. Anand dismissed members of the NPKC from the military, and pulled many military figures out of sinecures in state enterprises and public services. He appointed an army head who swore to keep the army out of politics – a litany repeated by his successors.

The military's political decline continued through the mid-1990s. When half the Senate came up for renewal in 1995, many military men were replaced by civilians. Generals disappeared from most boardrooms. The military's share of the government budget declined from 22 per cent in 1985 to 13 per cent in 1996. Unofficial income sources were also cut because arms buying, construction, and other military projects came under close public scrutiny. Several lower-ranked personnel freelanced as security guards, or by selling protection, particularly in the entertainment industry. Some 700 generals (almost half the total) had no substantive job. Many played a lot of golf, and some exercised their leadership skills by heading national sports associations.

The army was pushed back towards the barracks, but it still resisted internal change or greater supervision. It protected the convention that the defence minister should be a military man. It hung onto its lucrative control of the electronic media. Army units continued to run border areas which were channels for increasing flows, both legal and illegal, of goods and people. Meanwhile, the army cast around for a role which would rescue its prestige. In 1994 it issued a White Paper, arguing that 'the contest for markets and resources could . . . lead to the use of force in the future' and hence the army was important for 'protecting national economic interests'.[22] It pressed to resume a role in rural development, and in mediating the sociopolitical tensions which had escalated in the 1990s.

The military era seemed finally over. But the presumption of a political role, justified by 'national security', had become part of the military's internal culture.

REFORM VERSUS 'MONEY POLITICS'

The military's forced retreat from the political frontline opened up new political space which businessmen and activists hoped to fill. The fear that investors and tourists would flee Thailand in 1992 convinced businessmen that the globalized economy could no longer be entrusted to generals with outdated agendas. During the 1992 crisis, the three peak business associations of commerce, industry, and banking, which normally kept a distance from public politics, openly called for a return to parliamentary rule. Several prominent Bangkok businessmen announced their intention of entering politics.

At the same time, intellectuals argued that 1992 was a 'crossroads' (Chai-Anan Samudavanija) or the 'turning point of an era' (Thirayuth Boonmi), with the opportunity to sweep away the legacy of half-a-century of dictatorial rule. Democracy activists advocated comprehensive constitutional reform to change the balance of power between the state and civil society, liberation of the electronic media from military control, reform of education to emphasize skill and creativity rather than nation-building, and democratic decentralization in place of the Interior Ministry's centralized colonial-style system.

At first, it seemed that parliament would be the channel to achieve this 'turning point'. The press portrayed the elections to reinstall parliamentary democracy in September 1992 as a contest between 'devils' who had supported the junta, and 'angels' who represented hopes of reform.

Through the 1990s, the fragmented array of parliamentary parties and factions fell roughly into two groups. On one side, the 'angel' coalition at the September 1992 elections was headed by the Democrat Party. Over the 1991–92 crisis, the party refashioned itself to reflect the aspirations of businessmen and the urban middle class. It recruited bankers and technocrats who gave the party the credentials for managing the modern globalized economy. It also recruited a new younger generation of politicians who gave the party an image of urban modernity which differentiated it from other provincially based parties. It enjoyed support from Bangkok and from the southern region which had a high proportion of urban population clustered in old port towns down the peninsula, and which had an export-oriented economy based on rubber, tin, fishing, and tourism. The Democrats projected a liberal image; promised to modernize the economy through law and institutions; encouraged neighbouring countries (especially Burma) to democratize; and tried to complete the demilitarization of politics. The Democrats were the most successful party of the decade, heading the coalition for all but twenty-eight months between September 1992 and January 2001.

On the other side were the politicians who had supported Chatichai and switched to the military's Samakkhitham in 1992. They came mainly from the central and northeastern regions characterized by an agrarian economy and rather new provincial towns. Their interests were more parochial and commercial, focusing particularly on the distribution of budget to the provinces. They viewed neighbouring countries, as had Chatichai, as economic opportunities to exploit, not political problems to solve. They were not averse to cooperating with the military's efforts to revive its political fortunes.

Parliament failed to deliver on the post-1992 aspirations for change. Partly, this was because the pressure for reform soon faded. Once political instability no longer represented a threat to Thailand's globalized economy, big business lost its passion for taking a personal role in politics; making money out of the continuing boom consumed all of its attention. Similarly, broader middle-class support for reform waned once there seemed to be no political threat to continued urban prosperity. Besides, most MPs (including most in the Democrat Party) were still returned by rural electorates which were little moved by the issues behind the politics of 1991–92.

Thus, the final outcome of the events which began with Chatichai's attack on the bureaucracy in 1988 was a compromise between the senior bureaucracy and the new politicians. Chuan Leekpai, the Democrat leader who became prime minister in late 1992, was a small-town lawyer from the south. He affected the polite, restrained manner of a typical bureaucrat and always worked cautiously, with extreme respect for rules and laws. The aggressive attacks on bureaucratic power of the Chatichai era ceased. No policy-making think tank was formed, and the initiative in policy making returned to senior officials. Bureaucratic reform was constantly discussed but never formulated. Similar agreements to share power and profit between bureaucrats and businessman-politicians were negotiated down the ladder from nation to locality. Cabinets returned to the pattern of the 1980s, with reshuffles at roughly annual intervals to allow rival factions to rotate through ministerial posts.

Under this arrangement, the activists' agenda of reforms was quietly sabotaged. Constitutional changes were whittled back to some minor amendments; proposals for media liberalization were reduced to a single additional television station (ITV); discussion of decentralization was suppressed; and educational reforms were delayed.

The compromise between politicians and officials had two other results. First, it intensified the depletion of natural resources for both private and public benefit. Government agencies commandeered more land and rivers for dams and other infrastructure. The Forestry Department declared many new national parks, denying land rights to hill peoples and peasant 'squatters'. Politicians, officials, and their clients used influence to acquire land for developing industrial estates, pulp plantations, gravel quarries, golf courses, resorts, and residential development. Local peoples who depended on these resources were disadvantaged and provoked to protest. In 1978, the government had counted 48 demonstrations and protests. In 1994, the number was 998, mostly rural, and many over the control of natural resources.

Second, the 1995–97 Cabinets failed to manage the increasingly globalized and delicate national economy. This became apparent when Banharn, 'this new élite's representative *par excellence*',[23] became prime minister in 1995 at a time when the economic boom had begun to crumble. Banharn focused on the share-out of the budget among political factions, and had little awareness of the need to manage the national economy which had seemed to boom along of its own accord over the previous decade. For his finance minister, he appointed first a pliable young politician and then a pliable technocrat. He dismissed the stock exchange head over a personal quarrel, lost the central bank chief over a bank crash, and then struggled to find willing and qualified replacements. His successor in 1996, Chavalit Yongchaiyudh, promised to field a 'dream team' to manage the economy, but failed to recruit the technocrats he wanted. Within months he had lost his finance minister, central bank chief, and finance permanent secretary, and again was forced to accept mediocre replacements. As signs of the looming economic crisis appeared, academics and businessmen urged that macro-management 'is so urgent and technical it cannot be left to the politicians', and argued for 'depoliticization'.

The 1992 events had led, not to reforms to end the military era, but to a compromise between bureaucrats and business politicians which sabotaged the reform agenda, licensed profiteering at the expense of natural resources and local communities, and neglected management of the national economy.

DISCOURSES OF REFORM

The continued grip of 'money politics', and its consequences, spurred an intense debate on the future of Thai society. Although parliament had become a business club, politics *nok rabop* (outside the system) emerged to occupy the new political space created by the retreat of the military. The events of 1988–92 heightened the role of the press, academics, and public intellectuals as the voice of largely urban middle-class opinion. Through the 1990s, the press and academics unearthed the scandals of political deals and their impact on people and the environment. In 1995, the Democrat-led coalition fell after the *Thai rath* newspaper conducted a six-month campaign to expose a land reform scheme which had benefited Democrat Party members rather than poor farmers. In 1996, the Banharn government fell after the parliamentary opposition used scandals first aired by the press to flay the government in two no-confidence debates aired on live television.

In political and social debate, the focus was no longer on how to build democracy in the face of military dictatorship, but how to create a better society in the context of globalization, and how to engineer a more efficient political system. Two schools contended in these debates.

The first was broadly liberal. It believed that rapid economic growth, coupled with globalization, would convert Thailand into a modern society on the pattern of the advanced countries. 'Dynamic economy, open society' was the slogan adopted by a big-business campaign to bolster Thailand's confidence and international image in the wake of the May 1992 violence. The political scientist, Chai-Anan Samudavanija, who offered a Thai translation for the word 'globalization' and wrote a newspaper column on the theme, argued that globalization would undermine the state's role in economic development and social control, and ensure the old elites within the apparatus of the nation-state would soon be 'bypassed'.[24] Chai-Anan had earlier founded an Institute of Public Policy Studies which acted as a think tank for proposals of political reform.

Others in this liberal school put their faith in 'civil society'. For several observers, the coalition which came together to fell the military in May 1992 was evidence of a growing independent assertiveness, especially by urban society. Thirayuth Boonmi, the 1973 student leader turned 'social critic', predicted that Thailand would now experience 'a transfer of power and legitimacy from the state to society . . . from bureaucrats to businessmen, technocrats, and the middle class'.[25] Thirayuth's book on *Sangkhom khemkhaeng* (Strong society, 1993) pioneered a small industry of essays on how to develop civil society so that it could both supplement and change the state. Anek Laothamatas argued that 'money politics' arose because Thailand's democracy was founded on a peasant electorate which was a captive of the local patronage system (*rabop uppatham*). To overcome this problem, Anek argued, the peasantry had to be modernized out of existence by a mixture of prosperity and education 'so they become individuals like the people of the city and other modern classes . . . only such a civil society can deal with the state and truly control and reform the bureaucracy'.[26]

The second school in the reform debates of the 1990s was dubbed localist or communitarian. It began from the reaction against top-down, urban-biased development policies in favour of *phumpanya thongthin*, local wisdom, and *watthanatham chumchon*, community culture – the survival ethic and sharing practices of peasant society. But it used the metaphor of community to argue more broadly for an ethical, participatory, and egalitarian society. Thinkers like Prawase Wasi and Saneh Chamarik strengthened the movement's philosophical base by pointing out that Buddhism, in contrast to capitalism's urge to maximize production and consumption, taught that true well-being was found through moderation, restraint, self-reliance, and attention to spiritual as well as material improvement. The basis of a better society would be communities that had sufficient to survive so that they could be self-reliant and independent of market capitalism. The balance between centre and periphery, city and village, had to be redrawn by putting more emphasis on rights, participation, and decentralization.

Against the background of booming urban growth, continuing destruction of the environment, and rapid spread of consumerism, these ideas gained a much wider audience. Sympathetic technocrats began to seek community participation to reverse the growing economic gap between city and village. The National Culture Commission championed the community as a fount of 'Thai' values. The king's interest in rural development, and particularly his 1994 'new theory' model of a 'sufficiency' mixed farm, gave these ideas greater legitimacy.

A group of senior activists, academics, and retired technocrats brought these ideas to bear on policy making. They acted as intermediaries between NGOs and government bodies to press for a wide range of social reforms. They argued that middle-class activism had to work with local communities, both to achieve reforms which would improve social equity, and to reverse the trend of increasing conflict and violence resulting from the state's top-down approach. They formed the Local Development Institute to mobilize 'social energy' for reform. The institute championed the idea of *prachakhom* or people's assemblies in which officials, local peoples, and activists could evolve solutions to local problems. Prawase Wasi, a doctor and prominent lay Buddhist, worked with NGOs to persuade the Health Ministry to plan a system of universal health care. An ex-technocrat, Sippanond Ketudhat, fronted a project which raised business funding to research a comprehensive programme of education reform, and then badgered the government into adopting it. As a result of lobbying by localists and sympathetic technocrats, the Eighth Plan (1997–2001) for the first time was compiled by a long process of consultation with NGO leaders, development workers, academics, businessmen, community leaders, monks, and bureaucrats. The resulting document aimed to shift 'from a growth orientation to people-centred development' through 'measures to promote self-reliance in local communities and the creation of relatively secure community economies'.[27] The biggest barrier to this vision, noted the plan document, was the over-centralized government itself.

While the thinking of the liberal and localist schools was very different and often directly in conflict, they shared a common opposition to the strong, overpowerful state, and thus could cooperate while ignoring their differences. Also, this largely urban middle-class activism and the rural protest movements which swelled in the 1990s lived off each other. The rural protests tapped the services of NGO workers, journalists, and intellectuals to organize their campaigns, articulate their demands, and add a touch of legitimacy to their projects. The urban activists allied with the rural campaigners not only out of conviction but also out of a need for numbers to create political weight. By exploiting the new public space and negotiating directly with the bureaucracy, activists were able to bypass the business-dominated parliament and translate their agenda into legislation and policy commitments.

These two trends of reform thinking originated among liberal intellectuals. But, in the mid-1990s, they began to gather much wider support. Bangkok's big business became increasingly concerned about the capacity of parliamentary democracy, as currently constituted, to manage the modern economy. Many senior technocrats were simply disgusted by political corruption. Even the National Security Council embraced principles of decentralization and participation. Importantly for these groups, the monarchy could be imagined as a supporter of political reform. Enthusiastic analyses pointed to 1973 and 1992 as evidence of the monarchy's role as an agent of balance during Thailand's rapid change. In 1994, the King Prajadhipok Institute was founded with a mission to educate politicians, bureaucrats, community leaders, and ordinary people about the proper functioning of democracy.

Over 1994–97, these very varied agendas for reform came together in the demand for a new constitution. In 1994, Amon Chantharasombun, a senior bureaucrat, published a book on *Constitutionalism* with proposals for major reform. Amon argued that parliament had become too powerful, had subtracted too much authority from the senior bureaucracy, and was both unstable and inefficient, as indicated by the succession of squabbling coalitions and the poor record on legislation. In 1995, Prawase Wasi played a key role in persuading the prime minister, Banharn, to allow a Constitution Drafting Assembly (CDA) to prepare a new charter independent from the parliament. The CDA was headed by Anand Panyarachun, the former bureaucrat, business leader, and prime minister under the NPKC who had become a leading advocate of reform. The draft re-engineered

parliament along lines suggested by Amon. Election procedures were redrawn to encourage a more stable two-party system. The prime minister's
position was strengthened. An Election Commission, National Counter
Corruption Commission, Constitutional Court, and ombudsman were introduced to provide checks and balances on corruption and the abuse of
power. To upweight Bangkok's influence in parliament, 100 additional seats
would be filled by a national vote by party. To prevent the uneducated entering parliament, MPs had to have a tertiary degree – a provision which
excluded 99 per cent of the agrarian population.

NGOs lobbied for clauses to change the balance of power between the
state on one side, and the individual or community on the other. As a
result, the draft included an extensive catalogue of the 'rights and liberties
of the Thai people', formation of a National Human Rights Commission,
removal of the electronic media from the grip of military and government,
and democratic decentralization of power to local government.

THE ECONOMIC CRISIS OF 1997

In 1997, the context of these debates on Thailand's future was totally transformed by an economic crisis which changed people's perception of the
present.

By the early 1990s, four years of double-digit growth had created problems. The capital's chronic traffic jams symbolized a more general strain on
infrastructure. Real wages began to rise as reserves of slack labour were absorbed. Technicians and scientists were in short supply because education
planners had not foreseen the inflow of technology-based industries.

In the late 1980s, the World Bank had urged Thailand to liberalize its
financial system as the next stage in making the economy more efficient,
and more accessible to foreign capital. The reform technocrats concurred
with this theory. They believed financial liberalization would loosen the
grip of the existing conglomerates and allow new entrepreneurs to contribute to growth. Between 1989 and 1993, the baht was made convertible,
interest controls removed, the stockmarket made more accessible, and an
offshore banking system installed. These reforms coincided with a phase
of low growth and high liquidity in the advanced economies which made
international investors enthusiastic about 'emerging markets'. Brokerages
and offshore banks arrived from Japan and the west. Thailand was hit by a
flood of money. In 1990 alone, private capital inflows, net of foreign direct
investment, exceeded the total over the previous decade. Between 1988 and
1996, the private sector's foreign debt multiplied tenfold. The stockmarket

index rose from around 400 before the liberalization, to a peak of 1753 in January 1994.

Thailand already had a high rate of investment, and generated enough savings to cover it. Because of the strain on infrastructure and rising wages, profits in export manufacturing were already falling. Thus, although some of the capital inflow was used productively, a lot was diverted to projects based on very ambitious assumptions of future growth, and a lot went into speculative markets, especially for property. By 1995, the cracks were visible. The stockmarket had begun to slide, the property market had become detached from reality, and export growth was faltering. But foreign investment still surged, as many western firms belatedly tried to participate in what the World Bank had christened the 'East Asian miracle'. The reform technocrats, impressed by their own apparent success and goaded by businessmen gorging on cheap credit, refused to rein in the boom. They imposed only ineffectual controls on financial markets, and denied any need to float the currency.

In late 1996, foreign capital began to leak away, and international speculators began to attack the baht. The central bank contributed 500 billion baht to prop up financial institutions, and committed virtually the entire foreign reserves to protect the currency. But against the enormous funds of international speculators, these funds were puny. The government was obliged to seek the help of the International Monetary Fund (IMF), which raised a loan of US$17.2 billion, mostly from Asian neighbours. In return, it insisted that Thailand allow the currency to float on 2 July 1997, imposed an austerity programme of increased taxes and high interest rates, demanded the closure of weak financial institutions, and began reforms to further liberalize the Thai economy and facilitate access for foreign capital.

This package did nothing to soothe foreign investors. Most of the loan and portfolio money which had come to Thailand since financial liberalization fled the country within the next two years. The baht plummeted to less than half its value (against the dollar), before recovering to around two-thirds. Firms which had taken foreign loans were rendered illiquid as well as technically bankrupt. Banks which had intermediated the loans were wrecked. Creditors stopped paying their bankers. Consumers stopped spending. Over 2 million people lost their jobs. In 1998, the economy shrank 11 per cent – a dramatic end to the forty-year 'development' era during which the Thai economy had averaged 7 per cent growth and never fallen below 4 per cent.

In mid-1998, the IMF was forced to abandon its austerity programmes in the face of social distress, business anger, and international condemnation.

The government tentatively began a Keynesian economic stimulus (budget deficit, low interest rates), which was intensified by a new government installed in early 2001. In 2002, the economy began to revive.

The 1997 crisis resulted in the biggest change in business ownership since the Second World War. Many of the major conglomerates were crippled, especially those which had failed to modernize their management. Several businesses were transferred to foreign ownership. Restrictions on foreign holding in banks, property, and other sectors were eased. While loan and portfolio money flowed out, more foreign direct investment entered during three years of bust than in the previous ten years of boom. Foreign firms bought out their local partners in manufacturing joint ventures. Four middle-sized banks were sold to foreign interests, and the foreign share in other major banks rose to the range of 40–49 per cent. Two chains of large-scale modern retail were sold to their foreign partners, and three other chains entered to take advantage of low property prices. The collapse of the domestic economy and domestic firms in the crisis further increased the economy's dependence on exports, foreign capital, and tourism.

REACTIONS TO CRISIS

The shock of the crisis created a widespread demand for change, especially in the political system which had led the country into this disaster.

The constitution drafted over 1995–96 initially faced fierce opposition. Many politicians and bureaucrats saw it as an attack on their power. Police chiefs, army generals, senators, judges, and village heads all came out in opposition. Some provincial boss politicians began to mobilize the Village Scouts to block it. But the draft's fate became bound up with the economy's slide into crisis in 1997. Bangkok's businessmen and middle class began to blame the crisis on mismanagement by politicians, and seized on the constitution as the way to bring politics into line with the needs of the globalized economy. White-collar street demonstrations demanded passage of the constitution. The draft was passed on 27 September 1997, the same day that the government concluded an agreement with the IMF.

After the baht was floated in July 1997 and the economy slid rapidly into crisis, business and the urban middle class demanded the removal of the current Chavalit Cabinet, dominated by provincial bosses. They wanted the Democrats and their technocrat team to return and manage the economy. Some appealed to the army to intervene, but the generals held aloof. In November 1997, Chavalit resigned, and a reshuffle of minor parties enabled the Democrats to return without an election.

The Democrats lobbied the IMF to adjust the details of the package, but not before the economic slump had created widespread bankruptcy and social distress. In general, the Democrats cooperated with the IMF, and suffered a gradual erosion of support as the crisis deepened and lingered over the next three years.

The enthusiasm for globalization declined with the GDP figures. Some now pictured globalization as a malign force which had 'enslaved' Thailand and undermined its stability. Others concluded that the crisis showed Thailand was not prepared for globalization, and had been unwary of the dangers. Even devout liberal modernists, who initially protested that Thailand should not reject globalization and turn inwards, now admitted that the country needed to strengthen its internal institutions in order to survive and prosper in an unstable and rapidly changing world. In the pit of the crisis, localists dominated the debate. They blamed the crisis on the prior pattern of development. The monk-intellectual P. A. Payutto said the crisis had arisen because Thailand 'misguidedly developed the country in a way which relied too much on the outside'.[28] The king again legitimized this thinking in his birthday speech in December 1997:

Being a tiger is not important. What is important is to have enough to eat and to live; and to have an economy which provides enough to eat and live . . . We have to live carefully and we have to go back to do things which are not complicated and which do not use elaborate, expensive equipment. We need to move backwards in order to move forwards. If we don't do like this, the solution to this crisis will be difficult.[29]

In the short term, this was simply practical advice as people laid off from the urban economy were thrown back on the resources of the family and village. Many government departments launched community-based schemes to combat the crisis. NGO activists persuaded the World Bank not to disperse its main social relief loan through government channels, but instead through an NGO-established network to local communities for projects to build such 'social capital' as local welfare schemes, education projects, child-care centres, and environmental protection schemes.

Prawase called for 'a war of national salvation' to rebuild society from the local community upwards, based on a 'cultural economics which is not about money alone, but also about family, community, culture, and the environment'.[30] He and others called for the government to focus more on agriculture, which had been neglected in the rush to industrialization yet still served as the primary support for half the population. Rural protest groups made similar demands with a more immediate and practical bent.

They demanded the government bail out the debts of poor farmers rather than those of urban businessmen and bankers. They petitioned government to support falling crop prices. Some thrown out of urban jobs occupied vacant land, and activists demanded land reform to reverse the trend of transfer of land from farmers to urban use and speculation.

Another theme of protest developed among businessmen driven to bankruptcy. The IMF and much mainstream economic analysis blamed the crisis on the cronyism and inefficiency of 'Asian' capitalism, justifying its destruction and replacement by more advanced international capital. But local businessmen rejected this interpretation and felt abandoned by state, Democrats, and technocracy. In early 1998, they formed new organizations such as the Alliance for National Salvation, held street demonstrations, took delegations to Washington, and railed against the 'neo-colonial' policies of the IMF.

These efforts initially excited very little public support. But over 1998–99, the social impact of the crisis broadened, social divisions widened, and protests spread. Even leaders like Anand Panyarachun, who initially counselled Thais not to reject globalization, welcomed a more self-reliant approach to managing the crisis 'for the sake of the Thai way-of-life'.[31] Various projects were launched to overcome the crisis by self-strengthening. A revered senior monk, Luangta Mahabua, collected donations of 2 billion baht, including 1.7 tonnes of gold, to offset the national debt. Themes of national defence surfaced in popular culture. In 1999, the film *Bang rajan* became a huge hit by telling the schoolbook history of villagers defying the Burmese attack in 1767. Princess Suphankalaya, a semi-legendary sister of King Naresuan who won Siam's 'independence' from the Burmese in the sixteenth century, became a popular goddess who could save businesses from the crisis. A 'new nationalist' group of academics and businessmen hoped to 'plant the love of country in every person in every corner of the country' so that 'the power to rescue economic sovereignty will grow of its own accord'.[32]

In 2000, the economic crisis began to ease. But the shock of the event had thrown up powerful themes about national defence, self-strengthening, the neglect of rural society, the need for a new approach to development policy, and reassessment of Thailand's position in the context of globalization.

THAI LOVING THAI

Ultimately, this period of crisis and debate ended with resurrection of the tradition of the strong dictatorial state – this time promoted by big businessmen wanting the power of the state to manage the threats of both globalization and democratization.

In July 1998, Thaksin Shinawatra founded a new political party. Thaksin had been one of the most successful entrepreneurs of the boom, building a net worth of almost US$2 billion within five years from a batch of oligopolistic telecommunication concessions, and from deft exploitation of the rising stockmarket. He flirted with politics in the mid-1990s, projecting the image of a modern, technology-aware businessman. His new party in 1998 attracted the support of other business groups which had been battered by the crisis but had survived. These included the biggest conglomerate, CP, the leading bank, Bangkok Bank, and several firms engaged in service industries oriented to the domestic market – the major segment of the economy still protected in various ways from foreign ownership. This big-business enthusiasm for politics reiterated the pattern following national crises in 1932, 1946, 1973, and 1992. On those earlier occasions, the enthusiasm had proved short-lived, but business now was much stronger, and the crisis had convinced many business leaders of the need to control the state to manage globalization. Thaksin presented himself as a successful businessman who would help both small and large firms to recover from the crisis.

The new party played to the post-crisis mood. Its name, Thai Rak Thai (TRT), Thai love Thai, reflected the nationalistic reaction to the crisis. Its slogan, 'Think new, act new, for every Thai', and its manifesto promising to 'bring about reform in the fundamental structure of the country in all respects, so that Thailand is strong, modern, and ready to face the challenges of the world in the new era', embraced the theme of self-strengthening to manage globalization. The party contacted NGOs and rural activists to help compile an election programme of agrarian debt relief, village capital funds, and cheap health care which recognized the crisis impact on the countryside. The party's programme adopted the localist vocabulary of community empowerment and bottom-up grassroots development. Prawase Wasi, Luangta Mahabua (the monk who had organized nationalist self-help schemes), and several rural protest groups endorsed the party.

With evidence of this growing support, Thaksin gathered the support of many provincial bosses who understood that the Democrats and their allies were likely to be defeated because of their association with IMF-mandated policies. Thaksin also spent an unusually large budget on a more polished, coordinated, and powerful election campaign than hitherto seen. At the polls in January 2001, Thai Rak Thai won two short of an absolute majority, and subsequently converted that into a majority of almost

300 out of 500 seats by absorbing two other parties (including that of Chavalit). The Democrat Party hung onto its base in the south, and remained the only other major party.

Besides this strength in parliament, Thaksin benefited from new constitutional provisions designed to strengthen the prime minister and create more stable and long-lasting governments. He also conducted himself as a politician of the communications age, delivering weekly radio chats about his activity, and dominating press and television news. The government implemented its electoral programme within its first year in office, cementing public support.

The TRT government used this powerful position to launch an ambitious programme of reform which reflected its core of big-business support. Thaksin prioritized economic growth, not just to escape from the crisis but also to leapfrog Thailand to first-world economic status. Government began to support domestic business in a fashion which more resembled the developmental states of East Asia than ever before. Government financial institutions were ordered to provide credit to priority sectors and chosen firms. Foreign consultants were hired to identify priority sectors and propose programmes to increase their competitiveness. Individual firms associated with the government benefited from debt relief and promotional policies. The government also set out to deepen Thailand's capitalism by incorporating the peasant economy and black economy into the mainstream. As part of its election promises, the government distributed a million baht fund to each village, and created other sources of small credit designed to turn farmers into small entrepreneurs.

Thaksin also planned a political transition to move beyond the era of the bureaucratic polity and money politics. He copied Chatichai's example of making wholesale reappointments in the senior bureaucracy and state enterprises to intimidate officialdom into submissiveness; set up an extensive structure of advisory bodies to take control of policy making away from the ministries; and overhauled the bureaucratic structure. Thaksin talked of himself as a 'CEO premier' and promised to replace old bureaucratic practices with more efficient business methods. Diplomats and provincial governors were called for 'CEO style' retraining, and ordered to focus on economic growth. At the same time, he launched an attack on the 'influence' which dominated local politics and local elections. He first targeted the methamphetamine drug trade in a campaign which took over 2700 lives and served as powerful intimidation. He followed up on the electoral programme with a host of other populist schemes, including cheap urban housing and redistribution of land to the landless, which emphasized that the central government machine was a more powerful fount of patronage than the local boss. These attacks on the bureaucrats and provincial bosses, whose mutually beneficial compromise had shaped the politics of the previous decade, paved the way for a new politics dominated by parties appealing for mass support.

The Thaksin government also closed down the political space which had opened up over the previous decade. It neutralized the new bodies set up by the constitution to act as checks and balances on the enhanced power of the executive. It reasserted tight control over the electronic media. Newspapers were cajoled with favours, and threatened by the manipulation of advertising budgets. Thaksin's family bought a controlling stake in the single independent station (ITV) formed since 1992. Other channels were ordered to broadcast only 'positive' news. Public intellectuals who raised their voices were fiercely attacked. NGOs were accused of protesting only in order to attract foreign funding. Local groups which continued attempts to defend their local interests were described as 'anarchists' and enemies of the nation. Thaksin began to revive the prestige and expand the role of the military as an instrument of political control. He said he wanted *kanmueang ning*, quiet or calm politics, and expressed open admiration for the political systems of Singapore and Malaysia.

Thaksin also began to redefine the symbolic value of the nation. In 2002, he changed rules on the use of the national flag to allow a freer and more widespread use (Figure 24). He suggested the flag and other national assets should no longer be used to reinforce internal unity but to strengthen national identity and competitiveness in the external world. Increasingly he presented himself as a national leader in the tradition of Phibun and Sarit, and celebrated his pro-business policies as a national crusade. The flag was displayed on every Bangkok bus along with the Phibun-era invocation to 'unite the Thai blood-flesh-lineage-race'.

Thaksin built on the changes in the new constitution to move away from the political system which had revolved around the provincial boss politician, to one dominated by big parties supported by big money. He committed the government to support business in a way which businessmen had aspired to since 1932, but never fully achieved. He shrank the space for other agendas – especially those emphasizing rights, participation, rule of law – which might compete with rapid growth through expanding capitalism. Big business had finally come to the centre of Thai politics and appropriated the strong-state tradition to rearrange both state and nation in its own interests.

Figure 24: Waving the flag. Thaksin Shinawatra declares victory in a war against drugs in December 2003.

CONCLUSION

Previous decades were little preparation for the rate of change in economy, politics, and society from the 1970s onwards. The economy launched into a headlong boom and bust which transformed income levels, swelled urban areas, raised the status of business in the social order, and exposed Thailand more both economically and culturally to globalization.

Society became much more complex, especially with the growth of the white-collar middle class, and the ranks of shuttling urban–rural migrants. Local worlds were prised open by roads, buses, motorcycles, televisions, and internet. A new mass society emerged, especially in the reflective panels of national media. Old unitary discourses of race, nation, history, national character, and culture were fragmented by the diversity of reality.

The elite management of politics was undermined by the student–worker–peasant revolts of the 1970s, by the explosion of creative expression, by globalization, and by the multiplication of social demands. At first, senior bureaucrats and generals resisted these trends by imagining a managed 'democracy' united around the national symbol of the monarchy. But this simple vision could not contain rising social aspirations and political demands. Businessmen and urban activists drove a transition towards parliamentary democracy. The military sacrificed its special role in the polity over the past half-century in an attempt to stem this tide. The monarchy evolved towards a more independent moral leadership crafted from ritual practice, Buddhistic sermonizing, and social good works.

Business succeeded the military as the dominant force in the polity. At first, provincial businessmen rose through their ability to manipulate the rural electorate. But their tendency to make politics an extension of business, and their failure to manage the sensitive and globalized modern economy, spurred Bangkok big business and the middle class to outwit them through the media, scandalization, constitutional reform, and modern election techniques. By the early years of the new millennium, Bangkok big business had finally captured the state and begun to overhaul it to more effectively serve the needs of domestic capital. A new government launched ambitious programmes to protect business both from the threats of globalization revealed in the 1997 crisis, and from the challenges of local protesters and dissident intellectuals who aspired to a broader, more inclusive, and more equitable democracy.

Postscript: the strong state and the well-being of the people

Since the foundation of Thailand's nation-state in the late nineteenth century, two traditions have evolved over its primary purpose.

The first of these began from the original formulation in the reign of King Chulalongkorn. The need for a strong absolutist state was justified to overcome external threats (colonialism) and internal disorder so that Siam could achieve 'progress' and become a significant country in the world. The right of the existing royal elite to rule this strong state was explained by history (the continuity of monarchy since Sukhothai), and by the elite's selflessness, professionalism, and monopoly of *siwilai*. The role of the nation was to be unified, passive, and obedient.

The formula was revived and updated by military dictators in the mid-twentieth century. Phibun and Wichit removed the monarchy from its central place, but kept the main elements of the formula intact. The need for a strong dictatorial state was justified to overcome external threats (communism) and internal threats (the Chinese) so that Siam could achieve progress/development and survive in a world of competing nations and ideologies. The right of the military elite to rule was explained by history (the Thai as a martial race), and by its selflessness, professionalism, and monopoly of force. Sarit, with help from the US, reunited the royal and military strands of the tradition.

In this reformulation, the role of the nation had to be adjusted because of the emergence of new urban classes with their own interests and aspirations. Wichit imagined the Thai as a free people in a free-market economy with opportunities to better themselves and change their social station. Whereas the nation was invisible in royalist history, Wichit gave it an active role in 'great migrations' from the north, the cultural achievements of Sukhothai, and deeds of martial heroism. Phibun and Wichit gave the new men and women of urban Siam roles as the vanguard of progress, especially as paternal officials overseeing the mass of society which was still judged incapable of being modern and was thus expected to remain passive and obedient.

At the start of the twenty-first century, Thaksin Shinawatra and his business party again revived the formula, and also adjusted it to reflect the emergence of a national economy and mass society over the prior quarter-century. The need for a strong, authoritarian state was justified to overcome external threats (globalization) and internal threats (democratization) so that Thailand could leapfrog into the ranks of first-world countries. The right of the new business-political elite to rule this strong state was explained by its selflessness (commitment to 'the people'), professionalism (the use of business methods), and its command of the wealth needed to win elections. The mass now had an active role as an electorate and as the audience for continual political theatre. But otherwise it was expected to remain united and passive so that the goal of economic growth would not be disrupted by distractions such as rights, equity, or democracy.

Over its successive appearances, this tradition has acquired some distinctive features. It provides a cloak for rapid accumulation by the political elite – the absolutist monarchy's accumulation of property and investments; the generals' ability to exploit natural resources and favour business friends; and the overt and covert favours for big business under the Thai Rak Thai government. It portrays the nation both as a mystical unity (*samakkhitham*) and as a distinctly graded hierarchy in which some are more Thai, more 'national' than others. It tends to project a highly masculine and martial aura, and to license the exploitation of women through polygamy and its modern variants. The periods when this tradition dominates coincide with the use of state violence against the nation's own people – the suppression of revolts in 1899–1902; Phao's killings of political rivals in the 1950s; the massacres of 1973, 1976 and 1992; the drug campaign of 2003; and repeated violence in the peripheral areas of the hills, far south, and backward northeast.

While changing in line with the expansion of the political nation, this idea of a strong state justified by external and internal threats and by the need to progress and be internationally prominent has become the dominant tradition of Thailand's politics.

The second, opposing tradition emerged in the aspirations of commoner intellectuals in the late nineteenth century, and took firmer shape in the public sphere of the early twentieth. In this formula, the purpose of the nation-state is the well-being of the nation's members. The desire to be a significant country in the world is of little or no importance. The enemy is not any threat, internal or external, but the strong-state tradition itself.

This second tradition avoids attributing to the nation any mystical unity, but instead embraces its diversity. It has rewritten history to highlight the variety of peoples bundled together in the nation, and explode the myths of unity and continuity. It counters the assumptions of power and privilege in the strong-state tradition by promoting government based on principle, the rule of law, the importance of institutions, and especially the role of constitutions. This strategy was prefigured by the memorial of 1885, and first implemented by Pridi and the People's Party in 1932. Subsequent reiterations of this tradition have returned to the same method in 1946, 1974, and 1992.

This tradition has tended to look outwards for ideas to oppose the dominant, strong-state tradition. The commoner intellectuals of the late nineteenth century looked to Meiji Japan's self-strengthening movements. The early twentieth-century publicists and politicians absorbed ideas from European liberalism and socialism. The intellectuals, students, and nascent urban middle class of the Cold War era drew inspiration not only from communism but also from western ideals of liberalism and democracy. Reformers in the era of globalization have taken up discourses of human rights, civil society, the ideal community, and direct democracy. This internationalism gives both strength and vulnerability. Advocates of the strong state repeatedly revert to nationalist arguments to denigrate opposing ideas as 'un-Thai'. In response, the second tradition often tries to domesticate its ideas by finding parallels within Buddhism.

Each political culture builds its own traditions about the uses of the nation-state. In Thailand, the strong-state tradition inaugurated at the birth of the nation-state has remained so influential because it has been deeply embedded by decades of dominance, and remains available for future political generations.

Notes

I BEFORE BANGKOK

1 Some scholars believe this famous inscription, ostensibly dated to 1292, is wholly or partly a later creation. As an illustration of *chaiyaphum*, the dating is immaterial.

2 Guy Tachard, *A Relation of the Voyage to Siam* (Bangkok: White Orchid Press, 1981 [1688]), pp. 180–1.

3 Francois Caron and Joost Schouten, *A True Description of the Mighty Kingdoms of Japan And Siam*, ed. John Villiers (Bangkok: Siam Society, 1986 [1671]), p. 128; Nicolas Gervaise, *The Natural and Political History of the Kingdom of Siam*, tr. and ed. John Villiers (Bangkok: White Lotus, 1998 [1688]), p. 53.

4 'Sakdina' probably means 'power over fields' and may originally have referred to some kind of land grant. By late Ayutthaya, however, it had become a numerical ranking attached to each official post. Recently, the term has been adopted as a shorthand for the premodern social order, equivalent to 'feudal' in Europe.

5 Alain Forest, *Les Missionnaires français au Tonkin et au Siam xviie–xviiie siècles. Livre I: Histoire du Siam* (Paris: L'Harmattan, 1998), p. 115.

6 Richard D. Cushman and David K. Wyatt, 'Translating Thai poetry: Cushman, and King Narai's "Long Song Prophesy for Ayutthaya"', *Journal of the Siam Society* 89, 1&2 (2001), pp. 7, 11.

7 *Khamhaikan chao krung kao* (Testimony of the inhabitants of the old capital) (Bangkok: Chotmaihet, 2001), p. 157.

8 Luang Phraison Salarak, 'Intercourse between Burma and Siam as recorded in Hmannan Yazawindawgyi', *Journal of the Siam Society* 11, 3 (1915), p. 54.

9 F. H. Turpin, *A History of the Kingdom of Siam*, tr. B. O. Cartwright (Bangkok: White Lotus, 1997 [1771]), p. 109.

10 Henry Burney, 22 December 1826, in *The Burney Papers*, Vol. II, Pt. IV (Bangkok: Vajiranana Library, 1911), p. 34.

11 For 1911 onwards, this chart is based on census data, with smoothing. The earlier figures have been estimated with help from earlier calculations by B. J. Terwiel and L. Sternstein.

2 THE OLD ORDER IN TRANSITION, 1760S TO 1860S

1 Yotfa is an abbreviated form of his full official regnal name, Phraphutthayotfa Chulalok. For an explanation of regnal names, see 'Reigns and prime ministers'.

2 Puangthong Rungswasdisab, 'War and trade: Siamese intervention in Cambodia, 1767–1851', PhD thesis, Wollongong University (1995), p. 144.

3 *The Dynastic Chronicle Bangkok Era: The First Reign*, Chaophraya Thiphakorawong edition, tr. and ed. Thadeus and Chadin Flood, vol. I (Tokyo: Centre for East Asian Cultural Studies, 1978), p. 281.

4 'Natural governments' is a description invented by Nidhi Eoseewong in his magisterial study of Taksin, *Kanmueang thai samai prachao krung thonburi* (Thai politics in the Thonburi period) (Bangkok: Sinlapa Watthanatham, 1986).

5 Jean-Baptiste Pallegoix, *Description of the Thai Kingdom of Siam*, tr. W. E. J. Tips (Bangkok: White Lotus 2000 [1854]), p. 123.

6 *Dynastic Chronicle*, pp. 78–84.

7 Letter to Anna Leonowens, 6 April 1868, printed in *Sinlapa Watthanatham* 25, 5 (March 2004), p. 156.

8 Pallegoix, *Description*, p. 117.

9 Patrick Jory, 'The *Vessantara Jataka, barami*, and the *Boddhisatta*-kings: the origin and spread of a Thai concept of power', *Crossroads* 16, 2 (2002).

10 B. J. Terwiel, *Through Travellers' Eyes: An Approach to Early Nineteenth Century Thai History* (Bangkok: Editions Duang Kamol, 1989), p. 212.

11 John Crawfurd, *Journal of an Embassy from the Governor-General of India to the Courts of Siam and Cochin China* (London: Henry Colbourn and Richard Bentley, 1830), vol. II, pp. 162–3.

12 Nidhi Eoseewong, *Pakkai lae bai rua* (Pen and sail) (Bangkok: Matichon, 1984).

13 Phimpraphai Phisanbut, *Nai mae: rueang di di khong nari sayam* (Great mother: good stories of Siamese women) (Bangkok: Nanmee Books, 2003), p. 96.

14 M. Hardouin of the French Consulate in 1884, quoted in Rujaya Abhakorn, 'Ratburi, an inner province: local government and central politics in Siam, 1862–1892', PhD thesis, Cornell University (1984), p. 21.

15 From *Nirat mueang phet*, quoted in Nidhi, *Pakkai*, p. 315.

16 Anna Leonowens, *The English Governess at the Siamese Court* (Singapore: Oxford University Press, 1988 [1870]), pp. 14–15.

17 Hong Lysa, *Thailand in the Nineteenth Century: Evolution of the Economy and Society* (Singapore: Institute of Southeast Asian Studies, 1984), p. 60.

18 Mayoury Ngaosyvathn and Pheuiphanh Ngaosyvathn, *Paths to Conflagration: Fifty Years of Diplomacy and Warfare in Laos, Thailand, and Vietnam, 1778–1828* (Ithaca: Cornell Southeast Asian Program, 1998), p. 117.

19 Bernd Martin, 'The Prussian expedition to the Far East (1860–1862)', *Journal of the Siam Society* 78, 1 (1990), p. 39.

20 Note dated 12 July 1822, *The Crawfurd Papers* (Bangkok: Vajiranana Library, 1915).

21 Anthony Farrington (ed.), *Early Missionaries in Bangkok: The Journals of Tomlin, Gutzlaff and Abeel 1828–1832* (Bangkok: White Lotus, 2001), pp. 119, 123.

22 F. A. Neale, *Narrative of a Residence at the Capital of the Kingdom of Siam* (Bangkok: White Lotus, 1997 [1852]), pp. 67, 181.

23 A. Moffat, *Mongkut the King of Siam* (Ithaca: Cornell University Press, 1962), p. 57.

24 Henry Alabaster, *The Wheel of the Law: Buddhism Illustrated from Siamese Sources* (London: Trübner, 1871), p. 73. Alabaster was a translator for the British diplomatic mission who resigned to work for the Siamese government. Part of this book is a condensed translation of *Sadaeng kitjanukit*.

25 Andrew Turton, 'Thai institutions of slavery', in J. L. Watson (ed.), *Asian and African Systems of Slavery* (Berkeley and Los Angeles: University of California Press, 1980), p. 258.

26 Peter Vandergeest, 'Hierarchy and power in pre-national Buddhist states', *Modern Asian Studies* 27, 4 (1993), p. 855.

27 Pallegoix, *Description*, p. 153.

28 Junko Koizumi, 'From a water buffalo to a human being: women and the family in Siamese history', in Barbara Watson Andaya (ed.), *Other Pasts: Women, Gender and History in Early Modern Southeast Asia* (Honolulu: University of Hawai'i, 2000), p. 254.

3 REFORMS, 1850s TO 1910s

1 Attachak Sattayanurak, *Kan plian plaeng lokkathat khong chon chan phu nam thai tang tae ratchakan thi 4 thueng phuttasakkarat 2475* (Change in the Thai elite's worldview from the Fourth Reign to 1932) (Bangkok: Chulalongkorn University Press, 1994), p. 151.

2 H. Warrington Smyth, *Five Years in Siam: From 1891 to 1896* (New York: Charles Scribner's Sons, 1898), II, p. 19.

3 Decree quoted in D. K. Wyatt, 'The Buddhist monkhood as an avenue of social mobility in traditional Thai society', in Wyatt, *Studies in Thai History* (Chiang Mai: Silkworm Books, 1994), p. 212.

4 Letter dated 18 May 1864, printed in *Sinlapa Watthanatham* 25, 3 (January 2004), p. 85.

5 1874, quoted in N. A. Battye, 'The military, government and society in Siam, 1868–1910: politics and military reform during the reign of King Chulalongkorn', PhD thesis, Cornell University (1974), p. 118.

6 Quoted in Attachak, *Kan plian plaeng*, p. 134.

7 Leonowens, *English Governess*, p. 47.

8 This map is based on a 1866 document quoted in Rujaya, 'Ratburi', pp. 34–5.

9 In this era, the term 'Lao' was used to refer to the peoples of both Lanna (Chiang Mai) and Lanchang (Luang Prabang, Vientiane, Champasak).

10 Sratsawadi Ongsakun, *Prawatisat lanna* (History of Lanna) (Chiang Mai: Chiang Mai University, 1996), p. 359.

11 Quoted in C. F. Keyes, 'Millennialism, Theravada Buddhism, and Thai society', *Journal of Asian Studies* 36, 2 (1977), p. 298.

12 Thongchai Winichakul, *Siam Mapped: A History of the Geo-body of a Nation* (Honolulu: University of Hawaii Press, 1994).

13 Le Myre de Vilers, governor of French Indochina in 1881, quoted in Patrick Tuck, *The French Wolf and the Siamese Lamb: The French Threat to Siamese Independence 1858–1907* (Bangkok: White Lotus, 1995), p. 44.

14 Thongchai, *Siam Mapped*, p. 125.

15 Battye, 'Military, government and society', p. 428.

16 Davisakdi Puaksom, *Khon plaek na nanachat khong krung sayam* (Siam's international strangers) (Bangkok: Sinlapa Watthanatham, 2003), pp. 31–2.

17 *King Chulalongkorn's Journey to India 1872* (Bangkok: River Books, 2000), p. 8.

18 David Streckfuss, 'The mixed colonial legacy in Siam: origins of Thai racialist thought', in L. J. Sears (ed.), *Autonomous Histories, Particular Truths: Essays in Honor of John R. W. Smail* (Madison: University of Wisconsin, 1993), p. 131.

19 Streckfuss, 'Mixed colonial legacy', p. 150 fn. 66.

20 Chaiyan Rajchagool, *The Rise and Fall of the Thai Absolute Monarchy* (Bangkok: White Lotus, 1994), p. 96.

21 Thongchai, *Siam Mapped*, pp. 101–2.

22 Chaophraya Thammasakmontri, *Thammajariya II*, p. 99, quoted in Kullada Kesboonchu Mead, *The Rise and Decline of Thai Absolutism* (London: Routledge Curzon, 2004), p. 89.

23 Somrudee Nicrowattanayingyong, 'Development, politics, and paradox: a study of Khon Kaen, a regional city in Northeast Thailand', PhD thesis, Syracuse University (1991), pp. 148–50.

24 Streckfuss, 'Mixed colonial legacy', p. 143.

25 Battye, 'Military, government and society', p. 418.

26 Craig J. Reynolds, *Autobiography: The Life of Prince-Patriarch Vajirañana* (Athens, Ohio: Ohio University Press, 1979), p. 37.

27 Damrong quoted in Nakharin Mektrairat, *Kanpatiwat sayam pho so 2475* (The 1932 revolution in Siam) (Bangkok: Munnithi khrongkan tamra sangkhomsat lae manutsayasat, 1992), p. 64.

28 1899, quoted in Thamsook Numnonda, 'The first American advisers in Thai history', *Journal of the Siam Society* 62, 2 (1974), p. 122.

29 M. Peleggi, *Lords of Things: The Fashioning of the Siamese Monarchy's Modern Image* (Honolulu: University of Hawai'i Press, 2002), p. 64.

30 Tuck, *French Wolf*, p. 191.

31 Attachak, *Kan plian plaeng*, p. 38.

32 Attachak, *Kan plian plaeng*, p. 153.

33 Chris Baker, 'The Antiquarian Society of Siam speech of King Chulalongkorn', *Journal of the Siam Society* 89 (2001), p. 95.

34 King Vajiravudh, *Thiao mueang phra ruang* (Visiting King Ruang's cities) (Bangkok: Ministry of Interior, 1954), p. 9.

35 Saichon Sattayanurak, *Somdet kromphraya damrong rachanuphap: kan sang attalak 'mueang thai' lae 'chan' khong chao sayam* (Prince Damrong: creating

the identity of Thailand and classes of the Siamese people) (Bangkok: Sinlapa Watthanatham, 2003), p. 115.

36 Panni Bualek, *'Sayam' nai krasaethan haeng kan plian plaeng: prawattisat thai tang tae samai ratchakan thi 5* (Siam in the tide of change: Thai history from the Fifth Reign) (Bangkok: Muang Boran, 1998), p. 67.

37 Eiji Murashima, 'The origins of modern official state ideology in Thailand', *Journal of Southeast Asian Studies* 19, 1 (1988), p. 84.

38 Murashima, 'Origins', p. 86.

39 Murashima, 'Origins', pp. 86–8.

40 Saichon, *Somdet kromphraya damrong*, p. 149.

41 Kennon Breazeale, 'The historical works of Prince Damrong Rachanuphap', MA thesis, University of Hawai'i (1971), pp. 168–9.

4 PEASANTS, MERCHANTS, AND OFFICIALS, 1870S TO 1930S

1 D. B. Johnston, 'Rural society and the rice economy in Thailand, 1860–1930', PhD thesis, Yale University (1975), p. 81.

2 F. H. Giles in 1898 quoted in Johnston, 'Rural society', p. 125.

3 Joachim Grassi in 1892 quoted in Johnston, 'Rural society', p. 123.

4 H. S. Hallett, *A Thousand Miles on an Elephant in the Shan States* (Bangkok: White Lotus, 2000 [1890]), p. 131.

5 Chatthip Nartsupha, *The Thai Village Economy in the Past*, tr. Chris Baker and Pasuk Phongpaichit (Chiang Mai: Silkworm Books, 1999), pp. 69–70.

6 Carle C. Zimmerman, *Siam: Rural Economic Survey 1930–31* (Bangkok: White Lotus, 1999 [1931]), p. 52.

7 Government's main taxes came from the opium, liquor, and gambling consumed by urban Chinese who were mostly employed in the mills, port, and other enterprises connected to the export of rice and teak.

8 Prince Dilok Nabarath, *Siam's Rural Economy under King Chulalongkorn*, tr. W. E. J. Tips (Bangkok: White Lotus, 2000 [1907]), pp. xv, 169.

9 Phraya Suriyanuwat, *Sapphasat* (Economics) (Bangkok: Rongphim Pikhanet, 1975 [1911]), p. 73.

10 W. F. Vella, *Chaiyo! King Vajiravudh and the Development of Thai Nationalism* (Honolulu: University Press of Hawaii, 1978), p. 170.

11 Farrington, *Early Missionaries*, pp. 34, 37.

12 Smyth, *Five Years*, I, p. 9.

13 Smyth, *Five Years*, I, p. 15.

14 Nothing seems known of Nai But, other than that he wrote several such poems, mainly about Bangkok. From internal evidence, *Nirat chom sampheng* was composed between 1912 and 1921. Somthat Thewet, *Krungthep nai nirat* (Bangkok in verse) (Bangkok: Ruangsin, 1978), p. 44.

15 *Jek* is a word conveying the meaning of 'Chinese in Thailand'. With the rise of anti-Chinese attitudes, it was applied mainly to un-Thai-ified Chinese with pejorative intent, rather like 'chink'.

16 This translation from Somthat, *Krungthep nai nirat*, adapted from that by Kasian Tejapira in 'Pigtail: a pre-history of Chineseness in Siam', *Sojourn* 7, 1 (1992), p. 110.

17 In the simplest form, these names joined their *sae* name with *trakun*, a Thai approximation to the meaning of *sae*; hence Huntrakun, and so on. Others translated the *sae* name, and some joined a translation of part of their Chinese name with *wanit* or *phanit* meaning commerce, hence Sophonphanit.

18 Seksan Prasertkun, 'The transformation of the Thai state and economic change (1855–1945)', PhD thesis, Cornell University (1989), pp. 276–7.

19 The early estimates, summarized by Porphant Ouyyanont, have some guess-work. The counts, from the first census in 1909–10, are complicated by rapid changes in the city's area.

20 Arnold Wright and Oliver T. Breakspear, *Twentieth Century Impressions of Siam: Its History, People, Commerce, Industries and Resources* (London: Lloyd's Greater Britain Publishing Company, 1908), p. 244.

21 J. Antonio, *Guide to Bangkok and Siam* (Bangkok: Siam Observer Press, 1904), p. 24.

22 Wright and Breakspear, *Twentieth Century Impressions*, p. 244.

23 Sathirakoses (Phraya Anuman Rajadhon), *Looking Back: Book Two* (Bangkok: Chulalongkorn University Press, 1996 [1967]), p. 77.

24 Smyth, *Five Years*, I, p. 26.

25 Scot Barmé, *Woman, Man, Bangkok: Love, Sex and Popular Culture in Thailand* (Lanham: Rowman and Littlefield, 2002), p. 81.

26 A women's newspaper, *Satri sap*, in 1922, quoted in Barmé, *Woman, Man, Bangkok*, p. 166.

5 NATIONALISMS, 1910S TO 1940S

1 Scot Barmé, *Luang Wichit Wathakan and the Creation of a Thai Identity* (Singapore: Institute of Southeast Asian Studies, 1993), p. 21.

2 Vella, *Chaiyo*, p. 66.

3 Vajiravudh, *Pramuan bot phraratchaniphon* (Collected writings) (Bangkok: 1955), pp. 97–9.

4 Chanida Phromphayak Puaksom, *Kanmueang nai prawatisat thongchat thai* (Politics in the history of the Thai flag) (Bangkok: Sinlapa Watthanatham, 2003), p. 84.

5 *Si krung*, 1928, quoted in Matthew Copeland, 'Contested nationalism and the 1932 overthrow of the absolute monarchy in Siam', PhD thesis, Australian National University (1993), p. 61.

6 Attachak, *Kan plian plaeng*, pp. 273, 275.

7 Siburapha [Kulap's pen-name], *Songkhram chiwit* (The war of life) (Bangkok: Suphapburut, 1949), p. 245.

8 Attachak, *Kan plian plaeng*, pp. 250, 252.

9 Copeland, 'Contested nationalism', pp. 189, 191.

10 Nakharin, *Kanpatiwat sayam*, p. 83.

11　Nakharin, *Kanpatiwat sayam*, p. 80.

12　Copeland, 'Contested nationalism', p. 64.

13　Chaiyan, *Rise and Fall*, p. 156.

14　Chaiyan, *Rise and Fall*, p. 156.

15　Copeland, 'Contested nationalism', p. 65.

16　Nakharin, *Kanpatiwat sayam*, p. 94.

17　Copeland, 'Contested nationalism', p. 74.

18　Chaloemkiat Phianuan, *Prachathippatai baep thai: khwamkhit thang kanmueang khong thahan thai 2519–2529* (Thai style democracy: political thought of the Thai military 1976–1986) (Bangkok: Thammasat University, Thai Khadi Institute, 1990), pp. 20–1; Kullada, *Thai Absolutism*, p. 168.

19　Benjamin A. Batson, *The End of the Absolute Monarchy in Siam* (Singapore: Oxford University Press, 1984), p. 30.

20　Benjamin A. Batson, *Siam's Political Future: Documents from the End of the Absolute Monarchy* (Ithaca: Cornell University Data Paper 96, 1974), p. 15.

21　Nakharin, *Kanpatiwat sayam*, p. 104.

22　Batson, *End of the Absolute Monarchy*, p. 38.

23　*New York Times*, 27 April 1931.

24　Khun Wichitmatra, *Lak thai* (Origins of the Thai) (Bangkok: Hanghunsuan, 1928), pp. 6, 9–10, 345.

25　Copeland, 'Contested nationalism', pp. 209–15.

26　Seksan, 'Transformation of the Thai state', p. 276.

27　Asvabahu (pen name of Rama VI), *Phuak yio haeng burapha thit lae mueang thai jong tuen toet* (The Jews of the orient and wake up Siam) (Bangkok: Foundation in Memory of King Rama VI, 1985 [1913]), p. 81.

28　Batson, *End of the Absolute Monarchy*, p. 88.

29　Copeland, 'Contested nationalism', p. 179.

30　D. A. Wilson, *Politics in Thailand* (Ithaca: Cornell University Press, 1962), p. 173.

31　Nakharin Mektrairat, *Khwam khit khwam ru lae amnat kanmueang nai kan patiwat sayam 2475* (Thought, knowledge, and political power in the 1932 Siamese revolution) (Bangkok: Fa dieo kan, 2003), p. 326.

32　Batson, *End of the Absolute Monarchy*, p. 205.

33　Nakharin, *Khwam khit*, p. 222.

34　Pridi Banomyong, *Pridi by Pridi: Selected Writings on Life, Politics, and Economy*, tr. Chris Baker and Pasuk Phongpaichit (Chiang Mai: Silkworm Books, 2000), p. 70.

35　Thamrongsak Petchloetanan, *2475 lae 1 pi lang kan patiwat* (1932 and one year after the revolution) (Bangkok: Institute of Asian Studies, Chulalongkorn University, 2000), p. 80, quoting the memoirs of Prince Mahithon.

36　Thamrongsak, *2475 lae 1 pi lang*, p. 227.

37　Suphot Jaengreo, 'Khadi yuet phraratchasap phrabat somdet phrapokklao' (The case about appropriating the assets of King Prajadhipok), *Sinlapa Watthanatham* 23, 8 (June 2002), p. 68.

38　Vichitvong Na Pombhejara, *Pridi Banomyong and the Making of Thailand's Modern History* (Bangkok, 1979), p. 78.

39 Pridi, *Pridi by Pridi*, p. 188.
40 Barmé, *Man, Woman, Bangkok*, p. 234.
41 Copeland, 'Contested nationalism', p. 232.
42 J. A. Stowe, *Siam Becomes Thailand: A Story of Intrigue* (Honolulu: University of Hawaii Press, 1991), p. 84.
43 MC Subha Svasti Wongsanit Svasti, *1 sattawat supphasawat* (Subha Svasti centenary) (Bangkok: Amarin, 2000), p. 511.
44 Kobkua Suwannathat-Pian, *Thailand's Durable Premier: Phibun through Three Decades, 1932–1957* (Kuala Lumpur: Oxford University Press, 1995), p. 83.
45 Barmé, *Luang Wichit*, p. 162.
46 Saichon Sattayanurak, *Chat thai lae khwam pen thai doi luang wichit wathakan* (Thai nation and Thainess according to Luang Wichit Wathakan) (Bangkok: Sinlapa Watthanatham, 2002), pp. 40, 54.
47 Saichon, *Chat thai*, pp. 63, 122.
48 Barmé, *Luang Wichit*, p. 125.
49 Saichon, *Chat thai*, p. 49.
50 Saichon, *Chat thai*, pp. 78, 81, 82.
51 Eiji Murashima, *Kanmueang jin sayam* (Siam Chinese politics) (Bangkok: Chinese Studies Centre, Chulalongkorn University, 1996), p. 168.
52 Nakharin, *Khwam khit*, pp. 346, 358.
53 C. F. Goscha, *Thailand and the Southeast Asian Networks of the Vietnamese Revolution, 1855–1954* (London: Curzon, 1999), p. 116.
54 Saichon, *Chat thai*, p. 31.
55 Saichon, *Chat thai*, p. 31.
56 Kongsakon Kawinrawikun, 'Kansang rangkai phonlamueang thai nai samai jomphon po phibunsongkhram pho so 2481–2487' (Constructing the bodies of Thai citizens in the era of Field Marshal P. Phibunsongkhram, 1938–1944), MA thesis, Thammasat University (2002), p. 24.
57 Kobkua, *Thailand's Durable Premier*, p. 113.
58 Saichon, *Chat thai*, p. 135.
59 Dr Yong Chutima quoted in Davisakdi Puaksom, 'Modern medicine in Thailand: germ, body, and the medicalized state', unpublished paper (2003).
60 Kobkua, *Thailand's Durable Premier*, p. 102.
61 Murashima, *Kanmueang jin sayam*, p. 110.
62 Murashima, *Kanmueang jin sayam*, p. 140.
63 J. B. Haseman, *The Thai Resistance Movement during World War II* (Chiang Mai: Silkworm Books, 2002), p. 49.

6 THE AMERICAN ERA AND DEVELOPMENT, 1940S TO 1960S

1 From a memo dated 20 June 1947 in Subha Svasti, *1 sattawat*, pp. 514, 533.
2 Seni's memoir in J. K. Ray, *Portraits of Thai Politics* (New Delhi: Orient Longman, 1972), p. 171.
3 Tran van Giau quoted in Goscha, *Thailand and the Southeast Asian Networks*, p. 186.

4 Thak Chaloemtiarana, *Thailand: The Politics of Despotic Paternalism* (Bangkok: Social Science Association of Thailand, Thai Khadi Institute, Thammasat University, 1979), p. 31.

5 Kobkua, *Thailand's Durable Premier*, p. 23.

6 Kobkua, *Thailand's Durable Premier*, p. 39.

7 D. Fineman, *A Special Relationship: The United States and Military Government in Thailand, 1947–1956* (Honolulu: University of Hawaii Press, 1997), p. 117.

8 Fineman, *Special Relationship*, p. 89.

9 Fineman, *Special Relationship*, p. 173.

10 Saichon, *Chat thai*, p. 151.

11 The film, based loosely on the memoirs of Anna Leonowens as tutor to King Mongkut's children in the 1860s, is a classic of American pop orientalism. Hollywood inserted a romance between the king and governess and much else not present in the memoirs.

12 Fineman, *Special Relationship*, p. 257.

13 Surachart Bamrungsuk, *United States Foreign Policy and Thai Military Rule 1947–1977* (Bangkok: Editions Duang Kamol, 1988), p. 114.

14 Thak, *Thailand*, p. 229.

15 F. W. Riggs, *Thailand: The Modernization of a Bureaucratic Polity* (Honolulu: East–West Center Press, 1966).

16 Said by the patriarch, Tan Suang U, in the 1969 novel which captures the strains of this transition: *Letters from Thailand* by Botan, tr. Susan Kepner (Bangkok: Silkworm Books, 2002).

17 Takashi Tomosugi, *A Structural Analysis of Thai Economic History: A Case Study of a Northern Chao Phraya Delta Village* (Tokyo: Institute of Developing Economies, 1980), pp. 43–4.

18 'Setthi mueang suphan' (Suphanburi millionaire), sung by Phumphuang Duangjan on the album *Chut jup kon jak* (Kiss before leaving).

19 Mani Siriworasan, *Chiwit muean fan* (Life like a dream) (Bangkok: Kwanphim, 1999).

7 IDEOLOGIES, 1940S TO 1970S

1 Thak, *Thailand*, p. 157.

2 C. F. Keyes (ed.), *Reshaping Local Worlds: Formal Education and Cultural Change in Rural Southeast Asia* (New Haven: Yale Southeast Asian Studies, 1991), p. 112.

3 N. Tapp, *Sovereignty and Rebellion: The White Hmong of Northern Thailand* (Singapore: Oxford University Press, 1989), p. 37.

4 Prince Dhani Nivat, 'The old Siamese conception of the monarchy', *Journal of the Siam Society* 36, 2 (1947), p. 95.

5 Prince Dhani and Phraya Siwisanwaja quoted in Somkiat Wanthana, 'The politics of modern Thai historiography', PhD thesis, Monash University (1986), pp. 325, 326.

6 According to the British ambassador quoted in Kobkua Suwannathat-Pian, *Kings, Country and Constitutions: Thailand's Political Development 1932–2000* (London: RoutledgeCurzon, 2003), p. 155.

7 Kobkua, *Kings, Country and Constitutions*, p. 12.

8 Thak, *Thailand*, p. 156.

9 Phya Anuman Rajadhon, *Essays on Thai Folklore* (Bangkok: Thai Inter-religious Commission for Development and Sathirakoses Nagapradipa Foundation, 1988), p. 406.

10 Kasian Tejapira, *Commodifying Marxism: The Formation of Modern Thai Radical Culture, 1927–1958* (Kyoto: Kyoto University Press, 2001), p. 52.

11 Siburapha [Kulap Saipradit], *Behind the Painting and Other Stories*, tr. and ed. D. Smyth (Singapore: Oxford University Press, 1990), p. 170.

12 Somsak Jeamteerasakul, 'The communist movement in Thailand', PhD thesis, Monash University (1993), p. 278.

13 'An internal history of the Communist Party of Thailand', tr. Chris Baker, *Journal of Contemporary Asia* 33, 4 (2003), p. 524.

14 Saiyud Kerdphol, *The Struggle for Thailand: Counter Insurgency 1965–1985* (Bangkok: S. Research Center, 1986), p. 226.

15 Sulak Sivaraksa, *When Loyalty Demands Dissent: Autobiography of an Engaged Buddhist* (Bangkok: Thai Inter-religious Commission for Development, 1998), p. 80.

16 Christine Gray, 'Thailand: the soteriological state in the 1970s', PhD thesis, University of Chicago (1986), p. 692.

17 Kobkua, *Kings, Country and Constitutions*, p. 161.

18 D. Morell, 'Thailand: military checkmate', *Asian Survey*, 12, 2 (1972), p. 157.

19 Quoted in the script of the VCD, *14 Tula bantuek prawattisat* (14 October [1973], a historical record) by Charnvit Kasetsiri, tr. Ben Anderson.

20 Craig J. Reynolds, *Thai Radical Discourse: The Real Face of Thai Feudalism Today* (Ithaca: Southeast Asia Program, Cornell University, 1987).

21 Somboon Suksamran, *Buddhism and Politics in Thailand* (Singapore: Institute of Southeast Asian Studies, 1982), pp. 105–7.

22 K. A. Bowie, *Rituals of National Loyalty: An Anthropology of the State and the Village Scout Movement in Thailand* (New York: Columbia University Press, 1997), p. 283.

23 D. Morell and Chai-Anan Samudavanija, *Political Conflict in Thailand: Reform, Reaction, Revolution* (Cambridge, Mass.: Oelgeschlager, Gunn and Hain, 1982), p. 236.

24 Somboon, *Buddhism and Politics*, p. 150.

25 Gawin Chutima, *The Rise and Fall of the Communist Party of Thailand (1973–1987)* (University of Kent at Canterbury, Centre of South-East Asian Studies, Occasional Paper No. 12, 1990), p. 31.

8 GLOBALIZATION AND MASS SOCIETY, 1970S ONWARDS

1 M. K. Connors, *Democracy and National Identity in Thailand* (New York and London: RoutledgeCurzon, 2003), p. 91.

2 By Sakda Jintanawijit, quoted in Kasian Tejapira, 'The postmodernization of Thainess', in Shigeharu Tanabe and C. F. Keyes (eds), *Cultural Crisis and Social*

Memory: Modernity and Identity in Thailand and Laos (Honolulu: University of Hawai'i Press, 2002), p. 204.

3 Yos Santasombat, 'Power and personality: an anthropological study of the Thai political elite', PhD thesis, University of California Berkeley (1985), p. 196.

4 Thanawat, *Tamnan chiwit jao sua: 55 trakun phak 2* (Legendary lives of the *jao sua*: 55 families, part 2) (Bangkok: Nation, 2001).

5 Kasian Tejapira, *Lae lot lai mangkon* (Looking through the pattern of the dragon) (Bangkok: Khopfai, 1994), p. 16. The translation below of the drama's anthem is by Kasian from the same book.

6 Sawat Horrungruang in *The Nation*, 7 April 2003.

7 M. B. Mills, *Thai Women in the Global Labour Force: Consuming Desires, Contested Selves* (New Brunswick, NJ, and London: Rutgers University Press, 1999), p. 4.

8 *Ban* by Phongsit Khamphi on the 1997 album of the same name.

9 E. W. Gohlert, *Power and Culture: The Struggle against Poverty in Thailand* (Bangkok: White Lotus, 1991), p. 143.

10 Wiraphon Sopha quoted in Praphat Pintoptaeng, *Kan mueang bon thong thanon: 99 wan samatcha khon jon* (Politics on the street: 99 days of the Assembly of the Poor) (Bangkok: Krirk University, 1998), p. 150.

11 P. A. Jackson, 'The enchanting spirit of Thai capitalism: the cult of Luang Por Khoon and the postmodernisation of Thai Buddhism', *Southeast Asian Research* 7, 1 (1999), p. 49.

9 POLITICS, 1970S ONWARDS

1 Connors, *Democracy and National Identity*, p. 136.

2 Connors, *Democracy and National Identity*, p. 140.

3 National Identity Office, Office of the Prime Minister, *Thailand in the 1980s* (Bangkok: Muang Boran Publishing House, 1984), pp. 136–7.

4 Prajak Sawangjit quoted in Chai-Anan Samudavanija, *The Thai Young Turks* (Singapore: Institute of Southeast Asian Studies, 1982), p. 62.

5 Chavalit Yongchaiyudh quoted in Chai-Anan Samudavanija, Kusuma Snitwongse, and Suchit Bunbongkarn, *From Armed Suppression to Political Offensive* (Bangkok: Chulalongkorn University, Institute of Security and International Studies, 1990), p. 211.

6 Suchit Bunbongkarn (1987), *The Military in Thai Politics 1981–86* (Singapore: Institute of Southeast Asian Studies, 1987), p. 69.

7 Chai-Anan et al., *From Armed Suppression*, p. 198.

8 *Bangkok Post*, 1 September 2002.

9 *Royal Speech: Given to the Audience of Well-Wishers on the Occasion of the Royal Birthday Anniversary, Wednesday, 4 December 1991* (Bangkok: Amarin, 1992), p. 19.

10 D. D. Grey (ed.), *The King of Thailand in World Focus* (Bangkok: FCCT, 1988), p. 119.

11 Office of His Majesty's Principal Private Secretary, *A Memoir of His Majesty King Bhumibol Adulyadej of Thailand, to Commemorate the Sixtieth Royal Birthday Anniversary* (Bangkok, 1987), p. 7.

12 Grey, *King of Thailand*, p. 54.

13 *Matichon*, 27 August 1995.

14 Tongnoi Tongyai, *Entering the Thai Heart* (Bangkok: Bangkok Post, 1983), p. 18.

15 National Identity Office, *Thailand in the 1980s*, p. 139.

16 King Bhumibol Adulyadej, *Rueang Phramahajanok/The Story of Mahajanaka* (Bangkok: Amarin, 1999), p. 141.

17 *King Bhumibol Adulyadej: Thailand's Guiding Light* (Bangkok: Post Publishing, 1996), pp. 15–16, 97.

18 *Thai rath*, 12 May 1990.

19 Gothom Arya quoted in W. A. Callahan, *Imagining Democracy: Reading 'The Events of May' in Thailand* (Singapore: ISEAS, 1998), p. 114.

20 *Royal Speech . . . 4 December 1991*, p. 46.

21 Callahan, *Imagining Democracy*, p. 56.

22 *The Defence of Thailand 1994* (Bangkok: Ministry of Defence, 1994), p. 26.

23 Chai-Anan Samudavanija, 'Old soldiers never die, they are just bypassed: the military, bureaucracy and globalization', in K. Hewison (ed.), *Political Change in Thailand* (London and New York: Routledge, 1997), p. 51.

24 Chai-Anan, 'Old soldiers never die', p. 57.

25 Thirayuth Boonmi, *Sangkhom khemkhaeng* (Strong society) (Bangkok: Mingmit, 1993), p. 56.

26 Anek Laothamatas, *Song nakhara prachathippatai: naew thang patirup kan-mueang setthakit phua prachathippatai* (A tale of two cities of democracy: directions for reform in politics and economy for democracy) (Bangkok: Matichon, 1995), pp. 91–2.

27 Government of Thailand, *The Eighth National Economic and Social Development Plan (1997–2001)* (Bangkok: NESDB, n.d.).

28 Phrathammapitok (P. A. Payutto), 'Khwam romyen nai wikrit thai: phutthaw-ithi nai kan kae panha wikrit khong chat' (Shelter in the Thai crisis: a Buddhist way to solve the problem of the national crisis), in Phitthaya Wongkun (ed.), *Thammarat: jut plian prathet thai?* (Good governance: turning point for Thailand?) (Bangkok: Withithat Globalization Series 6, 1998), pp. 3–4.

29 Our translation from the unofficial Thai transcript at: <http://kanchanapisek.or.th/speeches/index.th.html>.

30 Prawase Wasi, *Setthakit pho phiang lae prachasangkhom naew thang phlik fuen setthakit sangkhom* (The sufficiency economy and civil society as a way to revive economy and society) (Bangkok: Mo Chao Ban, 1991), p. 18.

31 Thailand Development Research Institute, *Ekkasan prakop kan sammana wichakan prajam pi 2542 setthakit pho phiang* (Papers from the 1999 annual seminar on the sufficiency economy, 18–19 December 1999).

32 Narong Petchprasoet, *Kham prakat chatniyom mai* (Declaration of new nationalism) (Bangkok: Chulalongkorn University Political Economy Centre, 2000), pp. 13–29.

Reigns and prime ministers

LATE AYUTTHAYA

Prasat Thong	1629–1656
Chaofa Chai	1656
Sisuthammaracha	1656
Narai	1656–1688
Phetracha	1688–1703
Sanphet (Sua)	1703–1708
Phumintharacha (Thaisa)	1708–1732
Borommakot	1732–1758
Uthumphon	1758
Ekkathat	1758–1767

THONBURI

Taksin	1767–1782

BANGKOK: THE CHAKRI DYNASTY

Rama I	Phraphutthayotfa Chulalok	1782–1809
Rama II	Phraphutthaloetla Naphalai	1809–1824
Rama III	Phranangklao	1824–1851
Rama IV	Phrachomklao (Mongkut)	1851–1868
Rama V	Phrachulachomklao (Chulalongkorn)	1868–1910
Rama VI	Phramongkutklao (Vajiravudh)	1910–1925
Rama VII	Phrapokklao (Prajadhipok)	1925–1935
Rama VIII	Ananda Mahidol	1935–1946
Rama IX	Bhumibol Adulyadej	1946–

Traditionally, in his lifetime, a king was simply called the king. At death, he was given a regnal name. The sequence Rama I, Rama II, and so on was invented retrospectively in 1916. The kings from Rama IV to Rama VII have become better known in English by the names given them as princes (Mongkut, Chulalongkorn, Vajiravudh, Prajadhipok). Since King Rama VIII, the regnal name has been conferred at accession.

PRIME MINISTERS

Phraya Manopakon (Mano) Nithithada	June 1932 – June 1933
Phraya Phahon Phonphayuhasena	June 1933 – December 1938
Phibun Songkhram	December 1938 – July 1944
Khuang Aphaiwong	August 1944 – August 1945
Thawee Boonyaket	August 1945 – September 1945
Seni Pramoj	September 1945 – January 1946
Khuang Aphaiwong	January 1946 – March 1946
Pridi Banomyong	March 1946 – August 1946
Thamrong Nawasawat	August 1946 – November 1947
Khuang Aphaiwong	November 1947 – April 1948
Phibun Songkhram	April 1948 – September 1957
Pote Sarasin	September 1957 – December 1957
Thanom Kittikhachon	January 1958 – October 1958
Sarit Thanarat	October 1958 – December 1963
Thanom Kittikhachon	December 1963 – October 1973
Sanya Thammasak	October 1973 – January 1975
Seni Pramoj	February 1975 – March 1975
Kukrit Pramoj	March 1975 – April 1976
Seni Pramoj	April 1976 – October 1976
Thanin Kraivixien	October 1976 – October 1977
Kriangsak Chomanand	November 1977 – February 1980
Prem Tinsulanond	March 1980 – April 1988
Chatichai Choonhavan	April 1988 – February 1991
Anand Panyarachun	February 1991 – April 1992
Suchinda Kraprayun	April 1992 – May 1992
Anand Panyarachun	June 1992 – September 1992
Chuan Leekpai	September 1992 – July 1995
Banharn Silpa-archa	July 1995 – November 1996
Chavalit Yongchaiyudh	November 1996 – November 1997
Chuan Leekpai	November 1997 – February 2001
Thaksin Shinawatra	February 2001 –

Glossary of names

Anand Panyarachun (1932–). Born in Bangkok, descendant of noble Mon family and Hokkien *jao sua*. Educated in England at Dulwich College and Trinity College, Cambridge. Career diplomat, 1955–77, including ambassador to USA. Resigned government service, joined Saha-Union (textile-based conglomerate), and became chairman, 1991. Prime minister under NPKC coup junta, 1991–92. Head of Constitution Drafting Assembly, 1996–97.

Anuman Rajadhon, Phya (1888–1969). Born to Chinese family in Bangkok. Educated at Assumption College. Worked in Customs Department. Independent scholar and essayist on religion, Thai culture, philology, and folklore under pen-name Sathirakoses. Recruited to Fine Arts Department in 1933 and rose to director-general. Taught and lectured after retirement.

Banharn Silpa-archa (1932–). Son of moderately successful cloth traders in Suphanburi market. Chinese name, Tek Siang sae Be. Moved to Bangkok after secondary education, and gained patronage of senior officials in Public Works Department. Won contract to supply chlorine for water supply. Founded construction company, working mainly on PWD contracts. Also crop trader and business in construction materials. Elected MP for Suphanburi in Chat Thai Party from 1975. Party secretary-general, 1976–94. Various ministerial posts including finance and interior in Chatichai Cabinet, 1988–91. Party leader in 1994. Prime minister, 1995–96.

Bhumibol Adulyadej, King Rama IX (1927–). Born in Boston, USA, son of Prince Mahidol, half-brother of King Rama VII. Family moved to Lausanne, Switzerland. Entered Lausanne University, 1945. Ascended throne on mysterious death of elder brother in 1946. Returned from Europe in 1951. Assumed more prominent role after Sarit's rise in 1957–58. Built new role for monarchy through Buddhist ritual, development projects, gifting relationships, television exposure, and political interventions at times of national crisis (1973, 1976, 1992). Longest reigns of any Thai monarch (1988), and of any living monarch in the world (1992).

Boonchu Rojanastian (1921–). Born in Chonburi, son of Hainanese immigrant carpenter turned construction contractor. Educated at Xinmin School and Thammasat University. Started accountancy practice. Hired into Bangkok Bank by Chin Sophonpanich in 1953. Rose to executive vice-president. Patron of left-wing journalism in 1950s. Founder-member of Kukrit's Social Action Party in 1974. Elected MP for Chonburi, 1975. Finance minister, 1975–76. Deputy prime minister, 1980. Drifted through minor parties. Leader of Phalang Tham Party in 1992.

Borommakot, King (1681?–1758). Ascended throne of Ayutthaya in 1733 after bitter succession struggle. Patronized Buddhism strongly. Built or rebuilt many Ayutthaya *wat*. Sent missions to Sri Lanka in 1751 and 1755 to revive the Sangha.

Buddhadasa Bhikkhu (1906–1993). Born in Chaiya, son of Chinese shopkeeper. Attended *wat* schools and ordained in 1926. Studied in Bangkok but became disillusioned with monastic education. Founded Suan Mokh Khapalaram near Chaiya in 1932. Wrote series of reinterpretations of Buddhist texts. By 1940s, recognized as leading philosopher of this-worldly Buddhism.

Chamlong Srimuang (1935–). Born in Thonburi, son of Chinese immigrant fish merchant. Career soldier. Attended Chulachomklao Military Academy, 1953. Three training spells in USA. Saw action in Laos, 1962. Member of Young Turks. Joined ascetic Santi Asoke Buddhist sect around 1973. Present at 1976 Thammasat massacre. Secretary to prime minister, Prem Tinsulanond, in 1980. Broke with Young Turks over failed 1981 coup. Resigned from army in 1985 as major-general. Elected mayor of Bangkok on anti-corruption platform, 1985 and 1990. Formed Phalang Tham Party, 1988. Resigned as mayor, 1992. Led Black May 1992 protests. MP, 1992–95. Resigned Phalang Tham leadership, 1995. Founded leadership school.

Chanat Piyaoui (1922–). Born Kim Ngek sae Ui in Saraburi, third daughter of sawmill and rice-mill owners. Educated in Bangkok. Thammasat University. Went to New York to study after Second World War, but abandoned project. Built Princess Hotel in 1950, with land and investment mainly from family. Opened Dusit Thani Hotel in 1970, and developed Dusit hotel group over next two decades.

Charnvit Kasetsiri (1941–). Born in Ratchaburi. BA in diplomacy from Thammasat University, doctorate from Cornell University on Ayutthayan history, 1972. Lecturer at Thammasat from 1973. Shifted focus of Thai history from Sukhothai, kings, and wars to Ayutthaya, trade, and the Chinese. Went abroad after 1976 massacre. Rector, 1994–95. Publicized history of 1973–76 era in print and video. Promoted interest in regional culture and history.

Chatichai Choonhavan (1920–1998). Born in Bangkok, son of General Phin, leader of 1947 coup. Career cavalry officer. Leader of Ratchakhru faction. Retired from army as major-general after Sarit's 1957 coup and served as ambassador. Business interests in textiles and finance. Co-founder of Chat Thai (Thai Nation) Party in 1974. MP for Khorat from 1975. Deputy foreign minister, 1975–76. Prime minister, 1988–91.

Chavalit Yongchaiyudh (1932–). Born in Nonthaburi, son of army captain. Career army officer, in signals and intelligence. Leader of Democratic Soldiers, and architect of political strategy against communism in 1980. Army commander, 1986–90. Resigned under pressure from NPKC. Founded New Aspiration Party. Prime minister, 1996–97. Merged party into Thai Rak Thai Party in 2002.

Chin Sophonpanich (1910–1988). Born in Thonburi, son of Kwangtung immigrant. Schooled in China, 1915–27. On return, worked as barge coolie, clerk in rice mills and timber agents. Shuttled between China and Siam during 1930s. Opened construction materials shop in Bangkok in 1939. In 1944, part of nine-family consortium in gold trading, construction, cinema, ice, and finance. Consortium opened Bangkok Bank in December 1944 with Chin as compradore. Developed remittance business. Moved closely with Phao Siyanon, and financed business of Ratchakhru group. Boardroom coup against partners in 1952. Big capital injection from government funds. Fled after Sarit coup, but restored relationship with Praphat.

Chuan Leekpai (1938–). Born in Trang, son of a Chinese teacher and market trader. Took law degree from Thammasat University and qualified as a barrister, 1964. Elected MP for Trang under Democrat Party since 1969. Attacked as communist in 1976 polarization. Prime minister, 1992–95, 1997–2001.

Chuang Bunnag (1808–1883). Born in Bangkok, descendant of Persian lineage resident in Siam since seventeenth century which became premier noble family in early nineteenth century. Eldest son of Dit, *phrakhlang* and *kalahom* under King Rama III, and architect of Mongkut's succession. Trader and enthusiast for western knowledge. Became *kalahom* and Chaophraya Si Suriyawong in 1851. Managed accession of King Chulalongkorn and served as regent. Promoted abolition of slavery, but opposed financial centralization.

Chulalongkorn, King Rama V (1853–1910). Educated in palace. Succeeded in 1868 at age 15. Travelled to India, Malaya, and Java. Began reforms of finance, labour controls, and administration from 1873–74. Formed ministerial council, mainly of brothers and half-brothers, in 1892. Travelled to Europe in 1897 and 1907. Moulded a 'modern' and pro-western conception of the Thai monarchy.

Damrong Rajanuphap (1862–1943). Born in Bangkok, fifty-seventh son of King Mongkut. Educated in Royal Pages Corps. Government roles in education and army in 1880s. Appointed first interior minister in 1894. Architect of the provincial administrative system. Quarrelled with King Vajiravudh in 1916 and resigned. Chairman of Capital Library (later National Library) and Royal Academy. Wrote around eighty works, mainly on history and biography, especially *Our Wars with the Burmese* (1920). Recalled as adviser by King Prajadhipok. Opposed introduction of a constitution. Left Siam after 1932 and lived in Penang until 1942.

Dhani Nivat, Prince (1885–1974). Grandson of King Mongkut. Educated in palace, and at Merton College, Oxford, in oriental studies. Minister of justice, 1926–32. Lived abroad after 1932. Returned in 1945 and became regent, then chairman of the Privy Council. Co-architect of revived monarchy. Author of many articles on Thai history, monarchy, literature, and Buddhism.

Dhanin Chiaravanont (1939–). Last son of Kwangtung seed trader who established shop in Bangkok in 1921. Chinese name, Jin Kok Min. Studied in Bangkok and Swatow. Built animal feed subsidiary into integrated chicken business under name Charoen Pokphand (CP). Replicated pattern in Indonesia and other neighbouring countries. Entered telecom business in late 1980s. Major foreign investor in China, especially in agribusiness and property, with strong political links in Shanghai and Beijing.

Feroci, Corrado (1892–1962). Born in San Giovani, Italy, to trading family. Attended the Royal Art Academy of Florence. Recruited by King Vajiravudh in 1923 to train artists. Given name of Silpa Bhirasri. Commissioned to produce many sculptures by the post-1932 government including the bas-reliefs on the Constitution Monument, the Victory Monument, and the statue of Thao Suranari in Khorat. Inaugural dean of Silpakorn University, 1943. Died in Thailand.

Haji Sulong Tomina (1895–1954). Born in Pattani, son of Islamic teacher. Went to study in Mecca, 1907. Stayed twenty years and became renowned religious teacher. Returned to Pattani in 1927. Founded Islamic School. In 1940s, became leader of resistance to Phibun's cultural policies. Presented 7-point petition for self-governing state within Siam, 1947. Charged with treason. Jailed 1948–52. Disappeared in 1954, believed drowned by Phao's police in Songkhla lake.

Jit Phumisak (1930–1966). Born in Prachinburi, son of revenue clerk. Began writing on literature, philosophy, history, and art in magazines in late 1940s. Graduated from Chulalongkorn University in 1957, and soon after published *Art for Life, Art for the People* and *The Real Face of Thai Feudalism Today*. Poet, musician, and prolific essayist. Jailed 1958–64. Joined CPT in jungle in 1965. Shot by police in Sakon Nakhon.

K. S. R. Kulap Kritsanon (1834–1921). Born in Bangkok, son of minor official. Educated in *wat* and Royal Pages School. Worked fifteen years for foreign firms. In 1880s, became pioneer Thai language publisher and essayist. Published journal *Sayam praphet*, 1897–1908. Published texts from royal collections on history, genealogy, royal culture. Found guilty of falsifying texts in 1902, but pardoned because of age.

Khrong Chandawong (1908–1961). Born in Sakon Nakhon, son of well-off farmer. Qualified as teacher in Ubon, and became teacher in home locality. Joined Seri Thai. Jailed 1952–57 in Peace Movement sweep. Advocated abolition of anti-communist law, and elections of village headmen. MP for Sakon Nakhon, 1957–58. Arrested in 1961 on charge of promoting communism and Isan separatism. Executed on Sarit's order in 1961.

Kukrit Pramoj (1911–1985). Born in Bangkok, great-grandson of King Rama II. Suan Kulap School; Queen's College, Oxford (PPE). Returned to join Revenue Department in 1933, then Bank of Thailand. Formed Progressive Party in 1945, merged into Democrat Party in 1946. Junior minister, 1947–49. Founded *Siam rath* newspaper, 1950. Speaker of National Assembly, 1973–74. Founded Social

Action Party, 1974. Prime minister, 1975–76. Novelist, especially *Si phaendia* (Four reigns, 1950). Acted with Marlon Brando in *The Ugly American*. Enthusiast for traditional arts, especially *khon* masked drama.

Kulap Saipradit (1905–1974). Born in Bangkok, son of railway clerk. Thepsirin School. Worked as English teacher, translator of imported movie plots, and journalist. Pioneer novelist with *Luk phu chai* (A real man, 1928), *Songkhram chiwit* (The war of life, 1931), *Khanglang phap* (Behind the painting, 1936). Founded *Suphapburut* (The gentleman) magazine, 1929. Jailed 1942–44. Visited Australia, 1947. Jailed in Peace Movement sweep, 1952–57. Visited China in 1957, and after Sarit coup decided not to return.

Manopakon Nithithada, Phraya (1884–1948). Born Korn Huthasingh in Bangkok. Attended Suan Kulap School and Law School. Took government scholarship to study law in London. Minister of justice and privy councillor in 1920s. Prime minister, 1932–33.

Mongkut, King Rama IV (1804–1873). Entered monkhood in 1824 to avoid succession dispute. Engaged in debate with missionaries, especially Bishop Pallegoix. Fascinated with astronomy and astrology. Founded more rigorous Thammayut sect. Left monkhood to ascend throne in 1851. Promoted western education among next royal generation. Began study of Siamese history. Invented guardian spirit for the kingdom. Died from malaria after trip to observe eclipse.

Nidhi Eoseewong (1940–). Born in Bangkok to Teochiu merchant family. Attended Assumption School, Siracha, Chonburi. Doctorate from University of Michigan. Taught history at Chiang Mai University from 1966 until retirement in 2000. Author of *Pen and Sail*, and studies of reigns of King Narai and King Taksin. Prolific author of essays on contemporary culture and politics, and advice columns. Activist for people politics. Received Fukuoka Asia Prize, 2000.

Phahon Phonphayuhasena, Phraya (1887–1947). Born Phot Phahonyothin, son of army general from aristocratic family. Studied at military college in Germany and attached to German army. Leader of the senior military officers who supported the 1932 revolution. Prime minister, 1933–38. Commander-in-chief during Second World War.

Phao Siyanon (1910–60). Born in Phitsanulok, son of army officer. Career military officer. Aide and son-in-law to commander of Shan States campaign. Transferred to police. Participated in 1947 coup. Appointed chief of police in 1951. Patronized by CIA to build anti-communist forces. Maintained covert group, 'Knights of the Diamond Ring', for political assassinations. Fled to Switzerland after Sarit 1957 coup.

Phibun (Phibunsongkhram) (1897–1964). Born Plaek Khitasangkha in Nonthaburi. Given official title, Luang Phibunsongkhram. Infantry Cadet School, top of class at Military Staff College in 1921, Fontainebleau Military Academy, 1924–27. Attended founding meeting of People's Party in Paris, 1927. Army chief and defence minister, 1934. Prime minister, 1938–44, 1948–57. Fled after 1957 coup, and lived in Cambodia and Japan.

Phumphuang Duangjan (1961–92). Born Ramphueng Chithan, daughter of Chainat field labourers. Two years of schooling. Child labourer. Gained fame in local singing contests. Apprenticed to Waiphot Phetsuphan's *luk thung* ensemble, 1973. From 1978, under guidance of Wichien Khamcharoen and with new stage name, modernized rural *luk thung* singing style and presentation to reach wider urban audience. Died of blood disorder. Granted royal-sponsored cremation. Became centre of cult at Wat Thapkradan, Suphanburi.

Prajadhipok, King Rama VII (1892–1941). Born in Bangkok, last son of King Chulalongkorn. Educated in England at Eton and military colleges. Succeeded to throne in 1925. Abdicated in 1935 and lived in Surrey, England.

Prasoet Sapsunthon (1913–1994). Born in Surat Thani, son of farmer and trader. Educated and later employed as book editor at Chulalongkorn University. Elected MP for Surat Thani, 1946. Proposed bill to amend Anti-Communist Law. Joined CPT. Disagreed with party's rural strategy. Expelled from party in 1957. Offered services to Sarit. Collaborated with ISOC to design anti-communist strategy.

Prawase Wasi (1931–). Born in Kanchanaburi, son of farmer. Studied medicine at Sirirat Hospital, University of Colorado, and London University, specializing in haematology. Medical practitioner, researcher, and activist. Professor at Mahidol University. Lay follower and publicist of this-worldly Buddhism. 1981 Magsaysay Award winner. Chaired committee which began process leading to 1997 constitution.

Prem Tinsulanond (1920–). Born in Songkhla, son of an official. Suan Kulap School and Military Academy. Career army officer. Developed political strategy against insurgency as commander of Second Army in northeast from 1977. Appointed army commander, 1978. Prime minister, 1980–88. Privy councillor, 1988.

Pridi Banomyong (1900–1983). Born in Ayutthaya. Given official title, Luang Pradit Manutham. Studied at Law School, then law and political economy at the University of Paris, 1920–27. Attended founding meeting of People's Party in Paris, 1927. Interior minister, 1934; foreign minister, 1937; finance minister, 1938; regent, 1941; prime minister, 1946. Wrote anti-war novel, *The King of the White Elephant*, and directed it as a film. Left Thailand after failed Palace Rebellion in 1949. Lived in China, then Paris from 1970. Wrote extensively in exile on philosophy, philology, and politics.

Puey Ungphakon (1917–1999). Son of fish wholesaler. Entered first year at Thammasat University. Scholarship to study economics at London School of Economics. Parachuted into Thailand by Seri Thai in 1944, and captured. Completed doctorate at LSE, 1948. Governor of Bank of Thailand, 1959–71. Rector of Thammasat University, 1974–76. Forced to flee after Thammasat massacre, and lived in London.

Sarit Thanarat (1908–1963). Born in Nakhon Phanom, son of district officer. Educated in Bangkok. Career army officer. Commander of Bangkok troops in 1947 coup and Palace Rebellion. Deputy defence minister, 1951. Head of army, 1954. Field marshal, 1956. Led coup in 1957. Visited USA, 1958. Executed second coup and became prime minister, 1958. Promoted development and personal rule, including summary executions.

Seksan Prasertkun (1949–). Son of fishing-boat builder and market vendor. Student leader at Thammasat University in 1973. Fled to jungle in 1976. Surrendered in 1980, and went to acquire a doctorate from Cornell University, 1989. Taught political science at Thammasat. Prominent public intellectual and writer of poetry, stories, and autobiography including the film, *The Moonhunter*.

Seni Pramoj (1905–1977). Born in Bangkok, great-grandson of King Rama II, elder brother of Kukrit. Educated at Worcester College, Oxford. Qualified as barrister in Thailand. As ambassador to US in 1941, refused to deliver Phibun's declaration of war. Organizer of Seri Thai. Returned to Thailand in 1945 to oversee peace negotiations. Prime minister, 1945–46. Co-founder of Democrat Party, elected its leader in 1968. Lawyer and journalist. Prime minister 1975, 1976.

Sujit Wongthet (1945–). Born in Prachinburi, son of village headman and farmer. Archaeology BA from Silapakorn University. Journalist at *Siam rath*. Editor of *Social Science Review*. Leading cultural-nationalist critic of the American era. Writer of poetry, short stories, and novels. Performer of traditional music and drama. Editor and publisher of *Sinlapa watthanatham* (Art and culture) magazine and publishing house which developed a cultural-nationalist interpretation of Thai history. Author of *Made in USA* (1971, 1973), *The Thai Were Always Here* (1986), and *Jek pon lao* (Chinese mixed with Lao, 1987).

Sulak Sivaraksa (1932–). Born in Thonburi, son of accountant in Thai-Chinese family. Studied in missionary schools then in England, 1953–61, qualifying as barrister. Started *Social Science Review* in 1963, also publishing company and bookshop. Became devotee of Buddhadasa Bhikkhu, and got involved in early NGO work. Fled after 1976 massacre and again after 1991 coup. Accused of lese-majesty in 1984 and 1992, acquitted both times. Leading activist in inter-religious movements, NGOs, and environmental causes. Author of several books on themes of Buddhism and politics, especially *Siam in Crisis* (1990).

Sunthon Phu (1786–1856). Born in Bangkok. Brought up in palace where his mother was a wet-nurse. Clerical job. Jailed for love affair with palace lady. Wrote first great poem, *Nirat mueang klaeng*, in 1806. Patronized by King Rama II, and contributed to court compilation of *Khun chang khun phaen*. In jail again for a drunken quarrel, began *Phra aphaimani*, continually extended over subsequent years. Wrote many *nirat* and didactic works. Patronized again by King Mongkut and ended life with rank and fame.

T. S. R. Wannapho, Thianwan (1842–1915). Born in Bangkok, grandson of Ayutthaya noble. Educated on fringes of court. Worked as trader. Studied English and law. Lawyer, essayist, and briefly member of 'Young Siam' group. In 1882, framed on charge of authoring seditious petition, and jailed for seventeen years. On release, ran bookstore, and published journals 1902–09 criticizing old social order, lack of attention to development, and lack of representation.

Taksin, King (1734–1782). Possibly son of migrant Teochiu gambler. Known as Jeung sae Ing or Sin. Probably a cart trader who acquired governor post of border town, Tak. Brought troops to defend Ayutthaya in 1767, and left before fall. Rallied forces in east, expelled Burmese garrison, and established new headquarters at Thonburi. Defeated rival claimants over 1768–71. Adopted personal, charismatic style of rule. Overthrown in bloody coup hatched by old nobles in 1782. Executed.

Thaksin Shinawatra (1950–). Born in Chiang Mai in leading business family in silk, construction, and banking. Entered Police Academy. Scholarship for doctorate in criminal justice from Sam Houston State University, USA. Began computer leasing business. Resigned from police in 1987. Gained string of government concessions including first private mobile phone network and satellite. Estimated net worth of 60 billion baht by mid-1990s. Entered politics in Chamlong's Phalang Tham Party, and had three brief spells as minister. Formed Thai Rak Thai Party, 1998. Elected prime minister, 2001.

Thanom Kittikhachon (1911–2004). Born in Tak, son of an official. Attended Military Academy. Career army officer. Right-hand man of Sarit Thanarat. Prime minister, 1958, 1963–73. Deposed and exiled after 14 October 1973 uprising but returned in 1976.

Thiphakorawong, Chaophraya (1818–1870). Born Kham, son of Dit Bunnag, in Bangkok. Scholar, enthusiast for western knowledge, and associate of Prince Mongkut. Appointed *phrakhlang*, 1851–65. Compiled royal chronicles of First to Third Reigns, and edited the Royal Autograph edition of the Ayutthaya chronicles. Wrote articles on science and Buddhism in fledgling Thai press, collected in *Sadaeng kitjanukit* (1867).

Thirayuth Boonmi (1950–). Born in Nakhon Pathom, son of army sergeant and market vendor. As engineering student at Chulalongkorn University, headed National Student Centre. One of thirteen arrested for demanding constitution, sparking movement which led to 14 October 1973. Worked as engineer and activist. Fled to CPT jungle camp in Nan. Went to study in Netherlands and Germany, 1981–85. Self-appointed 'social thinker' and leading public intellectual. Books include *Strong Society* and *Turning Point of the Era*.

Vajiravudh, King Rama VI (1881–1925). Suan Kulap School. To England, 1894–1903: private tuition; Sandhurst Military College; Christ Church, Oxford. Succeeded to throne in 1910. Formed *Sua pa* (Wild Tiger Corps) as royalist paramilitary, 1911. Angered palace old guard by patronizing male commoners. Obliged to take foreign loan in 1920 to avoid personal bankruptcy. Founded Lumpini Park. Prolific dramatist, translator of Shakespeare, and writer on nationalism.

Wichit Wathakan, Luang (1898–1962). Born Kim Liang, son of orchard farmer in Uthai Thani. Took foreign service exams and appointed to Paris legation, 1921–27; studied part-time at University of Paris. Head of Fine Arts Department, 1934–42; foreign minister during Second World War; finance/economic affairs minister, 1951–53; special adviser to prime minister Sarit, 1958–62. Prolific playwright, radio broadcaster, and writer on history, religion, culture, and self-improvement.

Yotfa, King Rama I (1737–1809). Born in Ayutthaya, son of leading Mon noble and Chinese wife. Married into leading Ratchaburi family, and took post there. Recruited by younger brother to join King Taksin. Became leading military commander. Elevated to throne in 1782 coup against Taksin by old nobility. Convoked Buddhist Council to revise Tripitaka. Oversaw massive military expansion to south, north, and northeast. Commissioned collections of laws, state manuals, religious texts, and dramatic works.

Readings

1: BEFORE BANGKOK

Kennon Breazeale (ed.), *From Japan to Arabia: Ayutthaya's Maritime Relations with Asia* (Bangkok: Foundation for the Promotion of Social Sciences and Humanities Textbooks Project, 1999).

Charnvit Kasetsiri, *The Rise of Ayudhya: A History of Siam in the Fourteenth and Fifteenth Centuries* (Kuala Lumpur: Oxford University Press, 1976).

Georges Condominas, *From Lawa to Mon, from Saa' to Thai: Historical and Anthropological Aspects of Southeast Asian Social Spaces* (Canberra: Australian National University, 1990).

Lorraine Gesick, 'The rise and fall of King Taksin: a drama of Buddhist kingship', in Gesick (ed.), *Centers, Symbols and Hierarchies: Essays on the Classical States of Southeast Asia* (New Haven: Yale University Press, 1983).

Charles Higham, *Early Cultures of Mainland Southeast Asia* (Bangkok: River Books, 2002).

David Lieberman, *Strange Parallels: Volume I, Integration of the Mainland: Southeast Asia in Global Context, c. 800 to 1830* (Cambridge: Cambridge University Press, 2003).

Richard A. O'Connor, 'Agricultural change and ethnic succession in Southeast Asian states: a case for regional anthropology', *Journal of Asian Studies* 54, 4 (1995).

Richard A. O'Connor, 'A regional explanation of the Tai *müang* as a city state', in Mogens Herman Hansen (ed.), *A Comparative Study of Thirty City-State Cultures* (Copenhagen: Royal Danish Academy of Science and Letters, 2000).

David K. Wyatt, *Thailand: A Short History* (rev. edn, Yale University Press, 2003).

2: THE OLD ORDER IN TRANSITION, 1760S TO 1860S

Neil A. Englehart, *Culture and Power in Traditional Siamese Government* (Ithaca: Cornell Southeast Asia Program, 2001).

Volker Grabowsky (ed.), *Regions and National Integration in Thailand, 1892–1992* (Wiesbaden: Harrassowitz Verlag, 1995).

Hong Lysa, *Thailand in the Nineteenth Century: Evolution of the Economy and Society* (Singapore: Institute of Southeast Asian Studies, 1984).

D. B. Johnston, 'Bandit, nakleng, and peasant in rural Thai society', *Contributions to Asian Studies* XV (1980).

Junko Koizumi, 'From a water buffalo to a human being: women and the family in Siamese history', in Barbara Watson Andaya (ed.), *Other Pasts: Women, Gender and History in Early Modern Southeast Asia* (Honolulu: University of Hawai'i, 2000).

Craig J. Reynolds, 'Buddhist cosmography in Thai history, with special reference to nineteenth century culture change', *Journal of Asian Studies* 35, 2 (1976).

William G. Skinner, *Chinese Society in Thailand: An Analytical History* (Ithaca: Cornell University Press, 1957).

Andrew Turton, 'Thai institutions of slavery', in J. L. Watson (ed.), *Asian and African Systems of Slavery* (Oxford: Blackwell, 1980).

3: REFORMS, 1850S TO 1910S

Kullada Kesboonchu Mead, *The Rise and Decline of Thai Absolutism* (London: RoutledgeCurzon, 2004).

Eiji Murashima, 'The origins of modern official state ideology in Thailand', *Journal of Southeast Asian Studies* 19, 1 (1988).

M. Peleggi, *Lords of Things: The Fashioning of the Siamese Monarchy's Modern Image* (Honolulu: University of Hawai'i Press, 2002).

David Streckfuss, 'The mixed colonial legacy in Siam: origins of Thai racialist thought, 1890–1910', in L. Sears (ed.), *Autonomous Histories: Particular Truths* (Madison: University of Wisconsin, 1993).

Tej Bunnag, *The Provincial Administration of Siam, 1892–1915* (Kuala Lumpur: Oxford University Press, 1977).

Thongchai Winichakul, *Siam Mapped: A History of the Geo-body of a Nation* (Honolulu: University of Hawaii Press, 1994).

Thongchai Winichakul, 'The quest for "siwilai": a geographical discourse of civilizational thinking in the late nineteenth and early twentieth-century Siam', *Journal of Asian Studies* 59, 3 (2000).

Patrick Tuck, *The French Wolf and the Siamese Lamb: The French Threat to Siamese Independence 1858–1907* (Bangkok: White Lotus, 1995).

4: PEASANTS, MERCHANTS, AND OFFICIALS, 1870S TO 1930S

Mark Askew, *Bangkok: Place, Practice and Representation* (London and New York: Routledge, 2002).

Scot Barmé, *Woman, Man, Bangkok: Love, Sex and Popular Culture in Thailand* (Lanham: Rowman and Littlefield, 2002).

Ian G. Brown, *The Elite and the Economy in Siam c.1890–1920* (Singapore: Oxford University Press, 1988).

Chatthip Nartsupha, *The Thai Village Economy in the Past*, tr. Chris Baker and Pasuk Phongpaichit (Chiang Mai: Silkworm Books, 1999).

J. C. Ingram, *Economic Change in Thailand, 1850–1970* (Kuala Lumpur: Oxford University Press, 1971).

Pasuk Phongpaichit and Chris Baker, *Thailand: Economy and Politics* (2nd edn, Kuala Lumpur: Oxford University Press, 2002).

Akira Suehiro, *Capital Accumulation in Thailand 1855–1985* (Tokyo: Centre for East Asian Cultural Studies, 1989).

David K. Wyatt, *The Politics of Reform in Thailand: Education in the Reign of King Chulalongkorn* (New Haven and London: Yale University Press, 1969).

5: NATIONALISMS: 1910S TO 1940S

Scot Barmé, *Luang Wichit Wathakan and the Creation of a Thai Identity* (Singapore: Institute of Southeast Asian Studies, 1993).

Benjamin A. Batson, *The End of the Absolute Monarchy in Siam* (Singapore: Oxford University Press, 1984).

Stephen L. W. Greene, *Absolute Dreams: Thai Government under Rama VI, 1910–1925* (Bangkok: White Lotus, 1999).

J. B. Haseman, *The Thai Resistance Movement during World War* II (Chiang Mai: Silkworm Books, 2002).

Kobkua Suwannathat-Pian, *Thailand's Durable Premier: Phibun through Three Decades, 1932–1957* (Kuala Lumpur: Oxford University Press, 1995).

Pridi Banomyong, *Pridi by Pridi: Selected Writings on Life, Politics, and Economy*, tr. Chris Baker and Pasuk Phongpaichit (Chiang Mai: Silkworm Books, 2000).

Craig Reynolds (ed.), *National Identity and Its Defenders* (2nd edn, Chiang Mai: Silkworm Books, 2002).

E. B. Reynolds, *Thailand and Japan's Southern Advance, 1940–1945* (New York: St Martin's Press, 1994).

Thamsook Numnonda, *Thailand and the Japanese Presence, 1941–45* (Singapore: ISEAS, 1977).

6: THE AMERICAN ERA AND DEVELOPMENT, 1940S TO 1960S

D. Fineman, *A Special Relationship: The United States and Military Government in Thailand, 1947–1956* (Honolulu: University of Hawaii Press, 1997).

K. Hewison, *Bankers and Bureaucrats: Capital and the Role of the State in Thailand* (New Haven: Yale University Southeast Asian Studies, 1989).

P. Hirsch, *Development Dilemmas in Rural Thailand* (Singapore: Oxford University Press, 1990).

F. Molle and Thippawal Srijantr, *Thailand's Rice Bowl: Perspectives on Agricultural and Social Change in the Chao Phraya Delta* (Bangkok: White Lotus, 2003).

R. Muscat, *The Fifth Tiger: A Study of Thai Development Policy* (New York: M. E. Sharpe and United Nations University Press, 1994).

Thak Chaloemtiarana, *Thailand: The Politics of Despotic Paternalism* (Bangkok: Social Science Association of Thailand, Thai Khadi Institute, Thammasat University, 1979).

7: IDEOLOGIES: 1940S TO 1970S

D. Morell and Chai-Anan Samudavanija, *Political Conflict in Thailand: Reform, Re-action, Revolution* (Cambridge, Mass.: Oelgeschlager, Gunn and Hain, 1982).
Saiyud Kerdphol, *The Struggle for Thailand: Counter Insurgency 1965–1985* (Bangkok: S. Research Center, 1986).
Kasian Tejapira, *Commodifying Marxism: The Formation of Modern Thai Radical Culture, 1927–1958* (Kyoto: Kyoto University Press, 2001).
Thongchai Winichakul, 'Remembering/silencing the traumatic past: the ambivalent memories of the October 1976 massacre in Bangkok', in Shigeharu Tanabe and Charles F. Keyes (eds), *Cultural Crisis and Social Memory: Modernity and Identity in Thailand and Laos* (Honolulu: University of Hawai'i Press, 2002).

8: GLOBALIZATION AND MASS SOCIETY, 1970S ONWARDS

Anek Laothamatas, *Business Associations and the New Political Economy of Thailand: From Bureaucratic Polity to Liberal Corporatism* (Boulder, CO: Westview Press, Institute of Southeast Asian Studies, 1992).
D. Arghiros, *Democracy, Development and Decentralization in Provincial Thailand* (Richmond: Curzon, 2001).
Andrew Brown, *Labour Politics and the State in Industrializing Thailand* (London and New York: RoutledgeCurzon, 2004).
M. K. Connors, *Democracy and National Identity in Thailand* (New York and London: RoutledgeCurzon, 2003).
M. B. Mills, *Thai Women in the Global Labour Force: Consuming Desires, Contested Selves* (New Brunswick, NJ, and London: Rutgers University Press, 1999).
Bruce D. Missingham, *The Assembly of the Poor in Thailand: From Local Struggles to National Protest Movement* (Chiang Mai: Silkworm Books, 2003).
Shigeharu Tanabe and C. F. Keyes (eds), *Cultural Crisis and Social Memory: Modernity and Identity in Thailand and Laos* (Honolulu: University of Hawai'i Press, 2002).

9: POLITICS, 1970S ONWARDS

Anek Laothamatas, 'A tale of two democracies: conflicting perceptions of elections and democracy in Thailand', in R. H. Taylor (ed.), *The Politics of Elections in Southeast Asia* (Cambridge: Cambridge University Press, 1996).
W. A. Callahan, *Imagining Democracy: Reading 'The Events of May' in Thailand* (Singapore: ISEAS, 1998).
Kevin Hewison (ed.), *Political Change in Thailand: Democracy and Participation* (London and New York: Routledge, 1997).
D. McCargo, *Chamlong Srimuang and the New Thai Politics* (London: Hurst, 1997).
D. McCargo (ed.), *Reforming Thai Politics* (Copenhagen: NIAS, 2002).

Ruth McVey (ed.), *Money and Power in Provincial Thailand* (Copenhagen: NIAS, 2000).

Pasuk Phongpaichit and Chris Baker, *Thaksin: The Business of Politics in Thailand* (Chiang Mai: Silkworm Books, 2004).

Kasian Tejapira, 'Post-crisis economic impasse and political recovery in Thailand: the resurgence of economic nationalism', *Critical Asian Studies* 34, 3 (2002).

Index